Revivalism and Modern Irish Literature

Revivalism and Modern Irish Literature:

The anxiety of transmission and the dynamics of renewal

FIONNTÁN DE BRÚN

CORK UNIVERSITY PRESS

Published in 2019 by
Cork University Press
Youngline Industrial Estate
Pouladuff Road, Togher
Cork, Ireland

British Library Cataloguing in Publication Data

A CIP catalogue record for this book is available from the British Library

ISBN: 978-1-78205-314-9

Typeset by Dominic Carroll, Ardfield, County Cork
Printed by Hussar Books, Poland

www.corkuniversitypress.com

Do mo thuismitheoirí, Séamus agus Máire

Contents

Acknowledgements

The writing of this book was greatly facilitated by an Arts and Humanities Research Council (AHRC) (UK) Leadership Fellowship award received for 2016–17. I am indebted to the AHRC for this opportunity, and also to the Irish and Celtic Studies Research Institute, the School of Irish Language and Literature, the Faculty of Arts, and the Research Office of Ulster University, whose support was crucial during all stages of the award. My sincere thanks are also due to Maria O'Donovan, Dominic Carroll and Mike Collins of Cork University Press, and to the two anonymous readers whose perspicacious comments were a welcome steer during the progress of this monograph. I am also grateful to the staff of various libraries who generously assisted my research, particularly the libraries of Ulster University; Queen's University, Belfast; the Linenhall Library, Belfast; Maynooth University; Trinity College, Dublin; University College, Dublin; Boston College (John J. Burns Library); St Isodore's College, Rome; the National Library of Ireland; the Royal Irish Academy; the National Archives; the British Library, London; and the New York Public Library.

Numerous friends and colleagues have shared their expertise and enthusiasm with me in a manner that has been the very definition of fellowship. At Ulster University, A.J. Hughes, Ailbhe Ó Corráin, Séamus Mac Mathúna and Don McRaild have read drafts, discussed key concepts or contributed in myriad other ways to the journey of this book. Similarly, Brian Ó Conchubhair (Notre Dame), Máirín Nic Eoin (Dublin City University), Liam Mac Mathúna (University College, Dublin), Mícheál Mac Craith (St Isodore's, Rome), Breandán Ó Conaire (Dublin City University), Ian Ó Caoimh (Rannóg an Aistriúcháin), Gearóid Denvir (National University of Ireland, Galway), Paul O'Grady (Trinity College, Dublin), Aisling Ní Dhonnchadha (Maynooth University) and Philipp Rosemann (Maynooth University) all kindly read drafts of various sections. Chapter 5 is based on an article previously published in *New Hibernia Review* (winter 2013), whose editor, James Rogers, and anonymous reviewers made very valuable comments on the initial draft.

Needless to say that I am solely responsible for any shortcomings that remain. Some of those mentioned above gave talks at the Interdisciplinary Symposium on Comparative Revivalism held in November 2016 at Ulster University's Belfast campus as part of my AHRC-funded fellowship. I am also grateful to Regina Uí Chollatáin, Rob Dunbar, Judith Hill, Kayla Rose and Pádraig Ó Tiarnaigh, who gave presentations at this event, and to the many other contributors on that day, among whom the late Aodán Mac Póilin was typically incisive and inspiring. My recent PhD students, Tricia Carr, Sorcha de Brún, Ciarán Ó Dornáin and Marcas Mac Bhloscaidh, together with numerous MA students have all contributed to the conversations that have informed these pages.

Just as this book was being completed I took up a new post as professor of modern Irish at Maynooth University. My new colleagues have extended me a particularly warm welcome, which was of great reassurance as I made the tentative journey south. My wife Jacaí has not only supported all of my endeavours, she has endured them and remains my most trusted reader. Similarly, Dónal, Lochlann and Eoghan have kept me right on all things.

This book is dedicated to my parents, Séamus and Máire. Their wisdom and humour are among their many gifts that, as with all things, they share unfailingly. *Nár laga Dia sibh.*

Introduction

We begin with two types of letter. In late 1640 Spanish privateers boarded a French ship bound for Nantes and intercepted two letters that they considered to have been written in code. In an effort to decipher this code, the Spanish authorities interrogated one of the addressees, Nioclás (Fearghal Dubh) Ó Gadhra, an Irish Augustinian friar who was based in various Irish colleges in Spain and France. The Spanish were no doubt disappointed to learn that the letters were not actually written in cipher but 'in the ancient language and handwriting ordinarily used in Ireland'.[1] The content of the letters proved to be similarly lacking in intrigue. Apart from some references to the ongoing 'Bishops' Wars', they comprised mainly local news from County Sligo, an update on appointments in the Augustinian order, mention of the three shirts Ó Gadhra's mother had sent over for him, and so forth. A much more intriguing type of seventeenth-century letter, albeit a fictional one, is the subject and title of Liam Mac Cóil's historical novel *An Litir* (The Letter) (2011).[2] Set in 1612, *An Litir* centres on the fraught passage of a letter that may alter the history of Ireland and even Europe. This highly sensitive political message is entrusted to a young man whose fortunes, in the classic formula of espionage, are mortally bound to the letter he must carry across the seas from Ireland to Rome. Moreover, as the unfolding plot pits the young letter-bearer against the all-pervasive colonial forces, the imperilled message comes to represent the precarious fate of the Irish language itself.

There are two important insights to be gained from these two contrasting forms of letters. Firstly, the difference between the fictional, retrospective letter of Mac Cóil's novel and the real-life letters intercepted by the Spanish illustrates a change in the function of the Irish language in the centuries that separate them. What has changed is that the Irish language is not merely a means of conveying information but also a symbolic code that represents something much greater than the message it conveys. Thus, contemporary official signage in Irish often advertises services that cannot be transacted in the language itself; instead the language signifies the institution of state

rather than the practical business within. Secondly, the motif of the imperilled message in *An Litir* encapsulates a certain concern in Irish literature for
its own survival, something we might call an anxiety of transmission, which
increased in intensity from the seventeenth century onwards. These conditions
have engendered a self-awareness and a concern for how the Irish language
and its literature should prevail in the face of the most adverse circumstances.
Both of these are important starting points for our discussion of revivalism
and modern Irish literature.

Of course, while the Irish language has taken on a symbolic function
often overshadowing its practical use, it has not by any means lost its basic
communicative function. Text messages, tweets and e-mails in Irish can still
be about the shirts that someone's mother has sent them. Indeed, mass literacy
and digital media have helped users of minority languages, such as Irish, to
become more prolific than ever. Yet the language shift that occurred in Ireland,
particularly from the nineteenth century onwards, has undoubtedly brought
about a consciousness of language as a medium that other, more dominant
languages, do not register. It is no surprise that the experience of the displacement or decline of a language – that thing that hitherto was a naturally
acquired, universal inheritance – brings about an awareness of the fragility
and impermanence of the medium itself. Moreover, the initial realisation that
culture is a medium, a construct that is negotiable rather than fixed, brings
with it an appreciation of the role of agency in human affairs, in particular
the recognition that if a language can be lost it might also be recovered. This
active intervention in matters such as language and culture, matters that are
often assumed to be organic, naturally occurring phenomena, is what brings
us to revivals and revivalism.

The concern of this book is to explore how this active intervention in the
fortunes of the Irish language – that which we call revivalism – has helped
shape both the production of literature in Irish and its attendant discourse
from the early seventeenth century to the present day. An important pre-
requisite for this discussion is the interrogation of revivalism as a concept. Part
of the necessity of so doing lies in the absence of any fully developed theory
or theories of revivalism. Rather than speak of revivalism as an overarching
concept, we tend to speak of specific revivals: the Gothic Revival, the Islamic
Revival, the 1980s mod revival, and so on. The lack of a firm consensus about
what revivalism represents is also evident in the *OED* definition: 'belief in
or the promotion of a revival of religious fervour … A tendency or desire to
revive a former custom or practice'.[3] This wide understanding is indicative

of the range of spheres to which revivalism has been applied, encompassing religion, art, design, architecture, politics, literature, music, fashion, pop culture and other fields. Similarly, the semantic range of the verb 'revive' is somewhat broad, stretching as it does from 'restore to or regain life' to 'improve the position or condition of'. There is clearly some distance between restoring something to life and merely improving its condition. Yet it is this very latitude that creates the space in which the myriad interpretations of revivalism are realised. It is also this breadth of interpretation that animates the engagement of Irish literature with revivalism and the case study that this book entails.

While this book is primarily a conceptual investigation of revivalism using modern Irish literature as its case study, it follows a broad chronological path from the early seventeenth century to the present day. The rationale for beginning with the early seventeenth century is, firstly, that a particular tradition of revivalism is discernible from this period onwards, and, secondly, the need for a case study to set certain limits for the sake of coherence. It may have been possible to begin at a much earlier date, but this would have involved a much larger and, probably, less focused study. The choice of texts consulted has essentially been guided by their relevance to the discussion of revivalism rather than as an attempt to provide a comprehensive digest of literature in Irish. This means, of course, that the work of many influential Irish writers will not figure in these pages. Where more serious sins of omission may occur is with regard to the work of writers who have much to say about revivalism, but, again, these are risks inherent in any focused study. The definition of literature is liberally understood here, with essays, personal letters and reports considered alongside the corpus of poetry, prose and plays in Irish. Inevitably, given that this book is centred on a conceptual enquiry, ideas drawn from philosophy, psychoanalysis, cultural theory and other areas inform part of the investigation. This is particularly evident in the first chapter, which seeks to chart a path towards a theory of revivalism. Nevertheless, the larger part of this book is directed chiefly towards the corpus of literature in Irish.

Over the past two decades a range of studies have been devoted to what is generally referred to as the Irish Revival dating from the 1890s to the early 1920s.[4] Where this book differs significantly from these is in linking this admittedly spectacular period of activity to a wider tradition of revivalism in Irish literature. While the many excellent monographs on the Irish Revival have enlightened our understanding of literature in English, less attention has been given to literature in Irish. The great exception to this is Philip

O'Leary's magisterial, multi-volume study of prose literature in Irish. The scale of the project realised in O'Leary's series is breathtaking in range and significance. It also opens up a huge number of texts in Irish not only to non-Irish speakers but to readers of Irish. Alongside O'Leary's work, Declan Kiberd's landmark critical volumes are a brilliant and indispensable guide to understanding Irish literature in Irish and in English. Of course, critical discourse in Irish is essential to this book, and certain conceptually based works have provided particular inspiration. Of these, two pertinent examples are Breandán Ó Buachalla's *Aisling Ghéar* (Bright Vision) (1996), a study of Jacobitism and Irish literature of the seventeenth and eighteenth centuries, and Máirín Nic Eoin's *Trén bhFearann Breac* (Through the Speckled Land) (2005) on cultural dislocation in twentieth-century Irish literature. Similarly, Brian Ó Conchubhair's excellent *Fin de Siècle na Gaeilge: Darwin, an Athbheochan, agus smaointeoireacht na hEorpa* (Irish Language's Fin-de-siècle: Darwin, the Revival and European thought) (2009) illustrates how Darwinism and the pervading sense of cultural decline in late nineteenth-century and early twentieth-century Europe encouraged the revivalist response. Other recent studies, such as Pádraig de Paor's *Áille na hÁille: gnéithe de choincheap na híobartha* (Beauty of Beauties: aspects of the concept of sacrifice) (2013), have also significantly expanded the interpretative range of contemporary writing in Irish.[5] The ongoing work of Gregory Castle on revivalism in Irish writing in English is similarly innovative. In particular, his contention that the late nineteenth-century Irish Revival was not simply about repetition or return but a 'rectification and overcoming of misprision' points towards an understanding of revivalism as a dynamic, critical practice.[6] This view and P.J. Mathews' assertion that the Irish Revival was about an 'alternative modernity' will find much corroboration in the chapters of this book.[7]

Part of the rationale for a study of revivalism is the evidence of a certain commonality of motivations and aims among revivals in different spheres. The business of the first chapter is therefore to probe the theoretical discourse of revivalism before embarking on a case study of modern Irish literature. This initial conceptual discussion centres on ideas drawn from philosophy and psychoanalysis to consider how the notions of return, recollection and repetition underpin the idea of revival. The Platonic notion of anamnesis, by which all learning is recollection of previous knowledge, is an indication of the importance of anteriority in Western tradition. The concept of 'eternal return' – a prevailing feature of ancient religious traditions by which it is understood that the cosmos and society are constantly recurring and returning to earlier states – is a similarly important starting point for this discussion. Yet although revivals typically invoke a return to a particular past, they involve more than this initial return. A key distinction here is made between return and renewal, with renewal entailing not just a return to a past practice or value but, rather, a re-establishment of that practice or value after a period of interruption. The question that naturally arises at this juncture is how can this renewal or revival faithfully re-establish what has already ceased to be? If the continuity of a cultural tradition has been interrupted, can it ever be restored?

The issue of continuation or renewal in revivalism in many ways mirrors the difference between *being* and *becoming* in pre-Socratic philosophy. Parmenides maintained that the world was defined by a constant state of being. This argument countered the case made previously by Heraclitus that change is the only constant – in other words, that things are continually becoming rather than being. In a similar way, revivalist movements often oscillate between the desire for a faithful transmission of continuous tradition and the attempt to renew that tradition by means of an active, radical intervention. This raises the question of how we preserve the authenticity of something that we seek to continue or renew. Can a tradition be authentic if its continuity has been breached, or is it the case that continuity is itself an illusion if we hold the world to be in a constant state of flux? A compromise emerges in Hegel's notion of *Aufhebung,* or sublation, a dialectical transition in which both elements are negated but partially maintained.[8] By this analogy, revivalism brings the past and present into an active dialogue through which both are transformed. This may in itself seem impossible in that the past, by definition, is that which is already beyond us. Although the past appears irretrievable, however, its residue holds a certain latency that encourages the revivalist to revive elements of the past. Yet, crucially, this revival of the past takes place within the new circumstances of the present, and this is what transforms both elements. For example, Gothic Revival buildings of the nineteenth century were intended to faithfully reproduce the models of medieval architecture, but they were inserted into a radically different environment from their medieval antecedents. Moreover, part of the rationale for the nineteenth-century revival of the Gothic order was a critique of the present – in particular, the perceived loss of religious values in the industrial age.[9] It follows then that the Gothic order was not simply restored in the nineteenth century but was transformed by the new circumstances of the present.

The relationship between *being* and *becoming* and revivalism in the modern era is particularly evident in Nietzsche's philosophy. His first book, *The Birth of*

Tragedy (1872), engaged in a revival of sorts, specifically an attempted retrieval of elements of Western culture that had been lost or repressed, particularly the meaning and use of tragedy.[10] Nietzsche's subsequent interpretation of *being* and *becoming* and his model of 'eternal recurrence' speak to the interrelation of past and present in modernity, something that is fundamental to revivalism. His presentation of eternal recurrence as a continual return to what has already been, and his insistence on a form of radical becoming in response, reflect, in many ways, the essential challenge of revivalism – to make the revisitation of the past an act of creative renewal.

Besides its relevance to philosophy, the desire to revive the past also has a particular resonance in Freudian psychoanalytic theory, in which the nature of desire itself is especially relevant. Freud's great disciple Jacques Lacan considered human psychology to be marked by a primal loss or lack that he calls the *real*. The *real* is not reality but the *thing* that we always lack and can never recover, though we pursue it in an endless spiral of unrealised desire. Seen in this context, revivals may be a collective expression of the same interminable longing for that which we lack and will always elude us. Moreover, for Lacan desire is not a straightforward relation between subject and object – it is not simply a matter of a subject forming a desire independently. The subject, for Lacan, is formed by its relation to the *other*, and it follows that desire, like identity, is not a fixed point of reference but, rather, is constantly mediated.[11] It is not surprising that this model of subject formation has provided fertile ground for postcolonial theory. The ways in which colonial subjects imitate the colony are too numerous to mention, but the seventeenth-century poem 'A Fhir Ghlacas a Ghalldacht' (O Man Who Follows English Ways) and Douglas Hyde's landmark 1892 lecture 'The Necessity for De-anglicising Ireland' offer pertinent examples of how the Irish have been prone to imitate colonial culture, often in spite of themselves.[12] However, as Homi Bhabha has demonstrated, 'colonial mimicry' is a deeply ambivalent process that never results in a straightforward reproduction of the colonial culture.[13] Similarly, when revivalists seek to restore the pre-colonised native culture, their efforts are often marked by their relation to the colonial *Other*. For example, the revival of early Irish literature in the late nineteenth and early twentieth centuries served to assert the Irish nation as an autonomous entity with its own subject, but often did so with one eye fixed on the norms of colonial respectability.[14] Similarly, the postcolonial fervour for native purity and authenticity bespeaks a failure to escape the gaze of the colonising *Other*.

In other words, continuation, faithful transmission or renewal of culture are projects fraught with contradictions that reach back to the fundamentals of metaphysics and ontology, particularly the dichotomy of *being* and *becoming*. Such complexity is apparent in the myriad ways in which revivalism is expressed and pursued. This does not mean that revivalism is inscrutable, but, rather, that it cannot be simply reduced to any simple formula or programme, as the endless debates and ideological disputes between revivalists confirm. Nor should these theoretical considerations be mistaken for mere intellectual speculation with no practical application. After all, the desire to revive aspects of the past has been a catalyst for periods of profound societal change, such as the Renaissance, the Reformation and countless nationalist movements. All of these have led to seismic change, whether this be through enlightenment and liberation or conflict and repression, according to one's own perspective.

The second chapter hinges on the commonality between the Renaissance, the Reformation and the Counter-Reformation as movements that sought to reform the present by reviving aspects of the past – a return to sources classical or scriptural – with a shared concern for renewal being central to this. The Irish Counter-Reformation is specifically significant to literature in Irish as it was the movement that produced the first sustained publishing of Irish-language books as well as a radical renewal of both language and literary production in Irish. This seventeenth-century Irish revival, undertaken by Irish clerics in mainland Europe, was consciously grounded in current European theological, philosophical and historiographical discourses as expressed, most frequently, in the prefaces to the books and manuscripts the movement produced. Thus, the seventeenth-century cleric Fearghal Dubh Ó Gadhra (the addressee of the intercepted letters mentioned earlier) prefaces his collection of bardic poetry by noting that the regeneration or renewal (*athnuachradh*) of tradition from age to age is standard practice in both biblical and pagan literature.[15] What this convergence of imperatives evident in the Renaissance, Reformation and Irish Counter-Reformation tells us about revivalism per se is that it is not simply contingent on the emergence of modern nationalisms in the eighteenth and nineteenth centuries, as is often suggested, but is more likely to be a recurrent and regenerative concern. In this chapter, the deep legacy of this Irish Counter-Reformation inheritance, as a template for subsequent Irish revivalism, is traced from its origins through to contemporary Irish-language writing, particularly historical novels such as *An Cléireach* (The Clerk) (2007), *An Litir* (2011), *I dTír Strainséartha* (In a Strange Country) (2014), *An Colm Bán/La Blanche Colombe* ((The White Dove) (2014) and *Sliocht ar Thír na*

Scáth (2018) (Children for the Land of Shades),[16] all of which deal specifically with, or draw substantially on, the role of Counter-Reformation writers as champions of the regeneration of the Irish-language literary tradition. These texts share a concern for participation in the European intellectual tradition as a way of countering insularity and colonial subjection, drawing on the critical distance of the European Irish colleges as an enlightened vantage point. All of these novels seek to overlay the cultural crises of the seventeenth century onto those of the twenty-first century, where literary culture in the Irish language is besieged not just by the hegemony of English, but by the perceived decline of conventional literary culture in the digital age. In these, and in other contemporary prose texts, the legacy of the seventeenth century is revisited in an effort to resolve contemporary anxieties of transmission and historical truth, and, ultimately, to restore a certain ontological security to the Irish language.

The eighteenth century was an intermediary stage in the social history of the Irish language, presaging the decisive language shift of the nineteenth century. Chapter 3 considers the evidence of revivalist discourse in both these centuries, taking as its remit cultural memory, futurity and the instrumentalisation of culture. By the latter part of the eighteenth century the use of Irish as a literary medium was increasingly dependent on a bilingual readership or audience. One implication of this bilingualism was that the material basis for literary production in Irish was undermined. Concomitantly, these circumstances also led to conscious collective efforts to reverse the narrowing of the language's orbit. In the second half of the eighteenth century, notices of forthcoming poetic courts in north Munster explicitly announce the rationale for revival. Similarly, the founding of a now obscure Irish-language society in Dublin in 1752 was an important signal of a new revivalist impetus from within the bosom of the Protestant Ascendancy. Under the influence of the Enlightenment, antiquarian interest in preserving the Gaelic literary inheritance was bolstered by the establishment of the Royal Irish Academy in 1785, which now holds the largest collection of Irish manuscripts.[17] This period also witnessed crucial collaborations between largely Catholic 'native' scholars and Ascendancy scholars.[18]

Throughout the eighteenth and nineteenth centuries, there was an implicit revivalism in the dedication of native scholars to the transmission of their tradition in spite of the manifest challenges it faced. Their endeavours ensured that manuscripts were copied and shared not just among scholars but read aloud at social gatherings, where the oral tradition of storytelling and recitation was also a particularly rich conduit for the transmission of cultural memory. Drawing on Aleida Assmann's definition of the canon and archive of cultural memory, Chapter 3 also considers the role of Irish scribes in maintaining both an active canon and a reference archive of cultural memory. The importance of the latter was to preserve endangered materials in a state of latency and intermediate storage. By so doing, a door was left ajar through which the thread of cultural memory could be taken up again.

The revivalist concern for futurity was shared by the native tradition of messianic belief, institutionalised in the *aisling* (vision) tradition of poetry. In such poems a dream-maiden, often personifying Ireland, typically delivered a message of hope to the poet, a message that was underscored by the prophecies of native saints.[19] Like the millenarianist currents that buoyed the Catholic Irish, the continual reiteration of imminent relief sustained an anticipatory outlook that held the present to be full of latent possibility. The providentialism that underscored this discourse appears on the surface to preclude the realisation of agency, yet, crucially, it reminded its audience that present political and social woes were temporary. Although Irish poets from the seventeenth century onwards wearily asked if God was deaf to their concerns, their belief in Divine Providence as the ultimate arbiter of human affairs meant that this higher authority could still usher in a radical transformation at any time.[20] Events like the American Revolution and English defeats in European wars were welcomed by Irish poets as evidence of such a turning tide.

The turn of the nineteenth century in Ireland was a time of substantial political change: the United Irishmen Rebellion had been crushed in the summer of 1798 and the Act of Union came into being in 1801, creating the United Kingdom of Great Britain and Ireland. Just as Jacobitism had sustained a messianic tradition of imminent liberation in the previous two centuries, many Irish-speaking Catholics were encouraged by a millenarianism that promised victory over their oppressors in the year 1825. Yet it was to be the O'Connellite Repeal Association that galvanised the Catholic Irish in a constitutional movement that saw Catholic Emancipation enacted in 1829. Ironically, O'Connell was a native speaker of Irish who was famously 'sufficiently utilitarian not to regret its abandonment'.[21] This prevailing utilitarian ideology brings the question of revival sharply into focus – any attempt to arrest the decline of Irish would be dependent on a very different rationale to the bold materialist formulae of Benthamism. In areas where the Irish language was not the medium of communal exchange, its utility was more likely to be seen as an affair of the soul. Thus, the Romantic nationalist identification of language with the national spirit made language revival a political imperative for the leaders of Young Ireland. The arena in which matters of the soul were most clearly allied with language, however, was the Protestant evangelical movement, often referred to as the Second Reformation. From the beginning of the nineteenth century, Protestant Bible societies devoted themselves to scriptural instruction in Irish, and, in so doing, mobilised a large network of teachers and published a swathe of religious texts in the Irish language. This undertaking in itself demonstrated that a knowledge of Irish was a material necessity in large parts of the country, but, more pertinently, their campaign generated numerous reflections and insights concerning the emotional and spiritual attachments of the Irish language. An example of these is the remark made by the renowned Scottish cleric Rev. Norman MacLeod (1783–1862), who was a leading exponent of the Presbyterian 'Home Mission' in Ireland:

> Strange it is that this peculiar feature in the character of the Irish, viz. their enthusiastic love for poetry and music, has not been laid hold of by their best friends for conveying to them lessons of religious instruction.[22]

The instrumentalisation of the language, whether in the service of cultural nationalism or Protestant evangelicalism, generally entailed a certain objectifying distance that was crucial to the development of a revivalist consciousness.[23] The corollary of this objectifying distance was to bring the role of human agency in language survival into sharp relief. Rather than language being an autonomous entity, revivalism understood language to be subject to agency and contingency. For nineteenth-century Irish revivalists, this realisation meant that their initial jeremiads on the decline of the language were followed by a recognition of the need for a proactive, future-facing response.

Such a response was slow to bring any material change until the founding of the Gaelic League in 1893, the harbinger of a new era in which language revival was centre stage in a wider movement of cultural and political regeneration. The focus of Chapter 4 is on the legacy of the writer, educationalist and 1916 Rising leader Patrick Pearse (1879–1916), who was a pivotal figure in ensuring the success of the Gaelic League's bid to cultivate a new literature in Irish that would renew a once vibrant tradition. In both his life and work, Pearse oscillated between a solemn duty towards the past and the urgent demands of the present. Some indication of this disposition is evident in the intellectual patrimony of his father, James Pearse, an ecclesiastical sculptor in the Gothic Revival tradition, whose negotiation of the medieval and modern was clearly a formative influence on the younger Pearse. While James Pearse revered the pre-industrial, religiously endowed medieval inheritance, he was, somewhat paradoxically, an atheist. Similarly, the younger Pearse was a champion of medieval values in education, but, as founder and headmaster of the bilingual Sgoil Éanna (St Enda's School), was decidedly modern in his adoption of progressive educational methods. The Gothic Revival appears to have been not just an influence but something of a foil for Patrick Pearse against which to develop his own Gaelic revivalism. Part of the evidence of this appears in an important essay on the Irish Literary Revival ('About Literature'), where he rejects the conservatism of his father's tradition, declaring that 'we want no Gothic Revival'.[24]

In Patrick Pearse's literary output this Janus-faced relation to the medieval and modern is expressed through the liminality of characters like Eoghainín na nÉan (Eoineen of the Birds), who, in the short story of the same name, sits on a ledge speaking to the swallows that fly between Ireland and the 'place where it is always summer'.[25] Eoghainín, like other visionary children in Pearse's short stories, has an understanding that adults have lost, and inhabits a threshold between the revelation of childhood and the impending loss of otherworldly insight in adulthood. The common thread here is the negotiation of past and present, and, more specifically, the characterisation of that which is soon to be lost as a messianic revelation. Certainly, Pearse's literary and oratorical *oeuvre* is infused with the messianic urgency of the political *aisling* poem, the message of which was traditionally underwritten by the prophecies of the native saints. Alongside the prophetic, however, Pearse was also enthused by the threshold of possibility. Both of these elements can be witnessed in his attraction to the life of the early Irish saints and particularly St Enda, after whom Pearse named Sgoil Éanna. The early saints lived in a world of prophetic visions, but in their search for the ideal community they were also the forerunners of the modern tradition of utopianism or social dreaming. This world of possibility is epitomised in Pearse's poem 'The Fool', he whose life has been spent 'attempting impossible things', happy to be scorned as long as he can ask, 'O wise men, riddle me this: what if the dream come true?'[26]

If Pearse embraced modernity only after fortifying himself with the elixir of the heroic and spiritually rich past, there was a point when the glorious past would have to give way to the urgent present. This point was the 1916 Easter Rising, which, although conceived in the laboratory of nationalist history, was an entirely unpredictable and intractable event that appeared to Pearse's protégé Desmond Ryan (1893–1964) to be just like a dream. Not the perfectly formed dream of national deliverance, but, rather, one of the chaotic, surreal dreams to which the new science of psychology would devote much investigation. If Pearse began with the threshold of the medieval and modern, his final act was to bring his protégé and literary executor to a new threshold where the present was a rapidly unfolding scene, the outcome of which no one could predict. Reflecting on the Rising some fifty years later, Eoghan Ó Tuairisc's novel *Dé Luain* (Monday) (1966) is pregnant with an overwhelming sense of latent possibility. In the final analysis, this may have been the real import of Pearse's revivalism.

The issue of temporality, or specifically the relationship of revivalism to time, is one that permeates each chapter but which is the express concern of Chapter 5, 'Temporality and Irish Revivalism: Past, present and becoming'. While the discussion includes references to early and medieval Irish literature as well as some further discussion of nineteenth-century Irish literature, the texts studied in this chapter are drawn chiefly from the twentieth and twenty-first centuries. This is in keeping with the general aim of the case study of modern Irish literature, which is to follow a chronological path as far as possible within what is primarily a conceptually driven discussion. Besides the readings of literary texts, an important aspect of this chapter is the debate around the preservation or revitalisation of the oral tradition. In particular, the arguments proposed by the writer Máirtín Ó Cadhain (1906–70) are pivotal to what was a wider debate about state intervention in the fortunes of Irish oral culture.

The project of revivalism is marked by a paradox wherein it seeks to replace the 'natural' boundaries of time with an open-ended and negotiable temporality. Chapter 5 begins by tracing the dialogue of living and dead evident in early and medieval Irish literature, which becomes systematically expressed by a Gothic idiom in the nineteenth and twentieth centuries. The sense of Irish speakers being akin to the undead, and by definition out of step with Victorian 'public time', becomes almost axiomatic and is expressed both outside and within the Gaelic tradition during the nineteenth century. In the twentieth century the Gothic trope is engaged to express the betrayal of nationalist teleology. In the prose fiction, essays and unpublished papers of Máirtín Ó Cadhain and Seosamh Mac Grianna (1900–90), the spatio-temporal exile of anti-Treaty prisoners becomes the literal and figurative experience of a denial of this rightful nationalist teleology. Yet the prevalence of a linear deterministic view of history, by which the Irish language and its literary tradition are seen as bound to a certain teleology, is deeply problematic. The evidence of revivalism suggests that we consider a Bergsonian understanding of time where the past and present coexist. In his reinterpretation of Henri Bergson's ideas, Gilles Deleuze summarises such an alternative understanding in the following terms: 'Not only does the past coexist with the present that has been, but … it is the whole, integral past; it is all our past, which coexists with each present.'[27] Drawing on Nietzsche's interpretation of 'eternal recurrence', Deleuze also stresses the importance of 'becoming' over 'being', which he allies to a radical sense of possibility. The contemporary emphasis on 'new speakers' of Irish (people who need not have any connection with a traditional *Gaeltacht*) reflects the sense in which 'becoming' is seen increasingly as essential to language revival and revitalisation rather than an unbroken continuity.[28]

If revivalism involves a renegotiation of time, it can also instigate a reinterpretation of place. In particular, Irish revivalism has encouraged a view of the *Gaeltacht* as being both the physical site of authentic historical continuity and also the object of an unattained revivalist desire or utopian longing. The tension between these two apparently contradictory categories, the one a self-evident material authenticity, the other an elusive alterity, is the focus of Chapter 6, which considers the themes of utopia, place and displacement from the Corca Dorcha of Myles na gCopaleen's (1911–66) *An Béal Bocht* (The Poor Mouth) (1941) to Nuala Ní Dhomhnaill's (b. 1952) *Murúcha* (Merfolk) poems in *The Fifty-minute Mermaid* (2007). Displacement here is not just the physical phenomenon but also that process, as understood in psychoanalysis, by which interest in one object or activity is transferred to another, so that the latter becomes its equivalent or substitute. The *Gaeltacht* is the case study here, and our starting point is the semantic shift that brought about its current meaning. Having previously meant 'the state of being Gaelic', the word *Gaeltacht* came to mean, from the late nineteenth century Revival period onwards, a specific, if notoriously shifting, place in Ireland. In other words, the state of being Gaelic was assigned a particular physical space, and this redesignation became an official reality after the founding of the Irish Free State in 1922. The corollary was that being Gaelic, for the majority of Irish people, was officially something that happened elsewhere. All of this led to a sense in which the Irish language was displaced to the margins, where it came to represent the declared object of the state's desire – Irish having been designated the official first language in 1922 – without this desire ever being fulfilled.

As mentioned earlier, the understanding of desire as an unending, unresolved spiral is one of the hallmarks of Freudian and Lacanian psychoanalysis.

Accordingly, some discussion of Lacan's trinity of the *real*, the *imaginary* and the *symbolic* is necessitated at the beginning of this chapter. This, I hope, is jus-tified in the ensuing discussion of texts, particularly since Lacan also offers us an important interpretation of how identity is formed in relation to the other. Myles na gCopaleen's satirical novel *An Béal Bocht* is a key text here, depict-ing as it does a timeless dystopian *Gaeltacht* that is ironically the unattainable object of desire of revivalists such as Myles' uncle, Fr Gearóid Ó Nualláin (1874–1942), whose autobiography is discussed here in some detail. As well as being a satire on how the Free State had displaced Irishness to the margins, *An Béal Bocht* was also written by someone whose own identity had been formed in close relation to the *Gaeltacht* ideal. Being the son of revivalist parents, Myles na gCopaleen/Brian Ó Nualláin was essentially one of the first generation of non-*Gaeltacht* native speakers whose claim to native authentic-ity was never endorsed by the state. After all, the state of being Gaelic was now something that happened in a place to which Myles na gCopaleen/Brian Ó Nualláin did not belong, even though the state of being Gaelic was probably the defining aspect of his upbringing. Again, the conflict between continuity and authenticity on the one hand and creative renewal and becoming on the other looms large.

If Irish revivalism's fetishising of the *Gaeltacht* has created an ideal place that is always out of reach, it has also cultivated another, more productive, idealisation of place. Hope, for Máirtín Ó Cadhain, was the 'chain detonation' in Irish history – the non-rational force that allowed the Irish to break out of the straitjacket of colonisation. The spaces of hope, as imagined by Seosamh Mac Grianna in his autobiographical adventure *Mo Bhealach Féin* (My Own Way) (1940), are the key to a particular strain of utopian longing in Irish revivalist literature. Journeys like Mac Grianna's draw consciously on the early Irish tradition of otherworldly journey, as does Nuala Ní Dhomhnaill's highly influential series of *Murúcha* poems presented in the bilingual anthology *The Fifty-minute Mermaid* (2007). While Ní Dhomhnaill is somewhat chary of utopian longing, particularly where it is driven by the state, her allegorical poems are a powerful meditation on loss and recovery and the difficulties therein. The central trope of *teacht i dtír* (literally, 'coming ashore', but also 'surviving') is a constant reminder of the challenges of managing our relation to the past, whether personal or communal. Yet it is the imagining of alterna-tive spaces and histories that gives part of its impetus to revivalism and to its enterprise of creative renewal. The realisation of agency often requires us to imagine it first.

CHAPTER 1

Towards a Theory of Revivalism

The very notion of revival invites contradiction. After all, the literal meaning of revive (from late-Latin *reviver*, 'to live again') makes no material sense except perhaps in the A&E ward. Rather, the notion of a second life tends to be the province of religion or the imagination – an idea that transcends the hard evidence of mortality and rests instead on faith or fantasy. The belief in a second life or a restoration of a world that has ceased to exist are typical of the religious notion of revival. Yet one can also *imagine* a second life without believing literally in it, and, similarly, one can also attempt to revive elements of culture in a strictly material sense, for example by creating a piece of jewellery from a historical artefact or replicating the architectural style of a historical era. So it follows that the concept of revival can be supported by either religious belief or the imagination, or it can be a material and secular affair. Yet the idea that we can clearly demarcate the religious from the secular notions of revival is problematic. In secular art, the revival of practices, values or styles from the past can be a way of asserting legitimacy by invoking precedent or of renewing the present by reintroducing elements from the past. Religious revivals, such as the Islamic Revival or Christian evangelical revivals, can be said to do exactly the same thing. Thus, the revival of past values is a preoccupation that is often shared by the religious and the secular to the extent that the lines separating each can become blurred. An example of such a convergence of spiritual and secular concerns in revivalism is the Gothic Revival of the nineteenth century, whose revival of medieval architecture was frequently justified by a critique of soulless modernity. Although proponents of the Gothic Revival clearly appealed to religious values, its influence on secular institutions is evident in the building of train stations and universities in the Gothic style, as well as in its broader application to secular art.

The type of revival with which we are concerned in this book is predominantly cultural and linguistic, and is characterised by a common set of fundamental concerns centred on the will to reform the present by recourse to values associated with the past. Although such a revival is outwardly secular, the spiritual and secular often overlap in the history of Irish revivalism. As the evidence of the following chapters shows, forms of Irish literary and linguistic revival have sprung from movements of religious renewal such as the Counter-Reformation and even, what is at times called, the Second Reformation of the nineteenth century. Furthermore, there is another important sense in which revivals share common ground with religion. Given that revivals run counter to the linear progress of history by returning to a past that no longer exists, they appear to present an alternative to the material evidence of the finality of the past.

The desire to return to the past is an age-old concern, and, indeed, perhaps the earliest antecedents of revivalism are the various ancient beliefs in 'eternal return'. These are explored in Mircia Eliade's *The Myth of the Eternal Return: cosmos and history* (1954).[1] Eliade's seminal work on the history of religions sets out to show how in archaic societies, by virtue of paradigmatic models revealed to men in mythical times, the cosmos and society are periodically regenerated. In this way, 'for the traditional societies, all the important acts of life were revealed *ab origine* by gods or heroes. Men only repeat these exemplary and paradigmatic gestures *ad infinitum*.'[2] The similarity of this 'primitive ontology' to Platonic philosophy is noted by Eliade, as is its presence in the Iranian, Judaic and Christian religious traditions.[3] Eliade goes on to conclude that *modern* man is condemned to an ongoing crisis by which he no longer benefits from the solace of mythical time but, in his newly acquired freedom from mythical belief, has to face the vicissitudes of continuous, historical time without recourse to the consolation of any metahistorical meaning.

Just as Eliade's thesis relies on different ways of perceiving time – the 'Great Time' or cyclical time of myth and the linear concept of time and history that displaced it – the concept of revival entails a crucial critical engagement with temporality, which is the subject of Chapter 5. It is also important to note how the backward look, or 'return', in antiquity relates closely to what we now broadly call utopianism, discussed in greater detail in Chapter 6.[4] The promise of a return to a state of untroubled perfection, as represented by Eden, or the invocation of an ideal society from antiquity, such as Arcadia or Atlantis, are among the oldest and most pervasive forms of utopian belief. Their relevance to the notion of revival is immediately apparent, given that the basic premise of a revival is that a superior state of affairs, displaced by a fall or similar decline, preceded the present.

Eliade's survey of the myth of 'eternal return' identifies, as alluded to earlier, a strong similarity between the cosmology of a wide range of archaic traditions and the philosophy of Plato. In particular, Plato's theory of preordained ideas or forms is regarded by Eliade as an elaboration of an ancient belief in archetypes.[5] Another related feature of Plato's writings, which is of great relevance to our discussion here, is the concept of anamnesis, whereby learning is recollection or a return to previous knowledge. Plato's discussion of this concept occurs principally in the *Meno*, *Phaedo* and *Phaedrus*.[6] Although anamnesis is not precisely defined by Plato, the general consensus is that it refers to learning being essentially recollection – bringing to the forefront of the mind what lies at the back of it, or of recapturing a memory that we hazily retain. The most well-known explanation occurs in the *Meno*, in which Socrates succeeds in getting a slave boy to prove a geometrical theorem by asking the appropriate questions that allow the 'spontaneous recovery of knowledge that is in him'.[7] In discussing this part of Plato's theory of knowledge, I.M. Crombie refers specifically to anamnesis as a *revival* of true belief through experience, and also draws attention to two strands that arise from this concept, the first being religious notions of pre-existence, the second being logical notions about the status of necessary truths.[8] This mirrors the coexistence of a spiritual and rational *raison d'être* in many instances of revivalism.

It is clear that a belief in return was a dominant one in antiquity, and, indeed, part of the legacy of classical philosophy was the periodic return to ideas that had been first enunciated in antiquity. The Renaissance is by definition synonymous with both a return to sources and a revival of classical learning, just as the Reformation was particularly concerned with a return to scripture. The common thread in these latter periods in the history of Western civilisation is that temporal concerns were guided by the religious and spiritual view of the world. How, then, does the concept of return – a concept that owes much to the realm of the non-material and the spiritual – prevail in the age of modernity and secular discourse? Perhaps the best example of how return persists in modernity is available to us in Freudian psychoanalysis. The corollary of Freud's persistent observation of patterns of repetition and regression in human mental processes and behaviour is that a return to previous knowledge and experience is fundamental to the modern human condition. In summarising the significance of Freud's work, Adam Phillips remarks that:

in Freud's view, we can only look forward now by looking back; our longing is to recreate the past, and the future is the place in which we may be able to rework the satisfactions and frustrations of our childhood. Freud is preoccupied, in other words, by whether it is possible for modern people to have new experiences, to find new objects of desire, to improvise upon their pasts.[9]

'Looking back', in Freud's treatment of it, is typically the individual's reworking of his/her past in a multitude of different ways. This is not just the repetition or regression that occurs in neurosis but is, in Freud's account, fundamental to the general development of the individual. Thus, in his essay 'Family Romances', which discusses the separation of the individual, as he grows up, from the authority of his parents, Freud remarks that the progress of society in general depends on the opposition between the generations.[10] But in our effort to replace our parents with grander personages, what we actually do is look back, we seek out a past, idealised version of our parents. As Freud remarks:

> Indeed the whole effort to replace the real father by another who is more distinguished is merely an expression of the child's longing for the happy times gone by, when his father seemed to be the strongest and most distinguished of men, and his mother the dearest and loveliest of women. He turns away from the man he now knows as his father to the one he believed in as a child.[11]

The sense in which desire is a response to a primal loss is one that is particularly associated with Jacques Lacan, whose work represents an extensive reworking of Freudian psychoanalysis, influenced in part by the structuralist theories of linguistics and anthropology. For Lacan the primal loss, or rupture, which he takes as a universal feature of human psychology, is the *real*.[12] The *real* is not what we call reality, but the *thing* whose lack we constantly try to assuage through desire. This ever-present lack, or loss, becomes the focus of an unattainable desire that circles endlessly around its object without ever attaining it. The idea of the *real*, this all-pervasive lack that we endeavour in vain to resolve, allows us to gain an important perspective on the universality of revivalism. It is not simply about the specific language or custom or architectural practice that we want to revive, but, if we accept Lacan's ideas, the lack that in itself constitutes desire is a universal concern that we cannot escape.

The paradox of the *real* is also the paradox of revivalism – the seeming impossibility of trying to return to something that is no longer available to us.[13]

Of course, both Freud and Lacan, as well as being hugely influential twentieth-century thinkers, are also highly controversial figures. One criticism of the application of their theories to societal phenomena such as revivalism is that any contribution they have to make is strictly to our understanding of the psychology of individuals rather than societies. Yet the existence of what is called the 'Freudian left' and the 'Lacanian left' – essentially the application of psychoanalysis to political radicalism – is just one indication of their relevance to broader collective concerns.[14] Where literary discourse is concerned, the relevance of Freud and Lacan is less contestable than in other areas – the original exposition of their ideas frequently invoked the canon of Western literature, and they, in turn, have informed both the production of literature and literary theory in myriad ways.[15] Accordingly, references to Freud and Lacan in this book stem mostly from their significance to literary discourse, to which they have contributed an influential conceptual frame of reference.

Returning to the paradox of revivalism, the attempt to restore that which is no longer attainable, it is not surprising that the notion of return invites the same scepticism as utopianism – both are routinely dismissed as the product of wishful thinking with no material evidence to support them. Yet it is in the practical attempt to revive past values or practices that some possible solutions emerge to the paradox of revivalism. Before looking at these potential solutions we need to consider again briefly the impasse presented in an attempt to return to the past. A complete return to the past seems materially impossible. The Christian notion of *apocatastasis*, meaning the universal restoration of all rational beings in the end to God, depends entirely on religious faith in such a future event.[16] In the material domain, even a partial restoration of elements of the past – say, a state's restoration of former laws and economic policies – would not bring back the conditions of the past itself since these laws and economic policies would be inserted into a new and different context. If Prohibition laws were restored today in the US, they would have even less efficacy than they had in the 1920s and early 1930s, if only for the much greater availability of illegal drugs as an alternative to alcohol. So the question arises, if we attempt to revive elements of the past, how can we be sure of what we are restoring? If the continuity of a cultural tradition has been interrupted, can it ever be restored? Rather than a restoration of the past, it is much more plausible to speak of a 'renewal', or re-establishment of elements of the past, that takes into account that such a renewal involves an engagement between past and present, which potentially alters both.

The choice between faithful continuity on the one hand and renewal on the other is one that pervades the discourse of revivalism. The co-founder of the revivalist Gaelic League, Douglas Hyde (1860–1949), famously declared that the aim of his organisation was to 'render the present a rational continuation of the past', although he said this at a time, at the end of the nineteenth century, when *continuation* of an unbroken linguistic tradition applied to a much larger geographical base than it does today.[17] Nevertheless, much of the Gaelic League's programme entailed a renewal, in the sense of something that is re-established after an interruption, and the league's renewal of the Irish literary tradition can indeed be posited as one of its great successes. As mentioned earlier, the Gothic Revival movement in nineteenth-century Britain and Ireland aimed to restore the standards of medieval architecture, yet part of the rationale for this was a critique of the present and what many felt was the loss of religious values in the industrial age. As such, the Gothic order was not simply restored in the nineteenth century but, rather, renewed and transformed by the new circumstances of the present.

The difference between continuation and renewal is closely related to the difference between *being* and *becoming*. The question of whether or not things are bound by a resolute continuity or permanence that we call *being*, or are subject to a constant state of flux that we call *becoming*, is one of the most enduring questions to emerge from pre-Socratic philosophy. Heraclitus articulated the case for *becoming*, often summarised by his maxim that one cannot stand in the same river twice since the water is never the same but always flowing and changing. Parmenides, on the other hand, held that 'Being was never born and never dies' – that is, the divisions in the world are dissolved by the uninterrupted continuity of *being* that is 'one and continuous'.[18] Being, therefore, implies continuation, whereas *becoming* is literally 'coming to be' – that is, a new departure. In the case of revivalist movements, there is frequently an opposition between the faithful transmission of continuous tradition and the desire to renew that tradition through a radical new intervention between past and present. Part of the contention between these rival intentions centres on the question of authenticity. Can one ever insist on a faithful continuation of tradition that we call authenticity, or is it the case that things are in a constant state of flux and so bound to change and become different in order to exist at all? More fundamentally, can we revive something that has ceased to exist? The answer to these questions, where revivalism is concerned, is that revival is not merely a return to or restoration of the past but typically a dynamic engagement with the past. In this sense it resembles the type of transition that is central to Hegel's dialectic and, in particular, the Hegelian notion of *Aufhebung*.

The literal meaning of *Aufhebung* is, paradoxically, 'abolition' and 'preserving' as well as 'raising up'.[19] The obscure English term 'sublation' has been most commonly employed as a translation. An example of *Aufhebung* is presented in Hegel's discussion of how the family and civil society are 'sublated' through the development of the state. The state supersedes both institutions, the family and civil society, by cancelling them out but at the same time retaining them. The family is characterised by the bond of love, whereas civil society essentially comprises competing individuals. Within the state the divisions of civil society are overcome within a new, unifying polity that still, paradoxically, maintains the element of competition between individuals. Similarly, the state maintains the institution of family by securing its position, but at the same time cancels it out by allowing for a new, higher type of family in which people are bound together through their identification with the nation.[20] Just as the literal notion of revival is paradoxical, Hegel appears to have valued the inherent paradox of the word *Aufhebung* being simultaneously 'to abolish' and 'to preserve'.[21] Where revival is concerned, the transition described as *Aufhebung* reflects both the paradox and resolution of the attempt to revive past values in the present. Both the past and the present are transformed in this dialectical sequence, and what remains is both a negation and preservation of each.

An example of such a transition in Irish literary revivalism is Máirtín Ó Cadhain's 1949 novel *Cré na Cille* (The Dirty Dust/Graveyard Clay). Ó Cadhain was a native speaker of Irish whose literary career belonged to an era in which, as he himself remarked, everyone's Irish was revivalist.[22] As a writer, he was also aware that his greatest inheritance was not the Irish literary tradition but, rather, native speech.[23] It is fitting then that Ó Cadhain's *Cré na Cille* (discussed in detail in Chapter 5) eschews narrative conventions, such as a narrator/narrators and indirect speech, and is presented instead entirely as direct speech. By so doing, he engages retrospectively with one of the defining debates of the Gaelic League, namely, the *caint na ndaoine* (the speech of the people) versus *Gaeilge Chéitinn* (the Irish of Keating) argument.[24] The debate, which dominated revivalist polemics from the 1880s to 1920s, concerned which form the literary language of the new revivalist literature should take: the contemporary speech of the people or the historical corpus of the seventeenth century, exemplified in the writing of Seathrún Céitinn (Geoffrey Keating) (*c.* 1580–*c.* 1644). The lines were drawn between those who held that any new literature in Irish had to be based on a definite historical precedent and those who thought that any such return to the standards of the seventeenth century would be a contrivance and thus doomed to failure. Ó Cadhain's novel, comprised entirely of speech, is clearly an endorsement of common speech as a literary medium, but it also transforms that speech into an instrument of modernist literary expression. At the same time, it retains the prestige of the historical literary corpus by creating a novel that is so esteemed that it is now deemed peerless and therefore equal, if not superior to, the seventeenth-century 'gold-standard' of Keating. In so doing, it simultaneously cancels out and preserves both common speech and literary precedent, raising each to a higher level of development.

Rather than being a continuation of the Irish literary tradition, Ó Cadhain's novel represents a distinct renewal. This opposition of continuation and renewal in revivalism, underpinned by the pre-Socratic dichotomy of *being* and *becoming*, is a dichotomy that became a significant concern in the philosophy of Friedrich Nietzsche.[25] Nietzsche's work is relevant to our discussion of revivalism for two main reasons: his modern interpretation of *being* and *becoming*, and his application to modernity of the theme of eternal return, or 'eternal recurrence'. Eternal recurrence, for Nietzsche, was the obligation to relive the same events over and over again.[26] Although this appeared initially to be a nightmarish bind, he famously came to see it as a marvellous opportunity. For Nietzsche, the willingness to embrace the endless repetition of all of the trials of life was a test of strength and an opportunity to affirm a yea-saying attitude to living. Central to this attitude was Nietzsche's views on *becoming*, which he interpreted as a dynamic exercise of the will. Tellingly, in the following piece from *Beyond Good and Evil* (1886) he attributes *becoming* rather than *being* as a quintessentially German trait: 'The German himself *is* not, he is *becoming*, he is "developing". "Development" is thus the truly German discovery and lucky shot in the great domain of philosophical formulas.'[27] Of course, Nietzschean philosophy, with its 'will to power' and 'Übermensch', is all too often associated with the horrors of Nazism rather than with any progressive-minded programme. However, the passage quoted above is a discussion of German identity, about which there seems to Nietzsche to be no clear definition; rather, Germans were a mass of contradictions. Far from being a discourse on racial purity, Nietzsche attributes a distinct lack of definition and continuity to the Germans. The fact that their origins were obscure, that they were a 'middle people', lacking an unbroken continuity with the past, all of this meant that 'The German himself *is* not, he is *becoming*, he is "developing".'

Notwithstanding the argument made here for renewal rather than continuation, Douglas Hyde's wish for a 'rational continuation' was a valid one at the end of the nineteenth century, and remains so in twenty-first-century Ireland. Those who live in the *Gaeltacht* have a right to expect that their linguistic ecosystem should continue, and, where the state is concerned, enjoy whatever assistance its constitutional guarantee should afford. In this case, 'language revitalisation' is a more appropriate aim than revival. Outside of the *Gaeltacht*, a renewal of the interrupted linguistic tradition implies *becoming*, as indicated in terms like *Nua-Ghaeltacht* (Neo-*Gaeltacht*) and 'new speakers'. One of the criticisms frequently made of revivalism is its perceived inauthenticity, the idea that *becoming* involves a self-conscious reinvention of self and of the cultural or linguistic tradition to which one wishes to return. In this sense 'new speakers' are regarded as similar to 'new money' or nouveau riche – they are a shoddy imitation of those steeped in the social mores of 'old money', and their behaviour is consequently alien to the authentic aristocratic tradition. The Irish literary tradition is replete with similar criticisms made against those who are seen as lacking either the requisite pedigree or an awareness of what is authentic. Two noted examples from diverse periods are the seventeenth-century satire *Pairlement Chloinne Tomáis* (The Parliament of Clan Thomas) and, in the twentieth century, Máire Mhac an tSaoi's critique of Seán Ó Ríordáin's (1916–77) lyrical poems in his *Eireaball Spideoige* (A Robin's Tail) (1952) – the crude imitation of English manners and speech being the object of satire in the former, and a lack of native Irish authenticity the criticism of the latter.[28]

One counter-argument to the notion that revivalism merely produces inauthentic, invented traditions is that revivals need not claim to reinstate the past – something that is manifestly impossible – but that, rather, as in Hegel's notion of *Aufhebung*, or sublation, both elements are negated but partially maintained by means of being elevated to a higher level as part of a creative renewal. A practical example is the creative renewal of tradition exemplified in various cultural festivals in Celtic countries, such as the Welsh *eisteddfod*, the Scottish *mòd*, and the Irish Oireachtas na Gaeilge. All were inspired by historic festivals or gatherings that had long since expired. Yet their fidelity to their historical precedents is of little consequence; instead, each has generated an enormous amount of activity that allows elements of past traditions to survive in a new form while at the same time being the site of a new social and aesthetic dynamic that could not have come about without the initial 'reinvention'.[29] The distinction between a simple regurgitation of the past and a return to the possibilities of the past is expressed by Martin Heidegger in the concept of *Wiederholung*, literally 'repetition', but more properly understood in Heidegger's philosophy as 'retrieval' and 'non-identical repetition'. Heidegger developed this concept in *Being and Time* (1927) as part of his radical reassessment of the question of *being*, where he presented his understanding of the concept *Dasein* (literally, 'being there').[30] Heidegger's *Wiederholung* does not involve reinstating the past but, rather, 'going back into the possibilities of the *Dasein* that has-been-there ... Repeating of that which is possible does not bring again [Wiederbringen] something that is 'past', nor does it bind the 'Present' back to that which has already been outstripped.'[31]

Just as the contrast between *being* and *becoming*, continuation and renewal, are central concepts in revivalism, a belief in latency and potentiality are also crucial to its project. In particular, faith in the latent power of cultural memory is a pervasive motif in revivalism, and one that is given expression in the phrase 'cultural awakening'. Equally important is the sense in which revivalists see their mission as involving the exercise of agency. Often, as is the case with many nationalist revivals, this entails a recovery of agency previously denied through a period of subjugation. Revivalism takes the age-old belief in a return to a state of perfection (the world restored that we find in religion), and makes this instead a radical intervention in the present. Its antecedents may often be in religious belief, particularly the expectation of a glorious return, but its radical innovation is to exchange expectation for intervention, to attempt to exercise agency in the here and now. Revivalism's engagement of past and present leads to a sublation, or *Aufhebung*, involving both the progressive and the conservative – the perceived recovery of agency being its progressive element and its return to past values and practices the conservative. The accommodation of this contradiction is reminiscent of Terry Eagleton's phrase to describe the emergence of an Irish modernist sensibility in the late nineteenth century, 'the archaic *avant-garde*'.[32]

The important point here is that we need not fetishise an authentic past that becomes invalidated as soon as its pristine continuity is breached; rather, tradition typically involves periods of critical or creative renewal. Nevertheless, the expressions of revivalism discussed in this book frequently include a certain anxiety for the secure transmission of what is valued from the past, such as the aesthetic traditions of bardic poetry or the riches of the oral tradition. That preoccupation with fixed continuity with the past is discussed in Chapter 5, where the motif of preternaturally old survivors of the past in medieval Irish literature is compared with the phenomenon of totemic individuals in the modern Gaelic League era, such as the poet Colm de Bhailís (1796–1906), whose remarkable lifespan was taken as a physical expression of continuity. Yet the real value of such exceptional personages is to reveal the latency rather than the permanence of a tradition. They are figures of potentiality rather than perpetuity.

With all of this in mind, it seems clear that *becoming*, especially as understood by Nietzsche, is the really indispensable element of revivalism. While Hegel's notion of *Aufhebung* reflects the type of engagement of past and present that revivalism initiates, Hegel's belief that dialectical processes led to an ultimate resolution is at odds with Nietzsche's ideas on radical *becoming*. Nietzsche objected to the idea of any world-historical teleology, whether religious or connected with worldly progress, on the grounds that, as Lawrence Hatab remarks, 'a purpose implies an end point that resolves "becoming" into a state of "being"'.[33] Nietzsche insisted instead on:

> The absolute necessity of a total liberation from ends (*Zwecken*): otherwise we should not be permitted to try to sacrifice ourselves and let ourselves go. Only the innocence of *becoming* (*die Unschuld des Werdens*) gives us the *greatest courage* and *the greatest freedom*.[34]

Of course, many revivals are conceived as part of a distinct teleology such as the nation's destiny or the will of God. The revival of the Aryan race in Nazi Germany or the caliphate in the case of Islamic State are two such examples. Yet for all their faith in a glorious destiny, the proponents of those egregious movements clearly held human agency to be essential to the radical transformation of society. Therefore, revivalism's reliance on *becoming*, on the creative possibilities inherent in a radical departure, represents both its regressive as well as its emancipatory potential.

Besides agency, alterity is also of crucial importance to revivalism, in its insistence on the latent possibility of difference rather than passive acceptance of the linear progress of human affairs. As such, it is no accident that there should be much similarity between revivalism and utopianism. Both are predicated on the possibility of a critical intervention in human affairs to bring about a radical change of direction, and both rely on an alternative view of how the present and future might be configured. Again, utopianism, like revivalism, can just as easily be a socially and politically regressive critical practice as much as an emancipatory one. What it need not be, however, is a passive acceptance of the seemingly natural or inevitable progress of human affairs. All of this considered, revivalism is not so much about guaranteeing the continuity of the past as pointing to the agency of the present.

The ultimate aim of this discussion of the theoretical issues involved in revivalism is to pave the way for the conceptual case study of revivalism in modern Irish literature that follows. While it is important to locate revivalism within a broader context than might initially be expected, the intention here is not to lose sight of the specificity of the case study to which this book is devoted. One is reminded of the late Donnchadh Ó Corráin's warning that 'the disease of Irish history in modern times is the generic and the national'.[35] Nevertheless, it is the erroneous assumption that we know what we mean by 'revival' – so much so that it has become almost exclusively associated with a specific period of Irish history between the 1890s and 1920s – that requires us to first consider the generic concept of revival before proceeding any further. This is no less apparent when one attempts to assign a starting point to the discussion of Irish-language revivalism. A text such as *Auraicépt na n-Éces* (The Scholars' Primer), originating in the seventh century, is one example of a work that deals with the revival of past knowledge – in this case, the origins of the Irish language and the ogham alphabet are presented as a defence of the use of the Irish language based on its ancient and noble origins.[36] In a similar way, the great manuscript collections of the twelfth century, such as Lebor na hUidre (The Book of the Dun Cow) and Lebor na Nuachongbála (The Book of Leinster), were conceived as part of a renewal of cultural knowledge, just as James Carney considered fourteenth-century Ireland to have been marked by a distinct 'literary revival'.[37] While various forms of revival could be identified in the Irish literary tradition, from its earliest expression in the seventh century onwards, the specific concern of this book is the modern period. The logic of the preceding argument is that revival is perennial, and, as such, any attempt to seek a point of origin would be futile. My contention is that a distinct tradition of revival, that one might style 'revivalism', is discernible from the seventeenth century to the present day, but that one cannot fully detach this particular tradition of revivalism, no more than any other, from the more general expressions of 'return' in human culture. As Pádraig de Paor points out, if Irish revivalism is a sociopolitical movement, it also has a deeper metaphysical concern with being itself.[38] While there is a marked tendency not to see beyond the specific historical circumstances of Irish revivalism, this can only occlude those deeper connections that arise not just from speculative enquiry but from the historical evidence itself, which places Irish revivalism in dialogue with movements such as the Renaissance, the Reformation and the Counter-Reformation, utopianism, and so on.

As the title of this chapter implies, the discussion so far has been offered 'towards a theory of revivalism', there being no sustained theory of revivalism available to us. All of the issues discussed above are part of the complex that underlies the production of literature in modern Irish. The aim of presenting this conceptual case study is, therefore, to do justice to the critical legacy of revivalism in modern Irish literature, but, in so doing, to yield broader insights towards a theoretical frame of reference for revivalism. Although a 'return' to the past is part of what is initiated in revivalism, it goes far beyond this. It is typically a dynamic renewal that engages past values in the present, and by so doing alters both. For this reason, the charge of inauthenticity, of the 'invented tradition', is misplaced. Revivalism is not an attempt at seamless continuity but more properly an act of *becoming* that takes the residue of the past not as a sign of finality but, rather, of latency and possibility. In so doing, it allows us a certain objectivity in relation to language and culture where, rather than being simply part of our passive inheritance, both are seen to be actively acquired. The critical intervention that is revivalism is ultimately, then, the realisation of agency.

CHAPTER 2

The Anxiety of Transmission:
The lives and afterlives of
seventeenth-century Irish revivalism

The body of Counter-Reformation literature in Irish, which emanated from the Irish colleges of the European mainland during the seventeenth century, can be considered as a forerunner of later revivals, particularly from the nineteenth century onwards. The evidence that the collective aims and methods of this movement have been regarded as something of a touchstone, if not a template, for Irish revivalism up to the present day is the main focus of this chapter. But before beginning this particular discussion, it is important to note that the Counter-Reformation itself is especially relevant to the earlier discussion of revivalism as a concept, given that it draws on two periods of European history that share the homology of revivalism, namely the Renaissance and the Reformation. Renaissance humanism was founded on a revival of classical learning typified in the slogan *ad fontes*, to go 'back to the sources', and this imperative was taken up by the leaders of the Reformation in their emphasis on a return to the sources of scripture. The Counter-Reformation absorbed both of these aspirations as well as the Reformation's innovative use of the vernacular, a development that was, of course, of obvious significance to the revitalisation and incipient popularisation of the Irish language as a literary medium in the seventeenth century.

Indeed, it is clear that Gaelic Ireland did not have to wait for the advent of the Counter-Reformation in order to benefit from the innovative principles of Renaissance humanism. This much is evident in Brendan Bradshaw's examination of Renaissance influences on the life and work of Maghnas Ó Domhnaill (*c.* 1490–1563), which, Bradshaw contends, justifies a comparison with the typical Renaissance prince. In particular, the features that

characterise Ó Domhnaill's life of St Colm Cille, *Betha Colaim Chille*, as a
Renaissance work – its lay authorship, its antiquarian character and its vernacular language – are precisely those on which Ó Domhnaill comments in
his preface, thus reflecting the author's self-consciously unconventional cast
of mind and readiness to eschew off hidebound tradition, both of which are
typical of the Renaissance outlook.[1] Further evidence of the influence of the
Renaissance on Gaelic Ireland, albeit frequently mediated through English
sources, has also been meticulously traced by Mícheál Mac Craith.[2] Indeed,
the coexistence of tradition and innovation within the Irish bardic mindset
prior to the emergence of the Irish Counter-Reformation corpus has been
persuasively argued by Marc Caball, following a line of analysis established
by Bradshaw's discussion of the *Leabhar Branach* (The Book of the O'Byrnes)
and Breandán Ó Buachalla's commentary on the Gaelic literati's response to
the accession of James VI (as James I) to the English throne in 1603.[3]

In the light of such evidence, one might ask why we should begin a discussion of Irish revivalism with the Franciscan Counter-Reformation literature
of the early seventeenth century when it could easily be antedated? While recognising that the atemporality of revival as a concept may render any starting
point arbitrary, the rationale for beginning with the early seventeenth century
is based on the continuity of revivalist aims and motivations, which link this
period more than any other with subsequent manifestations of revivalism.
While the sixteenth century witnessed a rapid growth of national consciousness throughout Europe – itself a by-product of the classical revival of the
Renaissance that identified the homeland, or *patria*, as the centre of allegiance
– the convergence of a form of Irish literary revival with faith-and-fatherland
nationalism in the early seventeenth century bears frequent correlation with
later forms of revivalism, and has served as a model for later reflections on
revivalism. Important examples of this are Tomás Ó Flannghaile's essay on the
Franciscan scholar Mícheál Ó Cléirigh (*c.* 1590–1643) in his influential *For the
Tongue of the Gael* (1896) and Patrick Kavanagh's polemical poem 'Memory of
Brother Michael'.[4] Furthermore, the developed sense of national consciousness
that is evident in the early seventeenth century is exemplified, to some extent,
by the first recorded use of the word 'nation' in Irish in Tadhg Ó Cianáin's
diary of the Flight of the Earls in 1607 and their subsequent travels through
Europe.[5] It is also important to note that the devotion of Irish Franciscan
scholars in this period to the doctrine of the Immaculate Conception and to
the theological work of Duns Scotus (*c.* 1266–1308), whom they mistakenly
believed to be Irish, provided the context for the forging of a form of Irish

national identity that was tempered by a strong sense of Ireland's place in Europe's spiritual and intellectual inheritance.[6] The importance of the concept of nation and nationhood to revivalism in the intervening period is beyond doubt. Yet what is of equal significance is the sense in which the concept of revival itself is not only put into practice but consciously discussed at a theoretical level in seventeenth-century Irish literature.

The first Counter-Reformation book published in Irish was Giolla Brighde (alias Bonabhentúra) Ó hEódhasa's *An Teagasg Críosdaidhe* (Catechism), printed in Antwerp in 1611.[7] Previous to this, printing in Irish had been initiated by Protestant churchmen. Indeed, the first book printed in Irish was Seon Carsuel's *Foirm na nUrrnuidheadh* (1567), a translation of *The Book of Common Order*, which had been printed in Edinburgh.[8] Carsuel's envoy is addressed to the 'men of Scotland and Ireland' and identifies the Franciscans as the explicit enemies of Calvinism.[9] The use of the vernacular by Carsuel was consistent with the Reformationists' desire to give universal access to scripture rather than it being available only to learned elites. In keeping with this, he preempts criticism that his prose fell short of the standards laid down by the poets by declaring that he had 'made no special study of Gaelic except as any one of the common people'.[10] Carsuel's publication appears to have spurred the Established Church to enter the field with Seán Ó Cearnaigh's *Aibidil Gaoidheilge & Caiticiosma* (Gaelic Alphabet and Catechism) (1571), followed by Uilliam Ó Domhnaill's translation of the New Testament and *The Book of Common Prayer* in 1603 and 1608 respectively. The successful introduction of printing in Irish in the service of the Reformation undoubtedly encouraged the Catholic Counter-Reformationists to make print their medium. More pertinently for this discussion, the dynamics of reform and counter-reform, renaissance and renewal were crucial to both the development of print culture and a revitalisation of the literary medium in Irish in the early modern period.

In Ailbhe Ó Corráin's discussion of the poem 'A fhir léghtha an leabhráin bhig' (O man that reads the little book), Giolla Brighde Ó hEódhasa's address to the reader of his *An Teagasg Críosdaidhe* (1611), Ó Corráin explores the influence of northern European Renaissance humanism on Ó hEódhasa's poem, evident in its very opening lines, which encourage the reader to return *ad fontes* – '*féch an tobar ó ttáinig*' (take heed of its source).[11] Ó Corráin's close reading highlights the poet's desire to promote the virtues of renewal, initially a Counter-Reformationist renewal of the faith, but also a renewal of language and nationhood. Ó hEódhasa's poem reflects the universal principles of both the Counter-Reformation and Renaissance humanism, but its message is clearly intended for the specific needs of its Irish readership. The renewal of language implicit in the use of Irish rather than Latin for devotional and learned texts was a common thread of Irish Counter-Reformation literature. This insistence on vernacular versions of scripture was a feature of evangelical humanism, eagerly expressed by Erasmus (1466–1536): 'I wish that every woman would read the Gospel and the Epistles of Paul ... I wish these were translated into each and every language ... read and understood not only by Scots and Irishmen, but also by Turks and Saracens ...'[12] The Reformation took up this clarion call in its own fashion, championing the use of the vernacular in scripture and public worship. Following the Council of Trent (1545–63), the Irish Counter-Reformation authors endeavoured to outdo the reformers by producing a number of popular devotional texts in Irish and, like the reformers, exploiting the increased availability of printing presses, accessible in Spanish Flanders to the Irish Franciscans of St Anthony's College, Louvain.

Giolla Brighde Ó hEódhasa's renewal of the literary language involved a simplicity of expression that was all the more significant for his having been a bardic poet and one of the most respected scholars of his day.[13] This conscious renewal of language through the adoption of a more common idiom foreshadows the debates among Gaelic Leaguers in the late nineteenth and early twentieth centuries over the respective claims of *caint na ndaoine* (the speech of the people) and *Gaeilge Chéitinn* (the Irish of Keating) as an appropriate literary medium for the revival. Flaithrí Ó Maolchonaire (Florence Conry) (*c.* 1560–1629) also took up the radical standard of language renewal in the second catechetical text to be published by the Louvain Franciscans, his Irish version of the Catalan devotional text *Sgáthán an Chrábhaidh* (Mirror of Piety), more commonly known as *Desiderius* (1616).[14] In his foreword to this work, produced on the printing press acquired by St Anthony's College, Ó Maolchonaire provides a rationale for his zeal, *ar son simplidheachta na sttíli ... chum leasa na ndaoine simplidhe* (for simplicity of style ... for the sake of simple people.)[15] This was again all the more impressive a commitment for one who belonged to a family for which the profession of letters was hereditary and for whom erudition was generally paraded as a mark of social distinction.[16] Having spurned the Irish writer's predilection for archaic language and alliterative excesses when such temptations were accessible to him, Ó Maolchonaire was on a solid footing for the 'Mirror of Piety' that ensued. In this way, the renewal of language and faith is securely intertwined, just as it is in Ó hEódhasa's work. The third form of renewal, that of nationhood, or *patria*, is equally implicit in *Desiderius*, in which, among the many liberties taken with the source text, is the interpolation of a substantial section where Irish Catholics are encouraged to persevere in their faith.[17] The identification of faith and nationhood was typical of the confessionalism that dominated European affairs after the Reformation, a reflection of which is the motto inscribed above the entrance to St Anthony's College, Louvain: *Dochum Glóire Dé agus Ónóra na hÉireann* (For the Glory of God and the Honour of Ireland).[18] Indeed, it is significant that where the Established Church's 1571 Irish catechism was devoted to 'the glory of God and the commonweal', the Irish Counter-Reformationists increasingly deferred to the honour of the *nation*.[19]

The conscious renewal of language pioneered by Ó hEódhasa, Ó Maolchonaire and others, such as Aodh Mac Aingil (1571–1626), is essential to a movement that has been called the 'Louvain school of Modern Irish'.[20] Yet these writers' enunciation of the virtues of simplicity does not necessarily equate to an emancipation of the literary medium. The intended audience was undoubtedly all-embracing, but a deferential view towards the norms of the literary caste and their craft was largely retained. Thus, Mac Aingil, who appears to have had formal literary training himself, apologises to the reader for his simple style and poor writing in the foreword to his *Scáthán Shacramuinte na hAithridhe* (A Mirror on the Sacrament of Penance).[21] Indeed, it appears that Theobold Stapleton (*c.* 1589–1647), a secular priest and author of a catechism published in 1639, is unique in having explicitly criticised the learned class, whom he regarded as having cultivated obscurity.[22] Yet while such conscious challenges to the hegemony of the literary class were rare, there can be no doubt that this movement was responsible for a reform and renewal of language that accompanied the renewal of faith and fatherland. This much was also apparent in a renewal of literary forms, of which the diary of Tadhg Ó Cianáin (*fl.* 1602–08) is a striking example. Being the first use of the diary form in Irish, albeit not strictly a daily diary, Ó Cianáin's work is by definition innovative. His use of numerous neologisms from other European languages – including Latin, English, French, Spanish, Dutch, Italian – is a further instance of his originality.[23]

Besides the catechetical texts discussed above, grammatical and lexicographical works, such as Mícheál Ó Cléirigh's *Foclóir nó Sanasán Nua* (Dictionary or New Wordbook) (1643), met the need for a standardised language that accompanied printing. The other major areas of output for this period were hagiography, history and literary anthology. The printed books and manuscripts that were produced in these fields testify to the national project that underpinned them, as well as to a revival of sources that may otherwise have perished. While not part of the vernacular literature, John Colgan's (1592–1658) Latin lives of the Irish saints, *Acta Sanctorum Hiberniae* (1645), was clearly intended to secure the honour and general recognition of the Irish Catholic nation. The work Colgan edited was the fruit of research carried out by the trained historian Mícheál Ó Cléirigh, who had travelled around Ireland between 1626 and 1637 collecting, transcribing and studying material while based in a Franciscan friary on the Drowes River, County Donegal. As was also the case with the historical texts produced in this era, with their diligent attention to sources, the hagiographical works of this period bore the stamp of the Renaissance and its rallying cry of *ad fontes*.[24] While the eleven years spent by Ó Cléirigh in Ireland were initially devoted to the hagiographical material, this work was soon complemented by research towards the writing of secular history. The most important of these was *Annála Ríoghachta Éireann* (Annals of the Kingdom of Ireland), completed in 1636 with the assistance of three other eminent scholars, Cú Choigcríche Ó Cléirigh (*fl.* 1630–62), Fearfeasa Ó Maolchonaire (*fl.* 1630–46) and Cú Choigcríche Ó Duibhgeannáin (*fl.* 1630–41), leading to this work's more popular title, 'The Annals of the Four Masters'.

Added to the historical work of Ó Cléirigh and his collaborators, the completion in 1634 of *Foras Feasa ar Éirinn* (History of Ireland) by Seathrún Céitinn (Geoffrey Keating) marks a signal development in the progress of nation-building under the Counter-Reformation. Being himself of Anglo-Norman stock, Keating's highly influential work was particularly significant for the way in which it consolidated the new Irish Catholic identity under the collective name of *Éireannaigh*, or people born in Ireland, which included, crucially, those like Keating who were of Anglo-Norman stock, but excluded the recently arrived Protestants.[25] The ongoing project of renewal of language, faith and national identity is given powerful advocacy in Keating's work, testament to which are the numerous manuscript copies of *Foras Feasa ar Éirinn* and the persistent manner in which his history was absorbed and promulgated by Gaelic literati over the course of the next 250 years.[26]

The compilation of anthologies of the Irish literary canon was part of the same nationalising project observed in the other branches of Irish writing in the first half of the seventeenth century. However, while St Anthony's College, Louvain was a fulcrum for such activity, the impetus for the compilation of two of the most significant literary anthologies of the time emanated from that other mainstay of the Irish community in Spanish Flanders, the Irish

Regiment. *Duanaire Finn* (The Poem-book of Finn), a compilation of poems relating to Finn mac Cumhaill and the *Fianna*, and *The Book of the O'Conor Don*, a highly significant collection of bardic poems, were commissioned by Captain Somhairle Mac Domhnaill (*c.* 1586–1632) of the Glens of Antrim, and transcribed by a member of the Irish Regiment, Aodh Ó Dochartaigh. Besides being the most extensive collection of Irish bardic poetry in existence, *The Book of the O'Conor Don* differs from other such *duanaireadha*, or poembooks, in that it is not a collection of poems for a single patron or family but a collection in which the leading families of Ireland are venerated, and, as such, deserves to be seen as a 'national *duanaire*'.[27]

The lineaments of the great literary project of the Irish Counter-Reformation are succinctly represented in the Irish motto of St Anthony's College extolling faith and fatherland, mentioned earlier. Yet the specific Irish evocation of these values was underscored by the universal values issuing from the Renaissance revival of classical learning and the ideals of northern European humanism – the revival of the cult of *patria* and the return to sources being prominent examples. It was also deeply influenced by the movement that it initially sought to counteract, the Reformation, which itself championed a return to the sources of scripture. The sense in which the corpus of Irish writing in this period is a manifestation of the perennial return or revival in human culture and is, as such, homologous with movements such as the Renaissance that preceded it, and those that would follow, is supported by one further example. This is the preface to the manuscript of Fr Nioclás (Fearghal Dubh) Ó Gadhra OSA, an important collection of Irish bardic poetry that was mostly written in Lille between 1655 and 1659. In Pádraig Ó Macháin's discussion of the preface to this manuscript, written by its author in 1686, he draws attention to Ó Gadhra's reason for writing, where 'he establishes that the regeneration or recycling (*athnuachradh*) of tradition from age to age represents standard practice in both biblical and pagan literature'.[28]

One is reminded again of the issue outlined in the introduction, the challenge to the notion that revival is strictly contingent on the thing that is to be revived. Yet how likely is it that seventeenth-century Irish clerics, whose entire outlook and purpose in the world was circumscribed by devotion to the Christian faith, would have troubled themselves to record their reflections on the universal significance of the concepts of renewal and revival? It seems highly unlikely that they would have been so inclined, but that, for them, renewal or revival was indeed contingent on, entirely bound up with, their absolute commitment and service to their faith – their first allegiance being to the resurrection rather than cultural revival. It is reasonable to assert, however, that the preoccupation in religion with transcending the limitations of mortality, notably through resurrection or reincarnation, appears to prepare a path for cultural revivalism that is itself about giving new life to past cultural forms of expression. Eliade's thesis, in which eternal return is a common inheritance of religion, would appear to support the view that the concept of revival is firmly rooted in religious belief. Certainly, in the work of the Irish Counter-Reformation authors the act of renewal was grounded in matters of faith, but gradually came to include the non-religious sphere, particularly secular history, albeit in the service of confessionalism and the consolidation of an Irish Catholic nation. The eventual decoupling of the spiritual and secular in the modern epoch has been discussed by Anthony D. Smith in relation to the rise of the 'scientific state', which challenges the legitimacy of religious explanations, leading to situations of 'dual legitimation', of which those affected are 'the modern equivalents of pre-modern clerisies, the intellectuals'.[29] If the universal significance of revivalism has been more commonly explored by modern intellectuals rather than by pre-modern clerics, it is because the latter had less need to do so, their concept of universality being indivisible from their belief in God.

Having given a general survey of the Irish literature of the Counter-Reformation and its relation to the concepts of revival and renewal, it is worth examining the ways in which this particular movement has influenced subsequent manifestations of Irish revivalism. Of course, Irish revivalism did not depend solely on the Franciscans or on the legacy of the Counter-Reformation, but, as has been mentioned before, the writing and publishing project of this era has had an enduring influence on subsequent expressions of Irish revivalism, particularly from the nineteenth century onwards. Although important Irish publications emanated from the continental Irish colleges during the eighteenth century – the very first Irish-English dictionary was published in Paris in 1732 and included a resolutely revivalist envoy – the legacy of this specific strand of revivalism is less apparent in this century, as indicated in a recent history of the Irish Franciscans, where the eighteenth century has been subtitled 'the silent century'.[30] It is also worth noting that St Anthony's College, along with other Irish colleges, was forcibly closed in the aftermath of the French Revolution.[31] While the legacy of the Irish colleges endured in the eighteenth century, as evidenced, for example, in references to Louvain in the poetry of Séamus Dall Mac Cuarta (1650–1733), the revivalist strands of the century are less indebted to Louvain than to the doughty perseverance of native scholarship and arts and to the prevailing winds of the Jacobite, Enlightenment and Romantic movements.[32]

Where the Enlightenment is concerned, an unlikely alliance of Franciscan scholarship and free-thinking rationalism is presented in the intriguing figure of John Toland (1670–1722).[33] The scholar and polemicist was also a native Irish speaker from Inishowen, County Donegal who sought out the Irish Franciscans in Prague to vouch for his lineage. The entente between Eoghan na Leabhar (Eoghan of the Books), as Toland was also known, and the Franciscans was not as counterintuitive as it may appear. Besides the likelihood of local ties with the members of the Prague Irish college, Toland's work at times drew on his knowledge of Irish manuscripts, and his 'History of the Druids' was concerned with uncovering the occluded tradition of ogham writing, which, he argued, had been repressed by the introduction of Christianity to Ireland with its 'book burning and letter-murdering humor'.[34] To this extent, the recovery of suppressed letters and literacy was an aim that the rationalist Toland shared with his fellow writers, albeit to different ends.[35]

An indication of how the Franciscan inheritance would inform the progress of revivalism in the nineteenth century appears in the first issue of Philip Barron's *Ancient Ireland* (1835), itself an important manifesto of revivalism. Barron chose as his motto a line of poetry composed by the Franciscan author Froinsias Ó Maolmhuaidh (Francis O'Molloy; *c.* 1606–77) of St Isodore's College, Rome:

> The Rev. Francis O'Molloy, D.D. writing upon the Irish language
> in Rome in the year 1676, has the following prophetic line:–
>> '[Gaelic script] Beidh an Ghaodhailig fá mheas fós/
>> [roman script] beih an Gaohailig fa veas fos/ "the
>> Irish will yet be in great esteem"'
> It is near two centuries since the above was written. May we not
> now hope that the period for the fulfilment of this prophecy is
> arrived?[36]

Barron's 'plan for the revival of the Irish language' is discussed in greater detail in the next chapter, but one may say here in summary that his revivalist programme was much less successful in renewing the legacy of the seventeenth-century Irish colleges than the primarily scholarly endeavours of John O'Donovan (1806–61). O'Donovan's edition of *The Annals of the Four Masters* was published between 1848 and 1851 and followed the translation of parts of the work by Rev. Charles O'Conor (1764–1828) in his *Rerum Hibericarum Scriptores Veteres* (1814–28).[37] When we consider the influence of the scholarly work of O'Donovan and Eugene O'Curry (1794–1862) in this period, and the interest in Keating's *Foras Feasa ar Éirinn* (including a translation to English by the Fenian John O'Mahony in 1857), it is clear that the publication and translation of Irish-language historical sources did not just bolster a nationalist agenda but implicitly furthered revivalist aims.[38] These revivalist aims may not have been explicitly and systematically outlined, as they were in the case of Philip Barron, but their effect was no less for that. Nevertheless, our primary concern here is with the development and conscious expression of a revivalist ethic emerging from the Counter-Reformationist tradition, and there are few clearer examples of this than the poem by Ó Maolmhuaidh quoted by Barron.

The 'prophetic line' quoted by Barron is worth exploring in detail, being an example of the articulation of a revivalist call and one that carried great resonance for the future. For example, the same line was used as a motto for the Society for the Preservation of the Irish Language in 1876 and was quoted by Eoin Mac Néill (1867–1945), the co-founder of the Gaelic League, in one of his earliest essays on the Irish language.[39] The poem from which this line is drawn is the envoy to Ó Maolmhuaidh's *Grammatica Latino-Hibernica*, published in 1677 but with the author's foreword written in 1676.[40] The envoy is entitled *Soruidh go hAos Óg ⁊ Éata Oiléin na Naomh* (Hail to the Young and Old of the Island of Saints) and is remarkable for its combination of a pessimistic assessment of the fortunes of the Irish language with a rallying revivalist appeal to his fellow countrymen.[41] The context for this appeal is perhaps best explained in the preface to another of Ó Maolmhuaidh's books, the catechetical text *Lucerna Fidelium* (Lamp of the Faithful) (1676), where Ó Maolmhuaidh excuses his own deficiency in learned Irish, having been in exile for around forty years.[42] Following the example of the Louvain writers, he makes the case for a direct, simple style of Irish to serve the needs of the old and young of Ireland and Gaelic Scotland, who have been beset 'within a short period of time' by a 'fog of ignorance'.[43] This ignorance, he continues, not only pertains to a lack of learning but more critically to a lack of knowledge of the catechism and articles of faith. In the envoy to his *Grammatica Latino-Hibernica*, however, the subject matter allows him to direct himself primarily to the Irish language itself rather than to matters of faith. The *Grammatica* was the first printed grammar of the Irish language, but twelve of its twenty-five chapters are specifically devoted to the prosody of bardic poetry. The decline of the bardic schools, especially in the second half of the seventeenth century, together with the author's own forty years of exile, are the backdrop to Ó Maolmhuaidh's bleak lament for the loss of learned knowledge of the Irish language, typified in one line: *Ní thuig Gaoidhil Gaoidhealg féin* (The Irish do not understand Irish itself).

This lament for both the loss of literacy in Irish and the ignorance of the music and poetry of the bardic schools takes up the first five quatrains of the poem. The sixth quatrain, however, begins with a dramatic rallying cry:

> Fill anosa, a aos mh'anma,
> Nā bī go dian dogharmtha
> 's nach cian ō chathshaoirlios Chuinn
> Go mbia an t-athaoibhnios againn.

> [Return now, oh people dear to my soul,
> Do not be stubbornly resistant to the call
> and it shall not be long until Ireland [the noble fort of Conn]
> will have a second glory.]

These final two lines refer to a famous poem by Fear Flatha Ó Gnímh (*fl.* 1602–40) entitled 'Mo thruaighe mar táid Gaoidhil' (I pity the Gaels as they now stand), composed in the aftermath of the 1609 plantation of Ulster. Ó Gnímh asks the Holy Trinity if the Gaels are to be forever in exile from the 'seat-fort of Conn' (Ireland), or will there be a second glory?[44] Writing at least sixty years later, Ó Maolmhuaidh answers Ó Gnímh's question directly, and goes on to present a vista of miraculous transformations that will follow when the Irish heed his call for a 'return'. With the reinstatement of poetic schools, springs will turn to wine and

> Bia[i]dh an Ghaoidhealg fa mheas mhōr,
> I nĀth Cliath na bhfleasg bhfíonōl;

> [The Irish language will be greatly esteemed,
> In Dublin of the flasks of wine;]

Ó Maolmhuaidh's gloriously transfigured landscape is an inversion of the devastating alienation of Ó Gnímh's poem, in which Ireland no longer recognises itself after the natural order of things has been entirely usurped – beauty replaced by ugliness, law replaced by disorder, and the countryside where hunters' slim steeds once ranged now ploughed up by foreign oxen. Having promised a radically restored landscape in which 'every hero will range as he pleases', the last five quatrains of Ó Maolmhuaidh's poem return to the subject of his envoi – the emancipatory contents of his little book in which the means to write poetry are clearly laid out and the mysteries of the poetic class revealed. In recommending what amounts to a cultural catechism to his readers, Ó Maolmhuaidh makes good his earlier suggestion (fourth quatrain) that 'No death punishment would it be for the men of Ireland/ To keep the oblique rule (of poetic language).'[45] This reference to a metrical rule applied by the bardic poets is intended as a playful allusion to Ó Gnímh's phrase that the men of Ireland have accepted a crooked rule (*riaghail chlaon*).[46] The implication here is that, whatever depredations foreign rule has brought, the Irish can return to the venerable institutions and rules of the poetic schools by force of their own will, and thus restore their fortunes. If in Ó Gnímh's poem the men of Tara, the historic seat of native political power, have been displaced, Ó Maolmhuaidh's message is that the self-willed restoration of native cultural institutions will see the Irish language esteemed, even in Dublin, the historic seat of foreign rule.[47]

The emphasis in Ó Maolmhuaidh's poem on return (*fill anosa*/return now) and renewal (*an t-athaoibhnios*/a second glory) are of obvious significance to the earlier discussion of return and renewal in this chapter. Besides its invocation by Philip Barron in the 1830s, Ó Maolmhuaidh's revivalist appeal also bears striking similarities to later manifestos of revivalism, particularly in its appeal to reason, national honour and a utopian ideal. The abandonment of literacy in Irish is presented as an illogical aberration by reference to an apologue that deals with the eschewal of reason by the learned. The fable tells how, at the beginning of the world, thirty philosophers warned their fellow men of an impending deluge that would destroy all. Finding that no one would believe their warning, the philosophers took shelter in a cave only to find on emerging again that the men of the world had become fools through exposure to the showers of rain. Agreeing that their wisdom was now worthless, the philosophers duly resolved to stand under the rain shower themselves so as to be like everyone else.[48] It is this apologue that is referenced by Ó Maolmhuaidh where he says:

> Fódla liu do chuaidh man gcioth
> I n-aghaidh sluaigh a sinsior;[49]

[All Ireland has submitted to the shower
In contrast to their ancestors;]

Although in another well-known poem by Eochaidh Ó hEódhusa (*c*. 1568–1612) this fable is retold in order to persuade his patron of the virtue of being like everyone else, Ó Maolmhuaidh clearly intends the opposite – the Irish people's having 'submitted to the shower' is a rejection of both reason and continuity, 'in contrast to their ancestors'.[50] Having abandoned knowledge of the Irish language they have been left without honour:

Nī thuig Gaoidhil Gaoidhealg fēin;
Nī labhraid í gan aoinbhēim;
     Nī lēighid le cágaidh cōir;
     trēigid, nī fhāghaid onōir.[51]

[The Irish do not understand Irish itself;
They do not speak it without faultiness;
     They read it without due propriety;
     In abandoning Irish, they merit no honour.]

Again, apart from its conscious reiteration by Philip Barron and others in the nineteenth century, it is hard not to notice how the core rhetorical strategies of Ó Maolmhuaidh's poem figure in later manifestos of Irish revivalism. In Douglas Hyde's 1892 landmark lecture 'The Necessity for De-anglicising Ireland', he chides the Irish nation for the 'anomalous' and 'illogical position of men who drop their own language to speak English', bemoaning how 'one of the most reading and literary peoples has become one of the least studious and most unliterary'.[52] Furthermore, Ó Maolmhuaidh's rallying cry *Fill anosa* (Return now) has its modern echo in the famous twentieth-century revivalist poem 'Fill Arís' (Return Again) by Seán Ó Ríordáin, a piece that accords closely with Ó Maolmhuaidh's poem in its call for a return to a more enlightened state and its celebration of the complexities of the Irish language.[53] The portrayal of a utopian landscape is another feature common to both poems – Ó Maolmhuaidh's miraculous landscape having its equivalent in Ó Ríordáin's idealised west Kerry *Gaeltacht*.[54] If these similarities are coincidental, they nevertheless point to the recurrence of key elements common to revivalism.

However accidental these correspondences may be, there can be no doubt that a very conscious renewal of Ó Maolmhuaidh's legacy is to be found in the work of the scholar and revivalist Tomás Ó Flannghaile (1846–1916).[55] The latter published an English translation of the chapters relating to prosody in Ó Maolmhuaidh's *Grammatica Latino Hibernica* (1677), which he entitled *De Prosodia Hibernica* (1908) and to which he appended the same epigraph that Barron had adopted just over sixty years earlier, which promises that 'the Irish language will be greatly respected in Dublin of the flasks of wine'.[56] Ó Flannghaile's earlier popular collection of essays *For the Tongue of the Gael* (1896) also included an essay on the life and work of Mícheál Ó Cléirigh. This contribution was not only important for the popularisation of the Irish Franciscan inheritance, *For the Tongue of the Gael* had a decisive influence on the young Patrick Pearse, who attributed his decision to join the Gaelic League to the influence of Ó Flannghaile's book.[57] Perhaps the most enduring testament to Ó Maolmhuaidh and the Franciscan legacy was in Ó Flannghaile's central role in the founding of the Irish Texts Society, in many ways the heir to the seventeenth-century presses of Louvain and Rome. Ó Flannghaile was chair of the provisional sub-committee established in 1896 to initiate the Irish Texts Society, and had previously been vocal in the discussion that preceded this, advocating editions for the general public of 'cheap grammars, cheap dictionaries, history, biography, legends, stories, poems, sketches, books of religion and devotion etc.'[58] The origin of the Irish Texts Society in the London-based societies the Irish Literary Society and the Southwark Literary Club is an important facet of its connection to the seventeenth-century Franciscan project of publishing in Irish. The exile's perspective in both initiatives is part of their *raison d'être,* and this perspective is embodied in the figure of Tomás Ó Flannghaile.[59]

The son of Irish-speaking parents from County Mayo, Ó Flannghaile's family had left Mayo for Manchester when he was seven years of age. He succeeded in learning to read and write in Irish under the tutelage of a man named Corrigan, who printed the Manchester *Keltic Journal and Educator*, a pioneering but short-lived series originated in 1869 and aimed at giving basic instruction in Irish to the 'intelligent and studious working classes'.[60] Ó Flannghaile's affinity with his fellow exile, the Franciscan Froinsias Ó Maolmhuaidh, is clearly stated in the preface to *De Prosodia Hibernica* (1908) where he explains how the Franciscan ended his grammar by craving his readers' indulgence if, through many years spent far away from books and teachers, his work suffered from any errors or deficiencies. Ó Flannghaile petitions the reader on the same grounds since he, the translator, had also spent many years in exile – 'not so many, happily, as the author' – but, similarly, was unable to draw on the sources and expertise available to him had he lived in Ireland's capital city.[61] This preface ends with a portentous statement of the importance of the seventeenth century in general to the contemporary project of revival:

> Little by little and one by one we are gathering up the threads of that web that was so violently, so savagely torn asunder in the seventeenth century – picking them up and trying to piece them together again, so that we may realise something of the beauty and grandeur of that native Irish civilisation that was then thirty centuries old. It was the most famous century in all our late history, full of brave deeds and brilliant men – men of thought, men of action – a century that saw three great struggles for Irish liberty, and had enjoyed brilliant if brief periods of liberty. We do not know as yet a hundredth part of the life and characters and activities of that strenuous time.[62]

The sense of exile being the key to objectifying, through distance, one's native culture and history is of great importance to the nineteenth-century Fenian movement, whose development depended, to a very significant extent, on the patriotic ardour of the Irish diaspora. It is not surprising to learn that Ó Flannghaile and his father joined the Fenians in Manchester and that Tomás knew personally many of the leaders of the Fenian movement in Britain.[63] His vital contribution to a revival of publishing in Irish was complemented by the work of fellow exile and Fenian John Denvir of Liverpool, whose 'Irish Library' series was an attempt to provide popular Irish historical and biographical essays. Ó Flannghaile became one of its two 'Gaelic editors' and contributed biographical essays on two Gaelic luminaries of the nineteenth century, John O'Donovan and Archbishop John McHale (1791–1881).[64] Ó Flannghaile's revival of the seventeenth-century inheritance was very much in keeping with the translation of Keating's *Foras Feasa ar Éirinn* by the Fenian leader John O'Mahony, a translation that was also completed and published in exile.[65]

If the seventeenth-century Franciscan publishing project and the nineteenth-century Irish Texts Society and Denvir series are indebted to an exile's perspective, this is less apparent in the next stage of the Franciscan legacy – what Mary Daly has called its 'second golden age', in the half-century or so after the First World War. During this time, Daly remarks, 'the Irish

Franciscan community re-established itself as a significant pastoral and intellectual force in a newly independent Ireland'.[66] This process witnessed an increased physical presence in Irish life for the Franciscan order through a steep rise in vocations as well as a vigorous expansion of its estate. While the order's expansion in the newly formed independent state progressed at pace, a similar revival took place overseas, the most significant aspect of which was the reopening of St Anthony's College, Louvain in 1927. This physical expansion was accompanied by a remarkable increase of the Franciscans' public role in Ireland as custodians of Irish cultural and historical heritage and by a dynamic re-engagement with Celtic studies. At the centre of this re-engagement was the establishment, in 1946, of a school of Celtic studies by members of the order, and a permanent home for the valuable manuscripts then held in Merchants Quay, Dublin.[67] From this house of study – Dún Mhuire, in Killiney, County Dublin – Franciscan Irish scholars set about the task of creating new editions of the classic Franciscan texts of the seventeenth century in a series entitled *Scríbhinní Gaeilge na mBráthar Mionúr* (Irish Writings of the Friars Minor).

While this series represented the literal revival of the seventeenth-century project, that original project's popularising remit was reflected in the state-supported commemorations of Mícheál Ó Cléirigh and Luke Wadding (1588–1657) in 1944 and 1957 respectively. These events gave large-scale exposure to the Franciscan inheritance through the issuing of commemorative stamps, the commissioning of radio and television broadcasts, and the hosting of gala concerts and dinners. In both commemorations the state played the role of patron, as instanced in the radio broadcast by *An Taoiseach* Éamon de Valera at the Ó Cléirigh celebrations and the attendance of President Seán T. O'Kelly at a commemorative event in St Isodore's College, Rome on St Patrick's Day 1957. Indeed, it is striking to note how, in a special miscellany dedicated to Mícheál Ó Cléirigh (1944), the imprimatur is given by the president (Douglas Hyde) and *Taoiseach* (Éamon de Valera) rather than by a cardinal or bishop.[68]

Notwithstanding the contribution of groups such as the Donegal Men's Association to the celebrations, not everyone joined Church and state in paying homage to Mícheál Ó Cléirigh.[69] Patrick Kavanagh's poem 'Memory of Brother Michael' struck a decidedly discordant note in the *Irish Times* of 14 October 1944:

> It would never be morning, always evening.
> Golden sunset, golden age –

When Shakespeare, Marlowe and Johnson were writing
The future of England page by page
A nettle-wild grave was Ireland's stage.

It would never be spring, always autumn
After a harvest always lost,
When Drake was winning seas for England
We sailed in puddles of the past
Chasing the ghost of Brendan's mast.

The seeds among the dust were less than dust,
Dust we sought, decay,
The young sprout rising smothered in it,
Cursed for being in the way –
And the same is true today.

Culture is always something that was,
Something pedants can measure,
Skull of bard, thigh of chief,
Depth of dried-up river.
Shall we be thus for ever?
Shall we be thus for ever?

Kavanagh was later to disown this piece as 'bad history' – this assessment having apparently been first put to him by the renowned Franciscan Irish scholar Cainneach Ó Maonaigh (Canice Mooney). The poet also regretted 'how appallingly this poem accepts the myth of Ireland as a spiritual entity'.[70] Yet 'Memory of Brother Michael' has been hard to cast off. Its frequent inclusion in anthologies is the most obvious reason for this, but it has also become axiomatic to the counter-revival attitude of the 1930s and 1940s, most commonly associated with Kavanagh, Seán Ó Faoláin and Frank O'Connor. *Pace* its author's disavowal, 'Memory of Brother Michael' cannot be dismissed if only for its popularity, and, while the target of his polemic may have been misjudged, the poem's challenge to revivalism is not without merit. The essence of the poem's critique – that Irish revivalism was a redundant, nostalgic reflex that rejected the present and stifled progress – is the very same criticism expressed by Patrick Pearse in his famous essay 'About Literature', where he warns against a certain regressive revivalism, insisting instead on the primacy of the contemporary and concluding that 'we want no Gothic Revival'.[71] Indeed, Máirtín Ó Cadhain's attitude to Kavanagh demonstrates how a seemingly polarised discussion is much more layered than might immediately appear. Ó Cadhain was fulsome in his admiration for Kavanagh's *Tarry Flynn* (1949), welcoming its debunking of the romanticised Irish peasantry, and, in a singularly important critique of the state-funded Irish Folklore Commission, he denounced folklorists' morbid anteriority in the same terms as Kavanagh decries 'the nettle-wild grave'.[72] Where 'Memory of Brother Michael' is concerned, however, Ó Cadhain echoed Tomás Ó Flannghaile, claiming that Ireland would scarcely exist at all if it were not for the Franciscans. He goes on to remark that the Franciscans, if allowed, might save the contemporary *Gaeltacht*, but resigns himself to the bleak conclusion that ten years hence – that is, 1972 – Ireland would be 'a country without ruins or memory'.[73]

Ó Cadhain's remarks were made in a review of Cainneach Ó Maonaigh's seminal essay on Irish writers of the seventeenth century.[74] Here, recalling his conversation with Kavanagh in which he accused him of writing 'bad history', Ó Maonaigh responds directly to the poem's sentiments. Besides emphasising the renewal of learning and tradition that took place in the Irish language in the seventeenth century, Ó Maonaigh makes a number of crucial points that not only illustrate the privileged position of this era in the history of Irish revivalism but which enhance also our understanding of revivalism as a concept. In the first instance, Ó Maonaigh paints a mesmerising picture of the Irish presence in Europe, which was made up principally of soldiers in the armies of France and Spain as well as clerics. Summarising an incomplete list of the Irish in Europe drawn up in Paris in 1660, Ó Maonaigh provides a litany of Irish cleric-scholars in the universities of what are now Austria, Belgium, Bosnia, the Czech Republic, France, Germany, Hungary, Italy, Poland and Spain. Being more fluent in Irish than English was no disadvantage to these Irish cleric-scholars, Ó Maonaigh asserts; rather, they were able to progress freely to the highest positions in academia, having generally Irish, Latin and one or two of the other modern European languages at their disposal. Just as Louvain became a centre of Irish learning to which foreign scholars would direct enquiries into Irish literature and history, Ó Maonaigh argues that this period was distinguished by a mutual exchange of learning and insight that was of equal benefit to both the Irish and mainland Europe. With the Irish holding a position at the centre of European culture, the Irish language responded readily to the creative challenge of articulating new ideas. Moreover, Ó Maonaigh contends, in this productively open environment the Irish language had the potential to become one of the important learned languages of Europe. He concludes his essay with this observation, in support of which he cites a verse from an Irish poem apparently composed in France at the close of the seventeenth century:

> Ní hí an teanga do chuaidh ó chion,
> acht an dream dar dhual a dídion;
>   mon-uar, darbh éigin a ndán
>   's a nduan do thréigean go hiomlán.

> [It wasn't the language that fell out of favour,
> But those who should have given it shelter;
>   alas, they were obliged to forsake,
>   its poetry and verse forever.][75]

It is the last point, where Ó Maonaigh emphasises the latent potential of the language, that is of most interest to our conceptual discussion of revivalism. The language itself was never deficient; it simply lost the vital patronage of those in whose care it had formerly thrived. The corollary of this proposition is that history is not an autonomous succession of events but the product of agency. In this case the language requires agency to realise its latent potential. This same proposition underpins revivalism's belief in agency and intervention in both the loss and revival of language, and it is this that sets revivalism apart from the deterministic view of language that regards intervention as artificial and ultimately futile.

    This core revivalist premise, together with the many legacies of the Irish seventeenth century, are actively reflected upon in various works of contemporary Irish fiction. Historical novels such as Darach Ó Scolaí's *An Cléireach* (2007), Liam Mac Cóil's *An Litir* (2011) and *I dTír Strainséartha* (2014), the late Liam Ó Muirthile's *An Colm Bán/La Blanche Colombe* (2014) and Breandán Ó Doibhlin's *Sliocht ar Thír na Scáth* (2018) all deal specifically with, or draw substantially on, the role of Counter-Reformation writers as champions of the regeneration of the Irish-language literary tradition.[76] Undoubtedly, the four-hundredth anniversary of both the opening of St Anthony's College, Louvain and the 'Flight of the Earls' provided an encouragement here – *An Cléireach* was the winner of a competition to mark the anniversary of the opening of St Anthony's. This would not, however, account for the motivation for Pádraig Ó Cíobháin's novel *Desiderius a Dó* (Desiderius

Two) (1995), the title of which pays homage to Flaithrí Ó Maolchonaire's *Desiderius* (1616). It is certainly appropriate that the legacy of Louvain and the other Irish colleges should be entrusted to novelists given the primacy of prose over poetry that typified this movement.[77] More pertinently, each of the historical novels listed above provides a contemporary perspective, refracted through the prism of the seventeenth century, on a number of issues that are central to Irish revivalism. These are, principally, language marginalisation and loss under colonisation, the renewal of language under the regenerative power of literary production, and the anxiety of representation and transmission of native history. On a wider plane, these novels mediate the generic concept of revivalism, particularly where the secular and spiritual are concerned.

Language, letters and history permeate the narrative of Darach Ó Scolaí's *An Cléireach*, a novel that tells the story of Tadhg Ó Dubháin, the eponymous clerk and sometime master of arms in the regiment of Colonel Éamonn Ó Flatharta of west Connacht during the Cromwellian Wars (1649–53). Having fallen out of favour somewhat with his master, Ó Dubháin eventually ends up in Ostend, Spanish Flanders, where he combines the duties of guard and clerk, the latter role allowing him to keep faith with his own inclinations, which are to place a higher value on books and writing than on the counting of arms and munitions. This favouring of books over arms is the key to a process of self-realisation for Ó Dubháin as he witnesses the encroaching military failure of the Irish Catholic cause. The novel itself is centred on the retreat of Ó Flatharta's men from Templemore, County Tipperary to the woods at Áth an Chuilinn and a night of storytelling that ensues there among remnants of the anti-Cromwellian forces in September 1650. This night of discussion and stories acts as a window on the fortunes of Gaelic Ireland during the first half of the seventeenth century, in which soldiers from all four provinces take stock of their recent history and speculate on what their future might be. At a crucial juncture in the discussion the protagonists resolve to take control of their future by declaring the opening of a Gaelic university in which arts and learning will be cultivated as they are elsewhere in Europe.

This interplay of militarism and letters within the novel is illustrated by a central vignette, concerning the struggle of one Éamonn Ó Maoldoráin to preserve a sacred text, 'Saltair an Easpaig' (The Bishop's Psalter), of which he is its hereditary keeper. The exploits of Ó Maoldoráin, which range from the battlefields of Bohemia to Flanders and Ireland, reflect a journey of survival *in extremis*. It is this will to prevail, even to the extent of deserting his comrades in arms, that marks Ó Maoldoráin's devotion to the *saltair* and allows the novel's author to underline the narrative of persistence of Irish letters over great adversity. In a similar vein, Captain Somhairle Mac Domhnaill, that celebrated patron of Irish letters in Flanders, features prominently in the novel as a renowned military leader whose greatest legacy is his contribution to Irish writing.

The marginalisation of the Irish language under conquest and colonisation animates Liam Mac Cóil's *An Litir* (The Letter), the first of a series of novels, which begins with the brutal execution in 1612 of Cornelius O'Devany, the Franciscan bishop of Down and Connor. The latent power of the Franciscan legacy figures physically as well as symbolically here as the crowd presses forward after the execution to collect pieces of the martyr's flesh as sacred relics. Alongside the brutal progress of conquest, an equally powerful hegemonic shift is being registered by the Gaelic Irish in a chapter entitled *Clostrácht* (Hearsay), in which a court session is dramatised. Here the language of the English court overrules and subverts the native Irish system of land tenure, rendering any recourse to native custom simply 'hearsay'. Mac Cóil cleverly mimics the scathing political strictures of seventeenth-century Irish poets such as Donnchadh Mac an Chaoilfhiaclaigh, whose 'Do fríth, monuar, an uain si ar Éirinn' (It has been found this time in Ireland, alas) lists the means by which confiscation of land and property has been carried out: Court of Wards, Exchequer, *Seómra Réaltach* (Star Chamber), King's Bench, and so on.[78]

If language expresses hegemonic power in *An Litir*, it also provides the key to redemption. The letter around which the novel is centred is from the representative of Flaithrí Ó Maolchonaire, now archbishop of Tuam, and contains an urgent message to be delivered to the earl of Tyrone, Aodh Ó Néill, in Rome. Just as the novel's central motif is a letter, entrusted to a young man embarking on a precarious journey, Irish writing itself is an imperilled message on the seas between Ireland and Europe. The anxiety of transmission that this implies reflects another of the preoccupations of these historical novels, namely the concern for historical truth and representation. A recurrent motif in each of these novels is the entrusting of a message or text to an individual at a critical stage in their life. In *An Cléireach*, such a decisive intervention occurs when Tadhg Ó Dubháin is asked by a Franciscan priest to write the history of the wars that he has witnessed. The priest gives the rationale for his request by referring to 'the lies that are being put about to diminish the acts of valour that distinguish our nation'. The Franciscan tasks Ó Dubháin with writing the history of these wars 'For the sake of truth ... and so that other nations might have a record and true account of us'.[79] The text that the priest entrusts to Ó Dubháin is blank, a book whose pages he will write. Similarly, in Breandán Ó Doibhlin's *Sliocht ar Thír na Scáth*, a novel set in Tyrone during the Nine Years War (1593–1603), a cleric and relative of Giolla Brighde Ó hEódhusa encourages the narrator to give an account of his times and so be part of a new narrative of Ireland that will be created in the Irish colleges.[80] This young cleric brings the completed narrative with him as he leaves for mainland Europe, and the text becomes the novel, presented as a seventeenth-century manuscript recently discovered in the Irish college in Paris.

This same concern for historical representation and the anxiety of transmission are succinctly presented in another historical novel by Liam Mac Cóil, *Fontenoy* (2005). Set in the mid-eighteenth century, it is strictly speaking outside the purview of this chapter, but its insight into the anxiety of transmission is most instructive. Like Ó Doibhlin's novel, *Fontenoy* involves a recently discovered account in Irish by Captain Seán Ó Raghallaigh of the famous battle of Fontenoy in 1745 where an Irish regiment was among the French army that overcame the Duke of Cumberland's forces in Flanders. This eyewitness account is Mac Cóil's own creation, of course, which he juxtaposes with the story of Ó Raghallaigh giving evidence to a French historian based on Voltaire. Ó Raghallaigh, we are told, has emerged from a great forest to enter the palace in which the writer is seated at a desk, and it is to this forest that he will likely return. The palace is a site of post-baroque order carved out of the forest with precision and exactitude, so much so that the forest itself, for all it wildness, now submits to the palace's design and intellectual plan. With its striking contrast of latent potentiality with a state of advanced order, this *mise en scène* is followed by a narrative that alternates between the captain's giving testimony to the French historian, upon whose desk are strewn various Enlightenment texts, and the captain's own 'recently discovered' version of the battle of Fontenoy. The contrast between Ó Raghallaigh's inchoate sense of the need to create his own record and the fully calibrated historiography of the French historian is thus a recurring motif in *Fontenoy*. This contrast becomes a dialogue and meditation on the representation and transmission of history, typified by the following scene:

> Níor bhréag a rá nach raibh ceachtar den dá agallamhóir ag éisteacht lena chéile níos mó – bhí an Gael gafa in eangach a chuid cuimhní agus bhí an Francach ag iarraidh súilíochtaí polaitiúla a lucht léite a bheachtú. Is mar sin a bhí Oisín agus Pádraig riamh, gach duine acu ag tabhairt a insinte féin ar an scéal, mar a bheadh i

línte lúbacha, anonn is anall, amanna comhthreomhar, amanna ag
imeacht ó chéile, amanna eile ag teacht i dtreo a chéile, agus fiú ag
teacht trasna ar a chéile ag pointí éagsúla.[81]

[It was true to say that neither interviewer nor interviewee was
listening to the other anymore – the Gael was caught in the nets of
his memories while the Frenchman was trying to correct the political
expectations of his readership. So it was always with Pádraig and
Oisín, each giving his own version of the story, like looping lines,
back and forth, sometimes parallel, sometimes diverging, other times
converging, and even crossing one another at various points.]

Thus, the narrator questions *claoninsint na staire* – 'the oblique telling of
history' – and the reference to 'Pádraig and Oisín' recalls Acallam na Senórach
(Colloquy of the Ancients), in which St Patrick recorded narrative tales of the
Fianna from conversation with Oisín, son of Finn, and Caoilte Mac Rónáin.[82]

Returning specifically to the seventeenth century, the transmission of
native historical perspectives is of signal importance to the extended influence of this period. The writing of Irish history in Irish was, as discussed
earlier, a key element of the seventeenth-century legacy, as exemplified by
Annála Ríoghachta Éireann (Annals of the Kingdom of Ireland) and Keating's
Foras Feasa ar Éirinn (History of Ireland), both completed in the 1630s. In a
recent monograph, Vincent Morley examines the definitive Gaelic history of
Ireland written by Keating in the seventeenth century, and follows its transmission throughout the eighteenth century and into the nineteenth century,
as instanced in the epic historical poem *Seanchas na Sceiche* (The History of
the Thornbush) by Antaine Raiftearaí (1779–1835), which includes a digest of
Keating's history related in verse.[83] Part of this legacy is explained in a telling
remark by Pádraig Ó Fiannachta:

Nuair a chuaigh an saol Gaelach faoi thalamh dála Thuatha Dé
Danann sa seachtú haois déag, thugadar lón anama leo – Foras Feasa
ar Éirinn. Ba é seo an saothar a choiméad an spiorad beo. Scaip sé ó
cheann ceann na tíre, ó theach mór go bothán, ó bhothán go scairt.

[When in the seventeenth century Gaelic life went underground,
like the *Tuatha Dé Danann* they brought with them provision for
the soul – *Foras Feasa ar Éirinn*. This was the work that kept the

spirit alive. It spread from one end of the country to the other, from big house to hut, from hut to shelter.][84]

The fraught transmission of history here is a work of the soul, underlining the numinosity that often characterises revivalist discourse and reminding us again of the relationships between secular and spiritual that are never far from the surface. In the case of Ó Fiannachta, a clergyman and scholar, this recourse to the spirit might be explained by his clerical vocation. Breandán Ó Doibhlin shares the same vocation, and so it is unsurprising that his novel *Sliocht ar Thír na Scáth* should bring the promise of resurrection and the cultural practice of revival into a natural alignment. This is apparent in the title and epigraph of the novel, taken from the Book of Isaiah (26:19):

Beidh saol ag do chuid marbhánach arís [...]
[...] óir is geal é mar dhrúcht do dhrúchtsa,
agus tiocfaidh sliocht ar thír na scáth.
(Íseáia 26:19)

[Thy dead shall live, their bodies shall rise.
[...] For the dew is a dew of light,
and on the land of the shades thou wilt let it fall.]
(Isaiah 26:19)

The convergence of resurrection and revival as a way to spiritual as well as cultural survival reflects a key aspiration underpinning this novel's narrative, namely that the long-term survival of Gaelic culture and identity should be achieved through an alliance of the institutions of the Catholic Church and native learning, with both embracing the currents of contemporary European baroque culture. These aspirations are eloquently articulated in a baroque sermon given by Bishop Réamann Ó Gallchóir in which he reminds his belea-guered congregation that their survival will be best secured if they follow the best examples of their own history when '[bardic] school and [monastic] cell, poetry and faith worked hand in hand'.[85] The force of this enjoinder is magnified when the bishop, like the historical bishop of Derry upon whom this character is based, is killed by English soldiers soon after delivering his sermon.[86] Yet while Ó Doibhlin's novel typifies the concern for the existential or transcendental in contemporary Irish novels that deal directly with, or draw substantially on, the legacy of the seventeenth century, the novels under consideration here tend to be of secular provenance.

One such example is Pádraig Ó Cíobháin's *Desiderius a Dó* (1995), a novel set in the late twentieth century but which draws inspiration from the seventeenth century, both in its title – paying tribute to Flaithrí Ó Maolchonaire's *Desiderius* – and as a starting point for a peregrination of the soul. Referring to his novel's borrowed title, Ó Cíobháin ascribes the origin of the Latin *Desiderius* to a combination of the elements *de* and *sidus*, which he understands as 'being without guidance in a search for the golden stars of wisdom'.[87] Yet among the various historical, literary, musical and religious references that punctuate the opening chapter of Ó Cíobháin's novel is a quotation from Martin Luther.[88] Ó Cíobháin's journey may, therefore, begin with the Counter-Reformation but is not bound to it, his experience of religion being one that moves 'from one contradiction to another'.[89]

While Ó Cíobháin's homage to *Desiderius* is selective and idiosyncratic, he identifies strongly with the tradition of revival of which Ó Maolchonaire's work is one particular expression. Echoing Ó Fiannachta's remark about Gaelic culture going underground like the *Tuatha Dé Danann*, he compares the oral tradition to a tunnel that brings us back to a 'place-time' that gives us our own seal of identity.[90] Thus, Ó Cíobháin's 'preface' begins with the narrator as a child in bed at night, trying to get to know his soul and indulging the visions that will bring forth the future. Among the influences that inform this early soul work is what he calls 'the mysterious voice of the *id* of the common people' that he hears in the oral tradition and especially in love songs.[91] He recalls discovering how a previous generation had gone about gathering this music and other elements of the oral tradition, all of which are like the cloth in which man has covered himself since being expelled from the Garden of Eden. The recovery of 'our universal life jacket', he continues, was the work of 'a movement which was called the Revival. Observe how races move from folly to regrowth.'[92]

Ó Cíobháin's concern, like Proust's, is with a dialectics of memory in which he will be engaged to the very hour of his death.[93] Yet Ó Cíobháin wishes for nothing else, concluding that 'the search for where we are from leaves us eternally young, the intervening years being merely like the waves which beat against the bottom of a boat'.[94] The eradication of time that this implies is what Ó Cíobháin claims to have set out to achieve in his search for 'some sort of existential permanence'.[95] In seeking this dissolution of the division of past and present, he points towards a constant state of revival in which memory and actuality are mutually engaged. This concern with temporality is a key feature of revivalism and the focus of Chapter 5, but for the purposes of the present discussion Ó Cíobháin's use of the seventeenth-century inheritance is particularly revealing as an example of the integration of secular and spiritual discourses. The prominence of the concepts of renewal and regeneration in seventeenth-century Irish devotional literature are clearly attractive to secular Irish writers of the late twentieth and early twenty-first centuries who, faced with the ongoing uncertainty of their medium of expression, strive towards some form of ontological security. To this end, seventeenth-century Irish devotional writing has been arguably adopted not just for its obvious cultural value but for its ontological anchorage.

Such an integration of the traditions of faith and reason has been discussed by the philosopher Jürgen Habermas in the context of what he terms 'the post-secular age'. Habermas argues that the modes of faith and reason, represented respectively by the traditions of Jerusalem and Athens, are part of the history of the secular reason that provides the medium in which modern people discuss their place in the world. Speaking of 'the unexhausted force of religious traditions' in contemporary society, Habermas remarks that 'secularization functions less as a filter separating out the contents of traditions than as a transformer which redirects the flow of tradition'.[96] This analysis of the persistent influence of religious wisdom in largely secular societies clearly applies to societies at large. Perhaps the popularity of seventeenth-century themes in contemporary Irish novels is, therefore, merely a microcosm of this broader 'awareness of what's missing'. After all, the very phrase used by Habermas to speak about religion could easily be taken up as a slogan by language revivalists outside of the traditional *Gaeltacht*. In both cases the presence and value of an apparently discarded inheritance is being asserted.

Many of these issues, and particularly the sense in which the Franciscan inheritance is invoked by contemporary writers in Irish, become evident when reading Liam Ó Muirthile's novel *An Colm Bán/La Blanche Colombe* (2014). The novel is narrated by an Irish writer who, having lived in Paris for a while as a young man in the 1970s, has returned to the city some forty years later in order to investigate the story of a mysterious Irishwoman, a dancer who came to work in Paris at the end of the First World War. The novel is ostensibly concerned with unearthing the intriguing life story of the dancer, but hinges as much on a spiritual as on a temporal quest, this duality being represented in the dancer's two names, Nóra Buckley and Ellen Daunt. The latter is the name of her Protestant grandmother, who becomes Nóra's alter ego in her apprenticeship and eventual mastery of dancing. Indeed, dancing becomes very much an affair of the soul, in which the initial physical act brings on a sublime transcendental state that leads her eventually to choose a life of religious devotion.

This is a novel of revivals – Nóra Buckley reviving the spirit of her grandmother, the narrator reviving both his own youth in Paris and his artistic vocation. While the narrator labours to discover the full story of Nóra/Ellen, in the next room of his hotel the ghost of an American artist works on an unknown picture that, during the unfolding of the quest for Nóra/Ellen, is revealed as the artist himself as St Francis and the birds. The Franciscan motif is also reflected in the title of the novel *An Colm Bán* (The White Dove) as well as in Nóra's entering a Franciscan convent before her death in a Nazi concentration camp. Among the various significances of the title *An Colm Bán* is, of course, the name of St Columbanus (White Dove) whose founding of monasteries in Europe in the late sixth century epitomises a golden age of Irish missionary work. The continental Irish colleges that flourished in the first half of the seventeenth century are often seen as the inheritors of this legacy, not least because of their devotion to writing the lives of the Irish saints, epitomised by John Colgan's *Acta Sanctorum Hiberniae* (1645). Thus, when Nóra Buckley/Ellen Daunt enters the Franciscan convent it is appropriate that she should take the name of St Columbanus. Just as the realist mode of narration has to yield to the transcendental climaxes of the dancing scenes and the narrator's dialogues with the ghost of the American artist, the duality of secular and spiritual – the dancer who becomes a nun and martyr – pervades Ó Muirthile's novel.

Where the historical novels by Mac Cóil (apart from *Fontenoy*), Ó Scolaí and Ó Doibhlin deal directly with the seventeenth century in their subject matter, the Franciscan inheritance occupies a more liminal space in Ó Muirthile's *An Colm Bán* and Ó Cíobháin's *Desiderius a Dó*. Yet the theme of self-realisation through exile – one of the great pieties of Irish modernism in the twentieth century – is central to all of the novels discussed above, and is undoubtedly one of the most alluring features of the Irish colleges' legacy.[97] One of the obvious advantages of the Irish language's presence in mainland Europe is to circumvent the hegemony of English. While this was more of an urgent priority for Irish clerics in the seventeenth century, as graphically recalled in the *An Litir* execution scene, contemporary Irish-language activists often look to the European Union as a champion of linguistic diversity and minority-language rights. On a practical level, the successful campaign to have Irish recognised as an official language of the European Union has created employment opportunities for graduates of Irish, particularly through translation, and has created a small community of Irish-language professionals in Brussels. And so, in the same region where Ó Maolchonaire's translation of a Catalan devotional text was published in 1616, Irish translators now produce documents of a worldlier variety.

Conversely, the motivation for Irish novelists forging a European perspective grounded in the literary inheritance of the seventeenth century is more likely to be explained by a form of existential anxiety. The European Union may provide some political reassurance to minority-language users but it has little to offer in the way of metaphysical relief. The lure of the Franciscan legacy to Irish writers, however, is arguably as a spiritual as well as cultural compass by which to negotiate the challenges of minority-language existence in the present day. In other words, the Franciscan inheritance, rich in both faith and reason, can give weight and solidity – an ontological anchor – to the contemporary Irish-language writer. The significance of this, where our understanding of revivalism is concerned, is in the need to reconcile the modes of faith and reason, to address 'an awareness of what is missing'. Whether the focus is on lost religions, lost communities or lost languages, modern societies will harbour a regret for what has been discarded in the progress of modernity. For Jean Baudrillard, in the age of post-modernity this loss was history itself: 'history is our lost referential'.[98]

The legacy of the Counter-Reformation Irish publishing-and-writing project of the seventeenth century sheds much light on the nature of both revivalism as a concept and its specific Irish manifestation. Firstly, the movement emerged initially through a dialectical relationship with the Reformation, in common with which it adopted many of the features of Renaissance humanism. This debt to the Renaissance is especially important since the Renaissance was itself a revival of classical art and learning. Thus, having been conceived within a revivalist paradigm, the Irish Counter-Reformation movement has itself been revived as both a template and totem by subsequent revivalist movements from at least the 1830s onwards. The recurrent pattern of revival and the tendency of revivalist movements to be continually re-invoked is clearly part of the case for seeing revivalism as a perennial practice. The renewal of language through a literary revival, initially through religious and later secular texts, is also of great significance to future Irish revivals. The revivalist movements of the nineteenth century, in particular, mirrored the Irish Counter-Reformation's concern with providing popular editions of texts and facilitating the expansion of literacy. Indeed, the Free State government's publishing scheme An Gúm (established in 1926) set out to achieve similar aims by providing subsidised translations of the secular literary canon.[99]

Part of the enduring influence of the Counter-Reformation era is its latent power as an exemplar of cultural renewal and regeneration, a challenge to colonial domination grounded in a robustly European intellectual movement. Yet where the study of revivalism is concerned, an equally important feature of the Counter-Reformation legacy is its representation of the duality of secular and spiritual. Just as the 'eternal return' of religion is part of our universal inheritance, revivalism's inherent appeal to transcendence is part of the persistence of the spiritual in a post-secular age. As memorably instanced in the 1932 Eucharistic Congress, the newly independent Irish state was itself a model of the symbiosis of secular and religious, and, as such, the Franciscan inheritance was eagerly co-opted, alongside the eighteenth-century idyll of Daniel Corkery's *Hidden Ireland* (1924), as part of its developing sense of corporate identity.[100] Indeed, the state's inclination to hold the Irish language in pious regard is often adduced to its failure to provide either the material conditions or rationale for a communal revival of the language. The invocation of the Franciscan inheritance by contemporary Irish novelists marks a further stage in the adaptation of this legacy to contemporary needs. Part of the motivation of this particular revival is the desire to redress the occlusion of a critical historical era characterised by the mutual beneficence of Ireland and Europe, and, by so doing, to restore a certain ontological security to the Irish language. Regarding our conceptual understanding of revivalism, the evidence of Counter-Reformation revivalism and its protean afterlives points to the remarkable power of latency and renewal in human culture. The corollary of this evidence is that revival is not just an abstract counterfactual proposition but an active agency for the reform of the present and prefiguring of the future.

CHAPTER 3

Cultural Memory, Futurity and the Instrumentalisation of Culture in the Eighteenth and Nineteenth Centuries

In August 1825 a crowd gathered outside Limerick County Gaol to witness the execution of one Cornelius Keating. Keating was sentenced to hang for a pistol attack on the home of a man named Bourke at Rathnasere, near Rathkeale in west County Limerick. Having proclaimed his innocence to the sheriff, clergymen and the 'train of gentlemen' assembled on the platform, Keating 'turned to the populace, whom he addressed in the Irish language with great facility and correctness, and in a style above the common peasantry'.[1] He again professed his innocence and urged those before him not to keep arms lawfully or unlawfully on his account and to be attentive to the voice of the clergy. The report concludes that the condemned man died 'almost without a struggle'. This vignette is worthy of note for a number or reasons. Firstly, there is considerable irony in Keating's address in Irish 'in a style above the common peasantry' given that the surname Keating is synonymous with a form of scholarly Irish that distinguished the writing of Geoffrey Keating. One of the first great revivalist debates of the late nineteenth and early twentieth centuries was, of course, whether to use the Irish of (Geoffrey) Keating or *caint na ndaoine* (the speech of the people). Geoffrey Keating's *Foras Feasa ar Éirinn* (1634) had, as mentioned in the previous chapter, an enduring influence on the narrative of Irishness and native history for centuries after its appearance.[2] Secondly, the demise of Cornelius Keating 'almost without a struggle' was closely followed by the language that he spoke, according to a very well-known account by the folklorist, Liam Ó Danachair, from the same part of Limerick:

This old John Moylan [of Rathkeale], who lived from 1800 to

about 1890, thought that the decay of Irish really began in 1840 or so. He said that the older people agreed with him, that the influence of Daniel O'Connell worked silently against the speaking of Irish. Up to about 1830, or so, the entire Rathkeale countryside spoke Irish. Then the new schools, the pro-English clergy, the influence of the landlords and agents, as well as the political leaders, the use of English in the law-courts, at gatherings and public meetings, in sermons and religious functions, the growing public feeling that Irish was a dying language, a mark of a degraded people who were not 'decent' – all this combined to produce a new people who from youth were pledged to speak no Irish. And so in West Limerick you had many who persisted in trying to speak a broken English and never again uttered a word in the old tongue they knew so well.[3]

Finally, the year of Cornelius Keating's execution, 1825, was one of great significance for the Catholic Irish. This year was supposed to be the year of deliverance from Protestant domination and was the focus of a strong current of millenarianism that marked the end of the eighteenth century and initial decades of the nineteenth century. The poetry of Antaine Raiftearaí (1779–1835), Tomás Rua Ó Súilleabháin (1785–1848) and Máire Bhuí Uí Laoghaire (1774–1848), among others, testifies to the common belief in the prophecies of Pastorini (Charles Walmesley), published in 1771, which predicted the demise of Protestantism.[4] Indeed, the influence of millenarianism is one of the factors attributed to the 'Captain Rock' uprising of 1821–24, which began in Newcastle West, County Limerick, less than ten miles from Rathkeale.[5] Cornelius Keating's speech from the gallows appears to reference this tendency when he maintained that the arms that were found in his home were acquired 'in peaceable times'. Of course, adherents of Pastorini's prophecies found only disappointment in 1825, and while the years that followed were distinguished by the success of the O'Connellite Catholic Emancipation movement in 1829, the Irish language recorded no such success or progress. Rather, the downward trajectory of the Irish language in the nineteenth century has become a truism, and the evidence cited above, of its decline in rural Limerick, would appear to confirm this.

Yet a recent study by Nicholas Wolf, covering the years between 1770 and 1870, has sought to counter the well-established narrative of decline and obsolescence of the Irish language by presenting much evidence for the vitality of the speech community in this period, as well as its interaction with the authorities of Church and state.[6] Wolf's thesis mirrors the case made by

Breandán Ó Buachalla against the supposed predominance of the themes of death and decline in Irish poetry of the seventeenth century and after.[7] The importance of such counterpoints to the prevailing story of inexorable decline is to restore some balance to our view of the linguistic landscape. Yet the challenges faced by the Irish language, particularly in the period from the late eighteenth century through the nineteenth century, were undeniably severe, as the census figures available from 1851 onwards indicate – even when allowing for considerable levels of under-reporting in the nineteenth century.[8] Whereas at the beginning of the nineteenth century the number of monoglot Irish speakers was estimated to be between 40% and 50% of the population, this had been reduced to less than 5% in the 1851 census, or 319,602 from a total of just over 6.5 million.[9] The subsequent 93% decrease by the 1901 census in the total number of those who knew Irish only – to a total of 20,953 from a total population of just over 4.4 million – presents a stark vista of decline.[10] The total number of people recorded as speaking both Irish and English decreased by well over a half in the same period, from a little over 1.5 million (23.3% of the population) in 1851 to 641,142 (14.4% of the population) in 1901. Besides the relatively less dramatic scale of decline in this category, it is also clear that the tendency towards bilingualism was resolute in this period. While the incidence of adult monoglot Irish speakers is now essentially obsolete, the statistics for bilingualism during the course of the twentieth and twenty-first centuries show a reversal of the decline recorded in the nineteenth century. The latest all-Ireland census figures from 2011 show that in the Republic of Ireland 41% of the population are declared as able to speak Irish, while 11% is the corresponding figure in the Northern Ireland census.[11] Notwithstanding the caveat that must accompany the untested, voluntary declarations of language knowledge in Irish census records, this recorded reversal is a significant change in fortunes and one that can be attributed particularly to the success of revivalist initiatives, particularly the Gaelic League revival from 1893 onwards and the enhanced status of the Irish language with the establishment of an independent state in 1922.

It is unsurprising, under these circumstances of language decline and growing bilingualism, that revivalism has been a recurrent thread of Irish cultural life, particularly from the late eighteenth century onwards. In the case of those for whom Irish was their literary medium by necessity of birth and upbringing, an awareness of revivalism may not have always accrued. Yet for those who negotiated an active course between Irish and English and for those for whom Irish was a conscious choice, revivalism was a discourse with which they inevitably had to engage. Although Irish revivalism appeared to be contingent on other initial motivations, such as cultural nationalism, it is possible to gain insights into revivalism per se as a recurrent cultural practice. The evidence of what we might call overtly revivalist literature of the late eighteenth and nineteenth centuries, comprising essays and correspondence together with poetry and prefaces, reveals a number of distinct conceptual strands that are the focus of this chapter. These are primarily the negotiation and transmission of cultural memory, latency and the concern for futurity, the instrumentalisation of culture, and the importance of objectifying distance in the development of a revivalist consciousness. In the case of each of these areas the practical circumstances of ongoing language shift are of central importance. Of equal significance is the confluence of spiritual and secular. Just as revivalism in the seventeenth century was largely a spiritual concern, contingent on the dialectics of Reformation and Counter-Reformation, Irish revivalism in the late eighteenth and the nineteenth centuries very frequently engages the religious sphere. Perhaps the most obvious example of this is the way in which the publishing of religious texts in Irish became part of the battleground of the 'Second Reformation' in Ireland, during which Protestant evangelical societies sought to extend their scripture-based education to the Catholic population in the first half of the nineteenth century.[12]

Just as the prefaces to publications by the Irish Counter-Reformationist authors are a crucial source of insight into revivalism in the seventeenth century, the period from the mid-eighteenth century onwards, particularly, witnessed a broad spectrum of documents in which revivalism was explicitly avowed. Notwithstanding the implicit revivalism of much Gaelic scholarship, such as the Dublin Ó Neachtain scribal circle in the first half of the eighteenth century, or the importance of antiquarian traditions of seventeenth and eighteenth-century Ireland, epitomised by individuals such as Charles O'Connor of Belanagare, County Roscommon (1710–91), and the founding of the Royal Irish Academy in 1785, the progress of explicitly revivalist discourse is discernible throughout the eighteenth century. Thus, a devotional text written in 1736 is prefaced by the scribe's note that:

> It is a pathetic situation for anyone who has acquired any sort of true learning not to be able to read or write his native language; and for that reason all of us who have an understanding of that language should help each other, so that we can bring it back to use again since it was lost to us through the force of heretics.[13]

Among the most important early examples of overtly revivalist discourse in this period are the prefaces to Begly and MacCurtin's *English–Irish Dictionary* (1732) and Andrew Donlevy's *Catechism* (1742), both published in Paris. The preface to the *English–Irish Dictionary* echoes the polemic of MacCurtin's *A Brief Discourse in Vindication of the Antiquity of Ireland* (1717) by asserting the pedigree of the Irish language in defiance of its detractors, but goes on to express the wish that the Irish themselves 'recover out of their Error' of 'neglecting so sacred a Depository of the Heroic Achievements of their Country'.[14] Andrew Donlevy's (1680–1746) preface to his *Catechism* gives a stark appraisal, from Paris, of the eviscerating effects of marginalisation and neglect on the Irish language by 1742. Irish was on the 'brink of utter decay', having been a language 'of neither Court, nor City, nor Bar, nor Business' since the beginning of the seventeenth century:

> … what a Discredit then must it be to the whole *Nation* to let such a language go to wrack, and to give no Encouragement, not even the Necessaries of life, to some of the Few, who still remain, and are capable to rescue those *venerable Monuments of Antiquity* from the profound obscurity, they are buried in?[15]

Perhaps the earliest example of an organised response to this dilemma is found in the rules for a now obscure society, the Dublin 'Irish Club', dated 1752, in which the members are bound to speak no language other than Irish in the club room.[16] The preamble to the rules begins like a 'warrant' with the word 'whereas':

> Whereas the Irish, the mother Tongue of this Nation, has been long neglected and discouraged by the introduction of strange Languages not so full or Expressive, and that the Natives, not only find themselves alone among all the nations of the earth, ignorant for the most part, of the language of their forefathers, but suffer frequently in their Trade, Business, and accomplishments …[17]

The language of the legal warrant was used contemporaneously in Irish as part of a poetic genre known as *barántas* (warrant), usually humorous, which frequently began with the English 'whereas'.[18] The *barántas* composed in 1754 by the Limerick poet Seán Ó Tuama (*c.* 1707–75), calling on poets to gather to practise their arts 'to honour, through collection, revival and rehearsing' the work of the late Seán Clárach Mac Domhnaill (1691–1754), is significant for its specific mention of revival but also for its assessment of the crisis facing the language and the need for a means of gathering in friendly association to assure its preservation.[19] This summons to the poetic court is issued to 'whomever wishes to renew the old Irish customs' (*gach aon lér mian athnuadhadh na sean-nós nÉireannach*), and goes on to warn:

> Óir dá laighead mhaireas anois dár dteangain ghaois-bhriathraigh Gaedhilge gan dul i mbáthadh agus i mór-dhearmad tré gach doi-lgheas tré n-ar hionnarbadh í go nuige seo, rachaidh go comair go neimhnídh muna bhféacham meodhán dícheallach le cuidiughadh go caoin caomhchumainn le chéile go toileamhail re n-a coiméad ar bun.

> [For, what little remains of our eloquent language, the Irish, that has not gone into decline and great neglect through all the affliction by which it has been driven out to date, it will shortly be altogether reduced to nothing if we do not seek out an effective means of friendly assistance and deliberate association with each other in order to guard it.][20]

The choice of legal address and the patriotic preamble is expanded somewhat in Tomás Ó Míocháin's (*c.* 1730–1804) *gairm scoile*, or 'convocation', of 1780.[21] Ó Míocháin, from Ardsollus, County Clare, was a poet and teacher of mathematics who, from 1770 until his death in 1804, kept a school in Ennis, the principal town of the county.[22] Courts of poetry thrived in the province of Munster during the eighteenth century, and Ó Míocháin appears to have been well connected to some of these in the 1760s and 1770s, such as the court mentioned above, convened by Seán Ó Tuama at Croom, County Limerick, and the poetic court held by Pádraig Mac Giobúin at Garrán an Ridire, near Mitchelstown in north County Cork.[23] Ó Míocháin's *gairm scoile*, composed at Ennis in 1780, in many respects mirrors the preamble and rules of the 'Irish Club' in that it begins with an assessment of the critical state of the Irish language – a feature shared by Seán Ó Tuama's *barántas* – but also in its enumeration of a set of rules. It has been suggested that this was felt necessary given the decline of the Munster schools of poetry by the 1780s.[24] It may also be argued that the desire to formalise the functions of the court of poetry was a reflection of the heightened political atmosphere of the time, concurrent with the American War of Independence, the rise of the Irish Volunteers, and the focus on national issues in the Dublin parliament.[25] Several of Ó Míocháin's compositions of the period deal with events ranging from the British retreat from Boston in 1776 to the defeat of Cornwallis in Yorktown in 1781.[26] Besides writing a panegyric for the Irish Volunteers and a denunciation of the Fencibles (six battalions raised in 1782 by the Protestant Ascendancy and elements of the government to curb the drive for further parliamentary reform), Ó Míocháin recorded his enthusiasm for developments in the Irish parliament, where the discussion of constitutional issues contributed to a rise in national feeling.[27] Hence Ó Míocháin's *gairm scoile* declares from the very outset that it is 'both right and lawful' [*is cuí agus is dlitheach*] to convene a court of poetry 'at this time when the princely leaders and noble servants of our country are working resolutely for our freedom in the great parliament of Dublin'.[28] Yet while it is tempting to see an inchoate republican constitution in the rules attached to Ó Míocháin's *gairm scoile*, given his support for American independence, his political sympathies appear to have been primarily Jacobite rather than republican. His poem 'Ar dTréigean Bhoston d'Arm Shasana, 1776' (After the English Army's Abandonment of Boston, 1776), while celebrating Washington's victory, expresses the hope that Ireland will be reunited with her true spouse, Charles Stuart.[29] Commenting on the incongruity of Ó Míocháin's reference to Washington's imminent charge of his 'kingdom', Neil Buttimer argues that 'employment of the word *ríocht* [kingdom] probably reveals the difficulties involved in transmitting political ideas across conceptual and linguistic divides. The exact form government in the rebellious colonies would take was not yet clear.'[30] Ó Míocháin may have been open to an explicit conversion to the new republican principles espoused by the Society of United Irishmen, but he left us no evidence of his reaction to either the United Irishmen or the 1798 rebellion, although this may well have been a matter of expediency given his advanced age and the ferocity of reprisals at the time.

As mentioned in the previous chapter, the language of English law was satirised by poets of the seventeenth century, and it is no surprise that this rich vein of satirical invective continued into the eighteenth century after the introduction of the Penal Laws.[31] Alongside the many examples of resentment towards English laws that were expressed in Irish-language sources, the facetious adoption of English legal parlance by the various authors of the *barántas* was more in the manner of subversive wit than political remonstrance.[32] However, Ó Míocháin's linking of the revival of political fortunes with the revival of language and poetry adopts a more serious tone within the *barántas*

and *gairm scoile* conventions.[33] His initial comments invoking the then favourable political climate are followed by a vindication of the antiquity of the
Irish language, commentary on its historical use by saints and theologians for
bringing unbelievers to the Christian faith, and reference to the proud traditions of learning that prevailed in north Munster. All of this is cited in support
of the opening declaration of the intention to 'renew and reform our sweet
mother tongue, namely the splendid-worded Irish language' (*ár dteanga mhilis
mháthardha .i. an Ghaeilge ghléarfhoclach d'athnua agus do leasú*). Renewal and
reform is immediately reminiscent of the Counter-Reformationists' project;
so, too, in a certain measure, is the acknowledgment of duty incumbent on
'those few among us who have a knowledge of learning and arts to combine in
earnest faith to deliver this lucid, word-rich language from consternation and
clear it of choking weeds'.[34] The sense of the renewal or revival (Ó Míocháin
uses both terms) falling to a small band of the faithful is similar to that
expressed by Donlevy in the preface to his *Catechism* (1742). Notwithstanding
the references to renewal and reform of language in Ó Míocháin's *gairm scoile*,
the broad readership invited by the Counter-Reformationist writers is not in
evidence here. Ó Míocháin addresses 'sages and dear friends' (*A shaoithibh agus
a chairdibh ionúin*), and, as various of the nine rules of his poetic school make
clear, this will be an exclusive gathering of men of the learned classes. While
the first rule stipulates that only men with a 'true knowledge' of Irish can be
admitted, exception may be made for those who have knowledge of arts and
various languages who wish to learn Irish. The sixth rule declares it the duty
of members to bring to book those poetasters who pose as truly learned poets
in order to seduce the common folk with their ignorant blustering.

This insistence on the gradations of Irish poets is reminiscent of the sentiments expressed by Dáibhí Ó Bruadair (1625–98) in north Munster a century
earlier when he referred disparagingly to balladeers as *aos órtha an fhuairscei-
dill* (the chanters of frigid sheets).[35] Ó Míocháin's reference to the need for a
'revival' in his *gairm scoile* of 1780 – coming after his dismay the year previously, 'Our native Tongue most shamefully reject'd', and again fifteen years
later in 1795: 'Our Language dead – and all our Celtic bards' – is perhaps
more of a comment on the decline of poetic standards than an assessment of
the use of Irish in his area of Munster.[36] After all, Ó Míocháin was a contemporary of Brian Merriman (1750–1805), a fellow Clare man who may well
have attended his poetic court in Ennis and is thought to have completed his
comic masterpiece *Cúirt an Mheon-Oíche* (The Midnight Court) in the same
year that the court was convened, 1780.[37] Like Ó Míocháin, Merriman was

a mathematics teacher and occasional scribe who was living in Feakle, twenty miles east of Ennis, at the time of the Ennis court of poetry.[38] Breandán Ó Buachalla's critique of the supposed death knell of the Irish literary tradition from the seventeenth century onwards concludes that, in spite of the obviously profound changes to the sociolinguistic status of Irish and the narrowing of its registers, works such as Merriman's *Cúirt an Mheon-Oíche* were hardly the products of a literary tradition that was dying.[39]

The sense of liminality that pervades the late eighteenth and early nineteenth centuries, where language decline is accompanied by examples of literary virtuosity, is reflected in the imaginary legal or court settings evident in the *barántas, gairm scoile* and *Cúirt an Mheon-Oíche*. The society that produced these compositions increasingly occupied a position of alterity, where its institutions were maintained by the imagination as much as by tradition.[40] That is not to say that Irish speakers were unable to engage with the English-language institutions that dominated the public sphere – Wolf has shown how the courts from the mid-eighteenth century onwards accommodated the use of Irish through frequent use of interpreters.[41] Rather, the milieu of Ó Míocháin, Merriman and their contemporaries was defined by bilingualism, which most probably pertained to all levels of society at this period in east Clare.[42] Indeed, there are indications that some of the Gaelic literati considered competence in English to be a marker of social standing and learning. One example is the south-east Ulster poet Peadar Ó Doirnín's (1700–69) lampoon of the poor English of his rival Muiris Ó Gormáin, and the complaint in his *Mná na hÉireann* (The Women of Ireland) that a beautiful girl was the partner of a 'hideous, swarthy man without English'.[43] The picture of eighteenth-century Irish society clearly divided along linguistic lines that emerges from Daniel Corkery's *The Hidden Ireland* (1924) and, more recently, Joep Leerssen's *Hidden Ireland, Public Sphere* (2002) has been rightly challenged, not least on the evidence of literary genres and forms such as the *barántas* and macaronic verse. As Liam Mac Mathúna argues, the linguistic evidence for permeating bilingualism confounds the oversimplification by which 'a single English-only public sphere relegated Irish speakers to non-contiguous Irish-medium private spaces'.[44]

Nevertheless, the curious liminality of imaginary courts and warrants inevitably deserves closer scrutiny. Notwithstanding the tradition of medieval European 'court of love' poems that seems likely to have influenced *Cúirt an Mheon-Oíche*, this shadow world of fantasy courts and warrants marks an intermediary stage in the social history of the Irish language, with certain implications for the development of revivalism.[45] Bilingualism was, by the end of the eighteenth century, becoming the default situation for the majority of Irish speakers, a trend that, as noted previously, accelerated during the course of the nineteenth century. Moreover, it has been estimated that only 20,000 of 1.5 million Irish speakers were literate in Irish in 1806.[46] It is not surprising, therefore, that the mainstay of native culture in the nineteenth century was an oral tradition of storytelling and verse. Indeed, many of the poets most frequently associated with the nineteenth-century Gaelic tradition, such as Antaine Raiftearaí, Máire Bhuí Uí Laoghaire and Diarmuid na Bolgaí Ó Sé (1755–1846), flourished within this vibrant culture of orality.[47] Besides the relative paucity of literacy in Irish, the use of Irish as a literary medium was steadily becoming dependent on a bilingual readership or audience. What all of this meant was that the material necessity one expects to fuel a culture of literary production – chiefly the need to provide reading matter for the default language of a given readership – was increasingly less evident in the case of the Irish language from the late eighteenth century onwards.

Yet the various Protestant evangelical societies that brought their mission to Irish speakers, from 1806 onwards, chose to do so through Irish. Part of the motivation for this was undoubtedly rooted in the Reformation ideals of providing scripture in the vernacular, but it was also founded in the perceived *material* necessity of doing so.[48] In this sense the considerable investment of Protestant Bible societies in a vernacular mission, ranging as far afield as Lower Manhattan and New Jersey, can be taken as an objective assessment of the prevalence of the Irish language.[49] Another inadvertent consequence of the Bible societies' work was to provide an outsider's account of the attitudes and moeurs of Irish-speaking communities, particularly with respect to the strength of emotional identification with the language.[50] While contemporary nationalist accounts of cultural cohesiveness may have an inherent bias, the testimony of Protestant evangelists was hardly likely to be similarly inclined. In one instance, native attachment to heroic tales and verse is described as 'the cause of the frequent occurrence of disturbances, among a people who are pre-disposed to everything hardy and daring, and who are trained in their infancy, by such tales, to look forward to distinguish their manhood by emulating these romantic fictions'.[51] The accounts given by some prominent Scottish Protestant clergymen, discussed later in this chapter, place similar emphasis on the strong emotional attachments to the Irish language, to which were added an acute sense of intergenerational political grievance.

The recognition of not just the extent of the Irish language, in practical terms, but also the strength of the emotional and cultural attachments it engendered is of great significance to the intermediary stage in the social history of the Irish language, mentioned above. Even when the progress of bilingualism would reach a stage where Irish became less materially necessary, the cultural and emotional pull of the literature and lore of Irish would mitigate against its abandonment. As the Irish language became less materially relevant, particularly as the nineteenth century progressed, the language inevitably became increasingly reliant on those who beheld it with a conscious sense of responsibility and those who engaged in a series of revivalist interventions. Prior to the most significant revivalist phase, in the last quarter of the nineteenth century, those who exercised a sense of responsibility towards the written language were primarily the scribes and guardians of the literary heritage:

> Already amongst the Celtic, and exclusively Irish-speaking population, there existed a class called MS. men, whose pride it was to read, to study, to transcribe, and to preserve, any writings they could find in their beloved native tongue. These were generally old legends, bits of Irish history, or sometimes fragments of the classics.[52]

Where revivalists were concerned, they included those, like Philip Barron (*c.* 1801–44) and Robert Shipboy MacAdam (1808–95), who shared the native scholars' appreciation of the intrinsic worth of the language and its literary riches. To these we may add two main groups: those who were inspired primarily by patriotic zeal or cultural nationalism, and those who were involved in the Protestant evangelical societies. These divisions are merely suggestive, given that scribes were frequently ardent nationalists or affiliated to evangelical societies, or, indeed, both at the same time. However, in trying to identify the critical motivation behind Irish revivalism in the nineteenth century it seems fair to propose scholarly interest, cultural nationalism and evangelicalism as the main areas of engagement. When the evidence of overt expressions of revivalism or, indeed, 'manifestos' of revivalism are considered, we find that all three of these areas of interest are well represented. It is also clear that revivalism in the first three quarters of the nineteenth century bears witness to both the convergence of the spiritual and cultural and the importance of exile or displacement leading to an objective awareness of linguistic heritage.

The tradition of scribal activity that was the preserve of the 'manuscript men' was, as tradition itself implies, largely concerned with continuity and preservation. This is not to say that it was impervious to innovation or creativity, but the scribes were primarily devoted to the copying of well-established texts, the subject of which included history, genealogy, heroic tales, verse, law and medicine. Yet the scribal tradition was not in any sense a monolith. In their discussion of the circulation of manuscripts between 1625 and 1725, Bernadette Cunningham and Raymond Gillespie see those writing history in Irish as part of a 'multi-lingual sphere that embraced manuscript and print in a variety of languages and for diverse audiences'.[53] While the multilingual aspect was less relevant in the nineteenth century, clearly, scribal activity involved numerous levels of interaction between Irish and English, oral and print culture, patron and scribe, audience and readership, and so on. Certain changes are discernible in the nineteenth century, such as the manner in which a rural, locally based tradition became increasingly dependent on urban-based patrons.[54] In some cases this type of interaction involved scribes being engaged in revivalist enterprises, as was the case with the scribes employed by Robert S. MacAdam, one of the founders of the Ulster Gaelic Society in 1828. The foremost of these scribes, Aodh Mac Domhnaill (1802–67), described the project in which he was involved as *athghineadh*, or the 'regeneration' of the Irish language.[55] However, there is also a sense in which scribes perceived of their work, independently, as being implicitly a work of revival. Hence Mícheál Óg Ó Longáin (1766–1837), of the renowned Cork scribal family, who was also a member of the Society of United Irishmen, describes his vocation as being 'for the sake of the Irish language and in order to help release it from the pernicious, forgetful darkness in which she has been for so long'.[56]

This last statement, from the most prolific of the Irish scribes of this period, bespeaks a commitment to the preservation of cultural memory, about which the theoretical insights of Aleida Assmann, specifically on the distinction between 'canon' and 'archive', are particularly apt. Assmann ascribes two separate functions to cultural memory:

> … the presentation of a narrow selection of sacred texts, artistic masterpieces, or historic key events in a timeless framework; and the storing of documents and artefacts of the past that do not at all meet these standards but are nevertheless deemed interesting or important enough to not let them vanish on the highway to total oblivion. While emphatic appreciation, repeated performance, and continued individual and public attention are the hallmark of

objects in the cultural working memory, professional preservation and withdrawal from general attention mark the contents of the reference memory.[57]

To this distinction between the active 'cultural working memory' and the passive 'reference memory' Assmann assigns the respective categories of 'canon' and 'archive'. The work of Irish scribes services both of these categories – the canon of scribal production was repeatedly performed at social gatherings where manuscripts were read aloud and revered texts, such as Keating's *Foras Feasa ar Éirinn* and Seán Ó Conaill's *Tuireamh na hÉireann*, were consistently copied and adapted.[58] Similarly, the extant corpus of Irish manuscripts represents a large archive of 'reference memory', and there is little doubt that scribes would have recognised that some of their work was more likely to be intended for 'professional preservation' than for active, working use. Indeed, Ó Longáin's identification of the 'pernicious, forgetful darkness' that encumbered the Irish language reflects the liminality of the archive as Assmann understands this: 'The archive, therefore, can be described as a space that is located on the border between forgetting and remembering; its materials are preserved in a state of latency, in a space of intermediary storage (*Zwischenspeicher*).'[59] It is this latency, this potentiality that can be realised through the active agency of reclamation, that underwrites much of the project of revivalism. The latency of the area of culture that is to be revived is what allows the revivalist to overcome the paradox of reviving that which has already expired and is, therefore, seemingly beyond retrieval.

Those who maintained the Irish scribal tradition in the nineteenth century might be described as 'guardian angels of transmission', Assmann's epithet for those who have historically been the custodians of archives.[60] The common scribal practice of petitioning future readers to pray for the soul of the scribe might also be interpreted as a need to seek the affirmation of posterity for the fraught process of transmission. Such petitions often referred to the transience of human life, and were undoubtedly intended as an opportunity for the intercession of prayers for one's mortal soul. But, as the following observation by Pádraig de Brún demonstrates, an awareness of other considerations was evident:

> The scribes left us much that we have yet to scrutinise: 'that which is before me, it will be behind me – to him that has knowledge I leave the task of sifting.' This was how one of them [the scribes]

understood his responsibility. It is up to us to do the sifting if we have any interest in those who preceded us.[61]

Besides the implicitly revivalist labours of nineteenth-century scribes, all of whom were doubtless aware of the challenges to the tradition they laboured for, the manifestos of nineteenth-century revivalist societies and initiatives provide an essential source of reflection on the nature of revivalism. The various strands of antiquarianism and revivalism that proliferated from the mid-eighteenth century onwards can only be briefly summarised here. The mid-eighteenth century onwards is marked by the growth of antiquarian interest in the Irish language typified in the work of Charles O'Conor of Belanagare, County Roscommon, Sylvester O'Halloran (1728–1807) and Charles Vallancey (1731–1812), whose desire for an academy was realised in the founding of the Royal Irish Academy in 1785. The distinction between antiquarianism (the collection and study of relics of antiquity) and revivalism (the revival and active renewal of aspects of a culture) is often difficult to discern, particularly in the early stages of this period, from the mid-1700s to the 1820s, but clearer lines of demarcation emerge from the 1820s onwards, and these become much more obvious by the last quarter of the nineteenth century.

The publication of Joseph Cooper Walker's *Historical Memoirs of the Irish Bards* (1786), Charlotte Brooke's *Reliques of Irish Poetry* (1789) and the first Irish 'magazine', *Bolg an tSolair* (Miscellany) (1795) were important developments that emanated from the growth of antiquarian scholarship and the influence of the European Romantic movement, of which James Macpherson's (1736–96) *Fingal* (1761) and *Temora* (1763) were of obvious relevance to Gaelic literature. The blurring of distinctions between antiquarianism and revivalism is illustrated in the aims of the Belfast Harp Festival of 1792 'to revive and perpetuate the ancient music and poetry of Ireland'.[62] While this intention is clearly revivalist, the next phrase in this passage bespeaks an antiquarian aspiration: 'They are solicitous to preserve from oblivion the few fragments which have been permitted to remain as monuments of the refined taste and genius of their ancestors.' Here the intention is to secure a record of the past rather than to revive what is dead or dying so that it can live.

The various Dublin societies of the first half of the nineteenth century – particularly the Gaelic Society (1806), the Iberno-Celtic Society (1818) and later, the Irish Archaeological Society (1840) – tended towards antiquarianism in method and patriotism in motivation. Yet 'the revival of the language and literature of the Gaels' was one of the foremost objects of the Gaelic Society, and Thomas Davis (1814–45), in his famous essay on 'The National Language' in the *Nation* in 1843, remarked that 'through the labours of the Archaeological and many lesser societies, it *is* being revived rapidly'.[63] Nevertheless, in spite of the rhetorical enthusiasm of Davis' essay – 'A People Without a Language of Its Own Is Only Half a Nation' – his own practical ideas were markedly gradualist:

> If an attempt were made to introduce Irish, either through the national schools or the courts of law, into the eastern side of the island, it would certainly fail, and the reaction might extinguish it altogether. But no one contemplates this save as a dream of what may happen a hundred years hence. It is quite another thing to say, as we do, that the Irish language should be cherished, taught, and esteemed, and that it can be preserved and gradually extended.[64]

Although Davis' practical proposals appear retrospectively to be cautious, even timid in nature – besides recommending the establishment of a newspaper, he recommended that the upper classes have Irish taught to their children – his appreciation of revivalism's potential for creative renewal is significant:

> As to Irish not having a modern literature, we say, so much the better, if the present or coming generation have the energy to set about creating one. If they go to the work with strong passions, they will build a literature fast and firm enough; they will be greater, and the parents of higher excellence, than if they studied and repeated instead of originating songs, histories and essays. The old Irish literature is ample to give impulse, and character, and costume to a new literature.[65]

Given the prominence of Davis' ideas in the development of Irish cultural nationalism, it is unsurprising to find much of them repeated in a lecture by John O'Daly (1800–78) entitled 'On the Decline of the Irish Language and Means Suggested for Its Revival', given to the Irish Confederation in November 1847.[66] However, O'Daly goes further than Davis on education, recommending that the Commissioners of National Education be petitioned to have Irish classes in their schools throughout the country. Conversely, on the issue of creating a national literature he appears much less progressive: 'My next lecture will be on Modern Irish Bards but let it not be understood that I mean the rhymers of the day. I mean no such thing but the men who sung in sorrowful strain the unhappy fate of their suffering country.'[67]

This tendency to vacillate between a view of Irish as bound to anteriority and a view of it as a language with a stake in futurity is typical of the play between antiquarianism and revivalism. However, despite the apparently regressive view of modern literature, O'Daly was not only a dynamic and prolific force in the development of publishing in Irish from his bookshop in Anglesea Street but also represented a vital link between various strands of revivalism and the historic Gaelic tradition. Besides publishing landmark texts such as *Reliques of Irish Jacobite Poetry* (1844) and *The Poets and Poetry of Munster* (1849), he helped found, and was secretary to, both the Celtic Society (1840) and the Ossianic Society (1853). Thomas Davis' gradualist attitude to the revival of Irish contrasts with the more robust programme advocated by the Ossianic Society, whose membership was dominated by middle-class men from the south-west of the country who had grown up hearing the *Fenian* (Ossianic) tales and lays.[68] The Ossianic Society was also significant for its success in attracting the allegiance of post-Famine emigrants to Britain, North America and Australia, due in part to its publication of popular modern Irish prose and verse.[69] In assessing O'Daly's legacy, Proinsias Ó Drisceoil points to the years O'Daly spent working for the Protestant evangelical Irish Society between 1826 and 1842 as crucial to the enterprises of subsequent years, not least for the annual income it provided.[70] This long association with the Irish Society allowed O'Daly to marry the manuscript tradition with the tradition of print and to acquire an acumen for publishing and editing from his experience of the Irish Society's publication activities. Moreover, O'Daly's skills as an organiser and committee man were indebted to his background in the Irish Society. A final point on O'Daly's legacy is to note that after his death in 1878, some of his manuscripts were purchased by a young Douglas Hyde (then eighteen years of age), who, of course, went on to found the Gaelic League.

The cultural nationalism of Thomas Davis and the Young Ireland movement within the history of various waves of 'ethnic revival' has been scrutinised in John Hutchinson's influential study *The Dynamics of Cultural Nationalism: the Gaelic Revival and the creation of the Irish nation state* (1987). While Hutchinson identifies three such ethnic revivals in Ireland – the first in the mid-eighteenth century, the second in the 1830s and the third in the 1890s – such a schema is problematic. Firstly, Hutchinson's focus on the historic development of cultural nationalism in Ireland does not allow much scope for an examination of revivalism as a critical cultural practice in its own right. Moreover, the lack of investigation of seventeenth-century revivalism is symptomatic of the limitations of the supposed three periods of 'ethnic revival'.[71] Nevertheless, while Hutchinson's main concern is with the third of his phases (the Gaelic League revival of the 1890s onwards), he stresses the continuity and inter-relatedness of the various revivalist movements: 'As the self-conscious heirs of the preceding revivals, the movements of the 1890s can only be understood through a historical analysis that places them both as a *recurring* phenomenon of the modern Irish period and as a *culmination* of their precursors.'[72]

A clear expression of such a recognition of the continuity of a revivalist tradition is to be found in the editorials and reviews written by James MacKnight (1801–76) of the *Belfast News-letter* in the late 1820s and early 1830s. In one such piece, from 1832, MacKnight remarks that 'Belfast rescued the Irish Harp from oblivion and to perfect its fame a revival of the Irish language and literature is only wanted'.[73] MacKnight was an Ulster Presbyterian journalist and land reformer from County Down who was described by the Young Irelander and co-founder of the *Nation* Charles Gavan Duffy as being 'perhaps the most influential layman in Ulster'.[74] His is an interesting case in that he was a staunch unionist who had studied for the Presbyterian ministry, yet had become fluent and literate in Irish through the influence of his Irish-speaking father. In the nineteen years from roughly 1827 that he spent as editor of the *Belfast News-letter*, a prestigious newspaper that was founded in 1737 and is still in print, his editorial output frequently referenced matters pertaining to the Irish language, and included a notice on the death of the scribe and poet Mícheál Óg Ó Longáin in 1837.[75]

Besides recognising the evident continuity within revivalism, MacKnight's ideas on the Irish-language revival are remarkable for the converging strands of motivation they express – patriotic, civic, humanist and evangelical – as well as the occasional insights they give into the nature of revivalism itself. An example of such an insight can be found in an early piece from 1828 in which MacKnight remarks:

> There is something unaccountably fascinating in the language of past times, and though it may be difficult to resolve the emotion into its first principles or to pursue it through its ultimate divergencies of mental association, there is scarcely an individual who does not feel it.[76]

Developing this thought further, he considers the pleasure of reading the classics of Greece and Rome:

> It is because we LIVE in the past, and have the power of resuscitating in idea, the departed forms of mental mastership, that we imbibe their sentiments with deepened enthusiasm when poured into our minds through the medium of their own native articulation.

Thus a humanistic rationale for antiquarian pursuits is followed by practical ideas for the establishment of 'newspapers and cheap periodicals and other interesting works freely circulated in the Irish language' for the sake of the 'improvement of the Irish'.[77] By increasing literacy, such publications would assist the evangelical aims of the 'Irish Society for Promoting the Education of the Native Irish Through the Medium of Their Own Language' and would, as such, be 'among the most powerful pioneers of the Reformation'.[78]

Although a committed unionist who disdained the O'Connellite Repeal movement, MacKnight's view of Irish revivalism is generally framed by an overarching appeal to patriotic spirit followed by practical suggestions within the provincial or civic spheres. His admiration for the Highland Society of Scotland is based on its having promoted 'the intellectual regeneration of their country', and he urged societies in Ireland to see what 'Scottish patriotism has done for the Scottish highlands'.[79] Yet Irish patriotism was in some ways more problematic than Scottish patriotism in the light of religious and ethnic differences. This is illustrated in MacKnight's 1834 editorial on the progress of the new Ulster Gaelic Society, which is prefaced by an epigraph from the south County Armagh poet Art Mac Cumhaigh (1738–73):

> … cluinim an Gaoidheilg uile d'a treigbhail
> Agus casmairt bearla ann a bheil a gach aon[80]
>
> [… I hear Irish being all abandoned
> And a din of English in the mouths of all]

The lines that he has taken as his motto, MacKnight explains, are the conclusion of

> a beautiful lament over the fallen condition of the Gael … and the circumstance with which the poet closes his elegiac effusion, as if

it had been the ultimatum of national evil, is the general disuse
into which the impressive language of his country had unhappily
fallen.[81]

MacKnight's familiarity with Mac Cumhaigh's poem can only be explained
by his having access to a manuscript or oral version of 'Aisling Airt Mhic
Cumhaigh' (The Vision of Art Mac Cumhaigh), there being no printed edition
available at the time, and, indeed, not for another eighty years.[82] This fact
is testament to MacKnight's knowledge of the Irish language and its literature. The poem itself, composed while Mac Cumhaigh was living in Howth,
County Dublin between 1763 and 1767, is an *aisling*, or vision poem, in
which a beautiful maiden appears to the poet in a dream. In these poems the
poet acts as a mediator between the Irish people and its destiny, as revealed
through an otherworldly messenger, most often a beautiful maiden personifying Ireland itself.[83] In this case the maiden's message is that Mac Cumhaigh's
native province of Ulster had been delivered from the rule of planter stock and
the Gaelic noblemen of his native Creggan district had risen from their tombs
to take control of their ancestral lands. The verse from which MacKnight
quotes, in keeping with the poem's central message, is a stark reflection of sectarian sentiment in which *Bhullaigh is Jane* (Willy and Jane), Mac Cumhaigh's
shorthand for Protestants, are usurpers who speak the poem's only English
words, 'You're a Papist, I know not thee.'[84]

MacKnight would surely not have been ignorant of the context from
which he had drawn his 'motto'. It is possible, as Roger Blaney has spec-
ulated, that MacKnight was a descendant of native Irish converts to
Presbyterianism, something his Gaelic surname and his father's knowledge
of Irish may indicate.[85] However, the explanation for MacKnight's adoption
of Mac Cumhaigh's lament, in spite of its sectarian sentiments, may lie in his
willingness to place the Irish language in a new revivalist context in which the
language could be admired on humanistic or antiquarian grounds or instru-
mentalised in the cause of Protestant evangelicalism. The same article, which
begins with the epigraph from Mac Cumhaigh, ends with

the assured hope, that the public will not leave the existing relics
of what their country once was to the fate described by the Roman
poet –
... Phocaeorum,
Velut profugit exsecrata civitas

Agros atque Lares patrios, habitandaque fana
Apris reliquit et rapacibus lupis.
[... just as Phocaeans swore an oath and left their fields and gods
and shrines to be the homes of ravening wolves and boars.][86]

Again, the appeal to humanistic regard for the sources of civilisation is
proposed as the rationale for revival, thus reinforcing his earlier remarks on
'the intrinsic power and sweetness' of the Irish language and its 'essential
relation to the ancient history not only of Britain but of Europe itself'.[87] In
other editorials addressed at the use of Irish for evangelical aims, MacKnight
rues the historic failure of the Reformation in Ireland to recognise that the
vernacular was 'one of the most powerful instruments for good', while welcoming the Presbyterian Synod's decision to make Irish classes compulsory
for students of the ministry.[88] Summing up the case in this instance, he cites
'utility and patriotism' in support of the project of revivalism.[89]

This willingness to overlook political antagonisms where a common aim
is advanced is typical of MacKnight's open-ended view of revivalism, reflected
in the phrase 'divergencies of mental association' with which he associated
the fascination with the language of past times. The outlook he expresses
also poses some interesting considerations for the generic study of revivalism.
MacKnight was keenly aware of the ethnic divisions that persisted in Ulster
between the planter and the Gael, and remarked that his father's singing to
him in Irish would surprise many, coming, as it did, 'from an old black-
mouthed Presbyterian'.[90] Yet his readiness to ignore the ethnic provenance and
distinctions relating to the Irish-language tradition is similar to the attitude
of contemporary Protestant cultural nationalists, such as Thomas Davis, for
whom the Gaelic tradition was consciously co-opted as the basis of a unifying
national culture. In the case of Davis, a certain reinvention of self was necessary in order to embrace the native tradition, whereas in MacKnight's case
he could have easily regarded himself as a bearer of that tradition despite
the apparent anomaly of his religious affiliation. MacKnight's articulation
of a divergent set of motivating principles for the project of revivalism, and,
ultimately, the unaccountability of the fascination with the language of past
times all points to the universality of revivalism as a practice in its own right,
rather than a mere auxiliary to certain political or evangelical movements.
MacKnight's revivalism can be said to have both encompassed and transcended the three areas of language intervention mentioned earlier – scholarly,
cultural nationalist and evangelical. Admittedly, his cultural nationalism was

more often expressed as 'patriotism', and was at no time separatist, but he had no hesitation in welcoming 'the spirit of nationality' when it led to language revivalism.[91]

Part of MacKnight's liberal negotiation of language and ethnicity involved an enthusiastic recommendation of the affinities between Gaelic Ireland and Scotland. In this respect the towering figure of Rev. Norman MacLeod (1783–1862) represents a powerful instance of the combination of language revivalism and Protestant evangelicalism.[92] MacLeod was a native speaker of Scottish Gaelic from Argyleshire who was known in Scotland by the soubriquet Caraid nan Gaidheal (Friend of the Gaels) for his outstanding pastoral and charitable legacy in respect of Highland communities and the Gaelic-speaking population of Glasgow, where he was minister of Campsie. Besides being a highly effective advocate for Scottish Gaelic within the Church of Scotland, MacLeod made a very significant contribution to literary culture in Scottish Gaelic, and was responsible for the first significant Scottish Gaelic periodical *An Teachdaire Gaelach* (The Gaelic Messenger) (1829–31). MacLeod's intervention in Irish affairs was as an effective advocate of Presbyterian missionary activity to Irish speakers. His practical proposals to this end were informed by extensive travel in Ireland in 1833, after which he set about the publication of an Irish translation of the psalms of David for use in the missionary activity of the Presbyterian Home Mission.[93]

MacLeod's reasoning for this project shows how vernacular scripture and catechism were as much a battleground for Irish souls in the 'Second Reformation' as they were in the first. Writing to Rev. George Bellis, secretary to the Home Mission, in 1835, MacLeod prefaced his remarks by welcoming the decision to send forth to the Irish people missionaries who could address them in Irish:

> – that language, without the aid of which there may be in Ireland, at this moment, no fewer than a million and a half of people who cannot form an accurate conception on any subject, and through the medium of which they are alone capable of receiving moral or religious instruction.[94]

This estimate, given sixteen years before the 1851 census, where a language question was first included, is probably based on the views expressed by MacLeod's colleague and fellow Scottish Gaelic scholar Rev. Daniel Dewar (1788–1867) in his *Observations on the Character, Customs, and Superstitions of the Irish* (1812), and also Christopher Anderson's *Historical Sketches of the Native Irish and Their Descendants* (1828).[95] What is interesting is the qualitative assessment of the linguistic competence of those 1.5 million, particularly in regard to matters of morality and religion. The evidence of the pastoral work of Catholic clergy to Irish emigrants in the industrial centres of Britain and North America throughout the nineteenth century and into the twentieth century references the critical need for a knowledge of Irish to hear confession and the inability of many emigrants to use English in this sacrament.[96] The Irish language was the key to opening hearts, MacLeod argued, and poetry, the most treasured medium of all, was the best to encourage conversions:

> I need scarce remind you of the intense love which the Irish have for music and poetry – hence it is, that the dark and wild superstitions of ages long since passed away have come down to us and been preserved to this hour – hence it is that the remembrance of Erin's wrongs, and Erin's woes, in the most distant periods of her history, are so intimately known by all the classes of the unlettered Irish – they are handed down in song – they are recited at the firesides and at all their festive meetings – they are set to music, and sung to their own sweet and simple melodies. To the influence of poetry and music is to be attributed the continued and undiminished feeling of suspicion, of hatred, and disregard fostered by the Irish against the descendants of their early conquerors. They had no other sort of poetry or music to counteract the effects of those national songs and melodies, which, handing down from age to age tales and histories of no peaceful character or tendency, had the most injurious influence on the moral feelings of the people, and which may account, in some degree, for the difference which exists at present in their character and conduct from that of their neighbours in the Highlands and Isles of Scotland. Strange it is that this peculiar feature in the character of the Irish, viz. their enthusiastic love for poetry and music, has not been laid hold of by their best friends for conveying to them lessons of religious instruction.[97]

This account of the intergenerational transmission of national grievances is likely to have been borrowed from Dewar's *Observations on Ireland* (1812).[98] It may well owe something to the influence of Thomas Moore's *Memoirs of Captain Rock* (1824), in which the eponymous Captain recounts his family's experience of centuries of English misrule.[99] At any rate, whether based on secondary sources or fiction, such as Moore's, or on his own travels in Ireland, MacLeod's analysis of native attachment to poetry, music and history is most revealing. While clearly sharing the evangelical's instrumental view of the Irish language, there can be no doubt that his attachment to the language was instinctive. The natural character of the Highlanders and the Irish, he remarked, was precisely the same, as, too, was their love of story and song. If places like Galway – 'that *dark* place' – were evidence of the 'triumph of monkish superstition',[100] this situation could be reversed, as it had been centuries earlier in Scotland following the successful introduction of the metrical psalms:

> The Highlanders became enthusiastic in their love of psalmody. The hymns of the Druids, venerated for ages, and the wild legends of the fairies and mountain-spirits, yielded to the songs of Sion – the holy effusions of the contrite and chastened David supplanted the *coronach* for the dead, and the wail for the dying. The enthusiasm of the people was not destroyed, but it received a new and holy direction. Indeed, it forms a new era in the history of our country … These were days of marked revival.[101]

The word 'revival' here refers, of course, not to a cultural revival but, rather, a spiritual revival. In the 1830s such 'revivals' were associated particularly with America, and were the subject of considerable interest to Presbyterians in Ireland.[102] Ulster Presbyterians witnessed their own waves of revivals, most notably in 1859. Indeed, James MacAdam, brother and business colleague of the antiquarian and language revivalist Robert S. MacAdam, in his diary of the same year refers rather disparagingly to these as 'insane exhibitions'.[103] The tendency to associate religious revivals with a certain vulgarity or ignorance was partly due to the radical change involved, particularly where participants exhibited outward physical signs of spiritual conversion.[104] Yet this radical break with the current order and the perceived garish inauthenticity of such transformations are of particular relevance to the discourse of cultural revival. Robert S. MacAdam's own position, oscillating between revivalist and antiquarian, is a case in point. He referred explicitly to *aith-bhe-odhadh ar d-teanga* (the revival of our language), and the aims of his avowedly secular Ulster Gaelic Society, while couched in the contemporary language of improvement, could be deemed revivalist insofar as its stated purpose was to revive literacy in Irish by 'promoting the diffusion of elementary education and useful knowledge, through the medium of the Irish language, where that language prevails'.[105] Undoubtedly, a large part of his activity, in keeping with a man of his times and social background, was antiquarian and conservationist – particularly in his collecting of manuscripts, folklore and song. Accordingly, his first editorial for the *Ulster Journal of Archaeology*, which he founded in 1853, reflects this concern for salvaging the remains of a dying culture:[106]

> We are on the eve of great changes. Society in Ulster seems breaking up … We stand as it were at the threshold of a new social edifice in process of erection and not yet completed; while all around us lie scattered the ruins of the ancient structure fast hurrying to decay. Before these are altogether swept away let us gather a few fragments.

Besides echoing the wish to 'preserve from oblivion the few fragments' contained in the notice of the 1792 Belfast Harpers' Festival, itself an important revivalist milestone, the last phrase in this quotation is taken from John (6:12), where the parable of the loaves and the fishes is related, and is the instruction given by Christ to the apostles.[107] In an age of religious observance, it is unsurprising that MacAdam should ground the mission of a secular antiquarian journal in biblical quotation. Yet it is also reflective of the constant segueing of religious discourse into the discourse of culture, particularly where revivalism is concerned.[108]

The antagonism between conservationism and radical renewal, between antiquarianism and revivalism, is expressed equally in the religious and cultural spheres. The sense in which revivalism involves a radical departure from the present orthodoxy often relies on a critical distance between the revivalist and that which is to be revived. This distance can entail the physical distance of exile, as discussed in the previous chapter. It can also involve social distance, where the revivalist is from a different social background to the language community or any other relevant group that represents a continuous link with the endangered culture. With regard to this social distance, the case of Protestant evangelical missionaries is of obvious significance. The first product of the Presbyterian Home Mission's drive to train missionaries in the Irish language was Henry McManus (1817–64) from County Cavan, who recorded his experiences in Irish-speaking west Connacht, beginning in 1840, in *Sketches of the Irish Highlands* (1863).[109] Although undoubtedly encouraged by the work of Dewar, Anderson and MacLeod, McManus' account of the communities he sought to convert is marked by an outsider's perspective.[110] Connemara, he says, 'in common with the South and West generally', had 'no middle class', and, as such, we can infer that McManus had no social equivalent there.[111] He was constantly challenged by the distance he encountered between himself and the communities he engaged with, often making his mission appear like a journey into the past. He describes the liminality of Joyce Country in striking terms: 'the fourteenth century still lingered there on the skirts of the nineteenth; just as, near the summits of the Alps, you can touch with one hand a flower, and, with the other, the eternal snows'.[112]

The advantage of this distance from the object of his mission is that McManus finds it necessary to explain west Connacht to the reader, thus rendering his memoir a store of ethnographical detail, social customs, folklore, poetry and local legend. In some ways the middle-class revivalists that led the Gaelic League revival from the early 1890s onwards owed their curiosity about, and later appreciation of, Gaelic culture to the same social and cultural distance that animates McManus' memoir. Douglas Hyde was an eminent collector of folklore and song who typified the class difference between folklorist and folk, even though he was an individual who easily transcended social and religious divisions. While in Connemara, Patrick Pearse is reputed to have dressed up as a 'man of the roads' so as 'to mix quite freely with the country folk as one of themselves'.[113] Ironically, Pearse encountered the remnants of one of the nineteenth-century Connemara Bible-society colonies, of which one old man read his Irish Bible to him and argued with him for an hour.[114] While sharing the same social distance as the Protestant missionary, Pearse's views on spiritual and material wealth in Connemara are the inverse of McManus': 'Here alone perhaps in the world are these sights to be seen since the French Revolution, hovels still lingering at the gates of castles, a rich spiritual life with poverty, a poor spiritual life with riches living side by side.'[115]

A contemporary of Henry McManus who shared his outsider status from an opposite perspective was Aodh Mac Domhnaill, a native scholar among urban antiquarians and revivalists. In this respect Mac Domhnaill's position was similar to that of Muiris Ó Gormáin (*c.*1705–*c.*1794), who spent most of the latter half of the eighteenth century in Dublin in the employ of antiquarians, such as Charles Vallancey, and acted for some time as amanuensis to the Committee of Antiquities of the Royal Dublin Society.[116] On either side of a period between 1842 and 1856, which he spent in Belfast as scribe and assistant to Robert S. MacAdam, Aodh Mac Domhnaill had a long association with various Bible societies, including several years as a teacher and inspector with the Presbyterian Home Mission in the Glens of Antrim, where his books no doubt included MacLeod's *Psalms of David in the Irish Language* (1836). These years ended in a certain degree of calumny for Mac Domhnaill, during which he became embroiled in a visceral dispute between Rev. Luke Walsh of the parish of Culfeightrin, north Antrim and Rev. Allen, superintendent of the Presbyterian Home Mission.[117]

The years spent by Mac Domhnaill under the patronage of Robert S. MacAdam – at this stage a prosperous industrialist whose Soho Foundry employed 250 men – accounted not only for rescuing Mac Domhnaill's personal fortunes but for his production of a modest but significant body of around forty-five poems as well as a treatise on philosophy.[118] In this respect, Mac Domhnaill's own *oeuvre* was initiated within what he understood to be a revivalist project. As has been mentioned before, Mac Domhnaill saw his work as full-time scribe and collector of manuscript material, folklore, song, proverbs and assistant lexicographer in MacAdam's unpublished English–Irish dictionary as being in essence devoted to the 'regeneration' of the Irish language. Moreover, MacAdam's patronage was an opportunity that relatively few others of the 'manuscript men' of his time secured. It is no surprise, therefore, that a certain amount of jealousy exercised some of Mac Domhnaill's contemporaries. During a poetic contention between Mac Domhnaill and a fellow scribe and poet from south Armagh, Art Mac Bionaid (1793–1879), Mac Domhnaill was accused of being like the one-eyed man who is a king among the blind.[119] This barb was delivered to Mac Domhnaill's patron MacAdam, along with the remark that 'there is more Irish history slumbering in the rocks of Ballykeel than ever Belfast was possessed [of]. It was cradled and nursed there and most likely never will awaken.'[120] Mac Bionaid was referring to his own townland here, and was petitioning MacAdam for a commission to write a history of Ireland.

Personal ambition and jealousies aside, Mac Bionaid's depiction of Aodh Mac Domhnaill as one-eyed man among the blind deserves further scrutiny. Although Mac Domhnaill was essentially an outsider within the MacAdam circle, it is not true that MacAdam and his fellow Belfast antiquarians and revivalists were blindly ignorant of the Irish language and its historical and literary culture. Although not a native speaker of Irish like Mac Domhnaill and Mac Bionaid, MacAdam had clearly learned the language in his youth – he went to school at Belfast Academical Institution where Irish was taught by Rev. William Neilson (1774–1821), and as a young man he had already begun collecting manuscripts while travelling on his father's business through the northern part of Ireland.[121] Nevertheless, there was certainly a marked cultural distinction between the 'old Irish population' in Ulster and those 'chiefly of English and Scottish descent', as MacAdam himself noted: 'Among them, the appearance, manners, language, and tone of thought, differ as thoroughly from those of the first-mentioned class, as if they were separated by a wide ocean.'[122] Although antiquarianism and cultural revivalism had built many bridges across this 'ocean', it is clear that ethnic divisions were clearly demarcated.[123] With this in mind, Mac Bionaid's description of Aodh Mac Domhnaill's singularity within the company of MacAdam and his peers is all the more understandable as an expression of social, ethnic and cultural distance.

By dint of this anomalous position Mac Domhnaill's poetic *oeuvre* differs markedly to that of his peers in matters of audience, in that he was composing Irish poetry for a select, mainly Protestant, antiquarian and revivalist coterie rather than for a local Irish-speaking community. As Énrí Ó Muirgheasa remarks, 'the poets of Meath continued to sing, and the scribes to write their songs, until there was no longer an audience left to understand them'.[124] In a certain sense, the revivalist project of MacAdam freed Mac Domhnaill from dependence on such a local audience, and his extended sojourn in Belfast was typical of thousands of others throughout Europe whose relocation to urban centres led to societal as well as individual transformations. Although Belfast was merely a large provincial town, albeit one that registered rapid industrial expansion throughout the nineteenth century, Mac Domhnaill's case bears a certain resemblance to the nineteenth-century artists who became proto-modernists in the metropolis, as Raymond Williams remarks:

> The most important general element of the innovations in form is the fact of immigration to the metropolis, and it cannot too often be emphasised how many of the major innovators were, in this precise sense, immigrants. At the level of theme, this underlies, in an obvious way, the elements of strangeness and distance, indeed of alienation, which so regularly form part of the repertory.[125]

While Mac Domhnaill's release from the ties of local culture did not lead to formal innovations in his poetry, it appears that the relatively novel circumstances that his urban patron provided for him were responsible for his becoming a poet in the first instance. All of his poetry belongs to the period spent in Belfast. While his poetry is not distinguished by innovations of form, his *Fealsúnacht*, or Philosophy (written in 1853), is a striking departure from the typical preoccupations of contemporary native scholars.[126] On a thematic level, his exposure to the novel and dynamic environment of a modern industrial workplace (the Soho Foundry) also led to his penning perhaps the earliest testimony in Irish to the shock of industrialisation. Mac Domhnaill's burlesque take on this experience presents the foundry as a vision of frenzied pagan ritual in which the witness' physical courage and 'interest in women' are purged.[127]

A similar sense of displacement leading to innovation is witnessed in one of Mac Domhnaill's contributions to the *aisling* genre, wherein the conventional poem segues into a contemporary newspaper report. In 'Aisling ar Éirinn' (Vision Concerning Ireland), written at the time of Daniel O'Connell's imprisonment in 1844, the poet bemoans O'Connell's incarceration as one of the many wrongs suffered by Ireland, particularly the abandonment of the Irish language and the decline of poetry.[128] Just at the moment the poet fears that the Gael will remain in bondage until the day of judgement, he is greeted by Ireland herself in the form of a beautiful maiden bearing a letter with news of O'Connell's release. Yet Mac Domhnaill's poem does not finish with this conventional promise of deliverance received from Ireland herself. Rather, the poet is seemingly returned to the present with a jolt when, looking round, he sees no one but *bean bheag Bhéarlach* (a little English-speaking woman), who is given the last prosaic lines of the poem in English: 'If you see the papers you'll see 'tis true/ That all our heroes have left the jail/ And we'll have Repeal for all they can do.'[129] As the eloquent promises of the dream maiden give way to the elliptical message of the street woman – the letter carried by the dream maiden seems in reality to have been a newspaper read by an ordinary woman in the street – it is as though the traditional Irish-language political message has to be corroborated at the end by that most contemporary of documents, the English-language newspaper.[130]

The idea that a new urban-based school of Irish literature could follow a modernist trajectory might have been realised in the circle of the Cork exile and tailor Tomás an tSneachta Ó Conchubhair (1798–*c.* 1865), who emigrated to London in 1820 and lived and worked in London's West End (Piccadilly and Oxford Street area). A neighbour of Ó Conchubhair's in London was the brother-in-law of Brian Merriman, and, besides having taught Irish classes for the Irish Confederation, it has been claimed that Ó Conchubhair was part of a small *dámhscoil* (poetry school) in London, along with other Cork scribes and poets. Yet the evidence of Ó Conchubhair's *oeuvre* reveals no evidence of a break from tradition inspired by his metropolitan surroundings. Rather, he penned a number of *aisling* poems that generally carry a contemporary message of national deliverance under the leadership of William Smith O'Brien, but reveal little of the poet's own situation in London.[131]

As discussed earlier, the notion that native Ireland had no public sphere because it was supposedly cut off from English print culture has been robustly challenged by many scholars in recent years. The earlier discussion of Irish-language poems on the American War of Independence is in itself part of the ample evidence against such a claim. The *Nation* was an important promoter of material in Irish from its founding in 1844 onwards, and its galvanising influence on the discourse of cultural nationalism is well documented.[132] Nevertheless, it is also true that substantial print journalism in Irish was a very late development, generally taken to begin in 1881 with the publication in Brooklyn, New York of Mícheál Ó Locháin's (1836–99) bilingual paper *An Gaodhal*. Ó Locháin was a native speaker of Irish from County Galway who was a pivotal figure in the American philo-Celtic societies. Previous efforts, such as Richard D'Alton's *An Fíor-Éironach*, of which seven numbers are estimated to have been printed in Tipperary in 1862, failed to take root. Ó Locháin was keen to highlight the superior initiative of exiles, claiming that the successful launch of *An Gaodhal* in 1881 had 'shamed the Gaels in Ireland into founding the Dublin *Gaelic Journal*' the following year, 1882.[133] Again, the importance of the objectifying distance of exile is worth investigating. Two other landmarks in the nascent tradition of Irish-language periodicals were the product of the same circumstances. The earlier of these, the five numbers of Philip Barron's *Ancient Ireland* (1835) – part of an ambitious revivalist project that included founding a short-lived Irish College at Bonmahon, County Waterford – were inspired after a period of exile in Paris and Italy. Philip Barron was forced into exile after losing a libel case taken against his newspaper, the *Waterford Chronicle*, in 1827, and his travels in mainland Europe are thought to have been the catalyst for his wide-ranging revivalist scheme.[134] As mentioned in the previous chapter, Barron's *Ancient Ireland* adopted the oft-quoted line from Froinsias Ó Maolmhuaidh – '*Beidh an Ghaodhailig fá mheas fós* … the Irish will yet be in great esteem' – as a motto, and this example was followed by subsequent revivalists. Barron's views on Irish revivalism are an important part of the content of his magazine, whose main focus was in reproducing texts in Irish. His comparison of the revival of Irish to the revival of classical learning in Renaissance Europe is a recurrent feature of his rationale:

> The literature of ancient Greece and Rome (having been over-
> whelmed by the barbarians) lay buried in darkness for ages, until

it was restored on the revival of learning in Europe. The literature of ancient Ireland became similarly buried, and remains so to the present day ... But from this era [1 January 1835] we shall have to date the revival of learning in Ireland.[135]

A later example of the dynamic exile revivalist is seen in the figure of James Ronan, a wholesale tea merchant in Salford, Manchester who initiated and ran the *Keltic Journal and Educator* in 1869. While only stretching to seven numbers, its Irish lessons were provided by the redoubtable Canon Ulick Bourke (1829–87) of St Jarlath's, Tuam, County Galway, whose landmark 'Easy Lessons or Self-instruction in Irish' were first published in the *Nation* in 1858. Bourke's lessons were continued in the 1870s in various periodicals, including the *Tuam News*, the newspaper Bourke founded and which had the distinction of having its own 'Gaelic department' under John Glynn (1843–1915).[136] The alienating experience of exile is the first factor to which the Manchester-based James Ronan attributed his conversion to the cause of the Irish language, as he explained in a letter to Glynn dated June 1869:

> It is now, just 20 years since I saw my native land. The experience of *every day* during those 20 years, has fixed upon my mind the *fact* that I am a foreigner in England. No length of time of residence *can ever make* England the home or *country* of an Irishman. And – here is an important matter for all Irishmen, – *the Irishman*, whether educated or *uneducated can never speak English except as a foreigner*. So strange and *foreign* is the *Irish*-English in England that it is the subject of continual mockery and derision in family circles, workshops, concert halls, theatres etc. in fact a kind of national laughing stock for the English nation.[137]

Rather than blaming the English for the loss of the Irish language, Ronan regarded the language shift as a national disgrace: 'Of all the nations the *Irish nation* stands *alone* in its mean desertion, in its cowardly sneaking away, from the Irish language.'[138] In response to this situation Ronan proposed the formation of a National Language Association with 'branches throughout the globe' but with its headquarters in Tuam, County Galway, where the archbishop was John McHale, a champion of the Irish language, and where the president of its diocesan college, St Jarlath's, was James Ronan's collaborator, Canon Ulick Bourke.[139] What is perhaps most significant in Ronan's proposal is that his association should have branches throughout the globe. This ambitious phrase no doubt recognised the material advantage of harnessing the zeal of exiles, but it also bespeaks a confidence in the capacity of a minority language to be revitalised by global networks.

In reviewing the role of missionaries, the displaced and the exiled in the development of a revivalist consciousness, the significance of a critical objectifying distance is immediately apparent. Whether through the instrumentalisation of language and literature effected by Protestant missionaries and cultural nationalists, or the externalisation of linguistic tradition as experienced by the 'displaced' Aodh Mac Domhnaill and exiles such as Philip Barron and James Ronan, an objectifying critical distance is common to both. The existential crisis faced by a linguistic community and literary tradition is what initially spurs the revivalist to action. Paradoxically, it is this crisis that allows agency to come clearly into focus – the natural, embodied practices of a linguistic community are suddenly matters of contingency and agency rather than seemingly autonomous organic continuity. Consequently, the ability of human agency to bring about the 'desertion' of a language is as evident as the potential for that same agency to bring about the 'regeneration' of the failing language. Thus, James Ronan's coruscating denunciation of the abandonment of the Irish language is balanced by his global aspirations for its revival. Accordingly, in Homi Bhabha's postcolonial analysis, 'those who have suffered the sentence of history – subjugation, domination, displacement and diaspora' are precisely those from whom we have most to learn, by dint of the critical strategies that arise from their social marginality.[140]

The second salient point is the constant overlap, in revivalist discourse, of the religious and cultural spheres. Again, in an age of religious observance this may be simply an aspect of the pervasive influence of religion. Nevertheless, the similarity of methods used by both the evangelical societies and language-revivalist groups – particularly the publication and distribution of cheap reading material, the use of peripatetic teachers and organisers – is also reflected in the recurrent spiritual imagery of revivalist discourse. Just as Thomas Davis thought that losing the native language to then learn an alien one was 'the chain on the soul', James Ronan regarded the work of language revivalism as 'holy work', and Robert S. MacAdam quoted the words attributed to Christ, 'gather up the fragments', to exhort his collaborators.[141] Although MacAdam's words were intended for the readers of an archaeological journal, as mentioned earlier MacAdam's work was a combination of antiquarianism and revivalism that blurred the distinction between them.

A further example of this spiritual-cultural convergence is seen in one of the earliest essays by Eoin MacNéill on the Irish-language revival. His essay was published in the *Irish Ecclesiastical Record* in 1891, and undoubtedly was pitched at a clerical audience, whom he addresses directly, saying 'the future of the Irish language is almost wholly in the hands of the Irish clergy'.[142] Mac Néill outlines the historic bond between the Irish Catholic Church and the Irish language initially through its literature, of which 'the mass of Irish classical literature is the work of ecclesiastics' so that 'writer and cleric became convertible terms'.[143] Urging the priesthood to appreciate the depth of their own historic literary tradition, he remarks that

> it appears that between the Irish priesthood and the Irish language there exists an ancient ξενία, or perennial bond of friendship, a tie as sacred as any that can hold between men and things. It assorts ill with the spirit of that historic connection to allow the Irish language, now undoubtedly a strong link with the Christian past, to get rusty, and ultimately to break altogether.[144]

The historic guiding influence and control of the Irish clergy on Irish literature was a sure bulwark against the 'irreligion and immorality and folly that pervade other modern literatures; and not least among them English literature'.[145] Citing the inherent dangers presented by three fourths of the books emanating from the printing presses, Mac Néill confidently juxtaposed the literature of the Irish language: 'a literature healthy as mountain air in the past, and capable of being preserved so in the future'.[146] Since Mac Néill's article is so clearly an invitation to the Catholic clergy to take leadership and ownership of the Irish-language movement, its account of the clergy's 'perennial bond of friendship' with the Irish language should not be taken at face value.[147] Mac Néill may simply have been trying to secure the powerful patronage of the clergy for the language movement in order to guarantee its future success. Nevertheless, what is interesting is the similarity between the case MacNéill makes for the instrumentalisation of language preservation in the cause of morality and confessional solidarity and the case articulated by Protestant evangelists such as MacLeod and MacKnight in the first half of the nineteenth century.

The question arises as to whether the origins of revivalism in religion, evident in concepts such as the eternal return and renewal, are evidence of the essential numinosity of revivalism or, alternatively, does the frequent instrumentalisation of language revival by religious protagonists lead to a conflation of religious and cultural revival? Rather than being mutually exclusive, it appears more likely that both propositions carry their own validity. It is difficult for revivalism to be a purely secular discourse given the extent to which its terms have been formed within the discourse of spirituality. Just as explicit manifestos of Irish revivalism during the eighteenth and nineteenth centuries tend to carry the imprint of religiosity, the implicit revivalism of literary production in Irish reveals the same tendencies. The most obvious examples of this are in the *aisling* genre and in other historical and millenarianist currents that bespeak a duty towards the transmission of historical continuity and a concern for futurity.

Antaine Raiftearaí, the blind Mayo poet, is a totemic figure for Irish literature of the nineteenth century, described by Gearóid Denvir as 'the major Irish voice of his day'.[148] In his own time Raiftearaí was known throughout Connacht, and probably beyond, as a highly accomplished travelling oral poet whose compositions were eagerly memorised, sung and recited. The life and work of Raiftearaí, as it persisted in the oral tradition of Connacht, was assiduously collected and edited by Douglas Hyde as the fifth instalment in his *Songs of Connacht* series of books.[149] In this sense this duty towards Raiftearaí's oral legacy was an essential part of Hyde's development as a scholar revivalist. Similarly, the origins of the literary revival of Yeats and Gregory owed a great deal to their fascination with the persona of this last vestige of the 'wandering poets', whose life story they researched and co-opted as an emblem of the peripheral figures they fetishised: 'His life was always the wandering, homeless life of the old bards', Gregory remarked in her discussion of stories she had collected, beginning with the reminiscences of two old women in the workhouse of Gort, County Galway.[150] Ironically, Raiftearaí became best known for a short poem he did not compose but which was attributed retrospectively to him in Ó Locháin's *An Gaodhal* in 1882.[151] This poem, 'Mise Raiftearaí', became part of the repertoire of Irish schoolchildren in the twentieth century, and was incorporated into the design of one of the last Irish bank notes to be superseded by the euro in 2002.

Raiftearaí's retrospective adaptation in the service of revivalism is in many ways fitting since part of his own *oeuvre* adumbrated a revivalist thread. His long narrative poem *Seanchas na Sceiche* (History of the Thornbush) reiterates and distils the narrative of Keating's *Foras Feasa ar Éirinn* (completed in 1634), and ends with a reference to the ominous year of 1825, the year of Pastorini's prophesised demise of Protestantism.[152] The poem is based on the conceit that the thornbush has been a witness to the history of Ireland from the time of the Flood to the end of the Williamite Wars in 1691. Raiftearaí is ostensibly a conduit for this oral testimony of the history of Ireland. As mentioned previously, the tradition of narrative poems as a versified summary of Keating's history in subsequent centuries has been carefully charted by Vincent Morley.[153] Aodh Mac Domhnaill composed a narrative poem (probably in the late 1840s) in this same vein, *Príomhstair an Stocáin* (The Main History of the Stack), the history of Ireland in this case being related by a large limestone stack-like rock (Cloch an Stocáin) on the Antrim coast, known in English as The White Lady.[154]

Besides *Seanchas na Sceiche*, the reference to 1825, Pastorini and the influence of millenarianism is frequently attested in Raiftearaí's work, particularly in his poems concerning the Whiteboys (*Buachaillí Bána*), one of the most prominent of the agrarian secret societies originating in the 1760s and bearing many similarities to the later Rockites.[155] The same adherence to Pastorini is also evident in the oral poetry of Máire Bhuí Ní Laoghaire of Uíbh Laoghaire, County Cork, particularly her 'Cath Chéim an Fhiaidh' (The Battle of Céim an Fhiaidh), based on an engagement between the Whiteboys and the yeomanry in 1822. The 'battle' itself had been foretold by a prophecy, according to local tradition, and Ní Laoghaire's poem enthusiastically invokes Pastorini in its encouragement of the Gael to prepare for the imminent defeat of the Protestant usurpers.[156] In another poem, 'Fáinne an Lae' (The Dawning of the Day), Ní Laoghaire uses the *aisling* to present a message of pending release from bondage:

> Beir scéal anois gur daoradh sinn
> Ag tréadtha an uilc 'san chlaein,
> Gan bhréag anois tá an téarma istigh
> Beidh Éire againn fí réim
>
> [Take this message that we were enslaved
> By the bands of evil and deceit
> Without a lie our term is now done
> We shall have Ireland under rule.]

Having given this promise of deliverance, the muse is invited by the poet to a tavern, but replies that she cannot stop since *tá an fóghmhar ar leathadh im dhéidh* (the harvest is being reaped behind me). The harvest, she explains, is the slaughter of the Duke of York and his troop by the true Prince of the Gael. This reference has been linked to defeats suffered by the Duke of York during the Flanders Campaign (1793–95); it may also refer to the first half of the Napoleonic Wars (1803–15).[157] However, the urgent sense of current unfolding events is compromised by the poem's anticlimactic conclusion, where rising expectations are put into abeyance: *'S ar an mbliain seo chughainn beidh búir go lag* (And next year boors will be weak). The anticlimax merely reflects the deficit between the imagined future and the actual present, and is one that can only be assuaged by the constant promise of imminent victory. It is the latency of the times, embodied in prophecy and encouraged by contemporary signs, that must be continually reiterated in phrases such as 'this present year', 'next year', 'the year that is approaching' and so on.[158]

Together with the transmission of historical continuity, it is this concern with futurity in Irish literature of the eighteenth and nineteenth centuries, a concern institutionalised in the *aisling* genre, that corresponds most closely to the formal manifestos of revivalism emerging mostly in the English language during the same period. Yet while the practical measures outlined in revivalist essays and programmes tended to be gradualist, the implicit revivalism evident in a range of Irish poetry and song tended to be of a much more dramatic order. Just as many Protestant evangelical revivals were inspired by the words of the Book of Joel (2:28) – 'In the last days, I will pour out my spirit on everyone … Your young men will see visions and your old men will have dreams' – the messianic promises of the *aisling* poems predicted a spectacular rupture of the orthodoxy of the present.

Whether through the formal discourses of language revival or belief in the imminent deliverance of the historic language community, Irish revivalism of the eighteenth and nineteenth centuries represents a broad spectrum of intentions bound by a common set of concerns. The anxiety of transmission discernible within the scribal tradition is the same realisation of impending loss that urges formal revivalist interventions. Those who encounter the linguistic and literary tradition at a certain remove – typically social distance, displacement or exile – experience an objectifying distance that allows for the development of a revivalist consciousness. Here the paradoxical advantage of language loss or estrangement is the realisation of agency and an awareness of what may be missing. Like religion, it appears that language must first be lost in order to gain a true appreciation of how it can be maintained. Throughout the discourse of Irish revivalism in this period the apparent indivisibility of the religious and cultural spheres looms large. As has already been noted, the terms of revivalism have already been formed within the discourse of spirituality. Besides its concern with faithful continuity, it is perhaps revivalism's devotion to return and futurity, matters that transcend the material world, that explains its intimacy with religion. The confluence of these issues is apparent in a verse composed by the Galway poet Peatsaí Ó Callanáin (1791–1865), in 'An tSlis' (The Washing Beetle), his allegory on the apostasy of a local Catholic priest. Just as Cornelius Keating had addressed the Limerick populace from the gallows twenty years earlier, and numerous Gaelic poets spoke to *Clanna Gael* directly or through the conceit of a dream maiden, Ó Callanáin addresses the Catholics of Ireland:

> Bheirimse comhairle charadach,
> Do Chaitlicigh na hÉireann,
> Ná glacadh siad aon eagla,
> Mar ní anachain an scéal seo;
> Nuair a thiteas brainsí críona is lofa,
> Le fána den chrann saedar,
> Is ag daingniú a bhíos na rútaí,
> Is ag ardú a bhíos ón léadar.[159]

> [I hereby give admonition
> To the Catholics of Ireland,
> Let them not fear,
> For this case is no disaster;
> When foul and rotten branches
> From the cedar tree are suspended
> The roots grow all the stronger,
> And the trunk rises taller.]

Beyond the sectarian rancour that underscores this piece, typical of the cultural landscape of the time, Ó Callanáin's admonition to the faithful is also a meditation on the transmutation of human affairs and the anxiety that this engenders. The fact that 'An tSlis' was composed in 1845 on the eve of the Great Famine makes this meditation all the more pertinent. As the verse quoted shows, the apparent loss can be offset by forces that one cannot discern but that lie beneath the surface. It is this desire to engage an alternative, as yet unseen, dimension in the progress of human affairs, one that can ensure some measure of continuity in the future, that typifies the revivalist act of faith.

CHAPTER 4

Patrick Pearse, the Gothic Revival and the Dreams of Ancients and Moderns

In March 1909 Patrick Pearse took to the stage of Dublin's Metropolitan School of Art just before the performance of Alice Milligan's play *The Last Feast of the Fianna*. The young headmaster of Sgoil Éanna began a long discourse on the illustrious dead, the culmination of which was the recitation of Stephen Gwynn's 'A Song of Defeat', an ode to the 'ever defeated, yet undefeated' Irish nation.[1] Gwynn's poem recalls a long litany of Irish nationalist heroes and martyrs who would never receive the accolades of cheering crowds; rather:

> Theirs is to inherit
> Fame of a finer grace,
> In the self-renewing spirit
> And the untameable heart
> Ever defeated, yet undefeated,
> Of thy remembering race.

As Pearse talked his way through centuries of Irish history, the actors behind the curtain grew increasingly irritated at this unwelcome delay to their performance. Finally, as the orator appeared quite oblivious to the growing muttering and grumbling behind the curtain, a member of the cast, Pearse's younger brother Willie, came out to tell him to get off the stage. The elder Pearse blushed deeply and took his seat, allowing the performance to eventually begin.[2]

The bathos of this scene is in sharp contrast to Pearse's later oratorical triumphs that also invoked the generations of patriot dead, most notably his speech at the Robert Emmet commemoration in 1911 and his graveside eulogy for O'Donovan Rossa in August 1915. These were typically energising and transformative occasions in which Pearse excelled himself. Yet his last public speech, his reading of the Proclamation of the Irish Republic to 'an almost completely uncomprehending audience', recalls some of the bathos of the scene before Milligan's play, being, as it was, a somewhat incongruous prelude to the real action – the urgent present of the Easter Rising.[3] The sense in which the constant invocation of history would have to give way to the urgency of the present is a familiar theme in the multifaceted revivalism of Patrick Pearse in his career as a Gaelic Leaguer, educationalist, writer and eventual insurrectionist. The body of essays, prose fiction, plays and poetry that he authored consistently point to an attempt to reconcile the medieval and the modern. This particular preoccupation in Pearse's work reflects the inheritance of his father, James (1839–1900), an English church sculptor and devotee of the Gothic Revival, the movement that sought to counter the chaos of modern industrial cities by returning to the benign order and beneficence of medieval society.[4] If the Easter Rising was to mark the end of speeches and litanies and the beginning of a new era, where 'all changed, changed utterly', as Yeats styled it, this change also signalled a shift from the latency of pietas to the latency of the present.[5] In other words, the poems of future deliverance in a 'second glory', to which Pearse paid tribute in his anthology entitled *Songs of the Irish Rebels*, had served their purpose.[6] The continuity with the past had been necessary to maintain the potential of a revolutionary moment that had now arrived and was part of a dynamic present.

Pearse's pivotal role in the Gaelic League revival, until his execution in May 1916, merits a particular case study that is the intention of this chapter, but before turning to this it is worth considering the remarkable rise of the Gaelic League. Although a clear revivalist momentum had been gathering from the 1870s onwards, with the founding of notable societies such as the Boston Philo-Celtic Society in 1873 and the Society for the Preservation of the Irish Language in 1876, the four decades from 1880 leading to the founding of an independent Irish state in 1922 represent arguably the most important and transformative phase of Irish revivalism.[7] The coalescence of divergent revivalist projects in Irish cultural life lend this period a significance that extends well beyond the history of Ireland, if only for the coming to prominence of W.B. Yeats (1865–1939) and the anti-imperialist reverberations of the Easter Rising. The Irish Revival in theatre, literature and the arts, the founding of the Gaelic Athletic Association in 1884, and the growth of the Irish cooperative movement in the 1890s marked a period of sustained regeneration that bears many similarities to the myriad other nationalist revivals that appeared internationally from the late eighteenth century onwards.[8] The Gaelic League, founded by Eoin Mac Néill and Douglas Hyde in 1893, was profoundly interrelated to these various other revivalist strands, yet its provenance can be clearly traced to the linguistic revivalist initiatives of previous centuries. This much is evident in its two stated aims:

1. The preservation of Irish as the national language of Ireland, and the extension of its use as a spoken tongue.
2. The study and publication of existing Gaelic literature, and the cultivation of a modern literature in Irish.[9]

In essence, there is very little to distinguish this from the aims expressed by the range of eighteenth and nineteenth-century revivalist manifestos discussed in the previous chapter.

The foremost difference between the Gaelic League and its predecessors was its success as a genuinely national movement. This success was made possible in the first instance by the phenomenal growth of its membership in the initial decade of the twentieth century, to a situation where in 1904 an estimated 50,000 were members and in 1909 it attracted 100,000 people to a Dublin rally to make Irish a compulsory subject for matriculation in the National University of Ireland.[10] The league's emergence as a national movement was accompanied by an alignment of cultural revival and nationalism, making it 'the movement that changed the language from an optional to a mandatory component of Irish nationality'.[11] Alongside its decisive intervention in the realm of education, the league was highly effective in both its activities to increase literacy in Irish and in its generation of publications. Here the importance of print in the longer history of Irish revivalism is strikingly evidenced. Besides its contribution to modern print journalism in Irish, in its first twenty-five years the league was responsible for over 400 books and booklets, the great majority of which were in Irish or contained substantial text in Irish.[12] Yet it was its success in the 'cultivation of a modern literature in Irish', signalled by the appearance of the first novel in Irish, *Séadna* by Rev. Peadar Ó Laoghaire (1904), that set the league apart from previous revivalist interventions.[13] While the league committed itself to 'the study and publication of existing Gaelic literature', it was its success in cultivating a new modern literature that marked a real point of departure. It is not surprising that Pearse remarked of the arrival of *Séadna*, 'Here at last we have literature!'[14]

Besides being a member of the league's executive committee, as secretary of the league's publications committee from 1900 to 1903 Pearse was instrumental in the success of its publishing drive. His next post as editor of the league's weekly paper, *An Claidheamh Soluis*, held from 1903 to 1909, again placed him at the very heart of the regeneration of literacy and literature in Irish.[15] While still editor of *An Claidheamh Soluis* he had embarked on his greatest project to date, the founding in 1908 of the first bilingual school, Sgoil Éanna, in Cullenswood House, Dublin. The school was to be a radical initiative that allowed Pearse to extend the revivalist project in new directions, not least in progressive education theory, but above all in creating a model utopian community that appeared to actualise the league's social aspirations. Alongside his various responsibilities, of course, Pearse was the author of various plays, short stories and poems in Irish. While this body of work stands on its own merits, its continued influence is inevitably bound to the legacy of the Easter Rising.

In order to trace the development of Pearse's revivalism and the meaning of the decisive shift from the latency of the past to the latency of the present, discussed above, it is important to return to the legacy of Pearse's parents and, in particular, to the intellectual patrimony of his father, James. The principles of his father's Gothic Revival legacy permeate many of Patrick Pearse's ideas and literary motifs, particularly the revival of the sacred medieval as a panacea against the crass secularism of industrial society. The dialogue here between what was essentially an architectural movement and a movement of linguistic revival is of obvious significance to our broader understanding of revivalism as a critical cultural practice. Yet it seems in the case of the younger Pearse that this dialogue culminated in a parting of ways, at which juncture he declared, 'we want no Gothic Revival'.[16] Patrick Pearse's father could not have registered any slight to his own life's work in this remark, having died six years before his son penned his 1906 landmark article 'On Literature'. Here the young Pearse argued the case for an Irish literature distinguished by its intimacy with the mind of modern Europe and its dissimilarity to the backward-looking Gothic Revival. The irony of this is that Patrick Pearse was in some ways a child of the Gothic Revival, his father's emigration to Ireland in 1857 having been occasioned by the demand for his skills in the decoration of a swathe of new Catholic churches. Indeed, on his death in 1900 James Pearse was described in an *Irish Independent* obituary as 'the pioneer of modern Gothic Art as applied to Church work, in this country'.[17] Among the families that left England to service the need for ecclesiastical craftsmen in Ireland were the Earleys, Sharps,

McLouglins, Tonges and Pearses, all of whom shared close connections either through business or marriage.[18] These families were also bound together by their debt to the Gothic Revival in architecture, a movement that is associated most closely in Britain with Thomas Rickman (1776–1841) and A.W.N. Pugin (1812–52).

Although its origins were in the late eighteenth century, it was not until the 1830s that the Gothic Revival movement began to avail of a growing body of scholarship that allowed its practitioners to recreate with great fidelity the original designs of medieval churches.[19] An intrinsic element of the scholarly commentary that guided the movement was its contrasting of the structured social order of medieval society with the amorphous confusion of nineteenth-century industrial society. This was the theme of Pugin's famous essay *Contrasts; or a Parallel Between the Noble Edifices of the Fourteenth and Fifteenth Centuries, and Similar Buildings of the Present Day; Shewing the Present Decay of Taste* (1836). The idea that architecture could be a moral force informing a broader social programme was closely bound to the dominant intellectual debate of the time between romanticism and utilitarianism/Benthamism.[20] For Pugin, and for those who shared his view, medieval society was distinguished by its august ecclesiastical edifices, while industrial society was epitomised by grotesque, soulless prisons, of which the 'modern poor house', based on Jeremy Bentham's (1748–1832) 'panopticon' design, was an egregious example.

These diametrically opposed views of society were part of an ongoing debate characterised by Thomas Carlyle (1795–1881) as 'the Condition-of-England question', a debate to which Carlyle contributed a damning critique of the new 'mechanical age' in which men had become mechanical in head and in heart.[21] The growth of this morally detached age of machinery found justification in the prevailing utilitarian belief in the progress of humanity on purely empirical, rationalist grounds. As Carlyle remarked, 'We have called it an age fallen into spiritual languor, destitute of belief, yet terrified at Scepticism; reduced to live a stinted half-life, under strange new circumstances.'[22] It is worth noting here that Patrick Pearse, in common with the Young Irelanders, held Carlyle in high regard. One pupil at Sgoil Éanna recalls Pearse advising him to read two books that would teach him how to think, Carlyle's *Sartor Resartus* (1838) and *The Dialogues of Plato.*[23]

The profound influence of the contention between utilitarianism/Benthamism and romanticism was succinctly described in John Stuart Mill's (1806–73) remark that 'Coleridge used to say that everyone is born either a Platonist or an Aristotelian: it may be similarly affirmed, that every

Englishman of the present day is by implication either a Benthamite or a Coleridgian.'[24] By this reckoning, the Gothic Revival, with little hesitation, might be designated Platonist and Coleridgian, but, more importantly, its philosophical, religious and social dimensions ascribe to it a universal significance that transcended architecture. Central to its social programme was the reinstatement of medieval values marked by 'the indelible stamp of faith, love and devotion' as an elixir against the Godless 'spiritual languor' of industrial society.[25] Of all the English cities afflicted by this curse, Pugin reserved a particular revulsion for Birmingham, 'the most hateful of all hateful places, a town of Greek buildings, smoky chimneys, low radicalism and dissent'.[26] Ironically, this was the city in which James Pearse grew up in humble circumstances and went on to work assiduously in the service of the Gothic Revival. Birmingham was known as the 'city of trades' on account of its large population of skilled tradesmen, and its radicalism was particularly associated with this artisan class, many of whom, like James Pearse, devoted themselves to self-education and self-improvement.[27] It is no less ironic that James Pearse was first employed in Dublin by Thomas Earley, who had trained under Pugin. Before settling in Ireland Pearse had carved statues in the new Palace of Westminster under the supervision of Edward Barry, son of Sir Charles Barry.[28]

Not only did James Pearse owe much of his livelihood to the Gothic Revival, there is much evidence to suggest that he was infused by much of the same zeal that animated Pugin. In Patrick Pearse's fragment of autobiography he recalls that his father had 'entered on the hopeless task of trying to make Irish churchbuilders recognise what was beautiful and religious in sculpture', with the result that it was he 'who had in him (atheist though he was) more of the religious mind of the Middle Ages than any other'.[29] The contradiction recognised here by the younger Pearse is essential to understanding the intellectual legacy of James Pearse. In spite of his deep appreciation of the religiosity of the Middle Ages, James Pearse was an admirer of the free-thinker Charles Bradlaugh (1833–91), also self-educated, and a noted working-class radical and republican.[30] Among Bradlaugh's many intriguing associations with Ireland, it is worth noting, in connection with the Pearses, that Bradlaugh assisted with the drafting of the Fenian proclamation of 1867.[31] As an ecclesiastical sculptor, there were, of course, sound business reasons that precluded James Pearse from drawing attention to his allegiance to Bradlaugh or to his own atheism. This anomaly of atheism and religiosity in James Pearse's life resembles the character of Sean-Mhaitias (Old Matthias) in Patrick Pearse's story 'Íosagán'.[32] Sean-Mhaitias is an old man who refuses to attend Sunday

Mass but ultimately becomes reconciled with God after he is befriended by the Christ child Íosagán. As with Pearse's other short stories, 'Íosagán' is set in a quintessential Connemara *Gaeltacht* community, closely resembling Ros Muc, where Pearse had his cottage. Colm Ó Gaora, a native of Ros Muc who was deeply influenced by his friendship with Pearse, identified Sean-Mhaitias as his own father.[33] Nevertheless, the similarities to Pearse's own father's conflicted relationship with religion are striking. According to Patrick Pearse, his father became disillusioned with religion after arguing with a Sunday school teacher, but, like Sean-Mhaitias, '[he] groped painfully and pathetically to find by himself such light as he could; and through great darkness he did find light as his life drew to a close'.[34]

Pearse's fondness for 'the religious mind of the Middle Ages' espoused by his father is readily evinced in his own essays, particularly in the field of education. Like Pugin, Pearse tended to pit the virtues of the medieval against the sins of the modern in binary opposition. In his famous 'Murder Machine' essay, he remarks that

> It should be obvious that the more 'modern' an education is the less 'sound', for in education 'modernism' is as much a heresy as in religion. In both mediaevalism were a truer standard. We are too fond of clapping ourselves upon the back because we live in modern times, and we preen ourselves quite ridiculously (and unnecessarily) on our modern progress. There is, of course, such a thing as modern progress, but it has been won at how great a cost! How many precious things have we flung from us to lighten ourselves for that race![35]

Given his reverence for Thomas Davis, John Mitchel and Young Ireland, it is no surprise to find that nationality was an affair of the spirit for Pearse. In one of his political essays, 'Ghosts', he identifies the folly of the previous generation of Irishmen in having 'conceived of nationality as a material thing, whereas it is a spiritual thing'.[36] In this same essay the modern conception of an Irish nation is attributed to four evangelists, Wolfe Tone, Thomas Davis, James Fintan Lawlor and John Mitchel, who have been the 'fathers'.

In valorising religiosity Pearse was no different to those in the nineteenth-century British intellectual tradition – such as Pugin, Coleridge and Carlyle – who had deplored the diminished spirituality of their age. Matthew Arnold (1822–88) was a pervasive advocate of this same filiation whose likely influence on Pearse has been discussed by Seamus Deane, who remarks that 'Pearse's evangelism against mean-spiritedness, cowardice, caution, commercial wisdom is precisely the old Victorian-Romantic crusade against the spiritual atrophy of middle-class rule'.[37] Arnold's specific enlistment of Celtic literature in this cause was proposed in his *On the Study of Celtic Literature* (1867):

> Far more than by the helplessness of an aristocracy whose day is fast coming to an end, far more than by the rawness of a lower class whose day is only just beginning, we are emperilled by what I call the 'Philistinism' of our middle class. On the side of beauty and taste, vulgarity; on the side of morals and feeling, coarseness; on the side of mind and spirit, unintelligence – this is Philistinism. Now, then, is the moment for the greater delicacy and spirituality of the Celtic peoples who are blended with us, if it be but wisely directed, to make itself prized and honoured.[38]

The Gothic Revival's defence of spirituality was clearly part of the patrimony of James Pearse, tempered as this was by his atheism. Just as contemporary Irish novelists can invoke the values of the 'Louvain School of Modern Irish' without necessarily subscribing to its religious doctrines, James Pearse's legacy was a compromise between the aesthetics and idealism of religion on the one hand and actual adherence to the word of God on the other. While proud of his father's intellectual tradition, Patrick Pearse did not share his eschewal of religious belief. Where the principles of father and son do coincide is in the revivalist desire to connect with a past ideal, and in a profound respect for the religious expression of that ideal. The idea that early Irish literature, in particular, was distinguished by a spirituality that had since been occluded was certainly central to Pearse's understanding of the Gaelic tradition. This view was expanded on in his 'Some Aspects of Irish Literature', in which he claims that had the Renaissance been founded on a rediscovery of the old Celtic, rather than the Greek, tradition, Europe would not have lost the 'goodly culture and the fine mysticism of the Middle Ages'.[39]

Pearse's short stories allowed him to mine a rich vein of this mysticism in which the recurrent motif of the visionary child is set within the idealised *Gaeltacht* community he modelled on Ros Muc. In all of Pearse's ten published short stories the traditional storyteller's perspective inflects the authorial voice to a greater or lesser degree.[40] The introduction to 'Eoghainín na nÉan' (Eoineen of the Birds) is a case in point, where the narrator tells us that a conversation between Eoghainín and his mother was heard by the song thrush and the yellow bunting, who told it to the swallows, who then 'told the story to me'.[41] Owen Dudley Edwards has written about Pearse's debt to Oscar Wilde with particular regard to 'Íosagán' and 'Eoghainín na nÉan', which bear close resemblance to 'The Selfish Giant' and 'The Happy Prince', respectively. Yet the borrowing is itself originally Wilde's, since the stories were based on traditional Irish tales, as Dudley Edwards remarks: 'Pearse was borrowing from a source Puritan Ireland forbad his acknowledging, but he was also taking the spirit of the stories back to the tongue whence it came.'[42]

While the stories were typically based on real events and people, and faithfully recreated native religious traditions, a key innovation is what might be called Pearse's personal cult of anamnesis. Among the most celebrated literary adaptations of anamnesis is Wordsworth's 'Ode on Intimations of Immortality from Recollections of Early Childhood'. Here Wordsworth presents the journey to adulthood as a loss of innate, a priori understanding in which the celestial light that surrounds the child is gradually dissipated:

> Shades of the prison-house begin to close
>   Upon the growing Boy,
> But he beholds the light, and whence it flows,
>   He sees it in his joy;
> The Youth, who daily farther from the east
>   Must travel, still is Nature's priest,
>   And by the vision splendid
>   Is on his way attended;
> At length the Man perceives it die away,
> And fade into the light of common day.

The loss of intuitive knowledge announced in the poem's opening stanza, 'The things which I have seen I now can see no more', is characterised in the same way in Pearse's stories of visionary children. Thus, when Sean-Mhaitias tells Íosagán that he has not seen him of late, Íosagán tells him that this is because 'adults are blind'.[43]

Besides 'Eoghainín na nÉan', two other stories in particular, 'Na Bóithre' (The Roads) and 'Bairbre' (Barbara), juxtapose the otherworldly insight of children with the blindness of adults.[44] In 'Na Bóithre' the child Nóra is witness to a vision of the passion of Christ, having ventured out on the roads one night when everyone else is attending a feast hosted by 'the man from Dublin', based on Pearse himself. In 'Bairbre' the ability of children to transcend the reality of the adult world is reflected in a child's belief that her doll, Bairbre, has saved her from death and in so doing sacrificed her own life. 'Eoghainín na nÉan' is the most significant of these stories in its portrayal of the transcendental child. It is also a story that illustrates the propinquity of Pearse's idealisation of childhood to the contemporary late-Victorian/Edwardian cult of messianism.

The eponymous Eoineen of the Birds is so-called after his friendship with the birds, with whom he talks as they nest around the home he shares with his mother. He has a special fondness for the swallows, whose return from the 'land where it is always summer' he awaits with a singular devotion from the vantage point of a cliff or rock face beside his house. When the swallows arrive one evening in late April they are sad to find Eoghainín less lively than before. The local priest calls to enquire after the child, having noticed a worrying redness in the boy's cheek, which his mother has mistaken for a glow of contentment at the swallows' return. Although the narrator does not make the priest's fear explicit, the clergyman's private tears are an indication that Eoghainín has succumbed to an affliction from which he is unlikely to recover. The mother is unaware of the imminent danger, but expresses her surprise that the boy should have asked her what she would do were he to leave with the swallows in autumn. The priest joins the boy on the ledge, where he asks him about his conversations with the birds. The deficiency of adults arises again when the priest initially struggles to accept that Eoghainín has not been merely dreaming but has been in actual dialogue with the birds. Perhaps on account of his own vocation, the priest listens attentively as the boy describes in detail his vision of the swallows' other land, before the clergyman finally returns home pensively. In the story's conclusion Eoghainín bids farewell to his mother, having apparently followed the swallows on their long journey south to 'the land where it is always summer'.

'Eoghainín na nÉan' was first published in *An Claidheamh Soluis* in June 1906.[45] The story belongs, therefore, to the period during which Pearse's 'chief hobby' was 'the study of education in all its phases'.[46] The idealisation of childhood in this story and others was to become a familiar characteristic of Pearse's educational mission and of Sgoil Éanna in particular. The motif of the visionary child who foregoes the inherent decline of adulthood to enter instead into a land where it is always summer is indicative of Pearse's belief in childhood as a state of pristine enlightenment. Eoghainín's position on a ledge is a literal expression of the liminal world of childhood that adults cannot appreciate – the priest joining Eoghainín on the ledge in order to share his insight is in keeping with this. In his autobiographical fragment Pearse characterised the domain of childhood as a halfway house between reality and imagination: 'The real adventures of a man are like the adventures of a dream; they trail off inexplicably and end ingloriously or even ridiculously. The half-real, half-imagined adventures of a child are fully rounded, perfect, beautiful, often bizarre and humorous, but never ludicrous.'[47] While Íosagán, rather than Eoghainín, is the messianic child of Pearse's first collection of stories, Íosagán explains to Sean-Mhaitias that he may be found wherever children are playing – sometimes children see him, other times they do not.[48] The implication of this and of Pearse's other stories of visionary children is the same version of anamnesis as Wordsworth's – 'heaven lies around us in our infancy' – childhood retains a state of grace that gradually fades. Eoghainín achieves his apotheosis by avoiding this decline, and in so doing reminds the adults of the greater calling of that land where it is always summer.

Although Pearse's interest in messianism can be easily located in the Irish-nationalist tradition, particularly in the *aisling* tradition of which the intervention of a messianic figure was a recurrent motif, his search for transcendence and his faith in the particular agency of childhood were shared by some of those who might have been his political foes.[49] 'Summerland' was another name for the afterworld, used by the late nineteenth-century and early twentieth-century British spiritualists whose preoccupations included the conception of a messianic child.[50] In many ways the various theosophist and spiritualist groups of this era were heirs of the earlier Romantic movement's search for an alternative to soulless scientific enlightenment. Darwinism had revealed a world in which human mortality was no different to animal mortality, and, as John Gray notes, this was a vision intolerable to nearly all.[51] The concerted efforts of powerful elites in late-Victorian Britain and the early Soviet Union to circumvent mortality and use science for escape from the world that science had revealed have been vividly reconstructed in Gray's *The Immortalization Commission* (2011). The extent to which various members of the British establishment participated in spiritualism differs, but it is a matter of some significance to find that two prime ministers, W.E. Gladstone and Arthur Balfour, were members of the Society for Psychical Research, along with a list of prominent thinkers, writers and scientists including Henri Bergson, John Ruskin, Alfred Lord Tennyson and the Nobel Prize-winning physiologist Charles Richet.[52] Indeed, the British circle's belief in the years before the First World War in a messianic 'spirit-child', and their fully commissioned plan to create one, place Pearse's fixation with a messianic child/youth firmly in the shade. Apart from the cult of Jiddu Krishnamurti (1895–1986), whom Annie Besant and other British theosophists believed to be the world's next saviour, a messianic child was actually conceived by Winnifred Coombe-Tennant, suffragist and British delegate to the League of Nations, and Gerald Balfour, brother of the prime minister and himself a former secretary of state for Ireland. Both these protagonists and their theoso-phist colleagues believed that they were channels for a secret scheme of world regeneration involving cross-correspondences with the spirit world.[53] As John Gray notes wryly, neither the child born Augustus Henry Coombe-Tennant in 1913 nor Krishnamurti went on to save the world.[54]

The influence of Darwinism and of related currents of thought on the Irish Revival of the late nineteenth and early twentieth centuries has been illuminated by Brian Ó Conchubhair.[55] Ó Conchubhair has examined the predominant fear of decline that pervaded the *fin de siècle*, a fear that focused on the dangers of the dilution of race and the loss of masculinity, among other matters. The influence of this prevailing European fear of decline as well as the specific Romantic and Gothic revivalist inheritance of his father no doubt encouraged Pearse's view of the spiritual and moral decline of his age. As dis-cussed here, the agency of children in potential salvation is a recurring trope in Pearse's short stories and essays. It was in his various plays, however, that this concern was effectively placed in a dynamic relationship with his most profound engagement with youth, Sgoil Éanna.

The first of Pearse's dramatic productions was a pageant, *Macghníomhartha Chú Chulainn* (The Boyhood Deeds of Cú Chulainn), hosted and performed by the staff and pupils of Sgoil Éanna in June 1909, at the end of the school's first year.[56] As a dramatic spectacle and re-enactment of the past, the 'pageant' is similar to the Gothic Revival 'tournament', the most well-known example of which was the ill-fated Eglinton Tournament of 1839, the planned large-scale jousting and staging of other medieval scenes that fell victim to a violent storm, the Eglinton tournament then becoming a byword for the folly of the medieval craze.[57] Pearse's spectacle was much more auspicious, attracting over 500 people to the school grounds at Cullenswood House, including most of the people in Dublin who were interested in art and literature, by Pearse's own account.[58] This public pageant is significant for many reasons, not least of which is the cult of the mythological figure of Cú Chulainn in Sgoil Éanna, from which an endorsement of martyrdom has often been inferred. Indeed, Ruth Dudley Edwards' biography *Patrick Pearse: the triumph of failure* (1977) concludes with the words attributed to Cú Chulainn that Pearse had rendered in a fresco above the school door: 'I care not though I were to live but one day and one night provided my fame and my deeds live after me'.[59] Such was the ubiquity of Cú Chulainn as a model to which the boys should aspire that it was remarked that he was an invisible member of the staff.[60] Cú Chulainn was, along with the figure of Íosagán, Pearse's great model of messianic youth whose great function was to be a force for redemption:

> … the story of Cú Chulainn symbolises the redemption of man by a sinless God. The curse of primal sin lies upon a people; new and personal sin brings doom to their doors; they are powerless to save themselves; a youth, free from the curse, akin with them through his mother but through his father divine, redeems them by his valour; and his own death comes from it.[61]

Pearse's elevation of childhood to a source of redemption is an important extension of the myth of anamnesis. Not only does childhood figure in Pearse's writing as a source of innate wisdom to which one must return, the child is also a key to salvation. This exaltation of childhood and youth is at least partly responsible for the speculation that persists about Pearse in relation to children.[62] His poem 'A Mhic Bhig na gCleas' (O Little Lad of the Tricks) has been the most frequent focus of these doubts. It appears that when his Sgoil Éanna colleagues Thomas McDonagh and Joseph Plunkett warned of the potentially scandalous import of the poem, Pearse was bewildered and hurt.[63]

> Little lad of the tricks,
> Full well I know
> That you have been in mischief:
> Confess your fault truly.
>
> I forgive you, child
> Of the soft red mouth:
> I will not condemn anyone
> For a sin not understood.
>
> Raise your comely head
> Till I kiss your mouth:
> If either of us is the better of that
> I am the better of it.

There is a fragrance in your kiss
That I have not found yet
In the kisses of women
Or in the honey of their bodies.

Lad of the grey eyes,
That flush in thy cheek
Would be white with dread of me
Could you read my secrets.

He who has my secrets
Is not fit to touch you:
Is not that a pitiful thing,
Little lad of the tricks?[64]

Before responding to such a controversial composition, one is aware of J.J. Lee's weary remark that 'the task of rescuing Pearse from the clutches of his idolators and demonisers continues'.[65] A critical reading of 'A Mhic Bhig na gCleas' cannot hope to exonerate Pearse any more than condemn him outright. The convention of not assuming the author and narrator to be indivisible is sufficient grounds for discounting this approach. Undoubtedly, the poem suggests an adult in authority (such as a headmaster) speaking to one of his charges, and, as such, points to Pearse's own professional domain. Even so, to submit any poem to an exclusively literal interpretation seems self-evidently mistaken. What a critical reading can do is propose a number of interpretations based on the contextual evidence to hand. It cannot draw any firm conclusions about Pearse's inclinations or actions without firm material evidence to support them. The material evidence for Pearse being inclined to, or acting on, paedophilia does not exist. There are references to Pearse kissing some of the boys at Sgoil Éanna, which certainly encourage the doubts about his sexuality.[66] Yet, as ever, even kissing is a symbolically charged act in Pearse's world. Kissing on the mouth occurs in various situations in Pearse's *oeuvre*, such as a mother kissing her daughter, and a mother and siblings kissing their son/brother, as occurs in the play *The Singer*.[67] The symbolic act of kissing on the mouth in the Gaelic literary tradition has also been extensively examined in relation to 'A Mhic Bhig na gCleas' by scholars such as Cathal Ó Háinle and Gearóid Denvir.[68] Inevitably, interpretations of Pearse's poetry and recollections of contemporaries have led to speculation rather than firm conclusions.

One of Pearse's most recent biographers, Joost Augusteijn, contends that while 'there is no proof that Patrick's activities went beyond kissing, which could still be interpreted as an extreme expression of idealised love and not lust', it seems 'most probable' that Pearse was sexually inclined to paedophilia.[69] On the other hand, Elaine Sisson, in her study of the 'cult of boyhood' at Sgoil Éanna, concludes that 'the persistent interest in Pearse's sexuality is perhaps more suggestive of our own anxieties about men's relationships with children and has little to do with the facts of Pearse's life'.[70]

'A Mhic Bhig na gCleas' is also significant for other reasons. The poem's concern with the shame of the adult interlocutor is consistent with Pearse's view of adulthood as inherently flawed and childhood as inherently pure and redemptive. It also chimes with his reiteration, on a number of platforms, of the shame of the nation, of Dublin, and of the past generation – 'the curse of primal sin' alluded to in his reading of the Cú Chulainn story. The shame of the nation is the theme of his poem 'Mise Éire' (I Am Ireland), in which Ireland speaks of her great glory in having borne Cú Chulainn, but great shame at her family having sold its mother.[71] His essay 'Ghosts' proclaims that 'there has been nothing more terrible in Irish history than the failure of the last generation ... One finds oneself wondering what sin these men have been guilty of that so great a shame should come upon them.'[72] This theme was echoed by James Connolly in 1915 when he warned of the shame that would engulf the current generation if it did not take up arms against the British, and, indeed, Pearse also spoke before and during the Rising of the need to purge Dublin's shame in having allowed Robert Emmet to be executed.[73] Taken in this context, the burden of shame carried by the adult in 'A Mhic Bhig na gCleas' is a generational failure, one that can only be redeemed by the next generation, untainted and unaware of the dreadful 'secrets' of its forebears. The same sense of a new generation arising to purge the guilt of the previous generation was expressed in the mid-nineteenth century by John Mitchel, one of Pearse's 'fathers' of Irish nationalism.[74] The burden of responsibility was duly relayed to Pearse's own generation in the preface of A.M. Sullivan's highly influential *The Story of Ireland* (1867):

> When we who have preceded them shall have passed away forever, they will be the men on whom Ireland must depend. They will make her future. They will guide her destinies. They will guard her honour. They will defend her life. To the service of this 'Irish Nation' of the future I devote the following pages, confident my

young friends will not fail to read aright the lesson taught by 'The
Story of Ireland'.[75]

The irony of the nationalist's idealisation of the child is, as Declan Kiberd
observes, that the Empire's own image of the colony was that of an unruly
infant.[76] The infantilisation of native culture in Yeats' early work merely reas-
serted the colonial view of the Irish as lacking in moral authority or agency.[77]
However, just as Yeats complicated his understanding of childhood even
within the enchanted world of 'The Stolen Child', Pearse cherished a number
of ideals of which the transcendence of childhood was only one, albeit one
of great importance. Pearse also idealised nationalist heroes of the past, and,
sharing his father's reverence for the spirituality of the Middle Ages, looked
to the lives of the saints and to the ascetic devotion of the early monastic
tradition as a model to which to aspire. This particular ideal was attractive to
revivalists, and was the subject of Hyde's play *An Naomh ar Iarraidh* (1902),
translated by Lady Gregory as *The Lost Saint* (1903).[78] This attraction to the
monastic tradition can be explained on a number of counts, not least the
ascetic devotion to an ideal that may never be materially realised, an ideal of
obvious relevance to minority-language revivalists. The identification of Irish
monasticism with the scribal tradition is also significant, given the importance
of the motif of transmission in Irish revivalism and its prominence in the
Gaelic League's aims concerning the preservation of Irish literature. Inevitably,
the appeal of a venerable, historic spiritual tradition was bound to be felt
strongly by those, such as Pearse, who hoped to establish a new tradition in
education and other areas.

Pearse chose Hyde's *An Naomh ar Iarraidh* as one of the first productions
to be hosted by Sgoil Éanna, for which he penned an unremarkable introductory poem extolling the virtues of the eponymous saint, Aongas.[79] Several of
Pearse's own plays involve characters based on the anchorite tradition, and
Sgoil Éanna was, of course, named after one of the foremost Irish saints of the
fifth century. The life of St Enda has been somewhat overlooked as a source
for Pearse's educational project, but it bears a number of striking points of
interest. The manner in which Éanna chose a life of 'self-abnegation' – as
the life of the monk Ciarán is described in Pearse's 1915 play *The Master* – is
particularly noteworthy.[80] The story told of St Enda's conversion from a life
of worldly depredation relates how the young Enda returned from a battle
and presented himself at the gate of his sister Faichne's convent. Enda asked
to see a beautiful maiden, who was under Faichne's care, but was refused

entrance unless he would renounce his former ways. Knowing that the maiden was lying dead, Faichne ushered her brother in without warning him of the maiden's death but allowing him to expect to see her in all her beauty. The shock of seeing the maiden he had lusted after lying before him as a veiled corpse prompted Enda to give himself entirely to God and to seek out the remote Aran Islands, the better to fulfil this.[81] Pearse's poem 'A Chinn Álainn' (O Lovely Head) is based on the same motif, where the 'lovely head of the woman that I loved' is in reality being gnawed by the slender worm.[82]

In removing Sgoil Éanna to the outskirts of Dublin to a fifty-acre site known as 'The Hermitage', Pearse was replicating the saint's withdrawal to a place apart in which to found an ideal community. The original inspiration to found a school, Pearse's sister Mary Bridget recalled, occurred during her brother's first visit in 1898 to the Aran Islands, known as Árainn na Naomh (Aran of the Saints) after the legacy of St Enda and the numerous saints that spent time in his community: 'And there, with the musical Gaelic voices in his ears … the great dream of his life materialised.'[83] Prophetic dreams and visions were essential to the world of the early Irish saints – St Ciarán had a vision while in Aran that he would found his famous monastery at Clonmacnoise, and, indeed, *físeanna* or *visionae* are a genre closely associated with the monastic tradition. In Pearse's play *An Rí* (The King), the abbot warns of a vision that has revealed to him the imminent defeat of the king in battle.[84] Pearse's own recourse to the literature of visions is most apparent in his poems 'Mise Éire' and 'Fornocht do Chonac Thú' (Renunciation), which draw on the tradition of Jacobite *aisling* poetry. Yet even here the underlying influence of the early saints is in evidence, as the message delivered by the otherworldly maiden in the *aisling* was generally underwritten by the prophecies of the native saints.[85]

The significance of Aran as a place of visions extends also to the genre of voyage literature, most associated with St Brendan, who sought Enda's blessing on Aran before setting out to seek the *terra repromissionis*, or promised land. Pearse wrote his own vision of an ideal future land in a piece for *An Claidheamh Soluis* in 1906, in which he falls asleep and awakes in the Ireland of 2006.[86] The tongue-in-cheek style of this piece is largely based on references to contemporary events and people as forecast in a benign future where Ireland is an entirely Irish-speaking independent state in which English is only taught in three schools, Irish and Japanese being the dominant languages of West and East respectively. The temperature of the country has risen several degrees, not as a result of global warming but, rather, due to the draining of the bogs

and reforestation. These innovations have made Dublin a city of shady boule-
vards and open-air cafés in which outdoor events are de rigueur. Apart from
Washington Irving's *Rip Van Winkle* (1819) – which Pearse references – the
conceit of the sleeper who awakes in the future is a common premise of utopian
fiction, such as H.G. Wells' *When the Sleeper Wakes* (1899) (republished in
1910 as *The Sleeper Awakes*). The retrospective comparison that is also a feature
of the piece is equally reminiscent of Edward Bellamy's *Looking Backward,
2000–1887* (1888).

The utopian thought with which this type of fiction engages has been
paraphrased as 'social dreaming' by the pre-eminent utopian-studies scholar
Lymon Tower Sargent. The mutual concerns of utopianism and revivalism are
the subject of Chapter 6, but it is important to note briefly that Pearse's speculative vision of future society is an important counterpoint to the backward
look. The practice of 'social dreaming', even where it favours a return to past
values, implicitly bespeaks a concern for futurity. Yet this can also involve,
as in Bellamy's *Looking Backward*, an imagined retrospective account of the
future. We do not know if Pearse sensed that he might be in the last year of his
life when he wrote his poem 'The Fool', but the poem's defence of dreaming
appears to anticipate the posthumous charge that he was a fool in thrall to his
own peculiar visions:

> I have squandered the splendid years that
> The Lord God gave to my youth
> In attempting impossible things, deeming
> them alone worth the toil.
> …
> And the wise have pitied the fool that hath
> striven to give a life
> In the world of time and space among the
> bulks of actual things,
> To a dream that was dreamed in the heart,
> and that only the heart could hold.

The fool's dream can never be proven, but, as with 'Pascal's wager', it cannot
ever be dismissed:

> O wise men, riddle me this: what if the dream come true?
> What if the dream come true? And if millions unborn shall dwell

In the house that I shaped in my heart, the noble house of my
thought?[87]

Pearse was only one among his contemporaries to posit the latent power
of a dream or vision to bring about the future. Declan Kiberd has written of
'the age's penchant for the half-said thing, the symbol radiant with partially-
articulated possibility'.[88] Alfred Perceval Graves' anthology *The Book of Irish
Poetry*, published two years before the Easter Rising, is replete with references
to 'dreams', ranging from Arthur Shaunessy's 'We are the music makers/ and
we are the dreamers of dreams ... For each age is a dream that is dying/ Or one
that is coming to birth' to the prophetic political message of Lionel Johnson's
'Ways of War':

> A dream! A dream! An ancient dream!
> Yet, ere peace come to Inisfail,
> Some weapons on some field must gleam,
> Some burning glory fire the Gael.[89]

It is perhaps not surprising that the predominant metaphor for Pearse's greatest
legacy, the 1916 Rising, has been a dream or vision epitomised by Yeats in his
'Easter 1916': 'We know their dream; enough/ To know they dreamed and
are dead'.[90] So much of what preceded the Rising and of what preoccupied
Pearse as an educationalist and man of letters was framed by an ideal. Yet if
dreams are synonymous with ideals, their interpretation is, in Freud's view, the
royal road to understanding the unconscious.[91] In the new science of Freudian
psychology – still in relative infancy in 1916 – dreams were no longer the
form of expression of a grand collective vision but, rather, the complex out-
working of an individual unconscious. Rather than existing in a mysterious
ether as Platonic forms, dreams were the traces constantly issuing from the
unconscious desires of the individual. There is a similar sense in which a shift
took place from latent potentiality to actuality during the Rising. Pearse's
former pupil and colleague at Sgoil Éanna, Desmond Ryan, gave this intriguing account of the days directly before and during the Rising:

> Anyone who lived through the time must know it well, and it
> always comes back when arguments arise as to the rights or wrongs
> of the Rising of 1916. We felt that at any moment a spring, the
> spring of the whole Irish–Ireland movement might snap, and

nothing would ever in our lifetimes mend it again. Yet it seemed as if the whole chance of striking first had gone, and we talked and talked round it. It was the beginning of a curious feeling that we were in a dream.[92]

This dream was happening in real time, and, unlike the revelatory dreams and visions of the early Irish saints and the *aisling* poems, no one knew how, or even if, it would conclude. Consequently, the litanies of continuity with the past that promised a 'second glory' were no longer relevant. Just as Pearse had to give way to the impatient players in the Metropolitan School of Art, his own production was now being realised in the urgent present.

The Freudian understanding of dreams as involving a suspension of logic and distortions of time and space is particularly apt to this real-time dream of the Rising. Desmond Ryan was astounded to witness the looting of goods by the Dublin poor, who seemed to walk through the plate-glass windows of shops without any fear.[93] Charles Townshend's study of the Rising also comments on the 'bizarre and destructive saturnalia' that took place in a peculiar timeless zone, the clocks on public buildings having stopped, with no one to wind them up.[94] The rebels themselves witnessed these scenes as they went about their own suspension of the preordained order of things, and the surreality of their own situation was not lost on them. The Waxworks was beside the rebel headquarters in the GPO, and, as one witness reported, this became the source of an alternative reality:

> With the accessibility of all that the Waxworks had to offer, it was not long till a number of our troops were arrayed in various uniforms and costumes from the wax figures ... All this time the bombardment of the Post Office was going on, and fellows were being wounded and, I'm sorry to say, killed.[95]

Desmond Ryan also recalled how Pearse, Connolly, Plunkett, Mac Diarmada and Tom Clarke had to be given opium by a Red Cross worker before they could sleep. On the following morning, as they sat together, pale and tired but calm and humorous, Connolly announced that the rebels had captured the king and Lord Kitchener – 'in the Waxworks', he added with a twinkle in his eye.[96] Later on, as the rebels made their escape from the flames and smoke of the GPO, wax figures were mistaken for comrades, of whom directions were asked in vain.[97]

It is probably no accident that a former member of André Breton's 1920s surrealist circle, Raymond Queneau, wrote a bizarre burlesque novel based on the Rising, entitled *On Est Toujours Trop Bon Avec Les Femmes* (We Always Treat Women Too Well) (1947).[98] A large part of the inspiration for surrealism was Freud's systematic examination of the psychic activity of dreaming. Breton, however, differed significantly from Freud on certain issues, particularly with regard to the surrealist's contention that 'the world of dreams and the real world are but one'.[99] Indeed, Desmond Ryan's characterisation of the Rising as both dream and actuality is exactly the type of resolution of the dream state and reality that was proposed by Breton as the definition of surrealism.[100] Whatever the differences between Freud and the surrealists, the emerging modern understanding of dreams was of a similarly radical nature as the transformative legacy of the 1916 Rising. Ryan's waking dream represents the transformation of a tradition of nationalist visions of the future into an actual reality, but a reality that crucially bore the strangeness and unpredictability of a dream.

While Yeats' 'Easter 1916' recognises the seismic turn of the Rising, after which 'a terrible beauty is born', he also makes the insurrection the terminus for the rebels' dream. This may have simply been a desire to warn Maud Gonne of the dangers of blind attachment to an ideal or the realisation that death could not be transformed by a glib metaphor:

> What is it but nightfall?
> No, no, not night but death.
> Was it needless death after all?
> For England may keep faith
> For all that is done and said
> We know their dream; enough
> To know they dreamed and are dead.[101]

Nevertheless, the effect of these lines is to preclude any afterlife for the dream of Pearse and his comrades – just as the individual is bound by his own mortality, so, too, are his dreams. In this case, in spite of his spiritualist inclinations, Yeats mirrors Freud's materialist understanding of dreams as expressions of the individual unconscious.

An alternative reflection on the afterlife of the Rising, one that is much less conclusive than Yeats' 'Easter 1916', is Eoghan Ó Tuairisc's novel *Dé Luain* (1966), published to coincide with the fiftieth anniversary of the Rising.[102]

Ó Tuairisc's modernist, decentred narrative comprises a series of constantly shifting perspectives that, interspersed with internal monologues from Pearse, gives the novel an unsettling, chimeric quality. In a brilliant reassessment of *Dé Luain*, Philip O'Leary defends its 'polyphonous, anti-climactic, and open-ended narrative', and argues that by limiting the action to the first twelve hours of Easter Monday, Ó Tuairisc was able to present the Rising as 'still unresolved, its meaning as yet entirely potential'.[103] Ó Tuairisc achieves this, to a large extent, by returning to the fault lines of James Pearse's intellectual patrimony – what is referred to in the novel as 'the marble images of the dead', the Gothic Revival that Patrick Pearse honoured and rejected.[104] Thus, the architecture of Dublin is the literal and figurative battleground in *Dé Luain* for a conflict between the ideal and the material, in which the historical continuity and stability of the city's fixed coordinates are challenged by the stream of latent possibility and random potentiality. It is not surprising to find that, like Desmond Ryan, one of the characters likens the experience of the unfolding Rising to a vision in which he had suddenly found himself.[105]

Just as Yeats' 'Easter 1916' and Ó Tuairisc's *Dé Luain* ponder both the transcendent idealism of the Rising and the material condition of mortality, Pearse's revivalism was framed by a similar dialogue between Platonic idealism and material necessity. His rejection of his father's inheritance, proclaiming 'we want no Gothic Revival' as he outlined the shape of a new modern European literature in Irish, belied his instinctive affinity with the reimagined mystic religiosity of the Middle Ages. This affinity inhabits some of his plays, most notably *An Rí* and *The Master*, and in the latter, the choice between the 'phantom' of an ideal and the 'substance' of worldly life is argued between the monk, Ciarán, and the soldier king, Daire.[106] Yet just as Ciarán speaks of his life's 'quest', Pearse insisted on a dynamic revivalism that would avoid the stasis to which he likened the Gothic Revival, in merely reproducing the artefacts of the Middle Ages. Similarly, Pearse's great educational project Sgoil Éanna, while infused with the values of the heroic past, was founded on extensive research into then current educational practice, including visits to thirty educational institutions in Belgium. This often overlooked 'practical' side to Pearse was made explicit with the publication of his letters on the centenary of his death, prompting F.S.L. Lyons to remark that 'these are the letters of a man who knew exactly where he was going and what he was doing'.[107]

Pearse's defence of dreaming in 'The Fool' indicates an idealism that held out the prospect of dynamic regeneration in the question 'what if the dream come true?' Even the simplistic piety of his short stories is underscored by a sense of latent possibility that is carried towards an irresistible rupture of the material order. The agents of this rupture are predominantly children, occupying a liminal space that adults, by dint of their spiritual blindness, cannot properly access. In this sense the implicit 'social dreaming' of Pearse's short stories, in particular, points towards what Ernst Bloch called the 'ontology of not-yet-being'.[108] Pearse's anamnesis, his idealisation of the child savant, is typical of the revivalist's return to origins, but it was not simply a matter of return for Pearse but a threshold of radical possibility. Although his excessive *pietas* implies a stolid conservatism, Pearse's real and imaginary models of the past were not cast in stone as Gothic Revival statues but pliable and protean and fit to be refashioned. Although he imbibed the dreams of ancients, the fixed prophetic visions of the early Irish saints and the *aisling* poets, Pearse tended towards the fluid sense of latent potential, moving ever-increasingly from the 'fully-rounded, perfect' adventures of childhood towards 'the real adventures of a man', and so to the unpredictable immediacy of modernity – 'like the adventures of a dream; they trail off inexplicably and end ingloriously or even ridiculously'.

CHAPTER 5

Temporality and Irish Revivalism: Past, present and becoming

In Seamus Heaney's *Human Chain* (2010), his elegy for Colin Middleton (1910–83) – 'Loughanure' – becomes a Proustian exercise in remembrance as well as an examination of individual legacy, prompting him to return to his time at the *Gaeltacht* Irish college (Coláiste Bhríde) in Rannafast, County Donegal in 1953. In the final two parts of the poem, the young Heaney's inadequacy in Irish dovetails with the limitations of the elder poet's memory as he tries 'to remember the Greek word signifying/ A world restored completely: that would include/ Hannah Mhór's turkey-chortle of Irish'.[1] The Irish-college rite of passage is apt for many reasons – the elegy for Middleton centres on his painting of Loughanure, near Rannafast, which is part of the landscape the poet had recently travelled by ambulance, having suffered a stroke. Moreover, the Irish-college experience was, and still is, about trying to reconnect with the lost legacy of previous generations, a return to the source of language and identity in the *Gaeltacht*. In this context the phrase 'Hannah Mhór's turkey-chortle of Irish' carries an intriguing ambivalence, one that reflects the inherent contradictions of revivalism. On the one hand there is an overwhelming immediacy in Heaney's sound picture, but, on the other hand, there is an immutable distance commensurate with irretrievable loss. The 'turkey-chortle of Irish' is unmistakably described yet entirely incomprehensible and unattainable. Therein is the paradox of revival in its attempt not just to restore a world completely, as a frozen image, but to bring that world to life in the present. In the case of the young Heaney it did not quite work. Yet while he did not go on to become a fully engaged Irish speaker, the literature of the Irish language had been a constant source of productivity, as witnessed in his numerous translations from the Irish and other critical engagements.[2]

It seems most likely that the Greek word that eluded Heaney was *apoca-tastasis*, meaning 'complete restoration, restitution, re-establishment'.[3] The revisited *Gaeltacht*, in Heaney's poem, is the site where memory, restoration and revival are mustered together as though to challenge the finality of mortality, in this case the death of the artist Middleton, and the poet's own recent encounter with life-threatening illness. While memory cannot overturn mortality, *apocatastasis* and revival might. Yet the poet concedes that, whatever chance there might have been in 1953 for his own personal revival, this opportunity has passed. Had he had sufficient Irish in Rannafast in 1953, then 'Language and longing might have taken a leap'.[4] Now as he drives through the *Gaeltacht* 'unhomesick, unbelieving', no such magical return is in sight; rather, the one constant thing is Mount Errigal on the horizon.[5] Similarly, the only afterlife available to the painter and poet will be their earthly work.

Ultimately, Heaney's 'Loughanure' is a meditation on temporality and impermanence that considers revival as one of the possible resolutions to an existence crudely circumscribed by mortality. In rejecting the finality of death, in whichever sphere to which it pertains, revival replaces this finality with a radically different temporal scheme, one that allows for traffic or even synthesis between past and present, living and dead. In other words, revival replaces the 'natural' boundaries of time with an open-ended and negotiable temporality.[6] It is fitting that Heaney's meditation on time should lead him back to the *Gaeltacht* Irish college and thus to two coexisting time zones, the 1953 of adolescent infinite possibility and the preserved pre-nineteenth-century rural Ulster in which the shift to English had not yet happened. This curious dual time is at once reminiscent of the temporal idiosyncrasies of Gothic literature, in which historical time bleeds into the present, stifling progress and forcing an anomalous, unnatural set of circumstances that must be confronted.[7] It is no surprise that the temporal quirks of the Gothic are often identified with those of colonialism, which creates its own temporality in which the colonised are perceived to be out of step with 'public time'. This sense of alienation from the present was a feature of nineteenth-century Gaelic Ulster observed by Robert S. MacAdam in his remark that 'the lineal descendants of the former lords of the soil and their retainers vegetate, as it were, in ignorance of the wondrous changes going on in the world around them'.[8] In due course, when colonised peoples have attempted to retrieve their position and place in time, these efforts have often been dismissed as an attempt to fake or invent tradition. Inevitably, this has frequently led to a polarised view of revivalism as an exclusively progressive or regressive force.

Evidently, the progress of the Irish-language revival has been infused with considerations of temporality, as manifested particularly in literature and in the discourse surrounding native tradition. Much has already been written about the temporalities of the colonial condition with regard to Ireland.[9] The reference to 'becoming' in the title of this chapter reflects a desire to challenge the narrow, historicist view of revivalism as a misguided or contrived attempt to alter the natural course of history. A countervailing view of time and history is available to us in the work of the post-structuralist philosopher Gilles Deleuze. Besides reinterpreting the work of Henri Bergson on time and memory, Deleuze took up the Nietzschean notion of the 'eternal return', whereby repetition and endless recurrence are the rule. While some have chosen to see these conditions as a great burden, for Deleuze the repetition is ironically a guarantee of opportunity and of difference, wherein the only hope for mankind is a revolutionary becoming: 'Becoming isn't part of history; history amounts only to the set of preconditions, however recent, that one leaves behind in order to "become", that is, to create something new.'[10]

The concept of a radically different temporal scheme, one that allows for traffic or even synthesis between past and present, living and dead, is a very old one in Irish literature, predating the modern revivalist period by well over a thousand years. Joseph Nagy's study *Conversing with Angels and Ancients* (1997) examines the dialogue between the living and dead (or the supernaturally old) that forms the basis of a body of literature stretching from the seventh century to the twelfth/thirteenth centuries:

> From the realms of hagiography and vernacular literature predicated on hagiographic themes, talk with angels and ancients has provided the texts' legitimating core. Patrick, in the world of his lives and the world he inhabits in vernacular or metasaga, is sought out by an angel who speaks with him, and as a result of this conversion/ conversation, Patrick returns to his 'past', Ireland, and revives that past in order to speak with its representatives, convince them and reform them in a Christian image.[11]

Nagy gives particular prominence to Acallam na Senórach (Colloquy of the Ancients), the late twelfth-century text in which Caoilte and Oisín relate the deeds of Finn mac Cumhaill and his *Fianna* to St Patrick. Part of the function of this text is to provide a bridge between past and present, and to give legitimacy to the conservation and use of knowledge originating in pre-Christian Ireland. Recovering the past by reviving the dead is thus a way of revitalising the present by removing the boundary that separates past and present, and allowing instead the past to be 'productively open-ended'.[12] A key feature of the texts studied by Nagy is that the 'old news' is 'never conveyed or captured in its totality. There is always the tantalising prospect of a return visit, a resumption of the dialogue.'[13]

Further intriguing evidence of the Celtic penchant for dialogue between living and dead is attributed to the second-century-BC Greek poet Nicander of Colophon:

> And it is often alleged because of nightmare dreams that the dead truly appear, for the Nasamones receive special oracles by staying at the tombs of their parents ... The Celts also for the same reason spend the night near the tombs of their famous men, as Nicander affirms.[14]

This convention is immediately reminiscent of some of the *aisling* poems of the seventeenth and eighteenth centuries, in particular *An Síogaí Rómhánach* (The Roman Fairy Woman) (composed *c.* 1650), in which the fairy woman speaks to the anonymous poet at the Roman graves of the earls of Tyrconnell and Tyrone, and 'Úrchill an Chreagáin' (The Graveyard of Creggan, *c.* 1770) by Art Mac Cumhaigh, where the poet spends the night at the tomb of the O'Neills in Creggan graveyard whereupon he is visited by a dream-maiden.[15] In both poems an impassioned discussion of past and present ensues, in each case lamenting the loss of the Gaelic leaders, who would have given protection and sustenance in the past. While the motif of sleeping by the tombs of the dead as a prelude to supernatural encounter may be merely coincidental in these instances, the desire to initiate an exchange between living and dead is not. The *aisling* poetry that flourished in the eighteenth century was all about mediation between past and present, the dream maiden explaining the decline of fortunes in the present and the promise of future deliverance by recourse to the prophecies of dead saints.

All of these examples of dialogue between living and dead/supernatural, between past and present, give us an important context in which to assess the inclination to create a synthesis of past and present or, in Douglas Hyde's famous phrase, 'to render the present a rational continuation of the past'. Indeed, the desire to enter into direct dialogue with the dead is witnessed in the necromancy and various spiritualist proclivities of Yeats and other figures associated with the Celtic Twilight. What seems most obvious here is the common recurrence of a desire to renegotiate or reform the present through active engagement with the past, particularly the heroic or spiritually rich past. Just as Mac Cumhaigh was motivated by a lack of heroic leadership in the eighteenth century, Yeats was moved by disenchantment with spiritual impoverishment in the nineteenth century.

One of the most influential analyses of the modern Irish revivalist movement, John Hutchinson's *The Dynamics of Cultural Nationalism: the Gaelic Revival and the creation of the Irish nation state*, takes the view of revivalism as a recurrent 'movement of moral regeneration' rather than a regressive, atavistic phenomenon: 'For the revivalist, the past is to be used not in order to return to some antique order but rather to re-establish the nation at a new and higher level of development.'[16] Many would disagree with this view of the 1890s–1920s Irish Revival as being a movement of moral regeneration. It has become commonplace to speak of a counter-revival in the period following the establishment of the Free State in 1922, whose most persuasive exponent was undoubtedly Seán Ó Faoláin (1900–91). Ó Faoláin's critique of the revival often rounded on the attempted synthesis of past and present, which, he claimed, had created a faked tradition: 'We used the Gaelic past as an excitement to inspire us; we never examined it; we are not able, when we do examine it, to see what it has to offer us in our present state.'[17] Setting himself and Frank O'Connor at odds with their former teacher Daniel Corkery, Ó Faoláin remarks: 'To us, Ireland is beginning, where to Corkery it is continuing.'[18]

Yet the alternative view – that revivalism is a universal, recurring sociocultural force – was expressed succinctly by Michael Tierney in a discussion of Ó Faoláin's *King of the Beggars*:

> It would be a great pity if any large number of Mr. Ó Faoláin's Irish readers should be led, by a natural irritation with some of the crude and hasty methods now in vogue for reviving the Gaelic language, into concluding as he has done that there is no way out except the choice he presents between a 'fake' and the entire rejection of their own history. Democracy is no substitute for culture, and much of what is most precious and of highest quality in past civilisations was in fact the result of their enthusiastic devotion to, and attempt to recover, literary, linguistic, and artistic traditions that were not always genuinely ancestral to them. After all a surprising amount of

what adds most to the savour of life even at present has come to us from the obsession of the seventeenth and eighteenth centuries with the languages and cultures of Greece and Rome. How much poorer would be European literature and art if all the consequences of the Renaissance were suddenly to disappear? Yet the Renaissance was far more a 'fake', even in Italy, which could lay some claim to continuity with Rome, than the Gaelic Revival is in the original home of Gaelic culture, whose political destiny even in our own time has been changed by the half-recovered memory of its ancient 'otherness'.[19]

We might summarise these opposing views as being, firstly, a view of the past as closed off from the present and in which history and time are linear, additive and organic in nature; secondly, a view of the past and present as actively integrated, in such a way that history and time can be circular and overlapping. A common critique of nationalist movements and modern nations is that they rely on 'invented traditions' that are of very recent provenance and often of spurious origin, as opposed to other 'natural', organic 'continuities'.[20] Yet, as mentioned earlier, colonialism effects its own unnatural temporality where the colonised is, in Albert Memmi's phrase, removed from history, 'dropping him off by the side of the road – outside of our time'.[21] In the Irish context this phenomenon could be dated to various points, but it was arguably in the nineteenth century that it had its starkest realisation, as summarised by John Mitchel: 'the "nineteenth century" would not know itself, could not express itself in Irish'[22] – that is, the Gaelic language and culture of Ireland were out of step with 'public time'. What I understand here by public time is the sense that people have of belonging to a specific period of time. Jerome Buckley's classic study *The Triumph of Time: a study of the Victorian concepts of time, history, progress, and decadence* places this new awareness of time in the Victorian nineteenth century, where 'The notion of public time, or history, as the medium of organic growth and fundamental change, rather than simply additive succession, was essentially new.'[23] Similarly, Benedict Anderson makes an important distinction between the modern awareness of time and the medieval, although there is little doubt that he underestimates the medieval when claiming that there were no 'radical separations between past and present'.[24] In the eighteenth century the novel and the newspaper became indicative of this heightened awareness of time, but neither of these forms were produced by Gaelic Ireland until the late-nineteenth-century revival.[25]

So the awareness of public time is essentially a by-product of modernity or, perhaps more specifically, the Industrial Revolution since the establishment of standardised Greenwich Mean Time in the mid-nineteenth century came about through the development of railways.[26] The profound impact of industrialisation heightened the sense of the Victorians living in a distinct era, one characterised by relentless progress and, indeed, by a cult of progress. Under the influence of Darwin's *On the Origin of Species* (1859), time came to be equated with progress and decline, and, in these circumstances, the sense of peripheral languages and cultures being left behind, in a way that reflected natural selection, gained currency.[27] This was also the era of the positivist view of history, proposed by Auguste Comte, as comprising three stages of development leading to the final stage where science and rational thought would dominate. The Victorian cult of progress and imperial expansion is often associated with Lord Macaulay and Francis Bacon, whose ideas were reinforced in the National-school curriculum, as Séamus Ó Grianna (1889–1969) contends in his account of schooldays in 1890s Rannafast, County Donegal.[28] Ó Grianna remarks of his schooling that he 'would have been led to believe that the wisdom of classical philosophers was worth nothing compared with the wisdom of Bacon and Macaulay'.[29] The sense that Victorians had of belonging to an age of unprecedented material, scientific, imperial progress is almost axiomatic, as is its corollary, the age of decadence and spiritual decline, expressed by Thomas Carlyle, John Ruskin, William Morris and others. Whatever one's position on 'the condition of England', however, the view prevailed that a country like Ireland, peripheral and predominantly rural, was out of sync with public time, and that a language such as the Irish language was bound to be similarly out of step and destined to extinction.[30]

As mentioned in Chapter 3, there is much evidence of an anachronistic self-image in Gaelic Ireland itself from the seventeenth century through to the nineteenth; the messianic tradition in Irish poetry that constantly reiterates the desire for deliverance from the present by the Stuart Pretender, Bonaparte, and so on, provides a case in point. The decisive phase of colonial subjugation in the early seventeenth century was registered by various Irish poets as a humiliation scarcely distinguishable from death.[31] Thus, Eochaidh Ó hEodhusa, in his poem 'Beag Mhaireas do Mhacraidh Ghaoidheal' (Few Remain of the Young Men of the Gael), characterised the Gaels as 'living though not living' (*gé mhairid ní mhairid siad*), their life being comparable to death.[32] The same temporal disjunction in the consciousness of Gaelic poets is also witnessed in the letters and name books of the nineteenth-century Ordnance Survey, where there are numerous instances of the descendants of what MacAdam calls 'the former lords of the soil and their retainers' hanging on to their medieval lineage in spite of the poverty of their circumstances, almost as ghosts.[33] In the literature of the eighteenth and nineteenth centuries the same sense of fall is evident in the burlesque versions of heroic literature from the Ulster and Finn Cycle or in songs such as 'An Chrúbach' (The Cow with Turned-in Horns), where the mythical cow is a hapless and bony ghost.[34]

Ghosts are, of course, most readily associated with the Gothic, that branch of literature where liminality prevails and where the past cannot be relinquished but, rather, lingers and erupts in the present. W.J. McCormack's seminal essay on Gothic literature in Ireland explains its appeal in the fact that past and present were not separate in Ireland, and remarks that 'In the Gothic novel wrongful disinheritance is an explicit formula.'[35] As I have mentioned, something quite akin to wrongful disinheritance, the memory of dispossession, was an enduring legacy of the seventeenth century among the Irish-speaking population. There are many other ways besides this in which Gothic literature and its peculiar temporality reflects and overlaps the situation of the Irish language and its literature from the seventeenth century onwards. There is the representation of the Gaelic Irish in the nineteenth-century Irish Gothic novel, 'where Gaelic Ireland is set ... in an anachronistic time-warp', as Joep Leerssen puts it in his discussion of the novels of Lady Morgan and Charles Maturin.[36] This is a tendency that carries through into the late nineteenth-century revivalist period, where Yeats, Gregory and Synge valorise not only the spatially peripheral – wandering fiddlers and poets, fishermen, island communities, and so on – but ascribe a temporal detachment to these favoured types. In Synge's *The Aran Islands* we are told that

> Few of the people, however, are sufficiently used to modern time to understand in more than a vague way the convention of the hours, and when I tell them what o'clock it is by my watch they are not satisfied, and ask how long is left them before the twilight.[37]

There is a suggestion that Synge's observation might be his own primitivist projection, a naivety ready to be exploited by his subject, when one old man asks Synge to send him a clock so that 'they wouldn't forget me'.[38] Leerssen equates the tendency to deny contemporaneity to peripheral cultures – what the anthropologist Johannes Fabian calls 'the denial of coevalness' – to a sense of advanced metropolitan superiority, or else a primitivistic nostalgia for the more 'organic' and 'natural' past.[39]

We find a good example of prelapsarian nostalgia for the preindustrial world in the work of a contemporary of Yeats and Synge, Herbert Moore Pim (1883–1950). Pim was the author of some Gothic novels, as well as a series of sketches published as *Unknown Immortals in the Northern City of Success* (1917), in which he describes a fish seller in Belfast:

> There is a doubt about his origin, and there is a greater doubt about his destiny. No one ever saw the fish-man begin his day of song, because his day never ends. He carries curious treasures, and he is full of wisdom. His garments cling about him, and his eyes are guarded from the light.
>
> No man can tell his age, and he is without kith and kin in the world.[40]

Far from being 'without kith and kin in the world', it is most likely that this man was one of the 'Fadgies' from Omeath, an Irish speaker from a very old and tightly knit community that settled in the Smithfield area of Belfast during the nineteenth century.[41] In Pim's whimsical portrait, the fishman has more in common with the undead, such as John Melmoth of Charles Maturin's classic Gothic novel *Melmoth the Wanderer* (1820), who is 'independent of time and place'.[42]

The idea that the Irish language and its speakers were like the undead of Gothic novels is also expressed from within the language-revivalist movement. The native Irish speaker and revivalist Philip Barron strikes a Gothic note in the first number of his magazine *Ancient Ireland* (1835) where he announces his mission to revive the literature and study of Irish language from where it 'lay buried'.[43] Similarly, James Clarence Mangan's poem 'The Irish Language' predicts that the language shall win 'proud release from the tomb thou art sepulchred in'.[44] One of the most common conventions in the Gothic novel is the 'found document', often a will, diary or fragment, and, as such, Gothic novels frequently include 'meditations on textual accuracy and transmission as central problems of historical retrieval'.[45] This is precisely where the energies and focus of literary endeavours in Irish rested in the nineteenth century, rather than in creating a new body of prose. Besides the common ground with Gothic literature, the values of Irish revivalism in the nineteenth century were clearly consonant with those of the Gothic Revival in architecture, a connection that was to become critical later on in the case of Pearse. Thus, in his account of the Irish college he had built in County Waterford in the early 1830s, Philip Barron remarked that 'the ancient Gothic order has been adopted'.[46] It is significant that Barron gives details of the Gothic credentials of his Irish college, since, as discussed in the previous chapter, the principles espoused by the Gothic Revival in architecture were often a rejection of the industrial, utilitarian, secularised nineteenth century, and a return to the institutions and values of medieval society.

As ever, the desire to reinstate former values begs the question as to whether such a synthesis of past and present can ever be achieved. As one writer put it in 1904 in the *Leader*, 'Perhaps the greatest of all difficulties which underlie the whole of what is known as the Irish Revival is the length of time we are obliged to go back before we arrive at any mode of life that may with truth be termed distinctively Irish.'[47] This becomes a much more complex question when we consider that many parts of Ireland were still overwhelmingly Irish-speaking, and many more still in some intermediate stage of language shift. Seosamh Mac Grianna (1900–90) of Rannafast remarked in the 1920s of native Irish speakers who were fifty years older than him that their knowledge of Irish surpassed his to the same degree that Mac Grianna's surpassed the Irish of revivalists such as Pearse.[48] Evidently, alongside the conventional boundaries of past and present are those that are represented on the spatio-temporal plane of east–west, *Gaeltacht–Galltacht*, typified in Seán Ó Ríordáin's call to 'return again' to the Ireland of the sixteenth century by simply going west to the Kerry *Gaeltacht* in the early 1960s, where an ideal past existed in the present.[49] Heaney's sojourn in the Donegal *Gaeltacht* as a schoolboy in 1953 was part of the same well-established, westward return.[50]

Considered against the ambivalent temporality of the Gothic nineteenth century and the even greater temporal ambivalence of the twentieth century, where Irish revivalism becomes a major cultural force, the notion of history as linear, additive succession or as clearly demarcated stages, as expressed by positivism and historicism, becomes decidedly unconvincing. Nevertheless, the notion that history is driven by an inevitable linear progress has had and still enjoys great influence. The political scientist Tom Garvin typifies this attitude in his 1987 study *Nationalist Revolutionaries in Ireland, 1858–1928*:

> ... the nationalist's hatred of the recent past debarred him from taking up a Burkean incremental conservatism which treasured past ways while accepting gradual innovation. The separatist was, commonly, a restorationist of an extinct past rather than a preserver of continuity with the recent, genuine past.[51]

The phrase that jars here is 'the recent, genuine past' – is only the recent past genuine? Or do revivalists espouse a *false* past? Rather than the past and present being parcelled into discrete stages or phases, the evidence of revivalism suggests that we consider a Bergsonian understanding of time where the past and present coexist, as formulated by Deleuze: 'Not only does the past coexist with the present that has been, but … it is the whole, integral past; it is *all* our past, which coexists with each present. The famous metaphor of the cone represents this complete state of coexistence.'[52] For Bergson the 'pure present' is 'the invisible progress of the past gnawing into the future'.[53] Duration, in Bergson's view, is a dynamic process of pure mobility characterised by continuity of progress and heterogeneity.

A related feature of Deleuze's adaptation of Bergson's theory of time is his interpretation of the Nietzschean 'eternal return', which he sees as an opportunity and a guarantee of difference rather than repetition: 'Destiny in the eternal return is also the "welcoming" of chance.'[54] Drawing also on Heraclitus as a philosopher of flux, Deleuze affirms the importance of *becoming* rather than *being*.[55] Interestingly, Heaney's reflection on his time in the *Gaeltacht* centres on the notion of return. He has come to the *Gaeltacht* as a schoolboy as part of a spiritual return *ad fontes*. Indeed, his journey there is marked by a 'flit of the foreknown' and a sense of reincarnation.[56] His return to this scene in *Human Chain* leads him to ponder on a 'world restored', which, similar to Deleuze, he refers to as elsewhere as the 'world of the second chance'.[57] Admittedly, these are abstract reflections on time and duration, yet they provide a theoretical or imaginative frame of reference for the concrete actuality of revivalism – how, for example, in a city such as Belfast the Irish language has been in a constant state of revival from at least the end of the eighteenth century.[58] At the very least, these interpretations of temporality allow for a broader understanding of revivalism, one that goes beyond the oversimplification that presents it as an atavistic reflex or a mere contrivance that ignores the true or natural process of history.

More than any other, the Irish-language writer whose work engaged implicitly with Bergson's conception of time and with related concepts such as Nietzsche's 'eternal recurrence' is Máirtín Ó Cadhain. As Declan Kiberd notes in his penetrating essay on Ó Cadhain's novel *Cré na Cille* (1949), the border between living and dead had been all but erased by modernists such as Ó Cadhain and Beckett.[59] In *Cré na Cille* the time is *de shíor* (eternal), and the finality of death is dispensed with as the characters, all deceased, engage in an endless cycle of gossip and bickering. As Kiberd remarks, there is a circular structure to both *Cré na Cille* and Beckett's trilogy. The characters cannot step out of time, but they are also incapable of growth. There can be no beginning, middle or end in the ensuing narration, only the perpetual repetition of the same range of sentences, petering out into a dot-dot-dot.[60]

Death is an anticlimax in *Cré na Cille*, for as the character Muraed Phroinsiais explains, people simply continue the same life as they had in the 'ould country', except that they cannot leave the grave nor hear the living.[61] Yet far from leading to an eschewal of the faith or even a questioning of Christian eschatology, the characters continue to value the trappings of Christian burial (respectable plots and crosses, crucifixes and shrouds), albeit on a strictly material rather than spiritual basis, as a reflection of social prestige.[62] Similarly, there is no decline in the traditional belief in the prophecies of native saints that had for so long bolstered messianic hopes and on which the dialogue between living and supernatural was predicated in *aisling* poetry.[63]

The peculiar temporal scheme of *Cré na Cille* might be reasonably traced to many of Ó Cadhain's preoccupations and experiences, not least his concern that he was writing in a language that might die before him.[64] His internment in the Curragh prison camp, along with hundreds of other republicans during the years of the Second World War, seems to partly account for his fascination with Dostoyevsky's *The House of the Dead* (1860), the fictionalised account of the Russian author's incarceration in a Siberian prison camp. Describing this period of his life to his brother, Dostoyevsky wrote, 'I consider those four years as a time during which I was buried alive and shut up in a coffin.'[65] Just as the dead of *Cré na Cille* continue to live in a limited sense, Ó Cadhain spoke of his imprisonment in terms that suggest a period of spatio-temporal exile. In one account he refers to his temporary release as a return to Ireland, rather like Muraed Phroinsiais' reference to the land of the living as the 'ould country'.[66] While the sense of prison being a house of the dead may well be universal, in Ó Cadhain's case, and in the case of other republicans in newly independent Ireland, there was a strong feeling that the spatio-temporal exile of incarceration was part of a wider injustice that involved a disruption and betrayal of the nationalist teleology. Interestingly, Ó Cadhain refers to the entire project of national liberation as an *aisling*, a vision articulated by the leaders of the 1916 Rising and betrayed by the successive governments of the new independent state.[67]

In many ways, some of the Gothic motifs witnessed in representations of

Gaelic Ireland after political conquest and cultural subjugation in the seventeenth century – such as 'wrongful disinheritance', liminality and temporal alienation – become the province of anti-Treaty republicans in the twentieth century. This is expressed most vividly in Seosamh Mac Grianna's final, unfinished novel *Dá mBíodh Ruball ar an Éan* (1940) (If the Bird Had a Tail), in which 'wrongful disinheritance' is registered literally and figuratively at the novel's core. *Dá mBíodh Ruball ar an Éan* centres on the fate of a tortured artist, Cathal Mac Eachmharcaigh, who is essentially a prisoner in the house from which he has been wrongfully disinherited by his older stepbrother, a corrupt politician who is leader of the Laochra na Saoirse (Heroes of Freedom) party. A large part of Mac Eachmharcaigh's torment is the result of his vain attempt to keep the higher ideals of art separate from the worldly machinations of politics and propaganda. This struggle is doomed to failure as the house in which the artist lives and works is dominated by the dark forces presided over by his half-brother, and, as such, the artist's gradual decline is inevitable. What we learn of this struggle is revealed to us by a journalist, Mánas Mac Giolla Bhríde, who discovers Mac Eachmharcaigh's diary after the latter's death (the classic Gothic 'found document'), and becomes not only 'heir' to the artist's vexation but experiences a sense of physical possession as the diary takes over his mind and body: 'the torment and heat of the author was in my blood'.[68]

In mood and tone as well as in narrative structure, *Dá mBíodh Ruball ar an Éan* is remarkably close to film noir. Just as film noir owes much of its origins to the Gothic novel (the term itself is based on the French *roman noir*, or 'Gothic novel'), Mac Grianna's novel is in many ways a modern rendering of the earlier Gothic form, particularly where aspects of temporality, and more specifically chronology, are concerned.[69] The seemingly inevitable chronology of national deliverance is disrupted on various levels in *Dá mBíodh Ruball ar an Éan* – faced with the odious reality of Ireland under independence, the artist Mac Eachmharcaigh renounces his former service to the nationalist project and becomes instead a martyr for the cause of art, a type of Prometheus, as Mánas Mac Giolla Bhríde has it.[70] In this manner Mac Eachmharcaigh begins to produce works of a purgatorial nature that the narrator describes as 'cubist-classical' – radically modernist but drawing on classical tradition – and which carry ironic titles such as *In the Name of God and of the Dead Generations* – taken from the opening line of the 1916 Proclamation.[71] These paintings represent the temporal purgatory of the nationalist vision – free from foreign rule, yet as far as ever from ultimate salvation. The significance of Mac Eachmharcaigh's 'cubist-classical' style is to break entirely with the present's corrupt version of national independence and to keep faith retrospectively with a purer ideal, in the way that anti-Treaty republicans sought to adhere to the vision of 1916.[72]

There are indeed strong indications from the outset in *Dá mBíodh Ruball ar an Éan* that the progress of the nationalist teleology is belied by an alternative narrative of a distinctly Gothic bent. The narrator and journalist Mánas Mac Giolla Bhríde alludes to this on the first page, where he speaks of having a secret mien that prevented him from ever succeeding in life.[73] Here Mac Grianna borrows from a line written by one of his own ancestors, Aodh Ó Domhnaill, an oral poet of pre-Famine Ireland: 'If it were not for the fate under which I was born that prevented me from ever succeeding in life.'[74] The sense that a malign fate will ensure that the end will not be reached is obvious to the reader on arriving at the point where the novel tails off and is followed by a now famous postscript where the author tells us that 'the well has run dry' and he will write no more.[75]

A further reflection in *Dá mBíodh Ruball ar an Éan* of the abrogated chronology of national liberation is revealed through the novel's investigative structure, again reminiscent of film noir, where the full circumstances of a crime or injustice are revealed through flashback and reverse chronology. In film noir this investigation frequently involves a 'wrong man'-type character whose hitherto benign progress in life has been disrupted inexplicably at an as yet unknown juncture, and this is precisely the approach followed in *Dá mBíodh Ruball ar an Éan*, where both Cathal Mac Eachmharcaigh and the narrator/investigator Mánas Mac Giolla Bhríde are constantly preoccupied with retracing the chronology of events in the hope that the critical point at which betrayal took place can be revealed.

The injury of wrongful disinheritance and spatio-temporal exile, while certainly fictive in Mac Eachmharcaigh's case, clearly mirrors the author's own experience of imprisonment (in the Curragh, as an anti-Treaty republican, in 1922–23) and his profound disenchantment with the Ireland of the Free State. This embitterment prevailed up until his famous 1935 postscript to *Dá mBíodh Ruball ar an Éan*, a point marking the abrupt end of his literary career and the onset of severely debilitating mental illness. Although both Mac Grianna and Ó Cadhain present their fictional and literal incarcerations as part of the struggle between progressive art and repressive state authority (Ó Cadhain adds to his identification with Dostoyevsky's imprisonment by the tsarist regime by comparing his interrogation by state authorities in

Dublin with that described by Arthur Koestler in *Darkness at Noon*),[76] one should, of course, resist any reified notion of imprisonment as an exclusively abstract, metaphysical condition. Both of Ó Cadhain's parents died during his incarceration. On the occasion of his mother's death, which occurred six weeks after his initial imprisonment, he was allowed 'to come out to Ireland' to attend her funeral. When his father died a couple of years later, however, permission to attend the funeral was denied.[77] Ó Cadhain also gives a strong indication that the circumstances of his arrest and imprisonment either led to or contributed to his mother's death: *Chuala sí gur tugadh droch-íde sa mbeairic dom agus fuair sí bás tobann* (She heard that I was given a bad beating in the barracks and she died suddenly).[78] The personal cost of spatio-temporal exile could hardly be clearer here, but it is also part of the wider experience, evinced by some anti-Treaty republicans in the 1920s and anti-Dáil Éireann republicans from the 1930s onwards, of being removed from the entire project of national liberation and cultural revival while others directed its realisation in a way that, it was felt, was inimical to its original aims. Disinheritance, incarceration and its implicit spatio-temporal exile became the metaphorical, as well as the often literal, condition of those who opposed the abrogation of the original 'vision' of national liberation.

The proposition that the just course of the national-liberation narrative had been abrogated or arrested by those who had betrayed the original vision is one that underlay Ó Cadhain's lifelong public engagement on issues such as education, the preservation of national heritage and tradition (particularly folklore), economic and social policy, and, of course, the Irish language and the *Gaeltacht*. At the heart of this engagement is the inherent paradox of revival – how and if one can revive a language or any significant element of national culture in those places where it has died out. This question is of central importance to Ó Cadhain's controversial 1950 talk on folklore to Cumann na Scríbhneoirí (The Writers' Society).[79] Although its many ad hominem interjections and general condemnatory intensity were character-istic of Ó Cadhain's polemic style, the author's recent imprisonment by the state authorities is likely to have fuelled his coruscating critique of the state's intervention in the preservation of national culture. The charge of betrayal underscores the entire case. Nevertheless, Ó Cadhain's criticism of the state-funded Irish Folklore Commission is also founded on a deeply considered examination of the broader question of revival and temporality.

Essential to Ó Cadhain's argument was the notion that death was eve-rywhere synonymous with the study of Irish and folklore, to the extent that the collected forces of academia and state-sponsored heritage preservation amounted to a small triangle in Dublin city centre that one might call *Priomh-Chill Éireann: an Chré Mharbh* (The Chief Cemetery of Ireland: the Dead Clay).[80] Folklore was simply a study of the dead, and the *Gaeltacht* – the contemporary communities for whom Irish and its traditions were living and immediate – had been reduced to a mere branch of folklore.[81] If this image suggests the situation realised in *Cré na Cille* of a community buried and yet living, so also do the frequent references to *cré* (particularly the opposition of 'dead clay' and 'living clay') evoke the sense in *Cré na Cille* of clay as a synecdoche for the mysteries of time, creation and transformation.[82] In the novel this occurs chiefly through the naming of each of its ten interludes after a different organic process by which the initial *cré dhubh* (black clay) becomes eventually *cré gheal* (bright/white clay). It is also a recurring trope in the magnificent, declamatory monologues of 'Stoc na Cille' (Trumpet of the Graveyard), the oldest voice in the graveyard and the only one to express a deeper awareness of eternity:

> Here in the grave the spool is forever spinning; turning the brightness dark, making the beautiful ugly, and imbricating the alluring golden ringlets of hair with a shading of scum, a wisp of mildew, a hint of rot, a sliver of slime, and a grey haunting of mizzle. The vespertine veil of indifference and forgetfulness is being woven from the golden filaments of the setting sun, from the silver web of moonlight, from the resplendent cloak of fame, and from the departing wafture of fugacious remembrance. For this weaver's material is none other than the malleable and kneadful clay.[83]

For Ó Cadhain folklore was 'permanent', and what appeared to be dying was simply being transformed into something new. It was not a question, therefore, of rescuing the body but, rather, the spirit that lay deep below – the error was in trying to give life to something when what was required was a 're-cultivating of the soul'.[84]

The contradistinction in *Cré na Cille* between the grandiosely transcendental soliloquies of 'Stoc na Cille' and the relentlessly material preoccupations of the other dead voices are indicative of both Ó Cadhain's materialist view of culture and society and his distrust of the Romantic mysticising of peasant society.[85] The most enduring target of Ó Cadhain's public engagement was the hypocrisy of the Irish state in having elevated *Gaeltacht* culture to a spiritual ideal while overseeing the material neglect of its people, as was particularly evident in chronic emigration.[86] Nevertheless, while Ó Cadhain was unapologetically socialist and republican he was also a committed Catholic.[87] While of, and firmly on the side of, the tillers of soil, he was clearly open to the mysteries of the soil. It is perhaps this Catholic conviction that allowed Ó Cadhain to renounce the Celtic mysticism typified by Matthew Arnold and the Celtic Twilight and yet speak not only of 're-cultivating the soul' but also of that 'particular little island of spirituality in the human mind that is the Gael'.[88] Where the discourse of romanticism and cultural nationalism led to an obfuscation of material realities, Ó Cadhain was quick to oppose this. This did not, however, mean that he could not consider cultural revival to have a spiritual dimension or even function. Indeed, in the script of one of his last talks, entitled 'An Dá Leitríocht' (The Two Literatures), he described the business of contemporary Irish-language literature as being 'a work of bestowal, a spiritual act in a very particular way'.[89]

The combination in Ó Cadhain's approach to cultural revival of both material and spiritual sensibilities is suggestive of what Anthony D. Smith termed 'the crisis of dual legitimation' in nationalist discourse, 'legitimation in terms of received religion and tradition versus legitimation by appeal to reason and observation'.[90] Of course, to admit of a spiritual dimension is to be open to a concept of time as subordinate to deity or at least to some unknown entity. Yet one of the most consistent features of Ó Cadhain's writing on culture, and most particularly on approaches to cultural revival or preservation, is his belief in a material synthesis that was both a necessary and natural path towards continuity. Just as the eternal time of *Cré na Cille* is punctuated by the organic process of synthesis undergone by the graveyard clay, so, too, is the narrative of national liberation in Ó Cadhain's view dependent on a synthesis of history and folk tradition.[91]

In proposing the importance of synthesis to the well-being of national culture Ó Cadhain drew particularly on T.S. Eliot's understanding of the nature of both community and tradition. In his landmark essay 'Páipéir Bhána agus Páipéir Bhreaca' (White Papers and Written Papers) (1969), published the year before his death, his description of his native *Gaeltacht* community as a 'local organic community' is based particularly on his reading of Eliot, whom he also considered to be the most perceptive writer on literary tradition of his times.[92] The emphasis on synthesis and renewal expressed in 'Páipéir Bhána agus Páipéir Bhreaca' reiterates the main premise of Ó Cadhain's 1950 essay on folklore discussed above. Here particular attention is drawn to some of the conclusions reached by Eliot in his essay entitled 'What Is a Classic?' (1945), especially with regard to temporality: 'If we cease to believe in the future the past would cease fully to be *our* past: it would become the past of a dead civilization.'[93] The error of the government-sponsored Folklore Commission was, in Ó Cadhain's view, symptomatic of the state's betrayal of the original vision of national liberation – that is, it failed to effect a synthesis of past and present. Ó Cadhain quotes Eliot's warning against 'a new kind of provincialism', by which he meant

> … a provincialism, not of space, but of time; one for which history is merely the chronicle of human devices which have served their turn and been scrapped, one for which the world is the property solely of the living, a property in which the dead hold no shares.[94]

Although clearly deeply aware of the theoretical issues implicit in cultural revival, Ó Cadhain was by no means silent on the practical achievement of this synthesis of past and present. While acknowledging the importance of fidelity to historical precedent, he also recognised the practical value of 'false traditions', and cites the example of Iolo Morgannwg (1747–1826) in Wales, whose influence was in evidence in the modern *eisteddfod*.[95] As Mícheál Briody has shown, Ó Cadhain's attack on the Folklore Commission was grounded in many practical and strategic considerations, notably the almost twofold increase of government funding awarded to the Folklore Commission at a time (1949–50) when it was being proposed that the funding of Irish-language literary magazines should be decreased, and also his desire to rebuff public intellectuals such as Arland Ussher and Seán Ó Faoláin as well as Séamus Ó Duilearga (director of the Folklore Commission), all of whom were seemingly dismissive of contemporary literature in Irish while enthusiastic about the value of folklore.[96] Indeed, it seems at times that Ó Cadhain could be too practical, as when, in 'Páipéir Bhána agus Páipéir Bhreaca' he encouraged an abandonment of poetry for prose in Irish on the grounds that writing was integral to the revival of Irish and prose was the very cement and concrete of life.[97]

An interesting view of how the state could accomplish a practically grounded, revivalist synthesis was offered by Ó Cadhain in 1962 when he was part of an Irish group that visited the Kyrgyz Soviet Socialist Republic.[98] His chief interest, according to Ó Cadhain's account of the visit, was to 'try and find out something of the way the Soviets dealt with a minor culture'.[99]

Ó Cadhain's interest in the oral literature and extempore verse tradition of Kyrgyzia had been well established in his reading of the Chadwicks' *The Growth of Literature* (1940) and of other scholars who had written about the Kyrgyz tradition, most notably Vasily Radlov and George Thomson.[100] Explaining his debt to the Chadwicks, Ó Cadhain remarked:

> The Chadwicks taught me all I knew about Kirghizia. In teaching me about Kirghizia, they gave me a deeper insight into myself, into the milieu in which I was born, into the culture – minor it may be – which I inherited. Here in a God forsaken corner in Ireland were the same riddle contests as in Kirghizia; the extemporising and compositions of verse for all occasions; the same sparkling speech which I may say *en passant* are not Synge's playboyisms, the same heroic traditional tales which took hours and hours to recite and which were the comics as well as the detective novels of my youth. I do not exaggerate when I say that I had thousands of lines of formalised speech before I could talk English. This rich traditional life has been all but liquidated in our day.[101]

The trip to the Kyrgyz Republic immediately confirmed this perceived commonality between its rural culture and that of his native Cois Fharraige. Yet while an old peasant woman's lilting while milking a cow immediately reminded Ó Cadhain of his mother, the difference was that this old woman had been made a member of the Supreme Soviet.[102] Notwithstanding his disappointment at an apparent 'Russianisation' in regard to language policy, a recurrent observation in Ó Cadhain's talk on Kyrgyzia is how peasant culture had been brought into the modern technological age reasonably intact and treated with respect.[103] He was particularly enthusiastic about the evidence of modern infrastructure, and reserved the highest praise for the 'liquidation of mass and adult illiteracy'.[104] It appeared to Ó Cadhain that the soviet republic had achieved the successful transition from a predominantly oral culture to a literate one without apparently diminishing the active vigour of the oral tradition. A key indication of this was the inclusion of storytelling in the school programme in both Russia and the Kyrgyz Republic and the evidence of an active engagement with the native oral culture at the highest levels of officialdom:

> When I mentioned *Manas* [Kyrgyz epic poem] everyone began to recite it, even the Minister for Education. I'd like to listen to

his opposite number here recite a long extract from 'the Midnight Court', though there is documented evidence that our venerable *Uachtarán* learnt it by heart in the jails of long ago.[105]

This last reference to Éamon de Valera hints at the perceived betrayal of the original cultural aims of national liberation by the leaders of the independent state, and places prison at the source of fidelity to the original vision. De Valera had, of course, been *Taoiseach* when Ó Cadhain was interned during the Second World War.

The notion that a successful cultural synthesis of tradition and modernity had been achieved in the Kyrgyz Republic was eagerly proposed by George Thomson (1903–87), the English Marxist and renowned Classics and Irish scholar. In his *Marxism and Poetry* (1945), Thomson remarks that he had for many years worked unsuccessfully 'to save the culture of the Irish-speaking peasantry' before realising that 'you cannot raise the cultural standards of a people without raising their economic standards'.[106] Thomson's belief in the dialectics of history and human development was given realisation in the apparent synthesis of traditional culture and modernity in Central Asia, and in particular in the Kyrgyz and Kazakh republics. Through modernisation and the eradication of illiteracy, Thomson claimed,

> These peoples [the people of Central Asia] have ceased to be primitive. They have been industrialised. That is what happened to the English peasantry during the Industrial Revolution, and the result was that their culture was destroyed. That is what is happening to the Irish-speaking peasantry today, with the same result. What then is becoming of the culture of the Kazakhs and the Kirghiz and the other peoples of Soviet Asia? So far from being destroyed, it is bursting into new life, richer and more vigorous than ever before. The potentialities of this cultural renaissance are incalculable, and they will have repercussions all over the world.[107]

As mentioned at the outset, at the core of revivalism lies an attempt to reconnect with the lost legacy of previous generations and to create a form of intergenerational synthesis or continuity where this has been disrupted. Yet while spiritual and artistic beliefs can allow one to forego the naturally observed boundaries of time, and specifically the impossibility of conversing with dead generations, the demands of reason and observation remain. In both

Thomson's Central Asia and Pearse's west of Ireland, individuals were identified who embodied intergenerational continuity and who, in their extraordinary longevity, seemed almost to have defeated death – the ultimate desire of any revival. Thomson's example is the Kazakh 'primitive poet' Jamboul, whom he considered, at ninety-nine years of age, to be the 'oldest poet in the world'.[108] Born in 1846, Jamboul had been known in the nineteenth century as the 'greatest bard of the Kazakhs', but much of what he had composed had since been lost. The reversal of this loss, according to Thomson, had been permitted by the revolution of 1917 and the subsequent revival of oral literature: 'here we have a primitive poet who had hardly lost his status under tribal society when he recovered it under socialism'.[109]

A similarly totemic figure for Pearse is the Connemara folk poet Colm de Bhailís (1796–1906), whom he presented as being discovered by the Gaelic League's paper *An Claidheamh Soluis*.[110] Part of Pearse's great attraction to de Bhailís was his remarkable lifespan, spanning three centuries, which made him a living witness to generations of Irish historical experience. In the introduction to the first of his poems to appear in print, Pearse was eager to illustrate the exceptional life of the poet who had been an infant at the time of the 1798 Rebellion, a boy at the time of Robert Emmet's rebellion, a middle-aged man during the Famine years, an old man during the Fenian Rising, and had become a centenarian shortly after the founding of the Gaelic League in 1893. Indeed, de Bhailís resembles one of the supernaturally old figures of medieval Irish literature who can explain their origins to the present generation.[111]

Pearse's life and work is characterised by this quest for intergenerational continuity, be it literally and physically embodied – as in the case of de Bhailís – or, as was more likely, aspired to through a feat of the imagination and the will. The invocation in the 1916 Proclamation of the 'dead generations' is consistent with so much of what Pearse had written about and worked to bring about throughout his life.[112] The literal and imaginative influence of previous generations is attested to in his autobiographical fragment where he recounts the singular influence of his grandaunt, Margaret Brady, an Irish speaker who had inherited a tradition of insurgency going back to 1798, and whose songs, foretelling of Bonaparte's intervention in the fate of Ireland, inspired Pearse to write his own verses on the same theme. Margaret Brady's songs were of course part of the *aisling* tradition in which the promise of deliverance was reiterated by each generation, with the messianic figure changing in each case to suit present circumstances.[113]

The case of Pearse's Gaelic 'nursemaid' is strikingly similar to others in the history of Irish revivalism, such as those of Thomas Crofton Croker, Lady Gregory and Ernest Blythe, where the particular influence of a nursemaid or domestic servant had helped inspire a revivalist career.[114] Indeed, more generally, this phenomenon seems to have been part of the large-scale cultural transference or appropriation across class lines – typified by the work of the Grimm brothers as collectors of folk tales – that was essential to the development of cultural nationalism throughout Europe in the nineteenth-century. This was certainly the experience of Pushkin, who learned the folklore of his country, including songs of former peasant rebellions, from his beloved serf nurse, who appears as Filipevna, nurse to Tatiana, in his *Eugene Onegin* (1833).[115]

If this particular form of intergenerational continuity appears to be a natural occurrence, it is surely not accidental that in the late 1890s the Gaelic League advertised and implemented a scheme whereby urban Gaelic Leaguers could employ native Irish speakers from the *Gaeltacht* to act as nursemaids or domestic servants in their homes. Indeed, with the same intentions Pearse recruited a native Irish *seanchaí* (historian) from County Mayo, Mícheál Mac Ruaidhrí, as full-time gardener and teacher of horticulture to the boys of Sgoil Éanna, his bilingual school.[116] One might ask whether or not it made any difference if in one instance this intergenerational dynamic was accidental and the other manufactured. One is reminded here of Garvin's phrase 'the genuine past' and the frequent tendency to view revivalist initiatives as inauthentic behaviour to be treated with the same suspicion as 'social engineering'.

Again, conflicting notions of temporality complicate the issue. The linear deterministic model of progress encourages the view that the decline of specific languages and cultures is part of a natural order that cannot be reversed. This is not simply the view of history that prevailed in the age of Darwin and Comte; a similar historicism sustained the converse view of nationalist and cultural revivalists, and continues to do so. A good example of this is the text of a Gaelic League pamphlet issued in 1966 as part of the fiftieth anniversary of the 1916 Rising, in which the following statement occurs: 'We are certain that, because of *the recurrent historical rhythm*, the Irish people will inevitably and inexorably return to that which is culturally and idealistically their own.'[117] Yet because the inevitability of such a course of events could not be evidenced from a rational, scientific viewpoint, the authors invoke a quasi-religious authority for their claim in the same way that the *aisling* poets had done up to the nineteenth century:

> Unequivocally we state that we of Conradh na Gaeilge [the Gaelic
> League] are dedicated to the restoration of the Irish language so
> that unborn generations shall one day rejoice in the full possession
> of our national heritage.
>
> This is the national gospel proclaimed by Pearse. To this, we of
> Conradh na Gaeilge firmly adhere.[118]

It is perhaps no surprise that the authors refer to the vision of Pearse rather
than to the league's first president, Douglas Hyde. After all, Hyde saw the
league's work as being 'to render the present a *rational* continuation of the
past', whereas Pearse's 'gospel' depended, to a significant degree, on a non-
rational, imagined conception of the future. This is not to ignore the evidence
of Pearse as a pragmatic and practical individual or to yield to the crude
popular image of Pearse as whimsical poet but, rather, to acknowledge Pearse's
awareness of the very real and practical power of myth and utopian discourse.
Writing his own piece on the anniversary of the Rising, Ó Cadhain alludes
to the non-rational, utopian foundations on which the vision of 1916 was
created: 'what could be more unreasonable than Easter Week? Were the race
of the Gael not so unreasonable as they have always been, we would have long
since disappeared from history.'[119] Rather than reason, it is hope, remarked
Ó Cadhain, that has been the 'chain detonation' that runs through Irish
history.[120]

Besides the rational motivation for revival, such as the desire to improve
upon the present and, in the case of colonised peoples, to reverse an injustice, it is clear that the aim of achieving a synthesis of past and present relies
on a willingness to look beyond the boundaries of time observed in nature.
Walter Benjamin's phrase 'a tiger's leap into the past' from his 'Theses on the
Philosophy of History' encapsulates this confidence in our ability to actively
engage with the past. In this well-known essay, Benjamin reimagines the
boundaries of time and history, and proposes a radical, revolutionary engagement with the past in which past and present become simultaneous. A key
concept in Benjamin's argument is his belief in what he calls 'messianic time':
'There is a secret agreement between past generations and the present one.
Our coming was expected on earth. Like every generation that preceded us,
we have been endowed with a *weak* Messianic power, a power to which the
past has a claim.'[121]

The same sense of messianic prophecy and of the supernatural bond
between generations figures large in Irish history, and in Pearse found perhaps

its most successful advocate. The notion that there is a 'secret agreement between past generations and the present one' has many implications, particularly where the responsibility of each generation towards a broad transhistorical aim is concerned. In the 1966 Gaelic League pamphlet the authors pose the question of whether or not Ireland had the will to endure as a nation, and, in answering this, quote Dr Eoin McKiernan of the University of St Thomas, Minnesota: '... one generation more, and the world shall know whether Ireland had that will'.[122]

Just over fifty years later, and with the centenary of 1916 itself now in the past, the discourse surrounding the Irish language is dominated by the same focus on generational responsibility. A government-commissioned comprehensive survey of language use in the *Gaeltacht* in 2007 concluded that, without decisive intervention, the strongest *Gaeltacht* areas would survive for at most fifteen to twenty years in their current state.[123] This study was followed by a government-sponsored TV campaign urging young people in the *Gaeltacht* not to be the last generation to use Irish. It is hard to ignore predictions of terminal decline in Irish-language usage when evidenced in rigorously conducted research, as is the case with the 2007 survey and its subsequent updates. Nor is it easy to deny the grim implications this would have for the distinctive *Gaeltacht* communities to which generations of Irish people (including a young Seamus Heaney) looked as a source of unbroken cultural continuity. Yet if, as Frederic Jameson has written, postmodernity is characterised by the 'reduction to the present' and by the 'end of temporality', then what hold should the linear narratives of progress and decline exercise henceforth?[124] With regard to another closely related condition of postmodernity – the triumph of *petites histoires*, or micro-narratives, over grand narratives – it has been claimed that, under such circumstances, both Irish-language literature and folklore are ideally placed to flourish.[125]

Again, the dichotomy of the material and spiritual appears in sharp relief. It may well be that the Irish language can survive among countless future generations as an artistic medium even if its future as the medium of the material life of a community is not secure. It is perhaps for this reason that Máirtín Ó Cadhain regarded 'art is long and time is fleeting' as among the greatest of all truths.[126] Nevertheless, when, towards the end of his life, Ó Cadhain examined the purpose of what he had set out to achieve as a writer, he pointed to the material progress of the revival. Writing in Irish, he remarked, was part of the action required to enable communities that had been broken down to be re-established. Revivalism for Ó Cadhain was not about an essentialist quest for authenticity or a restoration of the past but, rather, a radical renewal of the present. For this reason it was clearly a matter of pride to him that the grandchildren of the non-Irish-speaking W.B. Yeats were 'native Irish speakers who had been raised in Dublin'.[127] In the same way, while discussing Irish revivalism in the twenty-first century, Seamus Heaney noted that for several generations it seemed there would always be a conflict between pietas and modernity. This, he felt, had now been replaced by composure and self-confidence, and, as such, the Irish language seemed now to bespeak 'parturition and the prospect of new life'.[128] With all of this in mind, it seems certain that those who value the Irish language may, as ever, be required to look beyond the irreversible, linear plane of progress and decline, and, after Deleuze, adopt a Bergsonian view of time where past and present are fully integrated and in which *becoming*, not *being*, is the thing.

CHAPTER 6

Utopia, Place and Displacement from Myles na gCopaleen's Corca Dorcha to Nuala Ní Dhomhnaill's *Murúcha*

In March 1952 a radio debate took place between Brian Ó Nualláin (Flann O'Brien/Myles na gCopaleen), Máirtín Ó Cadhain and the publisher Seán Ó hÉigeartaigh on the topic of 'Literature in Irish Today'. Ó Nualláin's remarks began with a decidedly bleak and paradoxical assessment of the subject: 'I agree with Bishop Berkeley who believed that there can be no sound without an ear listening, and that which cannot be seen – does not exist. There can be no literature without a readership. There is no readership worth speaking of in Ireland.'[1] Having resorted to metaphysics to prove that literature in Irish did not exist, Ó Nualláin had proposed a paradox that was rooted in his own upbringing as a 'native speaker' of Irish who was not native to any *Gaeltacht* or Irish-speaking community. The paradox extended to his adult life, where he was also a highly regarded writer in Irish, author of the celebrated satirical *Gaeltacht* novel *An Béal Bocht* (1941) – translated as *The Poor Mouth* (1973) – and numerous Irish articles in his renowned *Irish Times* column 'Cruiskeen Lawn'.[2] In citing Berkeley to express a fundamental metaphysical doubt about the existence of Irish literature, na gCopaleen/Ó Nualláin echoes a question asked by the narrator of his own *An Béal Bocht*, 'Are you certain that the Gaels are people?'[3]

Brian Ó Nualláin/Flann O'Brien/Myles na gCopaleen (1911–66) was a child of the Revival, one of the first generation of children whose parents were inspired by the Gaelic League to raise their family as Irish speakers outside of the historic Irish-speaking community. This anomalous position was one that caused Ó Nualláin to question and even resent the primacy of the *Gaeltacht* as the locus of Gaeldom. In so doing, he anticipated a still unresolved tradition of metaphysical doubt regarding the *Gaeltacht* itself. The origin of this uncertainty is intrinsically linked to the word *Gaeltacht*, the meaning of which changed during the late nineteenth-century Gaelic Revival from 'the state of being Gaelic' to denoting a specific, yet notoriously ill-defined, place where Irish was spoken.[4] What that place has come to represent has been, simultaneously, the seat of an authentic historical continuity and the object of an unattained revivalist desire or utopian longing. The tension between these two seemingly contradictory categories – on the one hand a self-evident material authenticity, and on the other an elusive alterity – is the focus of this chapter. What is being considered here, in other words, is how the real and the imaginary are represented by place and displacement in Irish literature of the twentieth and twenty-first centuries. As the title suggests, the range of texts discussed spans the early work of Myles na gCopaleen in the 1930s and the *Murúcha* (Merfolk) poems of Nuala Ní Dhomhnaill, a bilingual collection of which was published in 2007.[5] Tír Fó Thoinn (Land Under Wave) is the mythical place from which the Merfolk have been supposedly estranged, and the absence of which is played out in their new land-bound environment.

As the semantic shift brought about by the Gaelic League revival demonstrates, revivalism can involve a reinterpretation of place as much as a renegotiation of time. In both instances it seems that the trauma of loss leads to an attempted retrieval of the past time or a past place. Yet the possibility of retrieval, in both cases, is mired in doubt. How can we reinstate the past of an Irish-speaking Ireland or recover a place, such as the Blasket Islands community, that no longer exists except as a memory? The significance of the retrieval is more likely to lie in the impulse itself, in the desire rather than in the outcome. This desire is often characterised as impractical and illusionary, yet it is a persistent and universally attested mode of thinking generally referred to as utopianism. Although the term itself originates in Thomas More's *Utopia* (1516), utopian desire is an immemorial feature of human societies closely related to religious belief.[6] Indeed, the Hiberno-Latin voyage tale *Navigatio Sancti Brendani Abbatis* (Voyage of St Brendan), in which the eponymous saint seeks the *terra repromissionis* (promised land), has rightly been identified as an eighth-century precursor to More's classic text.[7] The *Navigatio* itself was part of a tradition of Irish and Hiberno-Latin voyage tales, known in Irish as *immrama* (ocean voyages; literally, 'rowings about'), and it is possible that More had read, or was at least aware of, an English translation of the *Navigatio*, which was printed by Caxton's Westminster Press between 1484 and 1527.[8] Wider afield, there are numerous expressions of utopian thought in antiquity, of which one might briefly mention the Sumerian clay tablets, the eighth-century-BC poetry of Hesiod, and Plato's *Republic* and *Laws*.[9]

The literal meaning of More's fictional island, 'no place', reminds us that utopia is primarily concerned with the quest rather than the discovery, with the imagining rather than the realisation. It is with this dichotomy of the imaginary and the real that we must begin our discussion of how a revivalist tradition of hope and desire is expressed through place and, indeed, displacement. If we are to understand a tradition of utopian desire, it seems natural that we should consult that body of thought for which desire is its stock-in-trade, namely psychoanalysis. The counterargument to this is that psychoanalysis is the province of the individual rather than the collective. On the other hand, as mentioned in Chapter 1, the so-called 'Freudian left' and 'Lacanian left' are evidence of how psychoanalytical theory can be applied to the broadest societal considerations. Quite simply, if Freud felt that modern people could only look forward by looking back, if he was preoccupied by 'whether it is possible for modern people to have new experiences, to find new objects of desire, to improvise upon their pasts', then he was preoccupied by the same issues that define revivalism.[10] The interdependence of literature and psychoanalytical theory is equally evident in the remark attributed to Freud: 'wherever I go I find a poet has been there before me'.[11] Similarly, Freud's illustrious heir Jacques Lacan was indebted to the interpretation of literature as a means of propagating his own theory of psychoanalysis. A prominent example of this is Lacan's analysis of Edgar Allan Poe's story *The Purloined Letter*, a seminal exposition of his method and the essay he chose to introduce his major collection of writings, *Écrits* (1966).[12] It is in Lacan's work that we find the most intriguing insights into the dichotomy of imaginary and real that animates revivalism, but in order to better explain this, the relevant aspects of Lacanian theory will be presented first in summary.

Crucially for this discussion, the imaginary and real are two parts of the trinity that underpins Lacanian psychoanalytic theory – that is, the real, the imaginary and the symbolic. As with Freud's id, ego and superego, Lacan's triad is proposed as a model that underlies all human psychology. However, the real in Lacan's scheme is not what we call reality but, rather, the part of human experience that constantly eludes us. Just as in Freudian theory the Oedipal myth and the childhood castration complex are part of the universal conditions of human development, in Lacan's work the real corresponds to a primal trauma or rupture that we struggle to apprehend. The real is also associated with the mother, since it is from the mother that the child must first separate. For Lacan the real is that elusive thing that haunts our psychic life: 'this something faced with which all words cease and all categories fail, the object of anxiety *par excellence*'.[13] The implications for the study of revivalism of Lacan's three orders of 'real, imaginary and symbolic' will hopefully become clear as we consider the imaginary, in particular. For the time being, the significance of the real in Lacanian theory is in its correspondence with that essential separation or trauma of loss that is a precondition for revivalism. The 'object of anxiety par excellence' for the revivalist is the language, custom, art, or other value that has been lost.

Lacan's 'imaginary order' is best understood in what he calls the 'mirror stage'. This is where a young infant first sees himself in a reflective surface and perceives a sense of unified wholeness. Yet this wholeness is mistaken given that the child has not yet mastered motor skills and is still essentially inchoate. Nevertheless, the child identifies with this false image of unified wholeness, and, in so doing, identifies with something other than that which he is. This has vital implications for Lacan's view of the subject – the 'otherness' of the mirror image becomes internal to the subject but is not recognised for what it is. In other words, 'recognition coincides with a profound misrecognition'.[14] The third and final order, the symbolic, generally denotes language, laws and the restrictions of society. It is closely related to the imaginary, and refers to that which is there before the subject and into which he has to be inserted.

Where revivalism is concerned, Lacan's 'imaginary order' speaks particularly to our understanding of identity formation. If we accept Lacan's account of the development of the subject and the inherent 'misrecognition' that pervades this process, then this casts the revivalist project of restoring a lost identity in a new light. The problem with restoring this identity is that it was never fixed to begin with but, rather, constantly mediated. Nevertheless, by imagining himself as something that he is not yet, the revivalist is simply engaging one of the three fundamentals of human existence, namely the imaginary order. Equally, the desire to rediscover is a universal concern, or as Lacan puts it, 'The subject is there to rediscover where it was – I anticipate – the real.'[15] However, the real is that which cannot ever be retrieved or fully apprehended, it is that which is impossible. This brings us back to desire, which, for Lacan, as with Freud, is never fulfilled but, rather, a constant.[16] Seen in this context the eternally elusive end of the revivalist project and the 'ever defeated, yet undefeated' spirit of revivalism are really just a reflection of the constancy of desire.[17]

Regarding our understanding of place, Lacanian theory has further insights for revivalism. If the real is the psychoanalytic equivalent of the Fall and expulsion of man from Eden, then the lost place is the object of our anxiety. In a similar way Lacan's split subject, whereby there is no anchored autonomous ego, marks a shift or displacement of the subject as a fixed, unambiguous point of reference.[18] 'Displacement' in psychoanalysis is also the term used to describe how interest in one object or activity is transferred to another, so that the latter becomes its equivalent or substitute.[19] How this relates to Irish revivalism is that place has become an abstraction, more a notional proposition than a fixed point of certainty – that is, place has been displaced. The *Gaeltacht* is our case study here. As mentioned earlier, prior to the late nineteenth-century revival era, the term *Gaeltacht* was not used in Ireland to speak of a place but, rather, a state of being Gaelic. The state of being Gaelic did not as yet need to be referenced to a place, although in Scotland the word *Gaeltacht* had been used to denote a place from the eighteenth century onwards. In Ireland the Gaelic League revival was largely responsible for this shift in both the meaning ascribed to *Gaeltacht* and the designation of a generally ill-defined place called *Gaeltacht*.[20] Although much of the west and far south of Ireland could be reliably deemed part of this *Gaeltacht*, many other areas existed in an indeterminate state of Gaeldom, for which the term *Breac-Ghaeltacht* (literally, Speckled *Gaeltacht*) was required. The founding of the Irish Free State in 1922 saw the *Gaeltacht* now become the responsibility of the state and, one might say after Lacan, its object of anxiety par excellence.

The official *Gaeltacht*, as it came to be known by the state, was notoriously elusive and required several government commissions to seek to define its physical coordinates and its essential characteristics – to determine, for example, how it was distinguished from the compromised *Breac-Ghaeltacht*.[21] Although the state regarded the *Gaeltacht* as the embodiment of its own self-image, like the infant in Lacan's mirror stage, recognition was marked by a profound misrecognition. For one thing, *Gaeltacht* areas continued to suffer high levels of economic deprivation and emigration, which belied the state's commitment to them. Moreover, the Irish language was not embraced by the state's ruling elite as the everyday language that it was in the *Gaeltacht*. Rather, too frequently the Irish language was a thing one aspired to rather than part of lived experience. Ultimately, the shift to *Gaeltacht* as a place allowed the state to kick the Irish language into touch – the language was now elsewhere. The signs reading *Gaeltacht* that have been erected over the past twenty years in uninhabited bogland are a bizarre testimony to the no-place that has been chosen to represent the unattainable desire of the state. Indeed, they epitomise the 'arbitrariness of the sign', one of the founding precepts of Saussurian structuralist linguistics under whose influence Lacan developed his psychoanalytic theory.[22]

The *Gaeltacht* construct has been explored in numerous literary and imaginative forms, the most celebrated being Myles na gCopaleen's satire *An Béal Bocht* (1941). Before considering this novel in detail, it is worth breaking with chronology to look at a more recent satire that affords us a panorama of the twentieth century and of the history of the state's acquisition and management of the *Gaeltacht*. This is Darach Ó Scolaí's play *Coinneáil Orainn* (2005) – literally, (We) Keep Going – the first in a trilogy of *Gaeltacht* plays.[23] *Coinneáil Orainn*'s central conceit is that the Department of Gaels, Gaelic and Gaelicism is endeavouring to keep the last two native speakers of Irish within their final enclave, a patch of land that later transpires to be the trees in the central reservation of a dual carriageway. For their part, the last two native speakers, a middle-aged male called *An Caiptín* (The Captain) and a young man called Seáinín, are under the impression that they are fighting a last-ditch guerrilla war against the state. In a verbal report to the department secretary, one of the department's inspectors uses a flipchart to explain just how this situation has come about. When the state was founded in 1922 there were 100,000 native speakers resident in the state and just two officials employed in the Department of Gaels, Gaelic and Gaelicism. The last available statistics, from 2005, show that there were, at that point, 10,000 native speakers left. The inspector has estimated that at present there are now just two native speakers and 99,998 officials in the department. As the secretary of the department remarks, 'The more Irish speakers that were hired to save the language, the less there were to speak it.'[24] When the inspector explains that he has discovered the last two native speakers and has managed to record their speech, the department secretary points out to him the existential dilemma that this evidence represents for the department. As she explains, 'When the last inspector finds the last [native] Irish speakers and gives them their [state] grant, the whole thing will be over.'[25] Needless to say that the evidence goes no further. In the final scene of the play the inspector consoles himself with the knowledge that, as long as the government thinks that Irish is being spoken in the hills out west, he will be kept busy pushing a pen and amassing paper.[26]

The sense of the *Gaeltacht* being a contrivance of the state was ironically forecast by J.P. Mahaffy (1839–1919), provost of Trinity College, Dublin, one of the Gaelic League's most powerful critics and sometime nemesis of its president, Douglas Hyde. In an 1899 essay entitled 'The Recent Fuss About the Irish Language', Mahaffy remarked:

> If we could still preserve in the few remote glens or moors the Irish which is still the natural speech of the natives, it would also preserve a peculiar and a charming type of man and woman, and I for one should be ready to make considerable sacrifices to do so. But I can only see one effectual method. The high roads leading into such a sanctum must be broken up; no light railways must be allowed to approach it by land, or steamers by sea; that noxious animal the tourist must be rigorously forbidden to profane it with his modern vulgarities and his demands for modern comforts. Such a policy might be effectual; it would at all events be honest; unfortunately it would also be absurd.[27]

The background to this article was the controversy over the 1899 Vice-regal Inquiry into Irish and Intermediate Education, during which Hyde successfully defended the Irish language from the disparaging representations made by Mahaffy and his colleague, Robert Atkinson. Hyde went on to write a satirical play inspired by the controversy, which he called *Pleusgadh na Bulgóide; or, The Bursting of the Bubble* (1903). The bubble here is the rarefied sphere of the Trinity College professor that bears no relation to the rest of the country. In Hyde's play the two professors are bewitched by the *Seanbhean Bhocht* (Poor Old Woman), an apple seller whose Irish-speaking and allegedly seditious intentions incite Mac Eathfaidh (Mahaffy) to roughly expel her from the college grounds. On so doing, however, Mahaffy and his colleagues in the college common room promptly find that they can speak only Irish. This, of course, leads to acute embarrassment, particularly when they are paid a visit by the viceroy and his wife. The farce is resolved when the Poor Old Woman returns and frees them of her spell with a final withering denunciation: 'You don't belong to this island in which God placed you, you are like people suspended half-way between the ground and the sky. You belong to neither country nor land.'[28] There was much justification in this epithet insofar as Trinity College, under Mahaffy, was a bastion of colonial exclusivity. The irony is that, after nearly 100 years of an independent state, the last foothold of the native Irish speaker should be similarly imagined in Ó Scolaí's play as the quintessentially liminal space – the trees of the central reservation of a dual carriageway.

It is little wonder that *An Caiptín* in *Coinneáil Orainn* articulates his various existential crises by asking if he is not like someone who has fallen asleep for three or four hundred years only to awake among strangers. Is he like the Japanese soldier who remained on guard on a little island for forty years after the end of the war, or, indeed, Oisín, who returns to Ireland to find the *Fianna* have long since died?[29] In Ó Scolaí's play the state's formula for maintaining the *Gaeltacht* as the fictional place to which the Irish language has been consigned is the revelation that the last two native speakers must never be discovered so that the fiction can be maintained indefinitely. This same paradox is discussed by Jean Baudrillard in relation to the Tasaday tribe of the Philippines. The Tasadays were discovered in 1971 having apparently spent 800 years in the forest without any outside contact. The government of the Philippines decided that the ethnological value of this find was so significant that the Tasaday's pristinely primitive state could not be disturbed. With this in mind, they prohibited any contact between the Tasaday and the outside world, with the exception of certain special visitors. Controversy has ensued ever since as to whether the Tasaday were the genuinely primitive isolated people they had appeared to be. For Baudrillard the purpose of preserving their state of isolation was so that ethnology itself could be preserved: 'in order to save its reality principle. The Tasady, frozen in their natural element, will provide a perfect alibi, an eternal guarantee.'[30]

Just as the title of Ó Scolaí's play, *Coinneáil Orainn* ((We) Keep Going), echoes the opening and final words of Samuel Beckett's *The Unnamable* (1953), the play makes numerous allusions to *Waiting for Godot* (1952).[31] More generally, the metaphysical farce set within an alienated landscape is unmistakably Beckettian, and, indeed, this treatment of the landscape of Connemara is anticipated in *Waiting for Godot* in lines spoken by Lucky: 'Stark naked in the stockinged feet in Connemara' and 'the skull in Connemara'.[32] Unlike Martin McDonagh's play *A Skull in Connemara* (1997), strictly speaking Connemara does not feature in *Coinneáil Orainn*, although the two native speakers speak Connemara Irish. The assumption is that this *Gaeltacht* area has shifted to a bleaker terrain. Accordingly, the metaphysical bind in which the protagonists of *Coinneáil Orainn* find themselves is reflected in a landscape that is starker still and from which there is no more prospect of relief. The central motif here is that place is now an abstraction that has lost all of its previous associations. In particular, the association between the Irish language and a specific ancestral territory has been completely dissolved.

It would be wrong to suggest that Connemara or the *Gaeltacht* in

Ó Scolaí's trilogy of *Gaeltacht* plays are in themselves being satirised. What is being satirised is the state's abstraction of the *Gaeltacht* into an object of unreachable desire. In this sense Ó Scolaí's plays follow the counter-pastoral of Liam O'Flaherty, Patrick Kavanagh and Máirtín Ó Cadhain in debunking, from the inside, the romantic illusion of rural Ireland. In Ó Scolaí's case his commitment to the Irish-speaking community within which he resides is indivisible from his own mortality, or, as he has put it, 'it is as difficult for me to think of the fate that hangs over us, never mind speak or write about it, as it is to imagine my own death'.[33] This unmediated identification with his linguistic community is what sets him apart from the state's flawed self-identification with the *Gaeltacht*.

While the state took responsibility for the *Gaeltacht* after the founding of the Irish Free State, as mentioned earlier, the initiation of the *Gaeltacht* construct itself has been attributed to the revivalist movement of the late nineteenth century. Thus, in one of the early satirical pieces by Myles na gCopaleen/Flann O'Brien/Brian Ó Nualláin, the inhabitant of a ludicrously stereotypical *Gaeltacht* area asks his local priest in abject exasperation who it was that created him and this miserable country.[34] The priest replies that God had no part in it, explaining instead that two Gaelic literati from Dublin were the creators of this dystopia. Peadar Dubh (Black Peter) promptly sets off for Dublin with his double-barrelled shotgun to put the situation to rights. *Eachtra Pheadair Dhuibh* (The Tale of Black Peter) is generally seen as a forerunner of the same author's satirical masterpiece *An Béal Bocht*, published in 1941 under the pseudonym Myles na gCopaleen.[35] Corca Dorcha, the setting of *An Béal Bocht*, is a seemingly timeless 'no place' that incorporates a composite *Gaeltacht* before and after 1922, when it became the responsibility of the state – in this way, both revivalists and the state are included as objects of the ensuing satire.[36]

The novel's main character, Bónapárt Ó Cúnasa, relates his life story to date in a rain-drenched, fate-ridden quagmire of *Gaeltacht* clichés. As his father has been imprisoned, Bónapárt is raised by his mother and *An Seanduine Liath* (The Old Grey Fellow). The series of episodes that unfolds largely follows an anarchic parody of the *Gaeltacht* autobiographies, particularly *An tOileánach* (1929), or *The Islandman*, by Tomás Ó Criomhthain, and the novels and short stories of Séamus Ó Grianna. An example of this is Bónapárt's first day at school, where the master beats him and his classmates into accepting that they are all called Jams O'Donnell. This is based on the episode in Ó Grianna's *Caisleáin Óir* (Castles of Gold) (1924) in which the schoolmaster beats the novel's hero on his first day at school when the latter gives his name as the local Irish patronymic Séimí Phádraig Duibh rather than the English Christian name and surname James O'Donnell.[37] Na gCopaleen's novel goes on to describe the arrival of urban Irish-language enthusiasts in Corca Dorcha and the various mishaps that befall Bónapárt until his final incarceration after a bizarre court appearance. It is in this final chapter that Bónapárt meets his father for the first time – just as his father is released after twenty-nine years in prison, Bónapárt is taken off to serve exactly the same sentence. Both the prison motif and circularity of this final episode are a fitting conclusion to a novel in which poverty, fate and language are trapped in an endless spiral of futility. The name of na gCopaleen' fictional *Gaeltacht* is most probably a play on Corca Dhuibhne (Dingle Peninsula), just as *The Islandman*, the autobiography of Tomás Ó Criomhthain from the outlying Blasket Islands, is its most frequently cited influence.[38] While *An Béal Bocht* parodies Ó Criomhthain's book, na gCopaleen described it in one of his *Irish Times* columns as 'the superbest of all books I have ever read'.[39] This is just one of the many contradictions and complexities with which we associate the multifarious voices of Brian Ó Nualláin. Where *An Béal Bocht* is concerned, however, if there is a key to understanding Ó Nualláin's motivations it lies arguably in his identification of the Irish language with family rather than with place, and the anomaly of his own family's non-*Gaeltacht* and, so, non-native provenance.

Crucially, the twelve children of Micheal O'Nolan and Agnes Gormley were one of the first generations of Irish speakers raised by parents who were non-native speakers attached to the Gaelic League revival. They were also one of a growing number of Gaelic League families who reclaimed the original Irish form of their surnames. When completing the family's census return for 1911, the year of Brian's birth, his father entered all of the details in Irish. The census enumerator, it appears, inserted English translations below each entry, but when it came to the children's names, no English translation was given – rather, they appear in Irish and then in Irish again, albeit in roman characters.[40] The impression being thus created, inadvertently or otherwise, was that the children's names could not be translated into English, as though to mark the new generation's reversal of language shift. One of a number of prominent Gaelic Leaguers who worked as customs and mail officers, Mícheál Ó Nualláin's job required him to shift the family home from its beginnings in Strabane, County Tyrone to various locations before the family finally settled in Dublin from 1923 onwards. Probably on account of the family's frequent relocation, Brian was not sent to school until he was twelve years of age. Instead, his father directed the education of the children, including Irish – by post when necessary. Reading Ciarán Ó Nualláin's memoir of his brother's youth, *Óige an Dearthár* (The Brother's Youth) (1973), it is clear that the Ó Nualláin children had a very different upbringing from their peers. While Ciarán regretted that they rarely played with other children, he considered the lack of formal schooling to be the key to an idyllic freedom.[41] In a similar way, the anomaly of their upbringing contained a potentially liberating development in that their Gaelic identity was not dependent on a relation to place but, rather, on the ideal of a national cultural revival. To this extent the Ó Nualláin family typified the stage of development in nationalism described by Ernest Gellner as the 'establishment of an anonymous impersonal society' held together by a shared culture in place of the previous myriad local groups sustained by folk cultures.[42]

Just as the eldest Ó Nualláin children had a very late and fraught initiation to the unwelcoming society of the schoolyard, as recounted in Ciarán's memoir, their place in newly independent Gaelic Ireland was subject to the same undermining doubt.[43] After all, they were not native speakers of Irish from the *Gaeltacht* but urban, non-native, native speakers without the continuity of connection to an ancestral Irish-speaking community. While their parents and extended family had a long-standing association with various Irish colleges in the *Gaeltacht*, this was as outsiders who travelled to the *Gaeltacht* to learn or perfect their Irish. This makes the first trips to the Donegal *Gaeltacht* from 1927 onwards, recalled by Ciarán Ó Nualláin, particularly intriguing.[44] Ciarán describes the life they witnessed as the end of an era depicted in the books of Séamus Ó Grianna, an *oeuvre* which Brian would later satirise in *An Béal Bocht*. Meeting girls whose daily language was the same as theirs was one of the few reassuring familiarities recalled in these sojourns in Donegal. More often, a sense of strangeness, both benign and bizarre, was registered. The sight of two old men dressed in traditional *glaisín* clothing and the attendance at a wake in which clay pipes and snuff were circulated seem to have confirmed their anticipation of the passing world they would encounter in the *Gaeltacht*. The bizarre, for well-heeled youths from Blackrock, was to be given a tiny piece of meat from their host as a special gift, or to witness an elderly woman hop for long distances on one leg, relieved only by short breaks when she threw herself into the nearest ditch to catch her breath.[45] These last incidents may have inspired some of the egregious poverty parodied in *An Béal Bocht*, just as the novel's 'hunting in the Rosses' episode may originate in the hunting expedition retold in Ciarán's memoir.[46]

If the daily language used by the girls in the *Gaeltacht* was the same one used by the Ó Nualláin children in Dublin, they clearly had very little else in common. To have encountered this profound otherness in the only continuous speech community available to them must have been, at the very least, a disconcerting experience. Given that their childhood identity had been marked by a certain social and linguistic separation, it might have been expected that going to the *Gaeltacht* would represent a return of sorts. Conversely, the inability to freely identify with the first Irish-speaking community they found may well have been an alienating experience. This would certainly have been compounded by the state's valorisation of the *Gaeltacht* as its own ideal self-image. Those who fashioned the state's self-image were predominantly the generation of the Ó Nualláins' parents, people who had learned Irish as a second language, whereas the Ó Nualláin children had known Irish as their first and most intimate language. This being the case, why should the state not have made the Ó Nualláin children and others like them their ideal? With all of this in mind, Ó Nualláin's disdain for the official revivalist project – a feature of his 'Cruiskeen Lawn' column and unpublished essay subtitled 'The Pathology of Revivalism', together with the parody of revivalists in *An Béal Bocht* – must be understood within the complex of the author's upbringing as a non-*Gaeltacht*, and thus unrecognised, native speaker of Irish.[47] With regard to the *Gaeltacht*, Ian Ó Caoimh's discussion of Brian, Ciarán and their classicist/folklorist brother Caoimhin's shared aesthetics is of signal importance, especially in the brothers' 'representation of Irish-speaking localities, both real and imagined, as places apart where the figurative is taken literally and the surreal implications explored'.[48]

Although the *Gaeltacht* autobiographies, referred to ironically in *An Béal Bocht* as the *dea-leabhair* (good books), are the most obvious source of parody, it is very possible that the author's uncle, Rev. Gearóid Ó Nualláin (1874–1942), provided at least some of the grist for his nephew's mill. Fr Gearóid was a favourite of his nephews, whose visits were a source of great amusement and diversion.[49] For one thing, he was a master of card tricks and legerdemain, and to this was added his dialect of Munster Irish that differed greatly from the Irish spoken by his brother's family, which was most influenced by the Donegal dialect of Cloughaneely. The mere fact that two brothers, the uncle and father of the Ó Nualláins, spoke radically differently dialects is testimony to the disconnection with place that marked the young Ó Nualláins' experience of Irish. Fr Gearóid was also a noted scholar of Irish, being professor of Irish at Maynooth and also president of the *Gaeltacht* Irish college at Béal

Átha an Ghaorthaidh, County Cork. In March 1938, four years before his death, he dispatched his autobiography, written in Irish, to the state publisher (An Gúm) asking for it to be considered for publication. Although the book was not published until 1950, there is evidence to suggest that Brian Ó Nualláin was aware of the contents of his uncle's autobiography *Beatha Dhuine a Thoil* (One's Life Is One's Will) when he was writing *An Béal Bocht* between February 1940 and April 1941. In a fascinating interlude between the death of Fr Gearóid and the book's publication, two of Brian Ó Nualláin's uncles, Feargus (a playwright and former teacher at Pearse's Sgoil Éanna) and Peadar (a priest of the Carmelite order), wrote to An Gúm as representatives of the Ó Nualláin and Gormley families to ask for certain parts of the book to be removed before publication. In the course of their subsequent correspondence they provided a very valuable insight into the author himself and his extended family. In one letter the brothers mention a 'relative' who had read the 'script' and criticised its many clichés and repetitions.[50] This seems unlikely to have been Ciarán Ó Nualláin since he is mentioned, in a letter to An Gúm in 1973, as one of the relatives asking to see the original manuscript so as to reveal what information had been excluded from it in publication.[51] As Brian Ó Nualláin had been well established as a journalistic writer in Irish at the time that his uncle had written and was revising his manuscript autobiography in consultation with An Gúm, it is quite possible that Fr Gearóid asked his nephew to give his opinion of it and that he, then, was the 'relative' who had read the original 'script'. This likelihood increases when we consider that the faults identified by this first reader – the abundance of hackneyed clichés and worn-out conventionalisms – were a celebrated target of Myles na gCopaleen's *Irish Times* column.[52] The fact that Fr Gearóid was a conscious imitator of Fr Peadar Ó Laoghaire, whom na gCopaleen castigated for having 'brought parochialism in language … to the stage of hysteria', adds further weight to the case.[53]

Even if it was not the case that Brian had read the manuscript, it is very likely that the numerous rambling anecdotes that make up the autobiography were the subject of his uncle's conversations with him and his siblings. Indeed, the entire book is marked and often marred by a highly digressive, conversational narrative style.[54] The first point of similarity between *Beatha Dhuine a Thoil* and *An Béal Bocht* is the name given to the latter's fictional *Gaeltacht*, Corca Dorcha – literally, [Place of] Dark People/Race. Describing his first trip to the *Gaeltacht* area of Béal Átha an Ghaorthaidh, County Cork, Fr Ó Nualláin recalls that 'although it was the month of July, it was very cold

and it was as dark as hell when we reached the place'.[55] The Corca Dorcha of
An Béal Bocht is, as its name suggests, a dark place whose unrelenting misery
is characterised by its eternally harsh weather and unrelieved poverty. The first
ray of sunlight that has ever come to Corca Dorcha coincides with the arrival
of the first *duine uasal* (gentleman) to speak Irish, a circumstance that is initially interpreted as a harbinger of the apocalypse but is soon followed by the
arrival of other gentlemen and ladies from Dublin, referred to afterwards as
Gaeilgeoirí (Irish speakers).[56] Fr Ó Nualláin's first trip to Coláiste na Mumhan
(Béal Átha an Ghaorthaidh Irish college) was made in the year of its opening,
1904, and like the city ladies and gentlemen who flock to Corca Dorcha to
waylay the natives with their incomprehensible Irish, he inflicted his limited
command of Ulster Irish on old people who spoke no English.[57] Yet in the case
of both Fr Gearóid and the fictional *Gaeilgeoirí* of *An Béal Bocht*, the initial
innocence is quickly succeeded by a mania for authenticity and a process of
unreciprocated appropriation where the language is concerned. An indication
of the former is when Fr Gearóid tells us that the jarvey who brought him to
Béal Átha an Ghaorthaidh did not really have as good Irish as he had initially
thought. The jarvey's use of the Ulster Irish interrogative *'tuige* was the telltale
flaw in the driver's speech.[58] Similarly, in *An Béal Bocht* one of the *Gaeilgeoirí*
queries the use of the word *meath* (decline) by one of the locals (*An Seanduine/*
The Old Grey Fellow) on the grounds that it was not to be found in the work
of Munster author Rev. Peadar Ó Laoghaire.[59] In Fr Gearóid's autobiography,
reading Fr Peadar's novel *Séadna* is the key to his rapid acquisition of the
Munster dialect, and Fr Peadar becomes for him, as he was to many in the
Gaelic League, the fountainhead of native authenticity.[60]

The cult of authenticity is undoubtedly part of the outsiders' appropriation of nativeness from the natives themselves. By developing and insisting
on a particular code of authenticity, the outsiders began to take possession
of the thing they had initially come to learn. In *An Béal Bocht*, not only
does the narrator describe how the affluent outsiders divest the locals of their
dea-Ghaeilge (fine Irish) and leave little in the way of remuneration, they
come to surpass the natives' own 'Gaelicness'. This happens when some of the
outsiders start to wear women's dresses – a reference to the Gaelic Leaguers'
mistaken revival of the kilt. This rapid appropriation of the native sphere is
reflected in Fr Gearóid's elevation from hapless learner to a professor of the
Irish college within two years of his first visit; he later became its president.[61]
In *An Béal Bocht*, although the initiative to hold a *feis* (festival) in Corca
Dorcha to raise funds for an Irish college comes from a local (*An Seanduine/*

The Old Grey Fellow), all the other officers are drawn from the ranks of the outsiders. Ultimately, allowing The Old Grey Fellow to be treasurer turns out to be a mistake as his only contribution is to steal the president's watch, perhaps an oblique reference to the old Aran Islands man who asked Synge for a clock.[62] Indeed, the class division that is accentuated in the *feis* scene (the poor natives arrive on foot with turnips and potatoes in their pockets, the *Gaeilgeoirí* arrive in their cars) presages the complete appropriation of the native sphere by the *Gaeilgeoirí* – with the exception of The Old Grey Fellow, the entire *feis* proceedings are conducted by the outsiders.

Perhaps the most telling likeness between Fr Gearóid Ó Nualláin's patronage of the Béal Átha an Ghaorthaidh *Gaeltacht* and the antics of the *Gaeilgeoirí* in *An Béal Bocht* is in one of the novel's most sublime episodes, the circumlocution and self-referential bombast of the *feis* speeches, beginning with the president's address. Here the gathering is exhorted to speak only about the Irish language when speaking Irish, a matter of such grave importance that an inaugural Irish-speaking competition is devoted to this very aim. The five competitors talk incessantly until midnight, at which point their faculties have been so exhausted that one competitor succumbs to a deadly fever while another becomes permanently dumb, having spoken all the Irish that was in his head. Fr Gearóid had himself been president of the *feis* as well as the Munster Irish college, and his discussions of all things Gaelic frequently exhibit the same repetitive, introspective vacuity that is lampooned in *An Béal Bocht*.[63] He even appears to have suffered the same fate as the dumbstruck *feis* competitor when, in sending his lengthy autobiography to An Gúm, he declared that he was tired of writing in Irish and wished to continue the correspondence in English.[64]

The sense of the *Gaeilgeoirí* appropriating the native sphere and surpassing the natives' own nativeness is alluded to quite directly in the correspondence of Fr Gearóid's brothers to An Gúm regarding their late brother's autobiography, where they remark that, 'Although his style was in its inception a meticulous imitation of the late Canon O'Leary's [Fr Peadar Ó Laoghaire], he soon outstripped and outshone his model, gradually shedding O'Leary's mannerisms and artificialities.'[65] The brothers even imputed the formless narrative adopted by Fr Gearóid to his eagerness to replicate the fusion of personality and style in the *oeuvre* of Fr Peadar, whom of course Fr Gearóid had exceeded.[66] Fr Gearóid's brothers were remarkably assured of their late sibling's genius, declaring him to be 'incomparably the greatest and most finished Gaelic scholar of his time', and their judgement of the literary triumph of his autobiography, certain troublesome chapters and general infelicities excepted, was to rank it among the six or seven best in the history of literature.[67] Reading such assured *ex cathedra* pronouncements, one wonders if Fr Gearóid's brothers were not engaging in the type of faux pomposity that was a staple of Myles na gCopaleen's column. Similarly, the penchant for comic incongruity in the brothers' commentary on their scholarly sibling is scarcely distinguishable from the 'Cruiskeen Lawn':

> [Fr Gearóid] was also a man of very wide and profound general culture; but to the end of his life he remained as simple as a child and never acquired a practical insight into actual human life … The notion of publishing the crossword puzzles in Chapter XL (with English solutions) was grotesque and would only have occurred to an author of the most sublime simplicity.[68]

Considering that entire sections of his uncle's autobiography could easily be slipped into *An Béal Bocht*, the distinct impression is that Brian Ó Nualláin's extended family provided him with boundless comic material. More pertinently, for our discussion, are the varying ways in which the revivalist identity of the extended Ó Nualláin family relates to the idealised places of Gaelic Ireland. Fr Gearóid Ó Nualláin had effectively appropriated the native *Gaeltacht* sphere, and was credited for this by his brothers, but the assiduous imitation of a model also precluded any originality. This fact was admitted by Fr Gearóid's brothers, who nevertheless concluded that such an abundance of clichés could be 'taken as approved by Gaelic taste', a judgement that was not shared by their fellow reader and relative, who seems most likely to have been Brian. That Brian Ó Nualláin/Myles na gCopaleen was not prepared to settle for a second-hand, clichéd mode of expression is unsurprising given that he was not a learner of Irish but a non-*Gaeltacht* native speaker. To accept entirely the identity of another as one's model would be to take the misrecognition in Lacan's infantile 'mirror stage' a stage further – rather than embracing a misleadingly unified image of himself, the Ó Nualláin infant would be embracing an entirely different child as his self-image. If Brian resolutely rejected the *Gaeltacht* as his model, refusing to become the 'simulacrum of a western farm labourer', its power as an ideal was nevertheless something that he clearly recognised, as is evident from his reaction to reading Ó Criomhthain's *The Islandman*, whose impact on him he described as 'explosive'.[69] It is interesting to note that, as a young man, Brian's brother Ciarán shared his parents' generation's idealisation of the *Gaeltacht*, commenting that the *Gaeltacht* was a place one approached with awe, 'as if the women should be more beautiful, the men more manly, the houses prettier, apples redder and fields greener than in any other place in the country'.[70]

In contradistinction to his brother, and the revivalist generation of his parents, Brian Ó Nualláin's portrayal of the *Gaeltacht* as dystopia is inevitably an assertion of his own authenticity. The name Myles na gCopaleen is itself, of course, ironically assumed from a stage Irishman in Boucicault's play *The Colleen Bawn* (1860).[71] In lampooning the *Gaeltacht*, Myles na gCopaleen is not only freeing himself from the imposition of an other's identity but he is also liberating the people of the *Gaeltacht* from their officially designated role as guardians of an unattainable and immutable ideal. *An Béal Bocht* is, in this sense, the double-barrelled shotgun with which *Peadar Dubh* dispatches his misguided creators. This motif of the character rebelling against his author is a familiar one in Brian Ó Nualláin's work, most particularly in *At Swim-Two-Birds* (1939). A closely related motif is that of the revenge killing in which the hero not only kills his oppressor but incorporates him. Thus, the short story 'Two in One' contains, as its editor Anthony Cronin summarises it, 'the story of a taxidermist who murders his hated employer, disposes of the body, retaining only the skin; and then assumes both skin and identity so that the missing person is himself, for the murder of whom he is hanged in the end'.[72] A similar tale is told in the 'Cruiskeen Lawn' column in which the narrator explains how he took revenge on his landlord by fulfilling a pledge to 'drink him under the table', in this case literally drinking him under the table, having first dissolved his corpse in acid and then consumed the contents while seated under a table.[73] This motif is at once a neat resolution of the paradox of identity formation as understood by Lacan, where the subject inevitably incorporates the *other*. It is also a reiteration of Stephen Dedalus' imagined encounter with the primordial other in Joyce's *A Portrait of the Artist as a Young Man*, the 'redrimmed horny eyes' with whom he must engage in a struggle to death for supremacy. The difference is Dedalus' realisation of the futility of such a contest: 'Till what? Till he yield to me? No. I mean him no harm.'[74]

As Maebh Long discerns in her discussion of *An Béal Bocht*, the power of naming is of crucial importance to the function of identity and subjectivity.[75] Hence the natives of Corca Dorcha are denied individuality and agency by English-language officialdom through the imposition of the universal name Jams O'Donnell. Conversely, the non-native *Gaeilgeoirí* are free to create their own fictitious personae by way of the curious monikers they invent for themselves, such as *Ochtar Fear* (Eight Men), *An Tarbh Teann* (The Formidable Bull) and *An Nóinín Gaelach* (The Gaelic Daisy). The fact that The Formidable Bull had the constitution of a mouse and The Gaelic Daisy was a sickly, corpulent fellow of utterly morbid complexion did not impede them. Again, the unintentional self-parody that, according to na gCopaleen, was a mark of the *Fíor-Ghaedhil* (True or Über-Gaels) since the beginning of the Gaelic League revival was also particularly true of Uncle Gearóid.[76] In submitting his autobiography, the mild-mannered and childlike Fr Gearóid called himself *An Gruagach Gréagach* (The Hairy Greek Goblin). He had done so as his original intention was to have his autobiography published pseudonymously, but abandoned this plan when it became clear that a renowned clerical Irish-language scholar could not retain his anonymity in an Irish-language autobiography of some 100,000 words.[77]

The spurious personal titles of *An Béal Bocht* originate in the prolific use of literary pseudonyms in the Gaelic League era, such as Douglas Hyde's own choice, *An Craoibhín Aoibhinn* (The Pleasant Little Branch), Séamus Ó Grianna's 'Máire', and Séamus Ó Dubhgaill's *Beirt Fhear* (Two Men). The latter is clearly the inspiration for *Ochtar Fear* (Eight Men), who, in *An Béal Bocht*, single-handedly conducts an 'eight-hand reel'.[78] Part of the explanation for literary pseudonyms lay in the need for those employed in the civil service to avoid any potential professional conflict that their literary output might create. It clearly added to Brian Ó Nualláin's resentment of the deference shown to *Gaeltacht* native speakers in the independent state that a significant number of Donegal authors of nostalgic *Gaeltacht* novels lived in suburban Dublin and worked in the civil service.[79] The most famous of these, Séamus Ó Grianna, refused to speak Irish to his civil service colleagues unless they were from the *Gaeltacht*.[80] This may explain the particularly merciless parodying of Ó Grianna's work in *An Béal Bocht* and na gCopaleen's unmitigated disdain for the 'loutish … present brood of Ulster "novelists"'.[81]

If the *Gaeltacht* was a construct that benefitted those who found it more convenient to have the Irish language located elsewhere, the irony that na gCopaleen had observed was that the *Gaeltacht* had itself been displaced to the capital city where the production of literature was concerned. Some of the most highly regarded *Gaeltacht* authors in the late 1930s – Séamus Ó Grianna, Seosamh Mac Grianna, Máirtín Ó Cadhain and Máirtín Ó Direáin – were based in Dublin, and all owed their livelihood to either the civil service or some other state-funded body, such as An Gúm. The somewhat disproportionate contempt with which Brian Ó Nualláin held many of these *Gaeltacht* writers must have stemmed from the lack of recognition for those, like himself, who were non-*Gaeltacht* native speakers with literary aspirations in Irish.

This frustration with the state and Irish-language establishment's valorisation of the native *Gaeltacht* speaker was apparent in the views expressed in the radio debate held between Ó Nualláin, Ó Cadhain and the publisher Seán Ó hÉigeartaigh in March 1952 on 'Literature in Irish Today'. Ó Nualláin elaborated on his criticism that literature in Irish was hampered by *Gaeltacht* parochialism, remarking that literary production in Ireland or elsewhere was a phenomenon of the city, whereas Irish-language authors were fixated on the *Gaeltacht*.[82] Naturally, the idea that literature owed its existence to cities was one that Máirtín Ó Cadhain readily contested, and seems more in keeping with one of the ill-advised pronouncements of the Ó Nualláin uncles. The notes for Brian Ó Nualláin continue, saying 'The native speaker is all very well, but he is a SPEAKER.'[83] This last emphasis is perhaps the most telling of all. In *An Béal Bocht*, speech and meaning are decoupled entirely – thus, the speaking competition finishes with the competitors mumbling incoherently, having exhausted any possible pretence towards meaning, and in the same way the overzealous folklorist mistakes the grunting of a pig for an example of pure Irish, the best Irish being itself incomprehensible.[84] Yet three years before the radio debate Máirtín Ó Cadhain had published his masterful *Cré na Cille*, which turned the relentless tide of *Gaeltacht* speech into the high art that Ó Nualláin so esteemed. Orality could no longer be disparaged as a blight on Irish literature and the *Gaeltacht* writer could no longer be dismissed as a mere medium for the fantasies of the state and the overzealous *fíor-Ghael*. Yet Ó Nualláin himself was not among *Cré na Cille*'s admirers – his brother Ciarán recalled how Brian was contemptuous of Ó Cadhain's novel, finding it completely unreadable.[85]

Nevertheless, it would be wrong to presume that Brian Ó Nualláin was unable to recognise talent and innovation among contemporary *Gaeltacht* writers. Since the early 1930s he had been an admirer of Seosamh Mac Grianna, whose *Mo Bhealach Féin* (My Way) (1940) was very different to the type of *Gaeltacht* autobiography that Ó Nualláin despised.[86] Mac Grianna, like Ó Nualláin, was utterly disillusioned with the state-led language revival, his main gripe being that since coming to Dublin to write original literature in Irish the state's publisher had instead set him translating English novels. This was compounded by An Gúm's censoring of Mac Grianna's debut novel *An Druma Mór* (The Big Drum), which, although submitted in 1930, was withheld until 1969, at which point the author was a patient of St Conall's

Hospital, County Donegal, to which he had been admitted in the late 1950s and remained until his death in 1990. Mac Grianna's acrimonious relationship with the state publisher had many origins, the most prominent being the ever-present civil-war hostilities – An Gúm was an initiative of the pro-Treaty Cumann na nGaedheal party of government; added to this was the fact that the editor was a cousin and neighbour from his native Rann na Feirste, whose familiarity with the characters and events on which *An Druma Mór* was based led him to alert An Gúm to the potentially libellous implications of publication. The thwarted development of Mac Grianna's creative output and the implicit denial of his originality was inextricably linked to the dependence of Irish-language publishing on the state. In just the same way Pádraig Ó Conaire (1882–1928) had blamed schoolchildren for ruining literature in Irish, for the reason that only literature deemed suitable for school curricula would be published in Irish.[87]

Ironically, Seosamh Mac Grianna's writer brother Séamus complained that his own books were read as mere 'collections of idioms':

> As I said in a recent article, I wrote in Irish because it was the only language that could adequately describe the life and the people I knew. I did not use Irish as a medium because it was the language of Pádraig, Brigid and Colmcille, or because it is a *'teanga bhinn bhlasta'* [mellifluous, sweet tongue]. I detest all that rubbish as does almost everybody from the Gaeltacht. The *binn-blasta-Pádraig-Brigid* mentality was and is like a *crann-smola* [blight] hanging over the Gaelic writer. No native thought, no creative talent could grow or develop under its blighting influence. I know it was useful as propaganda, perhaps necessary. But propaganda chokes art …[88]

This letter, written in 1932 to the anti-Treaty newspaper *An Phoblacht*, was in support of a previous piece by Peadar O'Donnell, who had complained that the dead middle-class mind was choking the new Gaelic voices.[89] Party politics aside, the sentiments expressed here, and by Seosamh Mac Grianna and others in this correspondence, reveal a much more self-aware cadre of Donegal *Gaeltacht* writers than na gCopaleen would credence in his acerbic assessment a decade later. The admission that the detested *binn-blasta-Pádraig-Brigid* mentality had been at one time useful as propaganda is striking. Clearly, the counter-revival polemics of Seán Ó Faoláin and others in the 1930s were not the only critical reassessment of the legacy of the Irish revolutionary period. Indeed, there was a well-established discourse of critique from within the *Gaeltacht*, exemplified by the socialist periodical *An t-Éireannach*, the first ever weekly Irish-language newspaper, which was published between 1934 and 1937. Its editors and most of its writers were from the *Gaeltacht*, and the paper had a strong *Gaeltacht* readership.[90]

The propensity of *Gaeltacht* writers to challenge the way in which the *Gaeltacht* had been reduced to a hermetically sealed space of unattainable desire is most evident in the assertion of their own creative identity. Again, the power of naming figures large. The very fact that Séamus Ó Grianna and Seosamh Mac Grianna used different prefixes (Mac/Ó) demonstrates that there was no established Irish form for their surname. Rather, they were known first and foremost by their local patronymics and English Christian names, Jimmy Fheidhlimidh and Joe Fheidhlimidh. The formal authorial convention of Christian name and surname would have been easily rendered in English as James and Joseph Greene, names that had already been standardised in census returns and other official documentation. However, the fact that no standardised Irish form of their surname existed illustrates the extent to which colonisation had stifled the organic expression of identity. In effect, colonisation was what made everyone a 'Jams O'Donnell', and this was of course the original point of this episode as described in Séamus Ó Grianna's novel *Caisleáin Óir*, a point somewhat obscured after Myles na gCopaleen had satirised it in *An Béal Bocht*. By choosing their own personal forms of their surname, both brothers were taking possession of that which had been withheld.

Perhaps the most profound attempt to forge a creative identity from within the *Gaeltacht* is Seosamh Mac Grianna's autobiography *Mo Bhealach Féin* (My Own Way) (1940). In the preamble Mac Grianna recalls, among other things, his fractious relationship with the state and the Irish-language revival that he went on to personify in the character of the martyr-artist Cathal Mac Eachmharcaigh in the unfinished novel *Dá mBíodh Ruball ar an Éan*.[91] His preamble is similar to the manifestos that were frequently employed by modernist artists to proclaim their break with convention and tradition. In Mac Grianna's case the convention and tradition that is being eschewed is primarily the bourgeois milieu of the Free State civil service to which he considered (like Brian Ó Nualláin) some of his *Gaeltacht* friends and relatives to have succumbed. However, what really sets Mac Grianna apart is that he does not replace the state's idealisation of the *Gaeltacht* with a hardened realism or counter-pastoral but, rather, makes his manifesto a declaration of the most

ardent utopianism. The ideal place that Mac Grianna seeks is beautifully visu-
alised in the opening paragraphs of *Mo Bhealach Féin* as the road of childhood
desire flanked by hillsides, more beautiful than those recalled in song, and
resting places where he would feel the life force of every stem and herb. This
was 'a road of no return', to which Mac Grianna committed himself with an
irrepressible zeal.[92]

   In following this alternative path Mac Grianna had to turn away from what
he calls his *leathchairde*, or 'half-friends'.[93] These were those, like his brother
Séamus, whom he considered to have given up on the radical spirit of the
revolutionary period and who were now in thrall to bourgeois respectability. In
declaring this break with his peers Mac Grianna literally creates new identities.
While fleeing his lodgings before settling his account, he strikes the son of his
landlady, and, fearing the blow to be fatal, imagines himself to be a pursued
man. He signs his name in the next lodging house as Art Mac Cumhaigh (the
eighteenth-century Ulster poet), and although he soon realises that he is not
being sought, the dynamic of pursuit and assumed identities drives him on.
Moving from lodging house to lodging house, Mac Grianna tries to lead a life
of adventure and philosophical enquiry, engaging with marginal, eccentric
figures and the politically radical. He attends a meeting of the Communist
Party and travels around the country with the IRA leader Seán Russell, but
declines a request to join the IRA, choosing instead to follow his own path.
Travelling to England and Wales he attends a seance in Cardiff and meets a
man in London who claims to be on the run from American dope gangs. A
feature of Mac Grianna's quest is the constant recourse to historical precedents;
he considers recreating the life of a seventeenth-century rapparee in Dublin,
and when he decides to walk the length of Wales it is to follow the example
of Finn and the *Fianna*. One might say that Mac Grianna's entire project is
inherently utopian, but it is in the episode where he and an accomplice steal
a boat that the historic tradition of utopian adventure is most consciously
invoked, namely the era of *immrama*, or rowings of otherworldly voyages.
Mac Grianna names the boat *Cúl re hÉirinn* (Back Turned on Ireland), the
name given to himself by Colm Cille (Columba), the renowned sixth-cen-
tury saint whose self-exile and sea voyage, as described in his biography *Vita
Columbae*, is closely related to the later *immrama*.[94]

   That the attempt to navigate the Irish Sea ends in mock-heroic farce is part
of the quixotic appeal of Mac Grianna's adventures. However, the insistence
on his own utopian longing is genuinely heroic. Lying on a mountain above
Tonypandy in Wales, his body trembling from lack of sleep, he is stirred by

a poem by James Clarence Mangan, 'The Sunken City', Mangan's translation from the original German of Wilhelm Müller (1794–1827): 'Hark! The
faint bells of the sunken city/ Peal once more their wonted evening chime
…'[95] The bells of the real city below are what brings the verse to mind, but
the distance is typical of the social isolation Mac Grianna would increasingly
endure, just as the imaginary sunken city is that other dimension, the city
beneath the waves that he was determined to seek. Like the imaginary road
where Mac Grianna's journey begins, the city in the Mangan poem is perfectly
formed in the imagination:

> Domes, and towers, and castles, fancy-builded
> There lie lost to daylight's garish beams
> There lie hidden till unveiled and gilded
> Glory-gilded, by my nightly dreams![96]

The triumph of Mac Grianna's autobiography is in creating his own dynamic
vision rather than serving the state's preconceived, static ideal of Gaelic
Ireland. The tragedy is that, like Mangan, he struggled with a debilitating
alienation born of a colonial crisis of identity.[97] In Mac Grianna's postcolonial
Dublin, the project of cultural reclamation to which Mangan and his fellow
contributors in the *Nation* had helped set in train was failing to reach the
expectations they had created. The loss and recovery of agency was a process
that was much more complex than might have initially been hoped.

While Freudian and Lacanian psychoanalysis see loss and attempted
recovery as universal features of human experience, postcolonialism locates the
trauma of loss and the displacement of culture specifically within the historic
experience of subjugated ethnic groups. The two perspectives are, of course,
closely related, and it is no accident that Frantz Fanon, one of the pioneers
of postcolonialism, was a psychiatrist whose profession gave him a particular
insight into the alienating effects of colonialism on indigenous people.[98] A
key feature of the colonial condition is a process of acculturation in which
the colonised typically compromises his native identity under pressure of the
colonial hegemony. The resultant dislocation or displacement of native culture
is something that subjugated peoples struggle to amend even when eventually free of colonial rule. Ironically, in the postcolonial era the longer-term
consequences of the colonial condition persist, perhaps indefinitely. One of
the themes of postcolonial studies is the process of reclamation, undertaken,
as Edward Said has it, to 'restore the imprisoned nation to itself', a project

in which the concept of the national language is central.[99] The conceptual framework of postcolonialism clearly offers many advantages to the discussion of identity, place and displacement in Irish literature, and Máirín Nic Eoin's landmark study of cultural dislocation in twentieth-century Irish literature is a case in point.[100] This central theme of dislocation ('dislocation' rather than 'displacement' is the term favoured in postcolonial studies) is exactly that which is expressed in Fear Flatha Ó Gnímh's early seventeenth-century poem 'Mo thruaighe mar táid Gaoidhil' (I pity the Gaels as they now stand), discussed in Chapter 2. Ó Gnímh's depiction of the physical displacement of Gaels in the wake of the plantation of Ulster focuses on the sense of internal exile that comes from witnessing the displacement of culture – hills that hunters ranged are now ploughed by oxen, haystacks stand where fairs were formerly held. The motif Ó Gnímh uses to reflect this is a semi-apocalyptic regression – beauty is replaced by ugliness, law replaced by disorder. It is apt that this same motif, taken from Yeats' 'The Second Coming', should give the title of Chinua Achebe's classic novel of colonisation in Nigeria, *Things Fall Apart* (1958).[101]

The title of Nic Eoin's book, *Trén bhFearann Breac* (Through the Speckled Land) – borrowed from the title of a poem by Colm Breathnach – reflects her contention that one of the consequences of cultural dislocation is that literature in Irish necessarily inhabits an in-between space that is closer to hybridity than purity. Thus, the mania for authenticity and a lost linguistic purity are unlikely to ever bear fruit. In this regard her critique of Seán Ó Ríordáin's 'Fill Arís' (Return Again) is especially pertinent: Ó Ríordáin's poem epitomises the embodiment of desire as an ideal place – in his case the Dún Chaoin *Gaeltacht* – where one can return to precolonial Gaelic Ireland.[102] Nic Eoin sees Ó Ríordáin's quest for an elusive authentic self as an ill-advised rejection of the hybridity of his own background in the *breac-Ghaeltacht* of Ballyvourney, County Cork, the son of an Irish-speaking father, who died when the poet was a child, and an English-speaking mother. In Nic Eoin's study of writing in Irish in the twentieth century the predominant circumstance is a cross-cultural, speckled landscape, the negotiation of which is itself a powerful creative catalyst.[103] In her discussion of the journeys undertaken in poems by Colm Breathnach ('Trén bhFearann Breac') and Seán Ó hÉigeartaigh ('Freudyssey na Gaeilge' (The Freudyssey of the Irish Language)) and in Breandán Ó Doibhlin's novel *An Branar Gan Cur* (The Untilled Field) (1979), all of which typify the sense of alienation experienced by Irish speakers, Nic Eoin points to Nuala Ní Dhomhnaill's 'Ag Tiomáint Siar' (Driving West), in which the journey itself is its own reward.[104] The ancestral landscape in Ní Dhomnaill's poem is not a static shrine to which one returns but a dynamic interlocutor in creative dialogue with the poet as she travels along the Connor Pass in County Kerry: 'Still I hear new stories from it every time/ flashes of understanding that make/ the rocks stand out in the middle of the road before me/ as though they were words.'[105]

In an illuminating reading of Ní Dhomhnaill's *Murúcha* (Merfolk) poems, Nic Eoin examines the restorative uses of memory as a response to cultural displacement or dislocation. The *Murúcha* series can be traced to Ní Dhomhnaill's 1981 poem 'An Mhaighdean Mhara' (The Mermaid), an allegorical meditation that the poet has linked variously to the debilitating isolation of young women, the consequences of language shift, and the experience of the Great Famine.[106] The central motif is inspired by a west Kerry version of the international folktale 'the man who married a mermaid', and this interpretation of the mermaid story has generated an extensive series of *Murúcha* poems in *Cead Aighnis* (Leave to Speak) (1998) and (with English translations by Paul Muldoon) *The Fifty Minute Mermaid* (2007).[107] The difficulty the Merfolk encounter in adjusting to their displacement from sea to land is represented in the Irish phrase *teacht i dtír* (literally, 'coming ashore', but also 'surviving'). The first poem in the sequence, 'Na Murúcha a Thriomaigh' (The Assimilated Merfolk), acts as a *mise en scène*:[108]

> Barely have they put in on this bare rock
> than their scales start drying out
> and they suffer such skin complaints as windgall and blotching
> and get pins-and-needles from the breezes, never mind the zephyrs,
> unaccustomed as they were to either

The attempted assimilation of the colonised to the hegemonic culture of the colonised is indicated in the same poem:

> The women wear heavy neck-ornaments
> While the men favour red kerchiefs,
> Anything at all that hides the signs of their gills

> … By now they've clean forgotten
> the dizzying churning of the deep currents
> and, from the abyss, the whales' antiphonal singing.
> From time to time they hear a snatch of it

on the wind and call it 'Port na bPúcaí'.

They make a sign of the cross between themselves and it.

In other poems unexplainable behaviour is linked to the emotional stress of repressed memory. In 'Cuimhne an Uisce' (A Recovered Memory of Water) a probing psychiatrist encourages the mermaid's daughter to speak the word that she cannot bring forth but can only refer to through comical periphrasis as a 'transparent liquid', a 'shiny film' and 'something wet'.[109] As Nic Eoin concludes of the *Murúcha* poems, they are best seen as a work of memory but one that provides an imaginative framework in which innumerable situations can be explored, not simply the Irish experience of colonialism.

The *Murúcha* poems also reflect on the expression of desire and alterity as tantalising lost or unattainable places. In particular, the land from which the Merfolk have originally come, *Tír-fó-Thoinn* (Land-Under-Wave), is taken from one of the otherworldly places in Irish mythology, and various of the *Murúcha* poems reference St Brendan, whose *Navigatio* depicts the otherworldly islands that the saint encounters in his search for the *terra repromissionis*. In the concluding poem in the series, 'Spléachanna Fánacha ar an dTír fó Thoinn' (Some Observations on Land-Under-Wave), the speaker follows the hope-bound tradition of otherworlds with its excess of wondrous allure, only to arrive at a very dark conclusion, literally in the 'deepest cellar under the earth'.[110] Referencing St Brendan's voyage and various mythological island otherworlds, such as Hy Breasail, the speaker admits to being spellbound. The reports by sailors and others who have glimpsed these magical places are like the 'Sunken City' of Mueller and Mangan, irresistibly formed but never actualised:

> Some of them have suggested that what they saw
> was a tall tower of crystal on an imposing cliff
> that couldn't be scaled from any side.
> Others said there were rows of windows
> cut into the rock itself, with light streaming out of them.
> The whole cliff-face was so honeycombed
> it resembled nothing so much as a beehive.[111]

As the speaker goes on to describe the place under the sea in which 'everything exceeds all expectations', the narrative turns ominously to the mermaid's guarded memory of the 'dark deeds' that are the true import of this supposedly ethereal realm. The final section of the poem marks a clear break with this misplaced tradition of utopian longing, replacing it instead with a sense of complicit shame:

> Besides which, anyway, those days are long gone.
> Anyone who might make his way
> sometime in the future
> into that fortress
> would find there
> only row upon row of empty rooms,
> one leading into the next.
> The heavy tread of his own shoes
> echoing up to the concrete beams of the roof
> would at once startle and shame him.
> He would follow on, for a long time,
> To the bitter end.[112]

The 'deepest cellar under the earth' does indeed contain 'the remnants of a complete world', but it is the sinister storehouse of the Third Reich's final solution, replete with heaps of 'gold teeth and earrings and eyeglasses' and a 'mountain of low-grade soap'.[113] Thus, what begins with St Brendan's quest for eschatological revelation concludes with the evidence of the Nazis' partially realised end of time.

While nothing in the *Murúcha* series compares with the devastatingly bleak climax of this final poem, there are ample hints in the preceding poems that Ní Dhomhnaill is wary of state-nurtured utopias. In particular, her references to the Blasket Islands include a cautionary scepticism. In 'Na Murúcha agus an Litríocht' (The Merfolk and Literature), the speaker explains how the Merfolk, although literate, have not created their own literature:

> And though their likes will never be seen again
> in any shape or form,
> they don't go writing screeds of poetry and prose,
> making a huge deal of it.
>
> They leave that kind of carry-on
> to the crowd from the Blaskets.[114]

The reference to 'their likes will never be seen again' is based on the phrase that occurs at the end of Ó Criomhthain's *An tOileánach* (The Islandman) and which in turn became a satirical refrain in Myles na gCopaleen's *An Béal Bocht*.

In Ríóna Ní Fhrighil's reading of the final poem in the *Murúcha* series, the silence of the mermaid is not just a symptom of the trauma she has endured but a strategy of resistance against the tyranny of reason.[115] This is consistent with the great thrust of Ní Dhomhnaill's *oeuvre*, which implicitly challenges the dominant patriarchal systems of knowledge and opens up other occluded discourses. This is most evident in her use of the oral tradition and other discourses in which women have not been intellectually disempowered. Yet, in another way, a rejection of the tyranny of reason is a precondition for embracing the same utopianism upon which Ní Dhomhnaill casts a weary eye in the *Murúcha* poems. Whether in religious or secular utopias, or in utopias brought about by divine or human agency, to place one's faith in a specific type of future is to look beyond the empirical evidence of actuality and to recognise the limits of reason. In his monumental study *Das Prinzip Hoffnung* (1959) (The Principle of Hope), Ernst Bloch took hope to be the defining and underlying principle in the history of the utopian vision of the future. From an Irish viewpoint it is significant that Bloch includes a detailed discussion of the *Navigatio Sancti Brendani*.[116] Where the history of the Third Reich and the final solution are concerned, it is striking to find that Bloch, a German Jew who had to flee Germany after the Nazis came to power, would devote his life to a philosophically and historically based radical utopianism. In common with his friend and colleague Walter Benjamin, who killed himself in 1940 when fleeing Vichy France, Bloch was deeply influenced by Jewish mystical and messianic traditions. Faced with the horrors of Nazism, hope or suicide was the only available resource to many, or, as Benjamin remarked, 'It is only for the sake of those without hope that hope is given to us.'[117]

Given that Bloch and Benjamin were both thinkers in the Marxist materialist tradition, their borrowing from spiritual traditions may seem counterintuitive. Yet the 'theological turn' in Marxism is a well-established development in our time, exemplified by writers such as Slavoj Žižek and Terry Eagleton.[118] Where literature in Irish is concerned, Máirtín Ó Cadhain epitomised both the Christian Marxist perspective and the belief in hope as an emancipatory force that transcends reason.[119] As mentioned in the previous chapter, in a lecture on the fiftieth anniversary of the 1916 Rising Ó Cadhain spoke of hope as the 'chain detonation' of Irish history, in which hope generated courage and vice versa. He also maintained that without a certain antipathy to reason the Gaels would have long since departed the record of history. The metaphor of the 'chain detonation' of history is shared by Bloch and Benjamin, who speak respectively of 'blasting [periods of awakening] out from the historical continuum' and the need to 'blast a specific era out of the homogenous course of history'.[120] Like Ó Cadhain, Bloch and Benjamin see hope as a radical alternative to the blind acceptance of the 'homogenous course of history', and, again, like Ó Cadhain inherited a tradition of messianism that allows for a cataclysmic rupture in the 'rational' progress of history. Of the influence of this Irish messianic inheritance Ó Cadhain remarked, 'I am a conveyor belt, no matter how frail, of this loaded passion of generations.'[121] This anticipatory disposition, which holds the latency of past and present as a source of hope and courage, is something that Ó Cadhain shares with Bloch's emphasis on the 'not yet' and, in particular, the 'ontology of not-yet-being'.

The concept of 'not-yet-being', sometimes translated as the 'not-yet-become', has obvious resonance for the conclusion of the previous chapter's discussion of temporality and revivalism and its emphasis on *becoming*.[122] Bloch's insistence on utopia as place, especially characterised as *Heimat* (homeland), is also of great relevance to this chapter's discussion of place and displacement in the discourse of revivalism. The final words of Bloch's *Principle of Hope* refer to this same spatial conception of hope, 'something which shines into the childhood of all and in which no one has yet been: homeland'.[123] If revivalism is viewed, in Lacanian terms, as part of the constant desire to retrieve the *real* – the primal absence or loss – then one might swiftly conclude that revivalism is a project that can never advance but, rather, simply repeats its own failures indefinitely. This conclusion would be to ignore the innately progressive elements of revivalism, not least its propensity to be an emancipatory discourse of alterity. This alterity is implicit in the preoccupation of the texts and traditions discussed here with the classic places of desire, such as Plato's Atlantis, More's Utopia, Hy Breasail or Tír-fó-Thoinn. Whether utopian or dystopian, as in Myles na gCopaleen's Corca Dorcha, the fact of having no fixed coordinates is what allows these places to become sites of alternative configurations. Rather than being barely perceptible horizons, these are places formed, refashioned and refined in the imagination. The expression of alterity and of contrapuntal readings of human progress is facilitated precisely by the space these places provide to hope and imagination. As Frederic Jameson remarks in his *Archaeologies of the Future*, 'utopia as a form is not the representation of radical alternatives; it is rather simply the imperative to imagine them'.[124] All of this has a very practical application to our own times, when many believe that the 'end of history' has already been reached in the West, and that it would be easier to imagine the end of the world than the end of capitalism.[125] Such an orthodoxy, precluding, as it does, alternative visions of the world, is implicitly opposed to progress. Revivalism, on the other hand, is inherently part of the alternative to this stasis and to the potentiality of 'not-yet-being'. It is for this reason, not least, that it may be considered an emancipatory discourse.

Conclusion

Much of the discursive trajectory of this book is reflected in the thematic development of two short stories by Pádraig Ó Conaire, 'An Sgoláire Bocht' (The Poor Scholar) and 'Bé an tSiopa Seandachta' (The Antique Shop Muse).[1] In particular, the tension between a desire for faithful, authentic continuity between past and present on the one hand and a creative renewal on the other, where past and present are actively engaged in a transformative sequence, is a central concern both of this book and of the two stories we will now consider. The first story, 'An Sgoláire Bocht' (originally published in 1905 as 'An Sean-Leabhar' (The Old Book)), tells of the last years of a wandering scholar in pre-Famine Connacht who yearns to find an heir for his learning before he can himself finally succumb to the grave.[2] He eventually finds such a person in the house of a family called Ua Flaithbheartaigh, by whom he is given shelter one night. The poor scholar quickly recognises in young Colm Ua Flaithbheartaigh one to whom his specialised knowledge can be entrusted, and the two form a friendship that may secure the passage of native learning from one generation to another. The sense of providence having guided this relationship is made more explicit again when the old scholar and his protégé discover a long-forgotten manuscript book in the loft of the house. The manuscript bears the title of Leabhar na bhFlaithbheartach (The Book of the O'Flahertys), and was written for an ancestor of Colm's, Donnchadh Mór Ua Flaithbheartach. The old scholar reads the prose tales and poetry to his pupil, and for many long, blissful days afterwards teaches him how to read the archaic Irish, until the young man has mastered the task himself. When the old scholar is blinded in a hunting accident he comes to rely entirely on Colm to read the manuscript to him. As with many of Pádraig Ó Conaire's short stories from this period, the blinding of the scholar is a prelude to an even greater disaster. Colm attends confession in a nearby town, only to be ordered by the priest to destroy the beloved manuscript. The priest's rationale for this command is that Protestant societies have been distributing Bibles and other books in Irish, thus making all forms of writing in Irish the subject of prohibition. Colm struggles valiantly between his supposed duty to God and his devotion to the manuscript, but is finally convinced that the book must be burned. This he does in a final pathetic scene where the blind scholar is left disconsolate, having failed to prevent the destruction of the revered manuscript.

As the negotiation of past and present lies at the heart of 'An Sgoláire Bocht', so, too, does it underpin the essential project of revivalism. Indeed, Ó Conaire's short story shares many of the preoccupations of this book – in particular, the anxiety of transmission that arises from a crisis of continuity between past and present. The convergence of the secular and spiritual also figures prominently in the form of the Bible societies' controversy, but also, more fundamentally, where Colm's dilemma is whether to secure continuity between the generations in this world or to ensure the safe passage of his own soul from this world into the next.[3] If the tragedy of 'An Sgoláire Bocht' is the failure to achieve the faithful transmission of an authentic tradition from one generation to another, a very different perspective on our relation to the past is presented in a story written by Ó Conaire in the direct aftermath of the 1916 Rising. In this case the relation with the past is one of latent possibility rather than faithful continuity. 'The Antique Shop Muse' is the story of how two men vie for the attentions of a beautiful young woman, the sales assistant in a Dublin antique shop. The first of these men, Peadar Ó Dónaill, is involved in organising the Easter Rising, and has a room facing the antique shop from which point he and the 'antique shop muse' begin to notice each other.[4] The second man is one of Dublin Castle's detectives, or G-men, tasked with tracking the activities of Peadar Ó Dónaill. Posing as a customer of the antique shop to monitor Ó Dónaill's room, the detective soon becomes infatuated with the young sales assistant. She, however, is attracted to Ó Dónaill, to whom she confides that a man has been observing him from the shop. The antique-shop muse agrees to flatter the detective's intentions, and attends a concert with him to divert his attentions from Ó Dónaill's activities. Four weeks later Ó Dónaill is dead, executed for his part in the Easter Rising, with the detective giving evidence against him. The story ends with the G-man's rejection by the young woman and his realisation that, unlike the heroic martyr Ó Dónaill, he will never win anyone's respect, much less the love of the antique-shop muse. This disillusionment descends into a state of torment during which he is confronted by hosts of mocking eyes whose relentless gaze hastens his eventual suicide.

Rather than a manuscript, the past in this second story is the antique shop into which all of the city's relics appear to have been consigned: old guns, rusty swords from the time of the parliament, books that were written, printed and never read, all manner of pictures, ornaments, vessels, big-bellied oriental idols and, finally, in the front window a statue of the Buddha under which the name of Queen Victoria had been written.[5] Both the foregrounding of this ironically named trophy from the Orient and the overburdened display of obsolete items allows Ó Conaire to designate the antique shop as the site of the decaying British Empire in Ireland. The antique-shop muse is its prisoner, or, as she herself despairs, 'A living flower such as her stuck in a small, dead world!'[6] But apart from the comment on the imminent demise of imperial rule in Dublin, the description of the antique shop is also a more general comment on how we engage with the past. The British Empire of the antique shop is a static past with which there is no prospect of engagement. It is a liminal space within the city, but far from being a threshold of possibility, it represents all that is moribund and redundant – it is the Empire rather than the colonised that appears, on this occasion, to be outside of time. Nevertheless, where 'An Sgoláire Bocht' speaks to the failure of a revival based on faithful continuity, 'The Antique Shop Muse' is all about latent potential as represented by the figure of the young woman. In a reversal of the traditional role of muse, and indeed the dream-maiden of *aisling* poetry, it is the muse herself who becomes inspired. Of course, this is part of the story's propagandistic content, being one of a collection of stories entitled *Seacht mBua an Éirí Amach* (The Seven Virtues of the Rising) in which awakening or release from blindness is a recurring trope, and the young woman, in this instance, is the Irish people whose potential has been revealed by the martyrdom of Peadar Ó Dónaill. Looking beyond the overtly political, however, 'The Antique Shop Muse' evinces a resolution to the impasse encountered by the path of revival in 'An Sgoláire Bocht'. The past cannot be restored miraculously or seamlessly reintegrated into the present. It can, however, re-emerge through a creative renewal in which the past ceases to be a static burden and becomes instead part of a dynamic dialogue with the present. The past, like Peadar Ó Dónaill, is beyond us, but its residue represents a site of latent possibility. What is required to bring it into play is a radical *becoming* that will allow the past to refigure within a dynamic present. If the muse at the beginning of the story is *being*, simply existing amidst the remnants of the past, the end of the story witnesses a radical *becoming* in which she realises her own agency, exemplified when she rises from her chair to order the G-man to leave.

The progress from thwarted continuity in 'An Sgoláire Bocht' to dynamic renewal in 'The Antique Shop Muse' reflects two central approaches to revival emerging from the chronological and conceptual discussion of revivalism in the first four chapters of this book. Equally apparent in the two stories is the sense of liminality of time and space, discussed in relation to revivalism in Chapters 5 and 6, respectively. Just as revivalism and Gothic fiction involve a critical engagement with temporality, both stories depict a present heavily encumbered by the past and a certain disruption of temporal boundaries typical of Gothic fiction. In 'An Sgoláire Bocht' the past of 'The Book of the O'Flahertys' – the classic Gothic 'found document' – returns like a ghost to the present, but only through the intervention of the mysterious poor scholar, a wandering, spectral figure whose name and origin he will not give.[7] When Colm burns the book he effectively drives a stake through the heart of its ghostly intermediary, and delivers both back to the past. In 'The Antique Shop Muse', however, the boundaries between past and present remain fluid, the reiterative legacy of martyrdom being asserted in the phrase 'Poor Peadar' that, at the end of the story, is repeated like a chorus by the muse, by men and women on the street and even the seagulls above the Liffey. A final point on the relevance of these two stories to our exploration of revivalism is to note the use of spatial liminality alongside temporal liminality in 'The Antique Shop Muse'. The antique shop is at once a place of material obsolescence but also a vantage point for alterity in that the muse observes another type of life and is in turn observed by it. The sense of possibility is intensified by the opportunity to monitor and then imagine the lives of other people from a safe distance. Indeed, the muse makes a hole in the curtain of the shop window to watch Peadar Ó Dónaill more discreetly, and the imagined world beyond the window becomes the object of her desire. Ultimately, the vantage point of her liminal position between the spaces of past, present and the imagined future is precisely what frees the muse from an acceptance of her fate as a set of fixed, immutable circumstances. Revivalism, centring as it does on renegotiating the boundaries between past and present, encourages an alternative view of how the future can be formed, and, in this way, places its faith in the potential of 'not-yet-being' rather than in a passive acceptance of the homogenous course of human history.

   Like the thematic progress of these two stories by Ó Conaire, the conceptual discussion of revivalism leads us back beyond the initial historical particulars and on to questions that are part of the discourse of metaphysics and ontology. This is itself an indication of the need to approach revivals not simply as discrete events but as part of a wider, recurring desire to reform the present by recourse to values associated with the past.

If the dichotomy of *being* and *becoming*, and Plato's notion of anamnesis are part of the metaphysical foundations of revivalism, then Nietzsche's body of thought is crucial to the role of revivalism in modernity. Nietzsche's *oeuvre* begins with a form of revival, his attempted retrieval of the meaning of tragedy and its potential rebirth in his first book, *The Birth of Tragedy* (1872). More pertinently perhaps, his work grappled with the notion of recurrence, and presented a model for the interrelation of past and present in the figure of eternal recurrence. The challenge envisaged by Nietzsche in eternal recurrence is ultimately the challenge of modernity itself, and one recognised in turn by Freud, whose work, as Adam Philips remarks, centres on 'whether it is possible for modern people to have new experiences, to find new objects of desire, to improvise upon their pasts'.

Moving from the broad question of how the present relates to the past within modernity, the problem of authentic continuity arises when we seek to successfully retrieve a lost element of culture – how can we retrieve what is already passed? The dichotomy of *being* and *becoming* suggests that continuity is a notion that is difficult to sustain, particularly if we tend, like Nietzsche, towards Heraclitus' philosophy of flux. If change is constant and the world is characterised by *becoming* rather than *being*, then this undermines the basis of Douglas Hyde's original hope for the Gaelic League revival, 'to render the present a rational continuation of the past'. Of course, rather than yielding conclusive answers, metaphysical questions tend to result in the adoption of positions for and against. In this sense Hyde's desideratum cannot be dismissed. Nevertheless, psychoanalytic theory problematises the notion of continuity further. Lacan presents identity as constantly mediated, in that the subject is never a fixed autonomous point of reference but, rather, part of a range of relationships with the *other/Other*. If we accept this model of subject development, then the desire to retrieve a lost identity or ensure an authentic, continuous identity appears increasingly conflicted. Coupled with this is Lacan's concept of the *real*, that perennial lack with which desire is engaged in an eternally unresolved quest. The resolution to this apparent bind is that an unproblematic continuity between past and present can be discounted in favour of the type of dialectical transition described by Hegel as *Aufhebung*, or sublation, in which both elements are negated but at the same time elevated to a higher stage of development. Yet this does not mean that there is some ultimate teleological solution to the integration of past and present in revivalism. If revivalism is not about guaranteeing the pristine continuity of the past, it is no more capable of guaranteeing a specific future. Its greatest innovation is to point to the agency of the present. The crisis of cultural or linguistic decline brings about a vital awareness of culture and language as not fixed but mediated. It is this objectifying distance that leads to an awareness of agency.

The crisis of continuity, from which this objectifying distance emerges, has been a fairly constant fixture in the Irish literary consciousness from the seventeenth century onwards. Like the seventeenth-century letters intercepted by Spanish privateers and the fictional imperilled message of Liam Mac Cóil's *An Litir*, Irish letters have encountered a steady degree of adversity over the course of the last four centuries. Whether registered as a full-blown existential crisis or merely a recognition of declining fortunes, this particular circumstance has been a critical influence on literary discourse in Irish. It has been a key to the transformative engagement with those movements of revival and reform, Renaissance humanism, the Reformation and the Counter-Reformation. Equally, the instrumentalisation of language and culture in the service of Irish nationalism or Protestant evangelicalism in the eighteenth and nineteenth centuries extended the sense in which the Irish language was a thing to be consciously regarded rather than being simply a medium of communication. Just as the active preservation of the canon and archive of cultural memory was a vital intervention in this era, the ongoing development of a revivalist consciousness with regard to Irish literature was explicitly cultivated and refined in various revivalist manifestos. These endeavours, together with the persistence of a radical, anticipatory outlook, exemplified in Irish *aisling* poetry, ensured that an alternative narrative could sustain those who refused to submit to the inevitability of linguistic and cultural decline.

This tradition of hope was reinvested in Gaelic Leaguers such as Patrick Pearse, who grappled with the seeming impossibility of retrieving a linguistic and literary inheritance that had already been lost to most of the Irish people. Yet the legacy of millenarianism and messianism could not be invoked indefinitely, and Pearse was instead forced to confront the urgent present. In so doing, he redirected Irish revivalism towards the latency of the present rather than the past, and towards an urgent sense of potentiality rather than pietas. Yet, in the aftermath of the 1916 Rising, a certain nationalist teleology that envisaged a future deliverance and neat resolution of all contradictions was also part of Pearse's legacy. Seosamh Mac Grianna and Máirtín Ó Cadhain both gave witness to the physical and figurative sense of spatio-temporal exile experienced by those who were alienated by the new independent state's stewardship of the ideals of 1916. Those who were shut out of nationalist history, like Mac Grianna's Promethean hero Cathal Mac Eachmharcaigh, were forced to re-evaluate it, and in both Mac Grianna and Ó Cadhain a new modernist ethic of renewal emerged in Irish. Accordingly, Ó Cadhain's magnum opus, *Cré na Cille*, challenged the linear determinism of nationalist teleology and opened up the prospect of an unrelieved present – his own version of the eternal present of modernity – as experienced by the deceased in his novel. The contribution of Mac Grianna and Ó Cadhain to revivalist discourse was thus a reorientation towards creative renewal and away from an elusive continuity.

Ó Cadhain's maxim that hope rather than reason was the chain detonation in Irish history is at once a recognition of the imperative of renewal but also a metaphor for revivalism as an act of radical *becoming*. The spatial representation of hope, often taking the classic utopian form of an island, is a prevailing feature of the canon of Irish-language literature in the twentieth century, witnessed in the veneration of Blasket Islands autobiographies and, more generally, in the state's valorisation of the *Gaeltacht* as the site of its own ideal identity. The state displaced its avowed revivalist aims by designating an alternative site of unattainable desire in the form of the *Gaeltacht*, creating the sense that Irish was always elsewhere. This duplicitous position had in many ways already been established by Gaelic Leaguers who had made *Gaeltacht* a place rather than a state of being. The anomaly of this situation inspired the sublime satire of Myles na gCopaleen's *An Béal Bocht*, in which its author's own experience as a non-native, native speaker gives to parody the relentless force of revenge. Yet the spaces of desire and alterity have also been a highly productive strain in Irish literature of the twentieth and twenty-first centuries. The utopian quest of Seosamh Mac Grianna's *Mo Bhealach Féin* and the anterior world of Nuala Ní Dhomhnaill's *Murúcha* are important examples of this. Those who have been displaced from public time and estranged from their own environment are given a perspective that is not perhaps available to those who have not incurred the depredations of colonial conquest or other similar adversities. These are the 'critical strategies' that Homi Bhabha attributes to those who have suffered the 'sentence of history'.[8] What the imagined spaces of revivalist literature provide us with is the window of alterity. This, taken with revivalism's capacity to bring about the realisation of agency and the prospect of a radical *becoming*, is ultimately what gives it its emancipatory potential.

While the Irish language has for a long time held a symbolic importance often overshadowing its communicative function, it is still an indispensable link with both the present of traditional and non-traditional Irish-speaking communities and the past of Irish history. If, in the manner of the mythical

Tuatha Dé Danaan, part of Gaelic Ireland went underground after the seventeenth century, it has also remained rooted to the landscape above ground. Like J.M. Synge's description of hearing Irish coming up through the floorboards of his room on the Aran Islands, the language may be characterised by its anteriority but is nevertheless part of a dynamic present. This Janus-faced disposition has accounted for much of the preoccupations of Irish revivalism in negotiating a present and past between which few clear-cut boundaries exist. What emerges from this ongoing tradition of revivalism is the recognition that, far from being a series of discrete historical events, Irish revivalism is part of a perennial concern with continuity and change, authenticity and alterity, agency and contingency, *being* and *becoming*. The literature of Irish revivalism is the ongoing record of this engagement, and its progress shows no signs of abating.

Notes and References

Introduction

1   Oscar Recio Morales, *Ireland and the Spanish Empire, 1600–1825* (Dublin: Four Courts Press, 2010), pp. 40–1. For a detailed analysis of the letters and their historical context as well as the full text of the original Irish letters with Spanish and English translations, see Éamon Ó Ciosáin, Pádraig Ó Macháin and Ciarán O'Scea, 'Two Letters in Irish from Domhnall Mac Suibhne OSA in Nantes (1640) [with index]', *Archivium Hibernicum*, vol. lxvii (2014), pp. 103–38.

2   Liam Mac Cóil, *An Litir* (Indreabhán: Leabhar Breac, 2011).

3   *The Concise Oxford English Dictionary* (Oxford: Oxford University Press, 2008), online edition.

4   Some examples are P.J. Mathews and Declan Kiberd (eds), *Handbook of the Irish Revival: an anthology of Irish cultural and political writings, 1891–1922* (Dublin: Abbey Press, 2015); Roy Foster, *Vivid Faces: the revolutionary generation in Ireland, 1890–1923* (London: Penguin, 2014); Brian Ó Conchubhair, *Fin de Siècle na Gaeilge: Darwin, an Athbheochan, agus smaointeoireacht na hEorpa* (Indreabhán: An Clóchomhar, 2009); Timothy G. McMahon, *Grand Opportunity: the Gaelic Revival and Irish society, 1893–1910* (Syracuse: Syracuse University Press, 2008); Richard Kirkland, *Cathal O'Byrne and the Revival in the North of Ireland, 1890–1960* (Liverpool: Liverpool University Press, 2006); B. Taylor-FitzSimon and J.H. Murphy (eds), *The Irish Revival Reappraised* (Dublin: Four Courts Press, 2004); Sinéad Garrigan-Mattar, *Primitivism, Science, and the Irish Revival* (Oxford: Oxford University Press, 2004); Margaret Kelleher (ed.), *Irish University Review* (special issue on the Irish Literary Revival) (Cork: Cork University Press, 2003); P.J. Mathews, *Revival: the Abbey Theatre, Sinn Féin, the Gaelic League and the co-operative movement* (Cork: Cork University Press, 2003).

5   In this case de Paor draws on the work of the anthropologist René Girard (1923–2015) and the philosopher Emmanuel Levinas (1906–95) to advance his thesis that culture centres on the concept of sacrifice and that the concept of escape underpins modern Irish literature and the revivalist movement from which it has emerged.

6   Gregory Castle, 'Irish Revivalism: critical trends and new directions', *Literature Compass*, vol. 8, no. 5 (2011), pp. 291–303.

7   Mathews, *Revival*, p. 2.

8   See Ermanno Bencivenga, *Hegel's Dialectical Logic* (New York: Oxford University Press, 2000), pp. 32–3. See also Ralph Palm, 'Hegel's Concept of Sublation: a critical interpretation', PhD thesis, Catholic University of Leuven, 2009.

9   See Rosemary Hill, *God's Architect: Pugin and the building of Romantic Britain* (London: Allen Lane, 2007); Tristam Hunt, *Building Jerusalem: the rise and fall of the Victorian city* (London: Phoenix, 2004).

10   See Chapter 2: 'Retrieving Greek Tragedy', in Lawrence Hatab, *Nietzsche's Life*

Sentence: coming to terms with eternal recurrence (London: Routledge, 2005), pp. 23–37.

11   Lacan makes a distinction between what he calls the 'Other' and the 'other'. For a brief discussion of this distinction and its relevance to postcolonial studies, see B. Ashcroft, G. Griffiths and H. Tiffin (eds), *Post-colonial Studies* (London: Routledge, 2000), pp. 169–71.

12   Osborn Bergin (ed.), *Irish Bardic Poetry* (Dublin: Dublin Institute of Advanced Studies, 1970), pp. 49–50; Douglas Hyde, *Language, Lore and Lyrics*, ed. Breandán Ó Conaire (Dublin: Irish Academic Press, 1986), pp. 153–70.

13   Homi K. Bhabha, *The Location of Culture* (London: Routledge, 1994), pp. 85–92.

14   See for example Lady Gregory's 'Apology', in her *Gods and Fighting Men*, where she addresses the criticisms of Irish literature made by Professor Robert Atkinson of Trinity College at the Commission of Intermediate Education. Lady Gregory, *Gods and Fighting Men: the story of the Tuatha De Danaan and of the Fianna of Ireland* (London: John Murray, 1904), pp. 461–2.

15   Pádraig Ó Macháin, '"One Glimpse of Ireland": the manuscript of Fr Nioclás (Fearghal Dubh) Ó Gadhra, OSA', in Raymond Gillespie and Ruairí Ó hUiginn (eds), *Irish Europe, 1600–1650: writing and learning* (Dublin: Four Courts Press, 2013), p. 155

16   The title of each might be rendered in English as *The Clerk* (2007), *The Letter* (2011), *In a Strange Country* (2014), *The White Dove* (2014) and *Children for the Land of Shades* (2018).

17   See Claire O'Halloran, *Golden Ages and Barbarous Nations: antiquarian debate and cultural politics in Ireland, c. 1750–1800* (Cork: Field Day/Cork University Press, 2005). For a recent study of the Enlightenment and Ireland, see Michael Brown, *The Irish Enlightenment* (Cambridge, MA: Harvard University Press, 2016).

18   The term 'native scholars' is used here to denote scholars who were native speakers of Irish.

19   See Breandán Ó Buachalla, *Aisling Ghéar: na Stiobhartaigh agus an tAos Léinn, 1603–1788* (Dublin: An Clóchomhar, 1996); Éamonn Ó Ciardha, *Ireland and the Jacobite Cause, 1685–1766: a fatal attachment* (Dublin: Four Courts Press, 2002); Seán Ó Tuama and Thomas Kinsella (eds), *An Duanaire: poems of the dispossessed, 1600–1900* (Dublin: Dolmen Press, 1994).

20   On poets in both the seventeenth and eighteenth centuries asking if God was deaf or blind to the injustices inflicted on the Gaelic Irish, see Ó Buachalla *Aisling Ghéar*, pp. 564–5.

21   Oliver MacDonagh, *The Life of Daniel O'Connell, 1775–1847* (London: Weidenfeld & Nicolson, 1991), p. 11.

22   Norman MacLeod, 'A Letter to the Rev. G. Bellis, by Norman McLeod D.D.', *Orthodox Presbyterian* [Belfast], vol. 6 (1835), p. 343. This letter was reprinted in full by James MacKnight in the *Belfast News-letter*, 21 August 1835.

23   The concept of objectivism, particularly with regard to anthropology, has been interrogated by Pierre Bourdieu in his *The Logic of Practice*, where he discusses the necessity of 'objectifying objectification'. Pierre Bourdieu, *The Logic of*

Practice, trans. Richard Nice (Cambridge: Polity Press, 1990), see especially pp. 30–41.

24 Patrick Pearse, 'About Literature', *An Claidheamh Soluis*, 26 May 1906, pp. 6–7.

25 'Ón Domhan Theas – an áit a mbíonn sé ina shamhradh i gcónaí' (From the Southern World – where it is always summer); Cathal Ó hÁinle (ed.), *Gearrscéalta an Phiarsaigh* (Baile Átha Cliath: Cló Thalbóid, 1999), p. 21.

26 P.H. Pearse, *Collected Works of Pádraic H. Pearse: plays, stories, poems* (Dublin: Phoenix, 1924), pp. 334–5.

27 Gilles Deleuze, *Bergsonism*, trans. Hugh Tomlinson and Barbara Habberjam (New York: Zone Books, 1988), p. 59.

28 For a recent report on new speakers of Irish, see J. Walsh, B. O'Rourke and H. Rowland (eds), *Tuarascáil Taighde ar Nuachainteoirí na Gaeilge* (Dublin: Foras na Gaeilge, 2015).

Chapter 1: Towards a Theory of Revivalism

1 Eliade's use of the phrase 'myth of the eternal return' is not to be confused with the Greek myth of eternal return or its modern interpretation by Nietzsche, nor does his use of the concept of 'archetype' refer to the Jungian understanding of that term; Mircea Eliade, *The Myth of the Eternal Return: cosmos and history*, trans. Willard R. Trask (New Jersey: Princeton University Press, 1954), p. xiii–xv.

2 Ibid. p. 32.

3 Ibid. pp. 34, 130.

4 While it is not possible to specify the first appearance of utopianism, its antiquity is evident in its early expressions that include the Sumerian clay tablets, the Old Testament, the poetry of Hesiod in the eighth century BC, and the political and philosophical debates of fifth-century BC Athens. See Lyman Tower Sargent, 'Utopian Traditions: themes and variations', in R. Schaer, G. Claeys and L.T. Sargent (eds), *Utopia: the search for the ideal society in the Western world* (New York: New York Public Library, 2000), p. 8. The very phrase 'looking backward' is the title of Edward Bellamy's celebrated novel of utopia, *Looking Backward, 2000–1887* (Boston, 1888). *The Backward Look* was, of course, the title of Frank O'Connor's renowned study of Irish literature; Frank O'Connor, *The Backward Look: a survey of Irish literature* (London: Macmillan, 1967).

5 Ibid. p. 123.

6 The specific sections are *Meno*, §80–6, *Phaedo*, §72–7, and *Phaedrus*, §247–50. See I.M. Crombie, *An Examination of Plato's Doctrines, Volume Two: Plato on knowledge and reality* (London: Routledge & Kegan Paul, 1963), pp. 135–47; Andrew S. Mason, *Plato* (Durham: Acumen, 2010), pp. 76–84.

7 Plato, *Protagoras and Meno*, trans. W.K.C. Guthrie (London: Penguin, 1970), §85d, p. 138.

8 Crombie, *An Examination of Plato's Doctrines, Volume Two*, pp. 138, 143.

9 Adam Philips (ed.), *The Penguin Freud Reader* (London: Penguin, 2006), p. xiv.

10 Ibid. pp. 422–6.

11 Ibid. p. 425.

12 See Jacques Lacan, *The Four Fundamental Concepts of Psychoanalysis* (London: Penguin, 1994), p. 55. See also Slavoj Žižek, *The Sublime Object of Ideology* (London: Verso, 1989), pp. 190–6.

13 For Žižek, 'the dialectics of overtaking ourselves towards the future and simultaneous retroactive modification of the past' inevitably stumbles onto a rock upon which it becomes suspended. This rock is the *real*, 'that which resists symbolization: the traumatic point which is always missed but none the less always returns, although we try – through a set of different strategies – to neutralize it, to integrate it into the symbolic order'; ibid. p. 74.

14 See Paul Robinson, *Freudian Left: Wilhelm Reich, Geza Roheim, Herbert Marcuse* (Ithaca: Cornell University Press, 1990); Yannis Stavrakakis, *The Lacanian Left: psychoanalysis, theory, and politics* (Edinburgh: Edinburgh University Press, 2007).

15 In the case of literature and critical discourse in Irish, the influence of Freud and Jung is more easily identified than Lacan. Two important critical studies that take a Freudian and Jungian approach, respectively, are Louis de Paor, *Faoin mBlaoisc Bheag Sin: an aigneolaíocht i scéalta Mháirtín Uí Chadhain* (Dublin: Coiscéim, 1991), and Gearóid Denvir, *An Dúil is Dual* (Indreabhán: Cló Iar-Chonnacht, 1991). The former is a study of Freudian influence on the stories of Máirtín Ó Cadhain, the latter a Jungian reading of Liam O'Flaherty's Irish-language short stories (Liam Ó Flaithearta, *Dúil* (Dublin: Sáirséal & Dill, 1953)). Probably the most important instance of Freud's reception in Irish-language fiction is Liam Mac Cóil's novel *An Dochtúir Áthas* (Doctor Joy) (Indreabhán: Leabhar Breac, 1994).

16 Ilaria Ramelli, *The Christian Doctrine of Apokatastasis*: *a critical assessment from the New Testament to Eriugena* (Leiden: Brill, 2014).

17 Douglas Hyde, *A Literary History of Ireland from Earliest Times to the Present Day* [1899] (New York: Charles Scribner's Sons, 1901), p. vii. While Chapters 2 and 6 of the present work include a more detailed discussion of language shift in Ireland, suffice to mention at this point that the historically continuous Irish-speaking community was much larger at Hyde's time of writing than it is now.

18 See Anthony Kenny, *A Brief History of Western Philosophy* (Oxford: Blackwell, 1998), pp. 6–13.

19 Michael Inwood, *A Hegel Dictionary* (Oxford: Blackwell, 1992), p. 283.

20 Glenn Alexander Magee, *The Hegel Dictionary* (London: Continuum Books, 2010), p. 238.

21 See Bencivenga, *Hegel's Dialectical Logic*, pp. 32–3. See also Palm, 'Hegel's Concept of Sublation'.

22 See Seán Ó Laighin (ed.), *Ó Cadhain i bhFeasta* (Dublin: Clódhanna Teoranta, 1990), p. 90.

23 Máirtín Ó Cadhain, *Páipéir Bhána agus Páipéir Bhreaca* (Dublin: An Clóchomhar, 1969), p. 15.

24 See Philip O'Leary, *The Prose Literature of the Gaelic Revival, 1881–1921: ideology and innovation* (Pennsylvania: Pennsylvania State University Press, 1994), pp. 45–9; Cathal Ó Háinle, 'Ó Chaint na nDaoine go dtí an Caighdeán

Oifigiúil', in K. McCone, D. McManus, C. Ó Hainle, N. Williams and L. Breatnach (eds), *Stair na Gaeilge* (Maynooth: Roinn na Sean-Ghaeilge, 1994), pp. 745–93, see especially pp. 754–64.

25 See Robin Small, 'Being, Becoming and Time in Nietzsche', in Ken Gemes and John Richardson (eds), *The Oxford Handbook of Nietzsche* (Oxford: Oxford University Press, 2013), pp. 628–44.

26 'Eternal recurrence' was first depicted in Nietzsche's *The Gay Science* (initially published in 1882), and was the basic conception of his *Thus Spoke Zarathustra* (published in parts between 1883 and 1892), but is dealt with to a greater or lesser extent in various other works, instances of which are collected together in a single section in R.J. Hollingdale (ed.), *A Nietzsche Reader* (London: Penguin, 1977), pp. 249–62. See also Hatab, *Nietzsche's Life Sentence*; Peter R. Sedgwick, *Nietzsche: the key concepts* (London: Routledge, 2009), pp. 52–3; Friedrich Nietzsche, *The Gay Science*, trans. Walter Kaufmann (New York: Random House, 1974); Friedrich Nietzsche, *Thus Spoke Zarathustra*, trans. R.J. Hollingdale (London: Penguin, 1969). The interpretation of Nietzsche's doctrine of eternal recurrence by Gilles Deleuze is discussed in Chapter 5.

27 Friedrich Nietzsche, *Beyond Good and Evil* (London: Penguin, 2003), p. 175.

28 In his discussion of the controversy that followed Mhac a' tSaoi's review, Barry McCrea considers the debate to be centred on 'questions regarding the ontological status of Irish itself'; see Barry McCrea, *Languages of the Night: minor languages and the literary imagination in twentieth-century Ireland and Europe* (New Haven, CT: Yale University Press, 2015), p. 99; N.J.A. Williams, *Pairlement Chloinne Tomáis* (Dublin: Dublin Institute for Advanced Studies, 1981).

29 The phrase 'invented tradition' is usually associated with the arguments put forward in Eric Hobsbawm and Terence Ranger (eds), *The Invention of Tradition* (Cambridge: Cambridge University Press, 1983).

30 The English translation of Heidegger's *Sein und Zeit* was first published in 1962. See Martin Heidegger, *Being and Time*, trans. John Macquarrie and Edward Robinson (Oxford: Blackwell, 1962).

31 Ibid. p. 437. I am grateful to Philipp Rosemann for his discussion of Heidegger's *Wiederholen*. See Chapter 5: 'Unfolding the Tradition', in Philipp Rosemann, *The Charred Root of Meaning: continuity, transgression and the Other in Christian tradition* (Michigan: Wm B. Eerdmans, 2018).

32 Terry Eagleton, *Heathcliff and the Great Hunger: studies in Irish culture* (London: Verso, 1995), Chapter 7, pp. 273–319.

33 Hatab, *Nietzsche's Life Sentence*, p. 62.

34 Ibid.

35 Foreword to Séamus Ó Ceallaigh, *Gleanings from Ulster History* (Ballinascreen: Ballinascreen Historical Society, 1994), p. i.

36 It is claimed, for example, that it was the first language to be brought from the Tower of Babel by Fenius Farsaidh, and was the most comprehensive of all languages, containing as it did every obscure sound from all of the languages of Babel. George Calder (ed.), *Auraicept na n-Éces: the scholars' primer* (Edinburgh: John Grant, 1917), pp. 3–5.

37   James Carney, 'Literature in Irish, 1169–1534', in Art Cosgrove (ed.), *A New History of Ireland, II: medieval Ireland, 1169–1534* (Oxford: Clarendon Press, 1987), pp. 268–707. Speaking of this literary revival that reached its peak in the early years of the fifteenth century, Carney remarks that its aim was 'to recreate Ireland as it was in the past, and as it should be in the present if certain events had never happened. Consequently, families of Anglo-Norman descent are not mentioned and Gaelic Irish families are shown as ruling over territories then under effective colonial control'; ibid. p. 690.

38   Pádraig de Paor, *Áille na hÁille: gnéithe de choincheap na híobartha* (An Daingean: An Sagart, 2013), p. 144.

Chapter 2: The Anxiety of Transmission: The lives and afterlives of seventeenth-century Irish revivalism

1   Brendan Bradshaw, 'Manus the Magnificent': O'Donnell as Renaissance prince', in A. Cosgrave and D. McCartney (eds), *Studies in Irish History Presented to R. Dudley Edwards* (Dublin: UCD Press, 1979), pp. 15–36, see especially pp. 25–6.

2   Mícheál Mac Craith, 'Gaelic Ireland and the Renaissance', in G. Williams and R.O. Jones (eds), *The Celts and the Renaissance: tradition and innovation* (Cardiff: University of Wales Press, 1990), pp. 57–89.

3   Marc Caball, 'Innovation and Tradition: Irish Gaelic responses to early modern conquest and colonization', in Hiram Morgan (ed.), *Political Ideology in Ireland, 1541–1641* (Dublin: Four Courts Press, 1999), pp. 62–82; Brendan Bradshaw, 'Native Reaction to the Westward Enterprise: a case-study in Gaelic ideology', in K.R. Andrews, Nicholas P. Canny and P.E.H. Hair (eds), *The Westward Enterprise: English activities in Ireland, the Atlantic and America, 1480–1650* (Liverpool: Liverpool University Press, 1978), pp. 65–80.

4   Brendan Bradshaw, 'Reading Seathrún Céitinn's *Foras Feasa ar Éirinn*', in Pádraig Ó Riain (ed.), *Geoffrey Keating's Foras Feasa ar Éirinn: reassesments* (Dublin: Irish Texts Society, 2008), p. 7; Tomás Ó Flannghaile, *For the Tongue of the Gael* (London: City of London Book Depot, Gill, 1896); Patrick Kavanagh, *A Soul for Sale: poems* (London: Macmillan, 1947).

5   Nollaig Ó Muraíle (ed.), *Turas na dTaoiseach nUltach as Éirinn: from Ráth Maoláin to Rome* (Rome: Pontifical Irish College of Rome, 2007), p. 92. See also Mícheál Mac Craith, 'Conry, Florence (Flaithrí Ó Maolchonaire)', in *Dictionary of Irish Biography: from the earliest times to the year 2002*, http://dib.cambridge.org/ (accessed 27 November 2018); Mícheál Mac Craith, 'The Political and Religious Thought of Florence Conry and Hugh McCaughwell', in A. Ford and J. McCafferty (eds), *The Origins of Sectarianism in Early Modern Ireland* (Cambridge: Cambridge University Press, 2005), pp. 183–203.

6   Mícheál Mac Craith, 'Clár Fichille agus Coinín Baineann Bán: gaibhniú féiniúlachtaí sa Róimh sa seachtú haois déag', in Ríona Nic Congáil, Máirín Nic Eoin, Meidhbhín Ní Úrdail, Pádraig Ó Liatháin and Regina Uí Chollatáin (eds), *Litríocht na Gaeilge ar fud an Domhain: cruthú, caomhnú agus athbheochan, imleabhar 1* (Dublin: LeabhairCOMHAR, 2015), pp. 59–84.

7 Bonaventúra Ó hEodhasa, *An Teagasg Críosdaidhe* [1611], ed. Fearghal Mac Raghnaill (Dublin: Dublin Institute for Advanced Studies, 1976). The importance of Irish literary culture to Irish nuns of the seventeenth century and their contribution to it has been discussed by Marie-Louise Coolahan with specific regard to the Poor Clares; see Marie-Louise Coolahan, *Women, Writing and Language in Early Modern Ireland* (Oxford: Oxford University Press, 2010), pp. 63–101.

8 R.L. Thomson (ed.), *Foirm na nUrrnuidheadh: John Carswell's Gaelic translation of the Book of Common Order* (Edinburgh: Scottish Gaelic Texts Society, 1970).

9 Ibid. pp. 10–13, 179–81.

10 Ibid. pp. 12, 180.

11 Ailbhe Ó Corráin, *The Pearl of the Kingdom: a study of 'A Fhir Léghtha an Leabhráin Bhig' by Giolla Brighde Ó hEódhasa* (Oslo: Institute for Comparative Research in Human Culture, 2011), p. 10.

12 J.P. McKay, B.D. Hill and J. Buckler (eds), *A History of Western Society: from the Renaissance to 1815* (Boston: Houghton Mifflin, 1987), p. 414.

13 Ó Corráin, *The Pearl of the Kingdom*, p. 1.

14 Seán Ó Súilleabháin's examination of Ó Maolchonaire's sources for *Desiderius* concludes that he used a Castillian and an Italian translation of the original Catalan text *Spill de la Vida Religiosa* (1529) and, it appears likely, a French edition entitled *Thesauras Devotionis*. Seán Ó Súilleabháin, 'Scáthán an Chrábhaidh: foinsí an aistriúcháin', *Éigse*, vol. 24 (1990), pp. 26–36.

15 Thomas F. O'Rahilly (ed.), *Desiderius, Otherwise Called Sgáthán an Chrábhaidh by Flaithrí Ó Maolchonaire* (Dublin: Dublin Institute for Advanced Studies, 1975), p. 2.

16 Ibid. p. xxxviii.

17 Mac Craith, 'The political and religious thought of Florence Conry and Hugh McCaughwell', see especially p. 190.

18 Bradshaw explains that 'By confessionalism is meant the system under which the polities of Europe identified themselves exclusively with one or the other of the credal communities into which Latin Christendom fragmented at the Reformation'; Bradshaw, 'Reading Seathrún Céitinn's *Foras Feasa ar Éirinn*', p. 8.

19 Mícheál Mac Craith, '… The false and crafty bludsukkers, the Observauntes: … na súmairí bréagacha beartacha: na hObsarvaintigh', in D. Finnegan, É. Ó Ciardha and M. Peters (eds), *The Flight of the Earls: Imeacht na nIarlaí* (Derry: Guildhall Press, 2010), pp. 219–20.

20 The foreword to *Desiderius* has been characterised by Anraí Mac Giolla Chomhaill as a manifesto for the 'Louvain School of Modern Irish' for its clear enunciation of the virtues of simplicity of language. Anraí Mac Giolla Chomhaill, *Bráithrín Bocht ó Dhún: Aodh Mac Aingil* (Dublin: An Clóchomhar, 1985), p. 40.

21 See Cainneach Ó Maonaigh (ed.), *Scáthán Shacramuinte na hAithridhe: Aodh Mac Aingil O.F.M.* (Dublin: Dublin Institute for Advanced Studies, 1952), p. 5.

22 Mícheál Mac Craith, 'Literature in Irish, *c.*1550–1690', in M. Kelleher and P. O'Leary (eds), *The Cambridge History of Irish Literature. Volume 1: to 1890*

(Cambridge: Cambridge University Press, 2006), p. 203. Concluding his examination of linguistic issues in the work of the Counter-Reformation authors, Ruairí Ó hUiginn remarks that 'In an age of reform a reformed medium was required'; Ruairí Ó hUiginn, 'Transmitting the Text: some linguistic issues in the work of the Franciscans', in R. Gillespie and R. Ó hUiginn (eds), *Irish Europe, 1600–1650: writing and learning* (Dublin: Four Courts Press, 2013), p. 104.

23 See Nollaig Ó Muraíle, 'Tadhg Ó Cianáin and the Significance of His Memoir: "The only work of its kind in Irish literature"', in Fearghus Ó Fearghail (ed.), *Tadhg Ó Cianáin: an Irish scholar in Rome* (Dublin: Mater Dei Institute of Education, 2011), p. 63.

24 Mac Craith, 'Literature in Irish, *c.* 1550–1690', p. 211.

25 For a reappraisal of the historical use of the term '*Éireannach*', see Ruairí Ó hUiginn, 'Éireannaigh, Fir Éireann, Gaeil agus Gaill', in C. Breatnach and M. Ní Úrdail (eds), *Aon don Éigse: essays marking Osborn Bergin's centenary lecture on bardic poetry (1912)* (Dublin: Dublin Institute for Advanced Studies, 2015), pp. 17–49.

26 This theme is the subject of Vincent Morley's *Ó Chéitinn go Raiftearaí: mar a cumadh stair na hÉireann* (Dublin: Coiscéim, 2011). It is not surprising to see devotion to Keating's work reaching into the twentieth century, insofar as it is mentioned in Pádraig Ó Conaire's portrayal of a London Irish immigrant community in the early twentieth century in his novel *Deoraíocht* (Exile) (1910); Pádraig Ó Conaire, *Deoraíocht* [1910] (Dublin: Talbot Press, 1973), p. 89.

27 See Pádraig Ó Macháin, *The Book of the O'Conor Don: essays on an Irish manuscript* (Dublin: DIAS, 2010) p. 1; Ruairí Ó hUiginn, 'Captain Somhairle and His Books Revisited', in Pádraig Ó Macháin (ed.), *The Book of the O'Conor Don: essays on an Irish manuscript* (Dublin: DIAS, 2010), pp. 101–2.

28 Ó Macháin, '"One Glimpse of Ireland"', p. 155; see also the appendix to this article, where the author gives the full text of Ó Gadhra's address to the reader with an English translation (pp. 160–2).

29 Anthony D. Smith, *Nationalism and Modernism* (London: Routledge, 1998), p. 189. This section is an updated summary of Smith's work on nationalism.

30 The dictionary was authored by Conchobhar Ó Beaglaoich (*fl.* 1732), a cleric who appears to have belonged to the Irish college of Paris, with some assistance from the County Clare historian, scribe and poet Hugh MacCurtin/Aodh Mac Cruitín (1680–1755). Mac Curtain's envoy *A Uaisle Éireann Áille* (Ye Nobles of Beautiful Ireland) is a rallying cry similar in many ways to Froinsias Ó Maolmhuaidh's *Soruidh go hAos Óg 7 Éata Oiléin na Naomh* (Hail to the young and old of the island of saints), discussed later in this chapter. See Vincent Morley, *Aodh Buí Mac Cruitín: Dánta* (Dublin: Field Day/Keough-Naughton Institute of Irish Studies, 2012), pp. 47–50; Joseph MacMahon, 'The Silent Century, 1698–1829', in E. Bhreatnach, J. MacMahon, J. McCafferty (eds), *The Irish Franciscans, 1534–1990* (Dublin: Four Courts Press, 2009), pp. 77–101. See Chapter 3 of the present work for a brief discussion of Andrew Donlevy's *Catechism* (1742), the influential Irish text authored by an illustrious County Mayo cleric who had spent twenty-four years as prefect of the Irish college

in Paris. See Proinsias Mac Cana, *Collège des Irlandais Paris and Irish Studies* (Dublin: Dublin Institute for Advanced Studies, 2001).

31 MacMahon, 'The Silent Century', p. 96.

32 See especially Mac Cuarta's poem 'Don Easpag Ó Siail' (For Bishop O'Sheil) in praise of the Franciscan James O'Sheil, who was bishop of Down and Connor between 1717 and 1724; Seán Ó Gallchóir (ed.), *Séamus Dall Mac Cuarta: Dánta* (Dublin: An Clóchomhar, 1971), pp. 51–3.

33 On Toland, see Alan Harrison, *Béal Eiriciúil as Inis Eoghain: John Toland, 1670–1722* (Dublin: Coiscéim, 1994); Philip McGuinness, Alan Harrison and Richard Kearney (eds), *John Toland's Christianity Not Mysterious: text, associated works and critical essays* (Dublin: Lilliput Press, 1997); Terry Eagleton, *Crazy John and the Bishop and Other Essays in Irish Culture* (Cork: Cork University Press/Field Day, 1998), pp. 46–67; J.A.I. Champion, 'John Toland, the Druids, and the Politics of Celtic Scholarship', *Irish Historical Studies*, vol. 32, no. 127 (May 2001), pp. 321–42.

34 Toland's 'History of the Druids' was published posthumously as 'A Specimen of the Critical History of the Celtic Religion and Learning', in idem., *A Collection of Several Pieces of Mr John Toland Now First Published, Vol 1* (London, 1726) (see p. 58); Champion, 'John Toland, the Druids, and the Politics of Celtic Scholarship', p. 335. Two years after its publication, an order was given to have Toland's *Christianity Not Mysterious* burned twice by the public hangman in Dublin in 1697.

35 The nineteenth-century scholar Edward O'Reilly began his 1823 lecture on the revival of Irish language and literature by quoting Toland's remark from the beginning of his 'History of the Druids': 'no language is really valuable but so far as it serves to converse with the living or to learn from the dead'; see Edward O'Reilly, 'On the Question Proposed by the Ollamh Fodhlean Society, "Whether the revival of the Irish language and Irish literature can be of any and what advantage to the country in general, and what utility to society in particular" read at a meeting of the society on Tuesday 4th March 1823', RIA 24 K 4. See Toland, *A Collection of Several Pieces*, p. 6.

36 *Ancient Ireland: a Weekly Magazine,* vol. 1, no. 1 (1835), p. 4.

37 The work was also translated in part by Owen Connellan in 1846 as *The Annals of Ireland.*

38 The retrospective epithet of 'nation-builders' was applied to O'Donovan, O'Curry and George Petrie (1790–1866) by Rev. Patrick MacSweeney in his study of their lives and work published by the Catholic Truth Society: P.M. MacSweeney, *A Group of Nation-builders: O'Donovan, O'Curry, Petrie* (Dublin: Catholic Truth Society, 1913). Geoffrey Keating, *The History of Ireland from the Earliest Period to the English Invasion. By the Reverend Geoffrey Keating, D.D.*, ed. John O'Mahony (New York: P.M. Haverty, 1857).

39 The membership card of the SPIL carried an adapted version of Ó Maolmhuaidh's line as its motto, reading *Biaidh an Ghaoidhilge faoi mheas fós i n-Eirinn uasal i n-innis na rígh* (The Irish language will yet be esteemed in noble Ireland, island of the kings); see National Library of Ireland, EPH A275. See also the Gaelic Union's adoption of this line in an article by Pádraic Ó Briain

on its aims, 'Beagán Focal Timchioll Aondacht na Gaedhilge', *Irisleabhar na Gaedhilge*, no. 25 (1887), p. 7. See also J. McNeill, 'How and Why the Irish Language Is to Be Preserved', *Irish Ecclesiastical Record*, vol. 12 (December 1891), p. 1105.

40   The one significant difference between Barron's quotation and the line from Ó Maolmhuaidh's poem is in the last word, where Ó Maolmhuaidh has *mhór* (great) while Barron has *fós* (yet). Assuming that this was Barron's source, whether intentional or otherwise, the effect of *fós* is to add latency to this 'prophetic line'. *Fós* may have been transposed for *mór* in one of the various manuscript copies that were made of this text in the following centuries. It is also possible that Barron is quoting some other of Ó Maolmhuaidh's works – a history of Ireland is attributed to him elsewhere, but this has not come to light; see Froinsias Ó Maolmhuaidh, *Lucerna Fidelium*, ed. Pádraig Ó Súilleabháin (Dublin: Dublin Institute for Advanced Studies, 1962), p. xiii.

41   Cuthbert Mhág Craith, *Dán na mBráthar Mionúr* (Dublin: Dublin Institute for Advanced Studies, 1967), pp. 227–9. For a recent discussion of Ó Maolmhuaidh's *Grammatica Latino-Hibernica* and its envoy, see also Claire Carroll, *Exiles in a Global City: the Irish and early modern Rome, 1609–1783* (Leiden: Brill, 2018), pp. 144–72.

42   Ó Maolmhuaidh, *Lucerna Fidelium*, p. 11.

43   'Fíor, ge doilgheasach le a aithris, leath asdigh do bheagan aimsire gur fhas a chomhmhor sin do cheo ainbhfis an-aos og agus eata Eirionn – ni airidhim Alban bhoicht na ngaoidheal …' (It is true, though sorrowful to relate, within a short space of time that such a fog of ignorance grew among the young and old of Ireland – not to mention poor Gaelic Scotland); ibid. p. 11.

44   'A Thrionnóid 'gá dtá an chumhacht/ an mbia an dream-sa ar deórdhacht/ níos sia ó chathaoirlios Cuinn/ nó an mbia an t-athaoibhneas againn?' See Tomás Ó Rathile (ed.), *Measgra Dánta II* (Cork: Cork University Press, 1927), pp. 144–7. Ó Gnímh's poem has been included in numerous anthologies of Irish poems rendered in English, ranging from Hardiman's *Irish Minstrelsy* to Patrick Pearse's *Songs of the Irish Rebels*. I have borrowed from Pearse the phrase 'a second glory' for the original *athaoibhneas*, which is comprised of the prefix *ath* = re- or new, and *aoibhneas* = bliss, delight; see James Hardiman, *Irish Minstrelsy or Bardic Remains of Ireland, Vol 2* (London: John Robins, 1831), pp. 102–13; P.H. Pearse, *The Complete Works of Pádraic H. Pearse: songs of the Irish rebels and specimens from an Irish anthology* (Dublin: Maunsel & Co., 1918), pp. 6–11. See also Sarah McKibben, *Endangered Masculinities in Irish Poetry, 1540–1780* (Dublin: UCD Press, 2010); John Minihane, 'Hiding Ireland', *Dublin Review of Books*, http://www.drb.ie/essays/hiding-ireland (accessed 6 September 2016). For a discussion of *aoibhneas* in eighteenth-century *aisling* poetry, see Peter McQuillan, 'Loneliness Versus Delight in the Eighteenth-century Aisling', *Eighteenth-Century Ireland/Iris an Dá Chultúr*, vol. 25 (2010), pp. 11–32. On Ó Gnímh's later accommodation with the political realities after the plantation, see A.J. Hughes, '*An Dream Gaoidhealta Gallda*: east Ulster poets and patrons as Gaelic and Irish Crown *personae*', *Études Celtiques*, vol. 34 (1998–2000), pp. 233–64.

45   'Ní breath dhaor dh'fhianuibh Fáil/ An riaghuil chlaon do chongbháil.' (No

death punishment would it be for the men of Ireland/ To keep the oblique rule [of poetic language]); see Mhág Craith, *Dán na mBráthar Mionúr*, p. 228.

46 'Tarla ó Bhóinn go bruach Lighean/ dligheadh is fhiú andligheadh/ gur bhreath shaor le fianaibh Fáil/ an riaghail chlaon do chongbháil' (Since from the Boyne to the Swilly Burn [County Donegal]/ a law equivalent to disorder prevails/ to which the men of Ireland have freely assented/ to keep the crooked rule of law); see Ó Rathile, *Measgra Dánta II*, p. 145, ll. 21–4.

47 'Mar lucht na Traoi ar n-a togbhail/ dá ndíchleith i ndíothrabhaibh/ fian Teamhra a-táid ó Thailtin' (Like the people of Troy after its destruction/ consigned to [concealed in] deserts/ far from Tailte are the Irish nobility [fighting men of Tara]). Tailte is Teltown in County Meath, but represents here an area typifying Ireland or the hereditary possessions of Irish rulers; see Ó Rathile, *Measgra Dánta II*, p. 146, ll. 61–3, and his notes on places, p. 271.

48 For a discussion of this apologue, see Mícheál Mac Craith, 'Cioth na Baoise', *Béaloideas*, vol. 5 (1983), pp. 31–54.

49 Mhág Craith, *Dán na mBráthar Mionúr*, p. 228.

50 The poem 'Bíodh Aire ag Ultaibh ar Aodh', in which Ó hEódhusa retells the fable, is given with an English translation by Lambert McKenna, in *Irish Monthly*, vol. 48, no. 569 (November 1920), pp. 593–8. See also Láimhbheartach Mac Cionnaith, *Dioghluim Dána* (Dublin: Oifig an tSoláthair, 1938), pp. 236–40, 457–8. See also Michelle O'Riordan, *Irish Bardic Poetry and Rhetorical Reality* (Cork: Cork University Press, 2007), pp. 251–8 for a discussion of Ó hEodhusa's use of this apologue in both *Bíodh aire ag Ultaibh ar Aodh* and *Ionmholta Malairt Bhisigh*.

51 Cuthbert Mhág Craith, *Dán na mBráthar Mionúr*, p. 228.

52 Douglas Hyde, *Language, Lore and Lyrics*, ed. Breandán Ó Conaire (Dublin: Irish Academic Press, 1986), pp. 153–4.

53 Seán Ó Ríordáin, 'Fill Arís', in idem., *Brosna* (Dublin: Sáirséal & Dill, 1964), p. 41. For an English version of this poem, entitled 'Return Again', see Seán Ó Ríordáin, *Selected Poems/Rogha Dánta*, ed. Frank Sewell (New Haven, CT: Yale University Press, 2014), pp. 162–3.

54 See Chapter 5 for a discussion of Ó Ríordáin's poem.

55 See Donnchadh Ó Liatháin, *Tomás Ó Flannghaile: scoláire agus file* (Dublin, 1940).

56 Tomás Ó Flannghaile, *De Prosodia Hibernica* (Dublin: Gill & Son, 1908).

57 See Joost Augusteijn, *Patrick Pearse: the making of a revolutionary* (Hampshire: Palgrave Macmillan, 2010), p. 73.

58 Riggs, Pádraigín, 'The Origins of the Irish Texts Society', *History Ireland*, vol. 6, no. 1 (1998), p. 8. The inaugural general meeting of the Irish Texts Society was held in 1898, and the first volume published the following year. Since then the society has published almost seventy volumes of key texts in Irish, and over twenty volumes in its subsidiary series.

59 *For the Tongue of the Gael* carried the dedication 'do chlannaibh Gaedheal cia bé áit a m-bíd ar dhruim an domhain' (to the children of the Gael wherever on earth they reside).

60 Established by James Ronan of Manchester, the Irish lessons were written by

Rev. Ulick Bourke of Tuam (1829–87), County Galway, and were aimed at 'Keltic Students in England, Ireland, Scotland, America, Australia, the Colonies and Throughout Europe'; *Keltic Journal and Educator*, no. 1 (1869). See Proinsias Ó Maolmhuaidh, *Athair na hAthbheochana: Uilleog de Búrca* (Dublin, 1981); Ó Liatháin's short biography of Ó Flannghaile mentions the tuition the latter received while a child in Mayo from his schoolmaster Peadar Ó hOisín, an ardent Gael (Ó Liatháin, *Tomás Ó Flannghaile*, p. 21).

61   Ó Flannghaile, *De Prosodia Hibernica*, p. vii.

62   Ibid. p. vii.

63   See Ó Liatháin, *Tomás Ó Flannghaile*, pp. 24–5.

64   See John Denvir, *The Life Story of an Old Rebel* (Dublin: Sealy, Bryers and Walker, 1910), pp. 113, 206. These two essays were included in the 1907 edition of Ó Flannghaile's *For the Tongue of the Gael*.

65   See entry for 'Seán Ó Mathúna (1815–77)' at Ainm.ie (www.ainm.ie), where the authors also remark that O'Mahony is reputed to have taught Irish to students of the Irish college in Paris after fleeing Ireland shortly after the Young Ireland Rebellion of 1848.

66   Mary Daly, 'A Second Golden Age: the Irish Franciscans, 1918–63', in E. Bhreatnach, J. MacMahon and J. McCafferty (eds), *The Irish Franciscans, 1534–1990* (Dublin: Four Courts Press, 2009), p. 132.

67   Ibid. p. 148.

68   Sylvester O'Brien (ed.), *Measgra i gCuimhne Mhichíl Uí Chléirigh* (Dublin: Assisi Press, 1944).

69   The Donegal Men's Association organised a banquet in the Gresham Hotel during the weekend of 24–25 June 1944; Daly, 'A Second Golden Age', p. 147.

70   Patrick Kavanagh, 'From Monaghan to the Grand Canal', *Studies: an Irish Quarterly Review*, vol. 48, no. 189 (1959), p. 33; Cainneach Ó Maonaigh, 'Scríbhneoirí Gaeilge an Seachtú hAois Déag', *Studia Hibernica*, no. 2 (1962), pp. 182–208. While Kavanagh ('From Monaghan to the Grand Canal', p. 33) attributes the line 'bad history' to J. McManus, Cainneach Ó Maonaigh ('Scríbhneoirí Gaeilge an Seachtú hAois Déag', p. 207) claims that it was he who had suggested this assessment while in conversation with the poet.

71   See Chapter 4 for a discussion of Pearse's essay and its context.

72   Máirtín Ó Cadhain, 'Tarry Flynn', *Comhar*, vol. 8, no. 3 (Márta 1949), p. 28. The essay on the Irish Folklore Commission is discussed in detail in Chapter 5.

73   Máirtín Ó Cadhain, '[Review of] *Studia Hibernica*, Uimh. 2 1962', in Seán Ó Laighin, *Ó Cadhain i bhFeasta* (Dublin: Clódhanna Teoranta, 1990), pp. 235–7. *Deich mbliana ó inniu is tír gan fothrach gan cuimhne a bheas againn.*

74   Ó Maonaigh, 'Scríbhneoirí Gaeilge an Seachtú hAois Déag'. Ó Maonaigh's essay was reviewed by Ó Cadhain as part of his review of *Studia Hibernica*, no. 2 (Ó Cadhain, '[Review of] *Studia Hibernica*, Uimh. 2 1962').

75   Ó Maonaigh explains that the only surviving manuscript copy of this poem, kept in the Franciscan library at Killiney, bears the inscription 'Irish rime written in '97' ('Scríbhneoirí Gaeilge an Seachtú hAois Déag', p. 208). For the full text and English translation of this poem, see Paul Walsh, *Gleanings from Irish Manuscripts* (Dublin: Sign of the Three Candles, 1933), pp. 88–95.

76 Darach Ó Scolaí, *An Cléireach* (Indreabhán: Leabhar Breac, 2007); Liam
    Mac Cóil, *I dTír Strainséartha* (Indreabhán: Leabhar Breac, 2014); Liam
    Mac Cóil, *An Litir* (Indreabhán: Leabhar Breac, 2011); idem, *An Colm Bán/La
    Blanche Colombe* (Dublin: Cois Life, 2014); Breandán Ó Doibhlin, *Sliocht ar
    Thír na Scáth* (Dublin: Coiscéim, 2018).

77 Anraí Mac Giolla Chomhaill cites the Franciscans' privileging of prose over
    poetry as an example of the modernising mission of the 'Louvain School';
    Mac Giolla Chomhaill, *Bráithrín Bocht ó Dhún*, p. 40.

78 Cecile O'Rahilly, *Five Seventeenth-century Political Poems* (Dublin: Dublin
    Institute for Advanced Studies, 1977), p. 8. See also Liam Mac Mathúna,
    *Béarla sa Ghaeilge: cabhair choigríche: an códmheascadh Gaeilge/Béarla i litríocht
    na Gaeilge, 1600–1900* (Dublin: An Clóchomhar, 2007), pp. 89–115; Lesa
    Ní Mhunghaile, 'An Dearcadh a Léirítear ar Fheidhmiú an Dlí in Éirinn i
    bhFoinsí Gaeilge ón 18ú agus 19ú hAois', *Studia Hibernica*, no. 36 (2009–10),
    pp. 105–34.

79 'Óir táid amuigh ansin, a deir sé, atá ag cur bréaga orainn agus ag déanamh beag
    is fiú dhe ghníomhartha gaisce is laochais ár náisiúin. Ar son na fírinne, a deir
    sé, agus ar son go mbeidh tuairisc is tuarascáil chruinn ag náisiúin an domhain
    orainn …' [For they are out there, he says, those who lie about us and disparage
    the heroic deeds of our nation. For the sake of truth, he says, and so that other
    nations might have a record and true account of us …]; Ó Scolaí, *An Cléireach*,
    p. 90. The *An Litir* series begins, as mentioned earlier, with the entrusting of
    a highly important letter to the hero, Lúcas. It is also significant that Lúcas'
    friend and classmate at the Galway school of Alexander Lynch is Dubhaltach
    Mac Fhirbhsigh (*c.* 1600–71), the celebrated antiquary whose great work of
    genealogy was carried out in Ireland rather than abroad. In Ó Muirthile's *An
    Colm Bán/La Blanche Colombe*, while living in Paris in the 1970s the narrator
    has been given a postcard with the name and alias of a mysterious Irish woman,
    Nóra Buckley/Ellen Daunt. The narrator returns to Paris four decades later
    to investigate the story of this elusive dancer; Ó Muirthile, *An Colm Bán/La
    Blanche Colombe*, p. 18.

80 Ó Doibhlin, *Sliocht ar Thír na Scáth*, pp. 256–7. The cleric in the novel is called
    Giolla Chríost Ó Heosa, and quotes from *Truagh an t-amharc-sa, a Éire* (This
    is a sorrowful sight, O Ireland), a poem of exile by his relative Giolla Brighde
    Ó hEódhasa (ibid. p. 251). For the text of this poem and an English translation,
    see Cuthbert Mhág Craith, *Dán na mBráthar Mionúr, Cuid 1*, pp. 28–31; idem,
    Dán na mBráthar Mionúr, Cuid 2, pp. 12–13.

81 Liam Mac Cóil, *Fontenoy* (Indreabhán: Leabhar Breac, 2005), p. 152.

82 Ibid. p. 152. The term *claoninsint* carries multiple significances here, all of which
    are germane to Mac Cóil's narrative. The literal meaning of *claoninsint* is 'indirect
    speech', but the prefix *claon* means variously crooked/sloping/inclined; perverse,
    unjust, evil; oblique, indirect; see Niall Ó Dónaill (ed.), *Foclóir Gaeilge–Béarla*
    (Dublin: Rialtas na hÉireann, 1977), pp. 239–40. The play of meanings here is
    reminiscent of Froinsias Ó Maolmhuaidh's use of the phrase *an riaghuil chlaon*,
    discussed earlier. Whitley Stokes, 'Acallamh na Senórach', in Whitley Stokes and
    Ernst Windisch (eds), *Irische Texte*, ser. iv, vol. 1 (Leipzig, 1900).

83 Morley, *Ó Chéitinn go Raiftearaí*. See also Bernadette Cunningham, *The World of Geoffrey Keating: history, myth and religion in seventeenth-century Ireland* (Dublin: Four Courts Press, 2000).

84 Morley, *Ó Chéitinn go Raiftearaí*, p. 107.

85 'Na rudaí móra a rinne ár muintir anallód, na rudaí móra is toil linn a dhéanamh go fóill, sin iad an bhunsraith is gá le sinn maireachtáil beo mar threabhchas. Níl am ar bith is mó a fíoraíodh an méid sin ná nuair a bhíodh Scoil agus Cill, Éigse agus Iris ag feidhmiú as láimh a chéile.' (The great things that our people did in the past, the great things which we wish to do yet, these are the basis on which we may survive as a people. This was never more fulfilled than when [bardic] school and [monastic] cell, poetry and faith worked hand in hand'.) Ó Doibhlin, *Sliocht ar Thír na Scáth*, p. 179.

86 Bishop Redmond O'Gallagher (*c.*1521–1601) was an important figure of the Counter-Reformation in Ireland, who enthusiastically introduced the decrees of the Council of Trent, and was considered central to the petitioning and securing of Spanish intervention in Ireland.

87 'Síolraíonn brí a theidil *Desiderius* on mbunús Laidne a bheadh le de a nascadh le sidus; is é sin a bheith gan treoir ag tóraíocht réiltíní óir an eolais.' (Its title *Desiderius* comes from the combination of the Latin *de* and *sidus*, that is, being without guidance in a search for the golden stars of wisdom); Pádraig Ó Cíobháin, 'Dúchas agus Toil mo Chinn', *Comhar*, vol. 57, no. 6 (1998), p. 24.

88 Pádraig Ó Cíobháin, *Desiderius a Dó* (Dublin: Coiscéim, 1995), pp. 13–14.

89 After considering the circumstances of his baptism, Ó Cíobháin remarks, Tá an chuid sin díom a rialaíonn an Dia sa mbith faoi pharasól Logos ó shin, an Focal a ghin gleannta mo dheor. Ó fhrithrá amháin go frithrá eile. (That part of me that the God in the world regulates has been under the parasol of the *Logos* ever since, the Word that generated the vales of my tears. From one contradiction to another). Ó Cíobháin, *Desiderius a Dó*, p. 15.

90 'Place-time' is a translation of 'áit-am'. Ibid. p. 12.

91 '… guth diamhair *id* uilíoch na cosmhuintire …' Ibid. p. 11

92 'Ár gcóta cabhlaigh uile. Gluaiseacht ar tugadh An Athbheochan uirthi. Féach mar a ghluaiseann na ciníocha ón mbaois go dtí an athfhás.' Ibid. pp. 11–12.

93 The first phrase in the following quotation presents certain difficulties to the translator where Ó Cíobháin has created two compounds using the noun *bith* which means both 'world' and 'existence'. 'Fanaim bithdhílis do mo bhithchuimhne. Deinim cumarsáid léi i mbéarlagar an leannáin. Caidreamh lena chéile a mhairfidh go bás'. (I remain existence/world-faithful to my existence/world-memory. I communicate with it in the language of a lover. A relationship with it will last until death.) Ibid. p. 15.

94 '… mar gurb í an tóir ar cad as dúinn a fhágann óg de shíor sinn, gan sna blianta idir dhá linn ach ar nós na dtonn ag bualadh tóin bháid dá ndroim …' Ibid. p. 16.

95 'Is ag an bpointe seo a thosnaíos ar a bheith ag iarraidh an ama a chealú. Sórt éigin bithbhuaine a bhí uaim.' (At this point I started to try to cancel time. Some sort of world/existential permanence was what I wanted.) Ó Cíobháin, 'Dúchas agus Toil mo Chinn', p. 23.

96 Jürgen Habermas, 'An Awareness of What Is Missing', in Jürgen Habermas et al., *An Awareness of What Is Missing: faith and reason in a post-secular age*, trans. Ciaran Cronin (Cambridge: Polity Press), p. 18.

97 In Ó Doibhlin's *Slíocht ar Thír na Scáth*, the text itself owes its existence to exile – it is commissioned by the character Ó Heosa as he prepares to leave for mainland Europe, and it is uncovered for a twenty-first-century readership in the Irish college in Paris.

98 Jean Baudrillard, *Simulacra and Simulation*, trans. Sheila Faria Glaser (Michigan: University of Michigan Press, 1994), p. 43.

99 It is worth noting that An Gúm published a modern edition of the Franciscan Counter-Reformation translation of *Introduction à la Vie Dévote* by St Francis de Sales, entitled *An Bheatha Chrábaidh*; Maoghnas Ó Domhnaill (ed.), *An Bheatha Chrábhaidh* (Dublin: An Gúm, 1939).

100 Daniel Corkery, *The Hidden Ireland* (Dublin: M.H. Gill & Son, 1924).

Chapter 3: Cultural Memory, Futurity and the Instrumentalisation of Culture in the Eighteenth and Nineteenth Centuries

1 'Execution', *Morning Post*, 24 August 1825.

2 In the early twentieth century, *Craobh an Chéitinnigh* (the [Geoffrey] Keating Branch) of the Gaelic League was dominated by physical-force republicans such as Tom Clarke, Seán Mac Diarmada, Michael Collins and Cathal Brugha; see Brian Feeney, *16 Lives: Seán Mac Diarmada* (Dublin: O'Brien Press, 2014), pp. 110–11.

3 Liam Ó Danachair, 'Memories of My Youth', *Béaloideas*, vol. 17 (1947), p. 59. See also Máirtín Ó Murchú, 'Language and Society in Nineteenth Century Ireland', in G.H. Jenkins (ed.), *Language and Community in the Nineteenth Century* (Cardiff: University of Wales Press, 1998), pp. 341–68.

4 Signor Pastorini (Charles Walmesley), *General History of the Christian Church from Her Birth to Her Final Triumphant States in Heaven Chiefly Deduced from the Apocalypse of St. John the Apostle* (1771). See James S. Donnelly Jr, 'Pastorini and Captain Rock: millenarianism and sectarianism in the Rockite movement of 1821–4', in Samuel Clark and J.S. Donnelly Jr (eds), *Irish Peasants: violence and political unrest, 1780–1914* (Wisconsin: University of Wisconsin Press, 1983), pp. 102–39. For an overview of literature in Irish during the nineteenth century and a discussion of the poets mentioned above, see Gearóid Denvir, 'Literature in Irish 1800–1890, from the Act of Union to the Gaelic League', in M. Kelleher and P. O'Leary (eds), *The Cambridge History of Irish Literature. Volume 1: to 1890* (Cambridge: Cambridge University Press, 2006), pp. 544–98.

5 See James S. Donnelly Jr, *Captain Rock: the Irish agrarian rebellion of 1821–1824* (Cork: Collins Press, 2009), and Seamus Deane's review of this work in *History Ireland*, vol. 18, no. 6 (November/December 2010), pp. 56–7. See also Thomas Moore, *Memoirs of Captain Rock*, ed. Emer Nolan (Dublin: Field Day/Keough-Naughton Institute of Irish Studies, 2008).

6 Nicholas Wolf, *An Irish-speaking Island: state, religion, community, and the*

linguistic landscape in Ireland, 1770–1870 (Wisconsin: University of Wisconsin Press, 2014), pp. 18–20.

7   Breandán Ó Buachalla, 'Canóin na Creille: an file ar leaba a bháis', in Máirín Ní Dhonnchadha (ed.), *Nua-léamha: gnéithe de chultúr, stair agus pholaitíocht na hÉireann c. 1600–c. 1900* (Dublin: An Clóchomhar, 1996), pp. 149–69.

8   Pre-1851 estimates are always very contestable, and census figures from 1851 onwards must also come with a caveat given the spectrum of under-reporting before the rise of the Gaelic League as a national movement in the early twentieth century, and of over-reporting after this point – i.e. from the 1911 census onwards. For a detailed demographic analysis of language shift based on census figures, see Garret Fitzgerald, 'Estimates for Baronies of Minimum Level of Irish-speaking Amongst Successive Decennial Cohorts: 1771–1781 to 1861–1871', *Proceedings of the Royal Irish Academy*, vol. 84C (1984), pp. 117–55, and also Garret Fitzgerald, 'Irish-speaking in the Pre-Famine Period: a study based on the 1911 census data for people born before 1851 and still alive in 1911', *Proceedings of the Royal Irish Academy*, vol. 103C [5] (2003), pp. 191–283.

9   See Seán de Fréine, 'The Dominance of the English Language in the Nineteenth Century', in Diarmaid Ó Muirithe (ed.), *The English Language in Ireland* (Cork: Mercier Press, 1977), p. 80. For a recent assessment of the estimates of numbers of Irish speakers in the nineteenth century, see Gearóid Ó Tuathaigh, *I mBéal an Bháis: the Great Famine and the language shift in nineteenth-century Ireland* (Connecticut: Quinnipiac University Press, 2015), pp. 9–11; Aidan Doyle, *A History of the Irish Language* (Oxford: Oxford Linguistics, 2015), pp. 128–32. See *The Census of Ireland for the Year 1851, Part VI. General Report* (Dublin: Thom & Sons, 1856), pp. xlvi–xlviii.

10   See Ó Tuathaigh, *I mBéal an Bháis*, p. 9.

11   See Merike Darmody and Tania Daly (eds), *Attitudes Towards the Irish Language on the Island of Ireland* (Dublin: ESRI/Foras na Gaeilge, 2015).

12   See Irene Whelan, *The Bible War in Ireland: the 'Second Reformation' and the polarization of Protestant–Catholic relations, 1800–1840* (Wisconsin: University of Wisconsin Press, 2005).

13   'Is claoidhte agus is bocht an cás do aon neach dá bhfuair ni air bith do fhior léighinn agus nach fios dhó theangaidh dhútheais fein do léughadh na do sgriobhadh; agus ar an ábhar sin ba chóir do gach duine againn ina bhfuil tuigse ansa teangaidh cheadhna, cuideadh re na cheile, ionnus go tiubhramaois í chum úsáide ris ó do chailleamur i re foirneart eiriceach'; RIA 23 I 30. I am grateful to Fintan Keegan for this reference. In a recent article based on her study of the Agallamh Oísín agus Phádraig (The Dialogue between Oisín and St Patrick) in the late manuscript tradition, Síle Ní Mhurchú highlights the paratextual evidence for a conscious awareness of the scribal mission that included an implicitly patriotic role and an active concern for the decline of the Irish language; Síle Ní Mhurchú, 'Agallamh Oisín agus Phádraig: léamha ón bparaitéacs', *Comhar Thaighde 2*, http://comhartaighde.ie/eagrain/2/nimhurchu (accessed 10 August 2017).

14   See Tony Crowley, *The Politics of Language in Ireland, 1366–1922* (London: Routledge, 2000), pp. 110–11.

15 Andrew Donlevy, *An Teagasg Críosduidhe do réir Ceasda agus Freagartha, air na Tharruing go Bunudhasach as Bréithir Shoilléir Dé, agus as Toibreacaibh Fíorghlana Oile. The Catechism, or Christian Doctrine by Way of Question and Answer, Drawn Chiefly from the Express Word of God, and Other Pure Sources* (Paris, 1742). See Crowley, *The Politics of Language in Ireland*, p. 115.

16 Joep Leerssen, *Mere Irish and Fíor-Ghael: studies in the idea of Irish nationality, its development and literary expression prior to the nineteenth century* (Cork: Cork University Press, 1996), pp. 330–1. Leerssen notes that a similar Welsh society, the Cymmrodorion, had been established the year previously in Wales (ibid. p. 340).

17 James Carney (ed.), *A Genealogical History of the O'Reillys* (Cavan: Cumann Sheanchais Bhreifne, 1959), pp. 21–2. Carney remarks that 'the spirit of the document anticipates that of the Gaelic League by well over a century' (ibid. p. 21).

18 See Leerssen, *Mere Irish and Fíor-Ghael*, p. 244. See also Pádraig Ó Fiannachta, *An Barántas* (Maigh Nuad: An Sagart, 1978). The *barántas* normally took the form of a preamble in prose followed by the main section in verse (ibid. p. 25).

19 'D'onórughadh re iar-chruinniughadh aithbheodhadh agus síor-aithris.' This piece is not strictly a 'warrant' but a summons to a poetic court, as Patrick Dinneen remarks in his *Filidhe na Máighe* (Dublin: Gill & Sons, 1906), p. 193. However, given its other similarities to the *barántas*, it is included by Dinneen in a section of *barántas* compositions in his *Filidhe na Máighe*, and also by Ó Fiannachta in his anthology of the *barántas*, *An Barántas* (cited above).

20 Leerssen, *Mere Irish and Fíor-Ghael*, pp. 244–5. I have modified the English translation slightly.

21 Brian Ó Cuív, 'Rialacha do Chúirt Éigse ó Chontae an Chláir', *Éigse*, vol. 11, 1965–66, pp. 216–18; Diarmaid Ó Muirithe, *Tomás Ó Míocháin: filíocht* (Dublin: An Clóchomhar, 1988), pp. 33–4, 89; Brian Ó Dálaigh, 'Tomás Ó Míocháin and the Munster Courts of Gaelic Poetry, *c.*1730–1804', *Eighteenth-century Ireland/Iris an Dá Chultúr*, vol. 27 (2012), pp. 142–61.

22 Although now known as Ardsollus, Ó Míocháin's native village was, in his time, called Assolas, from the Irish Áth Solais' (Ford of Light). See Ó Dálaigh, 'Tomás Ó Míocháin and the Munster Courts of Gaelic Poetry', p. 142. Ó Dálaigh provides extensive biographical details and a discussion of Ó Míocháin's poetry.

23 See ibid. pp. 145–6.

24 Ibid. p. 156.

25 For a comprehensive discussion of the representation of such contemporary international and national concerns in contemporary Gaelic sources, see Cornelius G. Buttimer, '*Cogadh Sagsana Nuadh Sonn*': reporting the American Revolution', *Studia Hibernica*, no. 28 (1994), pp. 63–101; Vincent Morley, *Washington i gCeannas a Ríochta: cogadh Mheiriceá i litríocht na Gaeilge* (Dublin: Coiscéim, 2005).

26 See Ó Dálaigh, 'Tomás Ó Míocháin and the Munster Courts of Gaelic Poetry', pp. 152–5; Morley, *Washington i gCeannas a Ríochta*.

27 'Moladh na Volunteers' (In praise of the Volunteers); 'Ar n-éirí do Fencibles' (After the rise of the Fencibles), Ó Muirithe, *Tomás Ó Míocháin*, pp. 78–81.

28 'san am seo ina bhfuil príomhcheannaibh prionsúil agus fostaibh fíoruaisle ár

dtíre ag saothrú ár saorgacht go fíordhíleas i mórdháil na hÉireann i mBéal Átha Cliath'; Ó Muirithe, *Tomás Ó Míocháin*, p. 33. On a more specific note, Buttimer asks whether the presence in the Dublin parliament of Sir Lucius O'Brien, a Clare man, may have influenced Ó Míocháin 'to seek an assembly of Gaelic scholars to cultivate Irish language and literature modelled after the parliament …?'; Buttimer, '*Cogadh Sagsana Nuadh Sonn*', p. 76.

29 Ó Muirithe, *Tomás Ó Míocháin*, p. 84.

30 Ibid; Buttimer, '*Cogadh Sagsana Nuadh Sonn*', p. 76.

31 Lesa Ní Mhunghaile has dealt extensively with attitudes evinced in Irish-language sources of the eighteenth and nineteenth centuries to the English common law that supplanted the native system from the sixteenth century onwards (see note in Chapter 1); Ní Mhunghaile, 'An Dearcadh a Léirítear ar Fheidhmiú an Dlí in Éirinn i bhFoinsí Gaeilge ón 18ú agus 19ú hAois'.

32 In an illuminating essay on the *barántas* and macaronic verse in the eighteenth century, Liam Mac Mathúna remarks of the *barántas* that it was 'explicitly satiric and as a *genre* it parodied the law, subverting respect for the *status quo*'; Liam Mac Mathúna, 'Verisimilitude or Subversion? Probing the interaction of English and Irish in selected warrants and macaronic verse in the eighteenth century', in James Kelly and Ciarán Mac Murchaidh (eds), *Irish and English: essays on the Irish linguistic and cultural frontier, 1600–1900* (Dublin: Four Courts Press, 2012), pp. 137–8.

33 See Ó Dálaigh, 'Tomás Ó Míocháin and the Munster Courts of Gaelic Poetry', p. 156.

34 'an beagán atá re léamh agus litir-ealaí in ár measc, cúnamh re chéile go dúthrachtach, dilchroíoch chum na léirtheangan líonfhoclach seo d'fhuascladh as anbhá agus do niamhghlanadh ó dhaorfhiailibh'; Ó Muirithe, *Tomás Ó Míocháin*, p. 33.

35 John MacErlean (ed.), *Duanaire Dháibhidh Uí Bhruadair: the poems of David Ó Bruadair. Part 2* (London: Irish Texts Society, 1913), pp. 138–9. Ó Bruadair's 'Is mairg nach fuil 'na dhubhthuata' (Woe to those who are not gloomy boors) is frequently cited as an example of increasing philistinism in the wake of the decline of bardic schools in the mid-seventeenth century; see John MacErlean (ed.,) *Duanaire Dháibhidh Uí Bhruadair: the poems of David Ó Bruadair. Part 1* (London: Irish Texts Society, 1910) pp. 130–3.

36 The first line of verse quoted is from Ó Míocháin's tribute to his friend and fellow scribe John Lloyd's (Seón Llúid) *A Short Tour or an Impartial and Accurate Description of the County of Clare* (Ennis, 1780); see Ó Murithe, *Tomás Ó Míocháin*, pp. 74, 93. The second is from Ó Míocháin's lament for Sir Lucius O'Brien published in a local newspaper; see Ó Dálaigh, 'Tomás Ó Míocháin and the Munster Courts of Gaelic Poetry', p. 158. Discussing the background to Merriman's *Cúirt an Mheon-Oíche*, Seán Ó Tuama remarks on the fact that while the Irish language was 'receding rapidly … there was probably a high degree of bilinguality at all levels of society at this period in East Clare'; Seán Ó Tuama, 'Brian Merriman and His Court', *Irish University Review*, vol. 11, no. 2 (autumn 1981), pp. 156–7.

37 Liam P. Ó Murchú (ed.), *Cúirt an Mheon-Oíche* (Dublin: An Clóchomhar,

1982). There are a significant number of English translations of Merriman's *Cúirt*, one of the most recent being by Ciarán Carson, *The Midnight Court* (Oldcastle: Gallery Press, 2005).

38 Ó Dálaigh, 'Tomás Ó Míocháin', pp. 156–7.

39 Ó Buachalla, 'Canóin na Creille: an File ar Leaba a Bháis', p. 166.

40 Buttimer makes a cogent argument for the sense in which issues such as the discussion of illegitimacy in *Cúirt an Mheon-Oíche* are reflective of contemporary national and international arguments concerning the legitimacy of various forms of government, the exclusiveness of certain social institutions and the desire for a more inclusive form of citizenship and the rejection of marginalisation. See Buttimer, '*Cogadh Sagsana Nuadh Sonn*', p. 89.

41 Wolf, *An Irish-speaking Island*, pp. 149–64.

42 Ó Tuama, 'Brian Merriman and His Court', p. 157.

43 'Tá cailín spéiriúil ag fear gan Bhéarla, dubhghránna cróin'; Breandán Ó Buachalla (ed.), *Peadar Ó Doirnín: amhráin* (Dublin: An Clóchomhar, 1969), p. 61; 'Muiris Ó Gormáin', in ibid. pp. 51–2. See Charles Dillon, '*An Ghaeilg Nua*: English, Irish and the south Ulster poets and scribes in the late seventeenth and eighteenth centuries', in James Kelly and Ciarán Mac Murchaidh (eds), *Irish and English: essays on the Irish linguistic and cultural frontier, 1600–1900* (Dublin: Four Courts Press, 2012), pp. 141–61.

44 Mac Mathúna, 'Verisimilitude or Subversion?', p. 138. Daniel Corkery, *The Hidden Ireland* (Dublin: M.H. Gill & Son, 1924); Joep Leerssen, *Hidden Ireland, Public Sphere* (Galway: Arlen House, 2002). Among the most recent studies that include counterarguments to Leerssen's thesis are Lesa Ní Mhunghaile, 'Bilingualism, Print Culture in Irish and the Public Sphere, 1700–c.1830', in James Kelly and Ciarán Mac Murchaidh (eds), *Irish and English: essays on the Irish linguistic and cultural frontier, 1600–1900* (Dublin: Four Courts Press, 2012), pp. 218–42; and Morley, *Ó Chéitinn go Raifteataí*.

45 See Ó Tuama's discussion of the affiliations between Merriman's poem and the medieval European 'courts of love'; Ó Tuama, 'Brian Merriman and His Court'.

46 Brian Ó Cuív, 'Irish Language and Literature, 1691–1845', in T.W. Moody and W. Vaughan (eds), *A New History of Ireland, IV: eighteenth-century Ireland, 1691–1800* (Oxford: Clarendon Press, 1986), pp. 374–473. See p. 381.

47 For a discussion of nineteenth-century literature in Irish, see Gearóid Denvir, 'Literature in Irish, 1800–1892: from the Act of Union to the Gaelic League', in Margaret Kelleher and Philip O'Leary (eds), *The Cambridge History of Irish Literature. Volume 1: to 1890* (Cambridge: Cambridge University Press, 2006), pp. 544–98.

48 See, for example, the detailed case made by the veteran itinerant Methodist preacher James McQuige to the Baptist Irish Society quoted by Pádraig de Brún, *Scriptural Instruction in the Vernacular: the Irish Society and its teachers, 1818–1827* (Dublin: Dublin Institute for Advanced Studies, 2009), pp. 11–13.

49 For a brief account of proselytising in New York, see Kenneth E. Nilsen, 'The Irish Language in New York, 1850–1900', in Ronald H. Bayor and Timothy J. Meagher (eds), *The New York Irish* (Baltimore: Johns Hopkins University Press, 1996), p. 257.

50 This emotional attachment is also evinced in the sources discussed by Liam Mac Mathúna in his study of 'code-mixing' (Irish and English) in Irish literature from 1600 to 1900; Mac Mathúna, *Béarla sa Ghaeilge*.

51 Pádraig de Brún, 'The Irish Society's Bible Teachers, 1818–27', *Éigse*, vol. 19, no. 2 (1983), p. 289.

52 Pádraig de Brún, '"Gan Teannta Buird Ná Binse": scríobhnaithe na Gaeilge, *c.* 1650–1850', *Comhar*, vol. 31, no. 11 (samhain 1972), p. 15. The quotation is from the biography of Rev. John Alcock by his daughter Deborah Alcock, *Walking with God: a memoir of the venerable John Alcock* (London, 1887).

53 Bernadette Cunningham and Raymond Gillespie, 'Cultural Frontiers and the Circulation of Manuscripts in Ireland, 1625–1725', in James Kelly and Ciarán Mac Murchaidh (eds), *Irish and English: essays on the Irish linguistic and cultural frontier, 1600–1900* (Dublin: Four Courts Press, 2012), p. 94.

54 See Meidhbhín Ní Úrdail, *The Scribe in Eighteenth- and Nineteenth-century Ireland: motivations and milieu* (Münster: Nodus Publikationen, 2000), pp. 77, 208–9.

55 Breandán Ó Buachalla, *I mBéal Feirste Cois Cuain* (Dublin: An Clóchomhar, 1968), p. 186.

56 'air mhaithe leis an nGaoidheilg agus d'fhonn coghnamh fuasgalta do thabhairt uirthi ón ndorchadas ndearmadach ndanardha ionna bhfuil le cian d'aimsir'; see Ní Úrdail, *The Scribe in Eighteenth- and Nineteenth-century Ireland*, p. 98.

57 Aleida Assmann, 'Canon and Archive', in Astrid Erll and Ansgar Nünning (eds), *Cultural Memory Studies: an international and interdisciplinary handbook* (Berlin: Walter de Gruyter, 2008), p. 101.

58 For a statistical discussion of manuscript copies of these two texts, see Vincent Morley, 'The popular influence of *Foras Feasa ar Éirinn*', in James Kelly and Ciarán Mac Murchaidh (eds), *Irish and English: essays on the Irish linguistic and cultural frontier, 1600–1900* (Dublin: Four Courts Press, 2012).

59 Ibid. p. 103.

60 Ibid. p. 104.

61 'D'fhág na scríobhaithe mórán againn nár scagamar fós: "An rud a bhí romham, beidh sé im dhiaidhse – ag an nduine is eolach fágaim an criathradh." Sin é an tuiscint a bhí ag duine acu dá chúram. Fúinne atá an criathradh a dhéanamh más suim linn an dream a chuaidh romhainn'; de Brún, 'Gan Teannta Buird ná Binse', p. 20.

62 Edward Bunting, *The Ancient Music of Ireland* (Dublin: Hodges & Smith, 1840), p. 63.

63 Thomas Davis, *Thomas Davis: essays literary and historical*, ed. D.J. O'Donoghue (Dundalk, 1914), p. 101 (emphasis in original text).

64 Ibid. pp. 98, 105.

65 Ibid. p. 104.

66 See Proinsias Ó Drisceoil, *Seán Ó Dálaigh: éigse agus iomarbhá* (Cork: Cork University Press, 2007), pp. 341–6; National Library of Ireland, MS G 416.

67 National Library of Ireland, MS G 416.

68 See R.V. Comerford, *Ireland (Inventing the Nation)* (London: Bloomsbury, 2003), pp. 139–40; Damien Murray, *Romanticism, Nationalism and Irish*

Antiquarian Societies, 1840–80 (Maynooth: Dept. of Old and Middle Irish, 2000), pp. 86–90. Oisín, son of Finn mac Cumhaill, was the narrator of Fenian tales and lays as most famously recorded in the late twelfth-century text *Acallamh na Senórach* (The Colloquy of the Ancients), in which Oisín and Caoilte Mac Rónáin were supposed to have related the exploits of Finn and his warrior band of *Fianna* to St Patrick. Ossian was the supposed bard whose compositions were presented initially by James Macpherson in his *Fingal* (1761) and *Temora* (1763).

69 See Murray, *Romanticism, Nationalism and Irish Antiquarian Societies*, pp. 92–5.
70 Ó Drisceoil, *Seán Ó Dálaigh*, p. 323.
71 See John Hutchinson, *The Dynamics of Cultural Nationalism: the Gaelic Revival and the creation of the Irish nation state* (London: Allen & Unwin, 1987), p. 49. Notwithstanding this specific criticism, Hutchinson's work is a major landmark, particularly in his development of the conceptual insights of theorists of nationalism, particularly Elie Kedourie, Ernest Gellner and Anthony D. Smith, as they apply to Ireland.
72 Ibid. p. 49.
73 See 'MacKnight (McKnight), James', *Dictionary of Irish Biography*, vol. 6 (Cambridge: Cambridge University Press, 2009), pp. 53–5; Roger Blaney, *Presbyterians and the Irish Language* (Belfast: Ulster Historical Foundation and Ultach Trust, 1996), pp. 143–59.
74 Blaney, *Presbyterians and the Irish Language*, pp. 143, 239.
75 Ibid. p. 148. The *Dictionary of Irish Biography* entry for MacKnight gives the dates *c.* 1830–46 for his editorship of the *Belfast News-letter*, while Blaney gives the dates 1827–46. The editorial pieces concerning the Irish language, discussed here, dating from January 1828 onwards, are clearly MacKnight's work.
76 'Improvement of the Irish Through the Medium of the Aboriginal Language', *Belfast News-letter*, 4 January 1828.
77 Ibid.
78 Ibid.
79 'Literature' [review of *Bibliothecha Scoto-Celtica*], *Belfast News-letter*, 23 October 1832. The Highland Society of Scotland was founded in 1784 and its library instituted in 1789. One of a number of improving societies founded in the late eighteenth century, its aims centred on a concern for the economic improvement of the Highlands and the preservation of its culture. It is now the Royal Highland and Agricultural Society of Scotland. See Ronald Black, 'The Gaelic Academy: the cultural commitment of the Highland Society of Scotland', *Scottish Gaelic Studies*, vol. 14, no. 2 (1986), pp. 1–38.
80 'Ulster Gaelic Society', *Belfast News-letter*, 25 November 1834.
81 Ibid.
82 The first printed edition of Mac Cumhaigh's poetry was Énrí Ó Muirgheasa, *Amhráin Airt Mhic Chubhthaigh agus Amhráin Eile* (Dundalk: Dundalgan Press, 1916). For the text of 'Aisling Airt Mhic Cumhaigh', see Tomás Ó Fiaich (ed.), *Art Mac Cumhaigh: dánta* (Dublin: An Clóchomhar, 1973), pp. 111–13. See also Art Hughes, 'Gaelic Poets and Scribes of the South Armagh Hinterland in the Eighteenth and Nineteenth Century', in A.J. Hughes and William Nolan

(eds), *Armagh: history and society: interdisciplinary essays on the history of an Irish county* (Dublin: Geography Publications, 2001), pp. 505–56.

83   See Ó Fiaich, *Art Mac Cumhaigh*, p. 156.

84   Ibid. p. 113.

85   Blaney, *Presbyterians and the Irish Language*, p. 143. MacKnight is also known to have used the Irish form of his name, Séumas MacNeachtain; see Séamus Ó Néill, 'Séamus Ó Néill Writes About the Tenant Right Leader and Gaelic Scholar, James McKnight', *Irish Times*, 7 May 1976.

86   The verse is from Horace's *Epodes* and the translation quoted is from Joseph Farrell and Damien P. Nelis (eds), *Augustan Poetry and the Roman Republic* (Oxford: Oxford University Press, 2013), p. 225.

87   'Ulster Gaelic Society', *Belfast News-letter*, 25 November 1834.

88   'Irish Language – Synod of Ulster', *Belfast News-letter*, 11 October 1833.

89   On another occasion, in which he castigates the politics of the Repeal movement and the *Nation* newspaper, he gladly acknowledges their success towards 'preserving and extending the aboriginal language of Ireland – a language the most intensely beautiful and philosophical, though simple in its construction, that was ever spoken by man'; 'The songs and ballads of the *Nation*', *Belfast News-letter*, 27 September 1844.

90   Ó Néill, 'Séamus Ó Néill Writes About the Tenant Right Leader and Gaelic Scholar James McKnight'.

91   'The songs and ballads of the *Nation*', *Belfast News-letter*, 27 September 1844.

92   See Colm Ó Baoill, 'Norman MacLeod: *cara na nGael*', *Scottish Gaelic Studies*, vol. 13, no. 2 (summer 1981), pp. 159–68; see also the biographical preface in Norman MacLeod, *Caraid nan Gaidheal/The Friend of the Gael: a selection of his writings* (Edinburgh: John Grant, 1910).

93   Ó Baoill, 'Norman MacLeod', pp. 162–4. At a special synod of the Presbyterian Church in Dublin in September 1833, it was agreed that MacLeod would go to Galway and other districts to ascertain, on behalf of the Presbyterian Home Mission, how best to use Irish as a medium of spiritual instruction. His experience of the difficulties of using Scottish Gaelic in Connacht was to inform his practical proposals for advancing the Presbyterian mission to Irish speakers. The following year, MacLeod decided to undertake the translation of the psalms of David into Irish with the help of an Irish scholar, Thaddaeus Connellan (*c.* 1780–1854).

94   MacLeod, 'A Letter to the Rev. G. Bellis, by Norman McLeod D.D.', p. 343.

95   Daniel Dewar, *Observations on the Character, Customs, and Superstitions of the Irish* (London, 1812), pp. 88–9; Christopher Anderson, *Historical Sketches of the Native Irish and Their Descendants* (Edinburgh, 1828), pp. 150–1. See also Whelan, *The Bible War in Ireland*, pp. 100–1.

96   See Fionntán de Brún, '"Society in Ulster seems breaking up": an tionsclú, an imirce agus pobal na Gaeilge sa naoú haois déag', in F. de Brún and S. Mac Mathúna (eds), *Éigse Loch Lao: teanga agus litríocht na Gaeilge sa naoú haois déag* (University of Ulster, 2012), p. 139.

97   MacLeod, 'A Letter to the Rev. G. Bellis', pp. 345–6.

98   See Dewar, *Observations on the Character, Customs, and Superstitions of the Irish*, pp. 57–8.

99 As Emer Nolan explains in her introduction to the Field Day edition, *Memoirs of Captain Rock* was an immediate success when first published in London in 1824, and numerous editions were printed in London and elsewhere, including French and German translations; see Moore, *Memoirs of Captain Rock*, p. xi.

100 Norman MacLeod, 'To the Rev. George Bellis, Secretary to the Presbyterian Missionary Society for Ireland', *Orthodox Presbyterian* [Belfast], vol. 5 (1834), p. 53 (emphasis in original text).

101 MacLeod, 'A Letter to the Rev. G. Bellis', pp. 346–7.

102 See, for example, the account provided in the *Orthodox Presbyterian* of 'Religious Revivals in America' by J. Hawes of Connecticut after a request from the editor; *Orthodox Presbyterian* [Belfast], vol. 4 (1833), pp. 133–9.

103 'Bigotry and religious nonsense are not confined to Irish Catholics, for the Presbyterians have made themselves conspicuous by insane exhibitions which they term Revivals and which have made them look ridiculous in the eyes of thinking persons'; diary entry from September 1859 quoted in Ó Buachalla, *I mBéal Feirste Cois Cuain*, p. 251.

104 See Paul Mervyn Darragh, 'Epidemiological Observations on Episodes of Communicable Psychogenic Illness', PhD thesis, Queen's University Belfast, 1988. Dr Darragh's wide-ranging study includes an in-depth historical medical case study of the 1859 Ulster Evangelical Revival. I am very grateful to the author of this thesis for the opportunity to consult his work.

105 See Ó Buachalla, *I mBéal Feirste Cois Cuain*, p. 85. The main aims of the Ulster Gaelic Society were stated as follows: 'I. To establish Schools, where reading, writing and arithmetic may be taught by means of the Irish language; II. To publish useful books in that tongue for the benefit of the lower classes; III. To collect books and manuscripts, for an Irish library, with a view of promoting the last mentioned subject and preserving the remains of Irish Literature, which are fast mouldering to decay. IV. To maintain a teacher of the Irish language in Belfast, that the educated classes in this town may be enabled to take an interest in the operations of the Society and to judge of its performances. See correspondence from Ulster Gaelic Society to the 1st Duke of Buckingham and Chandos in 1830, British Library, Add MS 70992, Morgan-Grenville Papers (ser. II), vol. I (f. 86). See also Blaney, *Presbyterians and the Irish Language*, pp. 119–22. Although Blaney detects, in the description of the society's aims, the influence of Thaddaeus Connellan – the scholar who assisted MacLeod in producing the metrical psalms in Irish and a pivotal figure in the Irish Bible societies movement – the Ulster Gaelic Society resolved 'not to interfere in the least degree with religion'. Blaney, *Presbyterians and the Irish Language*, p. 121.

106 Robert MacAdam, 'The Archaeology of Ulster', *Ulster Journal of Archaeology*, 1st ser., vol. 1 (1853), pp. 1–8.

107 Edward Bunting, *The Ancient Music of Ireland* (Dublin: Hodges & Smith, 1840), p. 63.

108 It is worth noting here that a Latin version of the same biblical quotation was adopted as the motto of the Irish Folklore Society of 1927.

109 See Blaney, *Presbyterians and the Irish Language*, pp. 99–102.

110 McManus describes his object as being 'to form, in connection with our

Church, the nucleus of a native congregation worshipping God in their own Irish language, and thoroughly Celtic in their sympathies, like the Highland congregations attached to the sister Church in Scotland'; Henry McManus, *Sketches of the Irish Highlands: descriptive, social and religious* (London, 1863), p. 237.

111   Ibid. p. 26.

112   Ibid. pp. 191–2.

113   Pearse's sister recalled that this disguise allowed Pearse to 'sit at their homely, hospitable turf-fires, drinking in all their beautiful stories and exquisite music to his heart's content'; Mary Brigid Pearse (ed.), *The Home Life of Pádraig Pearse* (Dublin: Mercier Press, 1979), p. 42.

114   Desmond Ryan, *Remembering Sion: a chronicle of storm and quiet* (London: Arthur Barker, 1934), p. 186.

115   Ibid. p. 185. For a discussion of Connemara as presented in Pearse's short stories, 'poor in material goods but rich in social and intellectual capital', see Angela Bourke, 'The Imagined Community of Pearse's Short Stories', in Róisín Higgins and Regina Uí Chollatáin (eds), *The Life and After-life of P.H. Pearse/ Pádraic Mac Piarais: saol agus oidhreacht* (Dublin: Irish Academic Press, 2009), pp. 141–55.

116   See Nioclás Mac Cathmhaoil, *Muiris Ó Gormáin: beatha agus saothar* (Cló Iar-Chonnacht, 2012).

117   For further biographical detail and a summary of this incident, see Fionntán de Brún, 'Expressing the Nineteenth Century in Irish: the poetry of Aodh Mac Domhnaill (1802–67)', *New Hibernia Review*, vol. 15, no. 1 (earrach/ spring 2011), pp. 81–106. For a full discussion of this particular episode, see Ó Buachalla, *I mBéal Feirste Cois Cuain*, pp. 104–13.

118   See Colm Beckett, *Aodh Mac Domhnaill: dánta* (Dublin: An Clóchomhar, 1987); Fionntán de Brún, 'Aodh Mac Domhnaill: tuiscint, cuimhne is toil shaor', in M. Ní Úrdail and C. Mac Giolla Léith (eds), *Mo Ghnósa Leas an Dáin: aistí in ómós do Mháirtín Ó Direáin* (An Daingean: An Sagart 2014), pp. 173–94; Colm Beckett, *Fealsúnacht Aodha Mhic Dhomhnaill* (Dublin: An Clóchomhar, 1967).

119   See Tomás Ó Fiaich and Liam Ó Caithnia (eds), *Art Mac Bionaid: dánta* (Dublin: An Clóchomhar, 1979), pp. 20–1, 55–9, 102–5.

120   Séamus P. Ó Mórdha, 'Arthur Bennett's Correspondence with Robert S. Mac Adam', *Seanchas Ardmhacha: Journal of the Armagh Diocesan Historical Society*, vol. 2, no. 2 (1957), p. 388.

121   MacAdam may also be said to have inherited an affinity for the language, if not a working knowledge, from his father's family, several of whom attended Irish classes in 1809. Of these, Robert MacAdam (uncle of Robert Shipboy MacAdam) was a collector of Irish songs. The Irish class referred to was taken by James Cody (Séamus Mac Óda), a scribe and piper, at 8 Pottinger's Entry, and was organised by the Irish Harp Society; see Brighid Mhic Sheáin agus Séamus Mac Diarmada, *Robert Shipboy MacAdam in Albain, 1848* (Dublin: Coiscéim, 2009), pp. 6–8; Ó Buachalla, *I mBéal Feirste Cois Cuain*, p. 70.

122   MacAdam, 'The Archaeology of Ulster', p. 2.

123 James MacKnight commented on the same divide: 'A *Scotchman* in the country districts of the North is synonymous with a *Presbyterian* – an *Irishman* with a *R. Catholic*'; 'Literature' [review of *Bibliotecha Scoto-Celtica*], *Belfast News-letter*, 23 October 1832.

124 Énrí Ó Muirgheasa, *Amhráin na Midhe* (Dublin: Cómhlucht Oideachais na hÉireann, 1933), p. 9.

125 Raymond Williams, *The Politics of Modernism: against the new conformists* (London: Verso, 1989), p. 45.

126 See Colm Beckett (ed.), *Fealsúnacht Aodha Mhic Dhomhnaill* (Dublin: An Clóchomhar, 1967). Mac Domhnaill's philosophy has been described as a treatment of 'the necessity and value of philosophy, the nature of the Deity, the mystery of the Blessed Trinity and its analogies in nature; generation, heredity and variation; the nature of man, the human senses, psychology; the nature of herbs and plants, and their healing properties; *Materia Medica* and Therapeutics, the names, peculiarities and habits of the various animals, birds, reptiles, and insects, the life of the bee, the trees and cereals of Ireland'; Canon F.W. O'Connell, 'The Philosophy of Aodh Mac Domhnaill', *Journal of the County Louth Archaeological Society*, vol. 3, no. 4 (November 1915), p. 315. See also de Brún, 'Expressing the Nineteenth Century in Irish', pp. 87–8.

127 See 'Fáilte Pheadair Uí Ghealacáin lena Eachtra agus a Ráfladh' (Peadar Ó Gealacáin's Welcome with [an account of] his Adventure[s] and Nonsense), in Beckett, *Fealsúnacht Aodha Mhic Dhomhnaill*, pp. 84–8.

128 Beckett, *Aodh Mac Domhnaill*, pp. 38–40.

129 Ibid. p. 40.

130 Liam Mac Mathúna has drawn attention to a similar phenomenon evidenced in the increased use of English in the *barántas* genre during the nineteenth century. See for example the *barántas* from 1813 in which the business of the 'warrant' is carried out in English (between the poet and the otherworld figure Clíona), while the narration is in Irish; Mac Mathúna, *Béarla sa Ghaeilge*, pp. 122–3.

131 See Eibhlín Ní Dhonnchadha, *Tomás Ó Conchubhair agus a Chuid Filidheachta* (Dublin: Oifig an tSoláthair, 1953), pp. 9, 16. See also Meidhbhín Ní Úrdail, 'Ón gCnocán Aoibhinn go dtí Londain Shasana: Tomás "An tSneachta" Ó Conchubhair (1798–c. 1870)', *Celtica*, no. 28 (2016), pp. 89–122.

132 In his survey of nineteenth-century Irish literature in English, Thomas Flanagan credits the *Nation* with having 'introduced into Ireland, in its specific terms, the modern notion of nationality'. This statement relies on a narrow interpretation of 'modern', but the *Nation* was certainly a driving force for the specific type of nationalism promoted by the Young Irelanders; see Thomas Flanagan, 'Literature in English, 1801–91', in W.E. Vaughan (ed.), *A New History of Ireland, V: Ireland under the Union, I, 1801–70* (Oxford: Clarendon Press, 1989), p. 496.

133 Úna Ní Bhroiméil, *Building Irish Identity in America, 1870–1915: the Gaelic Revival* (Dublin: Four Courts Press, 2003), p. 45.

134 See Dóirín Ní Mhurchú, 'Philip Barron: man of mystery', *Decies* [Waterford], no. 2 (May 1976).

135 *Ancient Ireland*, vol. 1, no. 1 (1835), p. 16; see also vol. 1, no. 4 (1835), p. 1.

The inclusion in *Ancient Ireland*, vol. 1, no. 2 (1835) of a dialogue entitled 'Is ceart dona boicht an Biobla leigheadh' (It is right that the poor should read the Bible) is significant, given that its interlocutors take the side of the Established Church against the Catholic Church in recommending that the Bible should be read by all. This may be a reflection of Barron's eagerness to encourage reading in Irish. An insight into Catholic views on the use of the Bible and its specific promotion by Protestant evangelical societies can be gained from a series of Irish poems composed in west Limerick. Initiated by Fr Uilliam Mac Gearailt (1789–1826), he asked fellow poets to compose verses in Irish to protect the Catholic faith. It appears Mac Gearailt accepted Irish Bibles from the Irish Society for use in his school at Newcastle West; see Pádraig de Brún, 'Forogra do Ghaelaibh, 1824', *Studia Hibernica*, no. 12 (1972), pp. 142–66; Tomás de Bháll, 'A West Limerick Anthology', *Irish Book Lover* (September/October 1936), pp. 105–6.

136 See Proinsias Ó Maolmhuaidh, *Athair na hAthbheochana: Uilleog de Búrca* (Dublin: Foilseacháin Náisiúnta Teoranta, 1981), pp. 99–106.

137 Letter from James Ronan to John Glynn, 28 June 1869. Letters to John (Mc) Glynn of the *Tuam News*, NLI, MS 3254 (underlined text in original text substituted with italics here).

138 Ibid.

139 In spite of the strident tone of Ronan's letter of 1869, his ideas in a later letter to Glynn on revival insist on neutrality and inclusivity: 'In the matter of the National Language we must be above all sects, personalities and politics'; letter from James Ronan to John McGlynn, 1 January 1874, letters to John (Mc)Glynn of the *Tuam News*, NLI, MS 3254.

140 Homi K. Bhabha, *The Location of Culture* (London: Routledge, 1994), p. 172.

141 Letter from James Ronan to John McGlynn, 1 January 1874, NLI, MS 3254.

142 McNeill, 'How and Why the Irish Language Is to Be Preserved', p. 1100.

143 Ibid. p. 1102.

144 Ibid.

145 Ibid. p. 1104.

146 Ibid.

147 Mac Néill's article predates the establishment of the Gaelic League by roughly two years, but it was clear that he recognised at the time of writing the existence of a movement that was growing in strength: 'Since the movement in favour of the Irish language first took shape, the names of bishops and priests have been at the head of it'; ibid. p. 1105.

148 Gearóid Denvir, 'Decolonizing the Mind: language and literature in Ireland', *New Hibernia Review*, vol. 1, no. 1 (spring 1997), p. 53.

149 Douglas Hyde, *Abhráin atá Leagtha ar an Reachtúire: songs ascribed to Raftery. Being the fifth chapter of the songs of Connacht* (Dublin: Gill, 1903).

150 Lady Gregory, *Poets and Dreamers: studies and translations from the Irish* (Dublin: Hodges, Figgis & Co., 1903), pp. 2, 34. See also Yeats' essay 'Dust Hath Closed Helen's Eye', in idem, *The Celtic Twilight* (London: A.H. Bullen, 1902), pp. 35–49.

151 See Gearóid S. Mac Eoin, 'Mise Raifterí 1', *Éigse*, vol. 12, pt 3 (1968), pp. 229–32.

See also Ciarán Ó Coigligh, *Raiftearaí: amháin agus dánta* (Dublin: An Clóchomhar, 1987), pp. 3–5.

152   Ó Coigligh, *Raiftearaí*, pp. 137–48.

153   Morley, *Ó Chéitinn go Raiftearaí*. See also idem, 'The popular influence of *Foras Feasa ar Éirinn*', pp. 96–115.

154   *Cloch an Stocáin* is also mentioned by Keating in his *Foras Feasa* to denote a northerly point of Ireland, and also by Seán Ó Conaill (*fl.* 1650) in his long poem that appears to draw extensively on Keating's history, *Tuireamh na hÉireann* (The Lament of Ireland). Apart from the many references to Keating and Ó Conaill in *Príomhstair an Stocáin*, the choice of this particular landmark as witness to Ireland's history was surely a recognition of Keating's historical tradition, a tradition that Mac Domhnaill, like Raiftearaí, strove to continue. See Colm Beckett, *Aodh Mac Domhnaill*, pp. 98–105, 159–64; David Comyn (ed.), *Foras Feasa ar Éirinn le Seathrún Céitinn/The History of Ireland by Geoffrey Keating, Part 1* (London: Irish Texts Society, 1902), p. 130; O'Rahilly, *Five Seventeenth-century Political Poems*, p. 76; de Brún, 'Aodh Mac Domhnaill', pp. 8–10.

155   See for example 'An Cíos Caitliceach', 'Bearnán Risteard', 'Na Buachaillí Bána', in Ó Coigligh, *Raiftearaí*, pp. 97–9, 103–6.

156   See Donncha Ó Donnchú, *Filíocht Mháire Bhuidhe Ní Laoghaire* (Dublin: Oifig an tSoláthair, 1931), pp. 28, 55–8.

157   Méidhbhín Ní Úrdail, 'Máire Bhuí Ní Laoghaire: file an "Rilleadh Cainte"', *Eighteenth-century Ireland/Iris an Dá Chultúr*, vol. 17 (2002), p. 150. Ní Úrdail also speculates that *priúnsa ceart na nGaedheal* (the true prince of the Gael) refers to Louis XVII of France. Given that the Duke of York was commander-in-chief of the British forces during the first six years of the Napoleonic Wars (1803–15), it is also possible that the 'prince' referred to was Napoleon Bonaparte, who was the object of much hope for the Gaelic Irish, and is described, for example, in the Munster song 'Ráiteachas na Tairngreachta' (The Saying of the Prophecy) as *aon-mhac phrionsa an chomhraic* (the only son of the prince of battle); see Mánus Ó Baoill (ed.), *Ceolta Gael 2* (Cork: Mercier Press, 1986), p. 74.

158   'Is an bhliain atá anois againn beidh rás ar gach smíste' (And in this present year all smiters shall be routed) in 'Cath Chéim an Fhiaidh'; see Ó Donnchú, *Filíocht Mháire Bhuidhe Ní Laoghaire*, p. 56.

159   Seán Ó Ceallaigh, *Filíocht na gCallanán* (Dublin: An Clóchomhar, 1967), p. 66. I have given my own translation here in preference to Ó Callanán's, the literal meaning of which diverges in places from the original: 'I hereby give admonition/ To the Catholics of Erin/ Let them not be terrified/ At their doctrine or teaching/ For, when foul and rotten branches/ Are suspended from the cedar/ The roots grow more extensive/ And contribute to the leader'; ibid. p. 126.

Chapter 4: Patrick Pearse, the Gothic Revival and the Dreams of Ancients and Moderns

1   Stephen Gwynn, *A Lay of Patrick and Ossian with Other Verses* (Dublin: Hodges, Figgis & Co., 1903), pp. 36–42.

2 This account was given by Desmond Ryan in a television interview for RTÉ's *Survivors* project recorded in 1964–65, http://www.rte.ie/archives/exhibitions/1993–easter-1916/2017–survivors/608845–the-survivors-desmond-ryan (accessed 21 June 2016).

3 F.S.L. Lyons, *Ireland Since the Famine* (London: Fontana Press, 1971), p. 369.

4 See Brian Crowley, '"His Father's Son": James and Patrick Pearse', *Folk Life*, vol. 43 (2004–05), pp. 71–88; Thomas Duffy, 'Artisan Sculpture and the Stone Carving Firms of Dublin, 1859–1910', PhD thesis, National College of Art and Design, Dublin, 1999.

5 'Easter 1916', in W.B. Yeats, *Michael Robartes and the Dancer* (Dundrum: Cuala Press, 1920), pp. 9–11.

6 One of those included is 'Ar Chéim Síos na nGaedheal' (On the Fall of the Gael) by Fear Flatha Ó Gnímh (*fl.* 1602–40), in which the poet asks the Holy Trinity whether the Gael will always be in exile, 'or shall we have a second glory?' (Nó an mbiaidh an t-athaoibhneas againn?). See Pearse, *Collected Works of P.H. Pearse: songs of the Irish rebels*, pp. 10–11.

7 On these societies, see, respectively, Úna Ní Bhroiméil, *Building Irish Identity in America, 1870–1915*; Máirtín Ó Murchú, *Cumann Buan-Choimeádta na Gaeilge: tús an athréimnithe* (Dublin: Cois Life, 2001).

8 See Mathews, *Revival*. The theory and history of nationalism was radically transformed during the 1980s and from the 1990s onwards, during which a number of key theoretical perspectives emerged. For a summary and discussion of these, see Smith, *Nationalism and Modernism*.

9 See the listed aims and means of the league in Gaelic League, *Imtheachta an Oireachtais/Full Report of the Proceedings at the Oireachtas* (Dublin: Gaelic League, 1897), pp. 4–5.

10 See Breandán S. Mac Aodha, 'Was This a Social Revolution?', in Seán Ó Tuama (ed.), *The Gaelic League Idea* (Cork: Mercier Press, 1993), p. 21; Proinsias Mac Aonghusa, *Ar Son na Gaeilge: Conradh na Gaeilge, 1893–1993* (Dublin: Conradh na Gaeilge, 1993), p. 96. See also McMahon, *Grand Opportunity*.

11 R.V. Comerford, *Inventing the Nation: Ireland* (London: Arnold, 2003), p. 141.

12 For a full list of the league's publications from 1893 to 1918, see the series of seven articles by Pádraig Ó Táilliúir, 'Ceartliosta de Leabhair, Paimfléid, etc. Foilsithe in Éirinn ag Connradh na Gaedhilge, 1893–1918', published in *Comhar* from February to August 1964. Although the list runs to 510 publications, numbers 429–510 list pamphlets mainly in English, followed by proceedings and programmes of the annual Oireachtas competition initiated in 1897. This latter section comprises significant material in Irish.

13 *Séadna* was serialised first in the *Gaelic Journal/Irisleabhar na Gaedhilge* between 1894 and 1897; see Peadar Ua Laoghaire, *Séadna*, ed. Liam Mac Mathúna (Dublin: Cois Life, 2011).

14 Patrick Pearse, 'Review: *Séadna* and the future of Irish prose', *An Claidheamh Soluis*, no. 24 (September 1904), p. 8.

15 For a comprehensive study of *An Claidheamh Soluis*, see Regina Uí Chollatáin, *An Claidheamh Soluis agus Fáinne an Lae, 1899–1932: anailís ar phríomhnuachtán Gaeilge ré na hAthbheochana* (Dublin: Cois Life, 2004).

16 Pearse, 'About Literature'.

17 David Thornley, 'Patrick Pearse and the Pearse Family', *Studies: an Irish Quarterly Review*, vol. 60, nos 239–40 (autumn/winter 1971), p. 338.

18 Ibid. pp. 335–6.

19 James Stevens Curl (ed.), *The Oxford Dictionary of Architecture* (Oxford: Oxford University Press, 1999), pp. 283–4.

20 See Hunt, *Building Jerusalem*; Hill, *God's Architect*.

21 Thomas Carlyle, *Critical and Miscellaneous Essays*, vols 1 and 2 (London: Chapman & Hall, 1888), see vol. 1, pp. 100–3.

22 Thomas Carlyle, *Critical and Miscellaneous Essays*, vols 3 and 4 (London: Chapman & Hall, 1888), see vol. 4, p. 160.

23 Kenneth Reddin, 'A Man Called Pearse', *Studies: an Irish Quarterly Review*, vol. 34, no. 134 (June 1945), p. 245.

24 John Stuart Mill, *On Bentham and Coleridge* (London: Chatto & Windus, 1950), pp. 102–3.

25 Hunt, *Building Jerusalem*, p. 107.

26 Ibid. p. 106.

27 See Crowley, '"His Father's Son"', p. 73. Brian Crowley, '"I am the son of a good father": James Pearse and Patrick Pearse', in Róisín Higgins and Regina Uí Chollatáin (eds), *The Life and After-life of P.H. Pearse* (Dublin: Irish Academic Press, 2009), p. 21.

28 See Duffy, 'Artisan Sculpture and the Stone Carving Firms of Dublin, 1859–1910', pp. 41, 184.

29 Patrick Pearse, 'Fragment of Autobiography by Patrick Pearse', unpublished typescript, Pearse Museum, Rathfarnham, Dublin, p. 6.

30 See Crowley, '"His Father's Son"', pp. 74–5.

31 See R.V. Comerford, *The Fenians in Context* (Dublin: Wolfhound Press, 1998), pp. 136–7.

32 Pearse published two collections of short stories, *Íosagán agus Scéalta Eile* (1907) and *An Mháthair* (1916), most of which were published originally in *An Claidheamh Soluis*. For the relevant dates, see Cathal Ó Háinle (ed.), *Gearrscéalta an Phiarsaigh* (Dublin: Cló Thalbóid, 1999), p. 20. I have retained the original names of characters in Pearse's short stories in Irish. The original text where quoted here is from Ó Háinle's edition, *Gearrscéalta an Phiarsaigh*, and textual quotations in English here are based on my own translations, except where otherwise indicated.

33 Ó Gaora, *Mise*, p. 36.

34 Pearse, 'Fragment of Autobiography by Patrick Pearse', p. 5. See also Crowley, '"His Father's Son"', p. 84.

35 Pádraic H. Pearse, 'The Murder Machine', in idem, *The Collected Works of P.H. Pearse: political writings and speeches* (Dublin, 1924), pp. 18–19.

36 Pádraic H. Pearse, 'Ghosts', in idem, *The Collected Works of P.H. Pearse: political writings and speeches* (Dublin, 1924), p. 224.

37 Seamus Deane, *Celtic Revivals: essays in modern Irish literature* (London: Faber & Faber, 1985), p. 65.

38 Matthew Arnold, *On the Study of Celtic Literature and Other Essays* (London 1910), p. 5.

39 P.H. Pearse, 'Some Aspects of Irish Literature', in idem, *The Collected Works of P.H. Pearse: songs of the Irish rebels etc* (Dublin, 1924), p. 133.

40 In his introduction to the first of his two collections, *Íosagán agus Scéalta Eile* (1907), Pearse attributes the source of the first three stories 'Íosagán', 'An Sagart', and 'Bairbre' to various people in 'Ros na gCaorach'. The introduction gives the same explanation for the source of *Eoghainín na nÉan* as that given at the beginning of the actual story; see Ó Háinle, pp. 150–1; see also Ó Gaora, *Mise*, p. 36.

41 Ó Háinle (ed.), *Gearrscéalta an Phiarsaigh*, p. 82; Pádraic H. Pearse, *Plays, Stories, Poems* (Dublin: Talbot Press, 1963), p. 289.

42 Owen Dudley Edwards, *Complete Works of Oscar Wilde* (Glasgow: Harper Collins, 1994), p. 14.

43 Bíonn na daoine fásta dall; see Ó Háinle (ed.), *Gearrscéalta an Phiarsaigh*, p. 58; Pearse, *Plays, Stories, Poems*, p. 240.

44 See Ó Háinle (ed.), *Gearrscéalta an Phiarsaigh*; Pearse, *Plays, Stories, Poems*.

45 Ó Háinle (ed.), *Gearrscéalta an Phiarsaigh*, p. 20.

46 Séamus Ó Buachalla, *The Letters of P.H. Pearse* (Gerrards Cross: Colin Smythe, 1980), p. 127.

47 Pearse, 'Fragment of Autobiography by Patrick Pearse', p. 14.

48 Ó Háinle (ed.), *Gearrscéalta an Phiarsaigh*, p. 58; Pearse, *Plays, Stories, Poems*, p. 240.

49 On the messianic hero, see Dáithí Ó hÓgáin, *The Hero in Irish Folk History* (Dublin: Gill & Macmillan, 1985).

50 John Gray, *The Immortalization Commission: the strange quest to cheat Death* (London: Penguin, 2012), pp. 35–6.

51 Ibid. p. 1.

52 Ibid. p. 9.

53 Ibid. pp. 80–4.

54 Ibid. p. 85.

55 Ó Conchubhair, *Fin de Siècle na Gaeilge*.

56 For the script of this production and a discussion of its background, see Róisín Ní Ghairbhí and Eugene McNulty (eds), *Patrick Pearse: collected plays/drámaí an Phiarsaigh* (Dublin: Irish Academic Press, 2013).

57 Hunt, *Building Jerusalem*, pp. 75–7.

58 Ní Ghairbhí and McNulty (eds), *Patrick Pearse*, p. 17.

59 Ruth Dudley Edwards, *Patrick Pearse: the triumph of failure* (London: Victor Gollancz, 1977), p. 344.

60 Pádraic H. Pearse, *The Story of a Success*, ed. Desmond Ryan (Dublin: Maunsel, 1918), p. 90.

61 Pearse, 'Some Aspects of Irish Literature', p. 156.

62 Joe Lee has spoken of Pearse's tendency to 'sanctify the cause of the moment and invoke the blessing of the Deity'; J.J. Lee, 'Pearse, Patrick Henry', in *Dictionary of Irish Biography: from the earliest times to the Year 2002*, http://dib.cambridge.org (accessed 12 April 2016).

63 Dudley Edwards, *Patrick Pearse*, p. 127.

64 Pearse, *Plays, Stories, Poems*, pp. 316–17. This poem is Pearse's own translation

of his Irish poem 'A Mhic Bhig na gCleas'; see Ciarán Ó Coigligh (ed.), *Filíocht Ghaeilge Phádraig Mhic Phiarais* (Dublin: An Clóchomhar, 1981), p. 31. Pearse translated fifteen of his original Irish poems into English; ibid. p. 78.

65 Lee, 'Pearse, Patrick Henry'.

66 Joost Augusteijn, *Patrick Pearse: the making of a revolutionary* (London: Palgrave Macmillan, 2010), p. 61.

67 This play was completed just before the 1916 Rising; see Ní Ghairbhí and McNulty (eds), *Patrick Pearse*, pp. 2, 203, 216.

68 Cathal Ó Háinle, *Scáthanna* (Dublin: Coiscéim, 2008), pp. 53–80; Gearóid Denvir, *Litríocht agus Pobal* (Indreabhán: Cló Iar-Chonnacht, 1997), pp. 185–92. See also Denvir's discussion of the trope of mortality and decline in Pearse's literary output: Gearóid Denvir, 'Ó Pheann an Phiarsaigh: athléamh ar shaothar liteartha Gaeilge an Phiarsaigh', in Gearóid Ó Tuathaigh (ed.), *An Piarsach agus 1916: briathar, beart agus oidhreacht* (Indreabhán: Cló Iar-Chonnacht, 2016), pp. 94–7.

69 Augusteijn, *Patrick Pearse*, pp. 61–2.

70 Elaine Sisson, *Pearse's Patriots: St Enda's and the cult of boyhood* (Cork: Cork University Press, 2004), p. 152.

71 Ó Coigligh (ed.), *Filíocht Ghaeilge Phádraig Mhic Phiarais*, p. 31; Pearse, *Plays, Stories, Poems*, p. 323.

72 Pearse, 'Ghosts', pp. 223–4.

73 Charles Townshend, *Easter 1916: the Irish rebellion* (London: Penguin, 2006), p. 113; Augusteijn, *Patrick Pearse*, p. 304. The Irish Republican Brotherhood's paper *Irish Freedom* warned of the sin of the current generation's not having taken up arms against England; see Townshend, *Easter 1916*, p. 37.

74 John Mitchel, *Jail Journal* [1854] (London: Sphere Books, 1983), pp. 5–7.

75 A.M. Sullivan, *The Story of Ireland* (Dublin, 1867).

76 Declan Kiberd, *Inventing Ireland* (London: Vintage, 1996), p. 104. See Chapter 6 for Kiberd's discussion of the theme of childhood, particularly in relation to Yeats.

77 Ibid. p. 104.

78 Douglas Hyde, *Selected Plays Douglas Hyde: 'An Craoibhín Aoibhinn'* (Gerrard's Cross: Colin Smythe, 1991), pp. 108–17.

79 Ó Coigligh (ed.), *Filíocht Ghaeilge Phádraig Mhic Phiarais*, pp. 23–4, 89. The play was performed in March 1909.

80 Ní Ghairbhí and McNulty (eds), *Patrick Pearse*, p. 191.

81 See Charles Plummer (ed.), *Vitae Sanctorum Hiberniae*, vol. 2 (Oxford: Clarendon Press, 1910), pp. 60–6.

82 Ó Coigligh (ed.), *Filíocht Ghaeilge Phádraig Mhic Phiarais*, p. 44; Pearse, *Plays, Stories, Poems*, p. 318. The origin of this poem has been imputed by some critics to Pearse's supposed love for Eibhlín Nicholls, a prominent Gaelic Leaguer who died in a drowning accident while on one of the Blasket Islands in 1909. See Sisson, *Pearse's Patriots*, p. 141.

83 Mary Brigid Pearse (ed.), *The Home Life of Pádraig Pearse*, p. 113.

84 Ní Ghairbhí and McNulty (eds), *Patrick Pearse*, p. 152.

85 See Ó Buachalla, *Aisling Ghéar*, p. 545.

86 Ní Ghairbhí and McNulty (eds), *Patrick Pearse*, pp. 324–32.

87 Pearse, *Collected Works of Pádraic H. Pearse*, pp. 334–5.
88 Kiberd, *Inventing Ireland*, pp. 201–2.
89 Alfred Perceval Graves, *The Book of Irish Poetry* (Dublin: Talbot Press, 1914), pp. 1, 177.
90 Yeats, *Michael Robartes and the Dancer*, p. 11. The lexicographer and scholar Pádraig Ó Duinnín (1860–1934) composed an extended poem in Irish drawing on the *aisling* tradition, entitled 'Spirits of Freedom: a Magical Vision of the Year 1916' – Pádraig Ua Duinnín, *Spioraid na Saoirse: aisling draoidheachta ar an mbliadhain 1916* (Dublin: M.H. Gill & Son, 1919).
91 Sigmund Freud, *The Standard Edition of the Complete Psychological Works of Sigmund Freud*, vol. v (London: Vintage, 2001), p. 608.
92 Bureau of Military History Witness Statements, WS 725, Desmond Ryan. The starting point for this feeling was Eoin Mac Néill's countermanding order which advised the Irish Volunteers not to mobilise as agreed on Easter Sunday 1916. Pearse and the rest of the Rising leaders famously decided to go ahead with the insurrection on the following day.
93 Desmond Ryan, *Survivors*.
94 Townshend, *Easter 1916*, p. 263.
95 Bureau of Military History Witness Statements, WS 889, James Kavanagh.
96 Bureau of Military History Witness Statements, WS 724, Desmond Ryan.
97 Bureau of Military History Witness Statements, WS 923, Ignatius Callender.
98 Queneau's novel was originally published using the nom de plume Sally Mara, and was later translated into English by Barbara Wright as *We Always Treat Women Too Well* [1981] (New York: New York Review Books, 2003). Queneau was also responsible for the French translation of Muiris Ó Súilleabháin's *Fiche Blian ag Fás* (Dublin: Clólucht an Talbóidigh, 1933) which he entitled *Vingt Ans de Jeunesse* (Paris: Gallimard, 1936), although he relied entirely on the very popular English translation, *Twenty Years A' Growing* (London: Chatto & Windus, 1933).
99 Jean-Pierre Morel, 'Breton and Freud', *Diacritics*, vol. 2, no. 2 (summer 1972), p. 20.
100 André Breton, *Manifestoes of Surrealism*, trans. Richard Seaver and Helen R. Lane (Michigan: University of Michigan Press, 1972), p. 14.
101 Yeats, *Michael Robartes and the Dancer*, p. 11. See R.F. Foster, *W.B. Yeats, a Life, Vol. II: the Arch-poet, 1915–1939* (Oxford: Oxford University Press, 2003), pp. 59–66.
102 'íomhánna marmair na marbh'. Eoghan Ó Tuairisc, *Dé Luain* (Dublin: Sáirséal & Ó Marcaigh, 1998), p. 24.
103 Philip O'Leary, 'Reasoning Why After Fifty Years: the Easter Rising in Eoghan Ó Tuairisc's *Dé Luain* (1966)', *Proceedings of the Harvard Celtic Colloquium*, vol. 31 (2011), pp. 256, 280.
104 Ó Tuairisc, *Dé Luain*, p. 24.
105 Ibid. p. 60. This character is based on Liam Ó Briain (1888–1974), the author of a memoir in Irish of the Rising that Ó Tuairisc used as part of his extensive research. See O'Leary, 'Reasoning Why After Fifty Years', p. 267; Liam Ó Briain, *Cuimhní Cinn* (Dublin: Sáirséal & Dill, 1951).

106 Ní Ghairbhí and McNulty (eds), *Patrick Pearse*, pp. 193–4.

107 F.S.L. Lyons, 'Foreword', in Séamus Ó Buachalla (ed.), *The Letters of P.H. Pearse* (Gerrards Cross: Colin Smythe, 1980), p. vii.

108 This is a central theme in Blochs' work, which is discussed further in Chapter 6; see pt 2 of Ernst Bloch, *The Principle of Hope, Vol. 1*, trans. Neville Plaice, Stephen Plaice and Paul Knight (Massachusetts: MIT Press, 1995).

Chapter 5: Temporality and Irish Revivalism: Past, present and becoming

1 Seamus Heaney, *Human Chain* (London: Faber & Faber, 2010), pp. 64–5. See also idem, 'Stations of the West', in idem, *Stations* (Belfast: Ulsterman Publications, 1975), p. 22; idem, 'The Gaeltacht', in idem, *Electric Light* (New York: Farrar, Strauss & Giroux, 2002), p. 51.

2 These include Heaney's *Sweeney Astray: a version from the Irish* (Derry: Field Day, 1983) and *The Midnight Verdict* (Oldcastle: Gallery, 2000), versions of the medieval tale *Buile Shuibhne* and of Brian Merriman's *Cúirt an Mheon-Oíche* respectively, as well as his translations/versions of poems attributed to Colm Cille, which are included in *Human Chain* (2010).

3 See Henry Liddell and Robert Scott (eds), *Greek–English Lexicon* (New York: Harper & Brothers, 1883), p. 183.

4 Heaney, 'Loughanure', *Human Chain*, p. 64.

5 Ibid. p. 65.

6 The term 'synthesis' is used in this chapter in a general sense. It is not intended to refer to the schema of 'thesis, antithesis, synthesis' that has been controversially used as a summary of Hegel's dialectics, even though Hegel did not himself use this triad; see Gustav E. Mueller, 'The Hegel Legend of "Thesis, Antithesis, Synthesis"', *Journal of the History of Ideas*, vol. 19, no. 3 (June 1958), pp. 411–14.

7 For a discussion of temporality in Gothic literature, see Jarlath Killeen, *Gothic Literature, 1825–1914* (Cardiff: University of Wales Press, 2009), particularly Chapter 1, 'The Ghosts of Time'. For a critical discussion of Gothic literature in the Irish context, see W.J. McCormack, 'Irish Gothic and After: 1820–1945', in Seamus Deane (ed.), *The Field Day Anthology of Irish Writing, Vol. 2* (Derry: Field Day Publications, 1991), pp. 831–949; Eagleton, *Heathcliff and the Great Hunger*; R.F. Foster, *Paddy and Mr. Punch: connections in Irish and English history* (London: Penguin, 1995), ch. 11: 'Protestant Magic'; Seamus Deane, *Strange Country: modernity and nationhood in Irish writing since 1790* (Oxford: Oxford University Press, 1997); Declan Kiberd, *Irish Classics* (London: Granta, 2000), ch. 22, 'Undead in the Nineties: Bram Stoker and Dracula'; Luke Gibbons, *Gaelic Gothic: race, colonization and Irish culture* (Galway: Arlen House, 2004); Jarlath Killeen, *Gothic Ireland: horror and the Irish Anglican imagination in the long eighteenth century* (Dublin: Four Courts Press, 2005).

8 MacAdam, 'The Archaeology of Ulster', p. 2.

9 Regarding temporality and the colonial condition in Ireland, see for example David Lloyd, *Irish Times: temporalities of modernity* (Dublin: Field Day, 2008); Kevin Whelan, 'Between Filiation and Affiliation: the politics of postcolonial

memory', in Clare Carroll and Patricia King (eds), *Ireland and Postcolonial Theory* (Cork: Cork University Press, 2003), pp. 92–108; Joep Leerssen, *Remembrance and Imagination: patterns in the historical and literary representation of Ireland in the nineteenth century* (Cork: Cork University Press in association with Field Day, 1996). For literature in Irish and postcolonialism, see Máirín Nic Eoin, *Trén bhFearann Breac: an díláithriú cultúir agus nualitríocht na Gaeilge* (Dublin: Cois Life, 2005), and Denvir, 'Decolonizing the Mind'.

10 Gilles Deleuze, *Negotiations* (New York: Columbia University Press, 1995), p. 171.

11 Joseph Nagy, *Conversing with Angels and Ancients: literary myths of medieval Ireland* (Dublin: Four Courts Press, 1997), p. 325.

12 Ibid. p. 323.

13 Ibid. p. 3.

14 From Tertullian, *Treatise on the Soul*, quoted by Philip Freeman, *War, Women and Druids: eyewitness reports and early accounts of the ancient Celts* (Austin: University of Texas Press, 2002), p. 35.

15 O'Rahilly (ed.), *Five Seventeenth-century Political Poems*, pp. 12–32, 108–20; Ó Tuama and Kinsella (eds), *An Duanaire*, pp. 176–81. As for the dating of Mac Cumhaigh's poem, this is regarded as being towards the end of his life, 1773. See also Ó Fiaich, *Art Mac Cumhaigh*, p. 170.

16 Hutchinson, *The Dynamics of Cultural Nationalism*, pp. 10, 198.

17 Sean O'Faolain in Michael Tierney, D.A. Binchy, Gerard Murphy, John Ryan and Sean O'Faolain, 'Politics and Culture: Daniel O'Connell and the Gaelic past', *Studies: an Irish Quarterly Review*, vol. 27, no. 107 (September 1938), p. 380.

18 Philip O'Leary, *Gaelic Prose in the Irish Free State, 1922–1939* (Pennsylvania: Pennsylvania State University Press, 2004), p. 441.

19 Tierney et al., 'Politics and Culture', p. 368.

20 See Hobsbawm and Ranger (eds), *The Invention of Tradition*, p. 14.

21 Albert Memmi, *The Colonizer and the Colonized*, trans. Howard Greenfield (1957; London: Earthscan, 2003), p. 156.

22 John Mitchel, 'The Famine Year', in idem, *Jail Journal* (London: Sphere Books, 1983), p. 415. See de Brún, 'Expressing the Nineteenth Century in Irish', p. 81.

23 Jerome Hamilton Buckley, *The Triumph of Time: a study of the Victorian concepts of time, history, progress, and decadence* (Cambridge, MA: Harvard University Press, 1967), p. 5.

24 Benedict Anderson, *Imagined Communities* (London: Verso, 2006), p. 23. This characterisation of the medieval view of time is clearly exaggerated; see Richard H. Godden, 'The Medieval Sense of History', in Stephen J. Harris and Bryon L. Grigsby (eds), *Misconceptions about the Middle Ages* (London: Routledge, 2008), p. 204; Jacques Le Goff, *Time, Work and Culture in the Middle Ages*, trans. Arthur Goldhammer (Chicago: University of Chicago Press, 1981).

25 This is certainly not to say that Irish-speaking Ireland did not interact with these forms, particularly the newspaper, in spite of Joep Leerssen's suggestion that Gaelic Ireland had no public sphere; Leerssen, *Hidden Ireland, Public Sphere*, p. 36. For a discussion of this issue and a pertinent critique of Leerssen's view, see Ní Mhunghaile, 'Bilingualism, Print Culture in Irish and the Public Sphere'.

26 In Ireland, Dublin Mean Time replaced Local Mean Time in 1880, before Greenwich Mean Time was eventually adopted in 1916; see F.W. Dyson, 'Standard Time in Ireland', *Observatory*, no. 39 (1916), pp. 467–8.

27 Charles Darwin, *On the Origin of Species by Means of Natural Selection* (London: Murray, 1859). For a detailed study of the influence of Darwinism and related currents of thought on the Irish language revival at the end of the nineteenth century and beginning of the twentieth century, see Ó Conchubhair, *Fin de Siècle na Gaeilge*.

28 This is, of course, the same Rannafast where Seamus Heaney came to study Irish as a youth.

29 'Bheadh sé creidte agam nárbh fhiú dadaidh an eagnaíocht a bhí ag fealsaimh an tseansaoil le taobh na heagnaíochta a bhí ag Bacon agus ag Macaulay'; Séamus Ó Grianna, *Saoghal Corrach* (Dublin: An Press Náisiúnta, 1945), p. 18.

30 An egregious example of this view was given in Robert Knox's *The Races of Man* (1850), where he remarks that the Irish were doomed to go 'the way of the dark races of the world'; see Ó Conchubhair, *Fin de Siècle na Gaeilge*, pp. 76–7. See also L. Perry Curtis, *Apes and Angels: the Irishman in Victorian caricature* (Washington: Smithsonian Institution Press, 1997); Michael de Nie, *The Eternal Paddy: Irish identity and the British press, 1798–1882* (Madison, WI: University of Wisconsin Press, 2004).

31 See Marc Caball, *Poets and Politics: continuity and reaction in Irish poetry, 1558–1625* (Cork: Cork University Press, 1999), pp. 83–113; see also Chapter 2 of McKibben, *Endangered Masculinities*.

32 Cáit Ní Dhomhnaill, *Duanaireacht: rialacha meadarachta fhilíocht na mbard* (Dublin: Oifig an tSoláthair, 1975), p. 99. See also the poem composed in the aftermath of the plantation of Ulster beginning with the line *Cáit ar ghabhadar Gaoidhil?* (Where have the Gaels gone?), in which the Gaels are likened to *cuirp bheómharbha* (half-dead corpses); William Gillies, 'A Poem on the Downfall of the Gaoidhil', *Éigse*, vol. 13, pt 3 (1970), p. 207.

33 MacAdam, 'The Archaeology of Ulster', p. 2.

34 See de Brún, '"Society in Ulster Seems Breaking Up"', pp. 145–6.

35 McCormack, 'Irish Gothic and After', p. 834.

36 Joep Leerssen, *Remembrance and Imagination: patterns in the historical and literary representation of Ireland in the nineteenth century* (Cork: Cork University Press in association with Field Day, 1996), p. 51.

37 J.M. Synge, *Four Plays and the Aran Islands* [1907] (London: Oxford University Press, 1962), p. 179.

38 Ibid. p. 180.

39 Joep Leerssen, 'Celticism', in Terence Brown (ed.), *Celticism*, Studia Imagologica: Amsterdam Studies on Cultural Identity (Rodopi: Amsterdam, 1996), p. 8.

40 Herbert Moore Pim, *Unknown Immortals in the Northern City of Success* (Dublin: Talbot Press, 1917), p. 18.

41 Writing of the Omeath *Gaeltacht* in the same era, Rev. Lorcán Ó Muirí [Ua Muireadhaigh] wrote: 'There was scarcely one of the old people in Omeath a decade ago who could not trace their descent back to the seventeenth century. I have tested several of these genealogical trees by means of the census returns of

1666 and 1766, and rarely have I found any error'; Lorcán Ua Muireadhaigh, *Amhráin Shéamais Mhic Chuarta* (Dundalk: William Tempest, 1925), pp. 13–14.

42 Charles Maturin, *Melmoth the Wanderer* [1820] (London: Penguin, 2006), p. 50.

43 Philip Barron, *Ancient Ireland: a Weekly Magazine*, vol. 1, no. 1 (1835), p. 6.

44 Jacques Chuto, Rudolf Patrick Holzapfel, Peter MacMahon, Patrick Ó Snodaigh, Ellen Shannon-Mangan, Tadhg Ó Dúshláine and Peter van de Kamp (eds), *Collected Works of James Clarence Mangan, Vol. IV: poems, 1838– 1844* (Dublin: Irish Academic Press, 2002), pp. 88–90. Mangan's poem is based on an original Irish poem published as 'Dán Mholadh na Gaoidheilghe' by John O'Daly in his *Reliques of Irish Jacobite Poetry* (Dublin: Samuel J. Machen, 1844), pp. 1–3. The lines quoted above do not appear in O'Daly's version, and, as such, 'either O'Daly found a more complete text, with which he provided Mangan, or the poet played his own variations on the theme'; Chuto et al. (eds), *Collected Works of James Clarence Mangan, Vol. IV*, p. 279.

45 Katie Trumpener, *Bardic Nationalism: the Romantic novel and the British Empire* (Princeton: Princeton University Press, 1997), p. 111.

46 Barron, *Ancient Ireland*, vol. 1, no. 1, p. 3. This should not be confused with Ollscoil na Mumhan, one of a number of Irish-language colleges for teachers of Irish founded between 1904 and 1906.

47 Quoted by Tom Garvin, *Nationalist Revolutionaries in Ireland, 1858–1928* (Oxford: Clarendon, 1987), p. 117.

48 Iolann Fionn [Seosamh Mac Grianna], 'Filí Gan Iomrá', in Gearóid Mac Giolla Domhnaigh and Gearóid Stockman (eds), *Athchló Uladh* [1926] (Muineachán: Comhaltas Uladh, 1991), p. 137; this was originally published as a booklet in 1926.

49 Ó Ríordáin, 'Fill Arís', in *Brosna*, p. 41; idem, 'Return Again', in idem, *Selected Poems /Rogha Dánta*, pp. 162–3.

50 For a discussion of this motif in the contemporary poetry of Cathal Ó Searcaigh, see Pádraig de Paor, *Na Buachaillí Dána: Cathal Ó Searcaigh, Gabriel Rosenstock agus ról comhaimseartha an fhile sa Ghaeilge* (Dublin: An Clóchomhar, 2005), pp. 100–101.

51 Garvin, *Nationalist Revolutionaries in Ireland*, p. 109. See also McMahon, *Grand Opportunity* for a counterpoint to the over-dependence, in Garvin's thesis, on a consideration of the separatist's mentality to the neglect of the broader revivalist motivations of the Gaelic League.

52 Deleuze, *Bergsonism*, p. 59. Explaining the schema of the cone, Bergson says, 'If I represent by a cone SAB the totality of the recollections accumulated in my memory, the base AB, situated in the past, remains motionless, while the summit S, which indicates at all times my present, moves forward unceasingly, and unceasingly also touches the moving plane P of my actual representation of the universe. At S the image of the body is concentrated; and, since it belongs to the plane P, this image does but receive and restore actions emanating from all the images of which the plane is composed'; Henri Bergson, *Matter and Memory*, trans. N.M. Paul and W.S. Palmer (New York: Zone Books, 1991), p. 152.

53 Bergson, *Matter and Memory*, p. 150.

54 Gilles Deleuze, *Nietzsche and Philosophy*, trans. Hugh Tomlinson (London: Athlone Press, 1983), p. 28.

55 Ibid. p. 24.

56 'Wraiths', in Heaney, *Human Chain*, p. 67. The sense of the *Gaeltacht* college being a spiritual rite of passage is most explicit in the poem 'Stations of the West', mentioned above.

57 Dennis O'Driscoll, *Stepping Stones: interviews with Seamus Heaney* (London: Faber & Faber, 2008), p. 351.

58 The Belfast Harpers' Convention of 1792 sought to 'revive and perpetuate the ancient music and poetry of Ireland', and the first Irish 'magazine' *Bolg an tSolair* was printed in Belfast in 1795 as part of a revivalist initiative; Fionntán de Brún (ed.), *Belfast and the Irish Language* (Dublin: Four Courts Press, 2006), p. 8.

59 Declan Kiberd, *Irish Classics* (London: Granta, 2000), p. 574. *Cré na Cille* is literally 'Graveyard Clay', and has recently been made available in translation as *The Dirty Dust* (trans. Alan Titley (New Haven, CT: Yale University Press, 2015)) and *Graveyard Clay* (trans. Liam Mac Con Iomaire and Tim Robinson (New Haven, CT: Yale University Press, 2016)). Passages quoted here are taken from the former.

60 Kiberd, *Irish Classics*, p. 580.

61 Ó Cadhain, *The Dirty Dust/Cré na Cille*, p. 6.

62 The opening line is a pertinent example of this, where Caitríona Pháidín wonders if she has been buried in the 'pound place', according to wishes expressed before her death, or in the cheaper 'fifteen shilling' area of the grave-yard; Ó Cadhain, *The Dirty Dust/Cré na Cille*, p. 3. See also the discussion of this point in Gearóid Denvir, *An Cadhan Aonair: saothar liteartha Mháirtín Uí Chadhain* (Dublin: An Clóchomhar, 1987), pp. 41–3.

63 Ó Cadhain, *The Dirty Dust*, pp. 176–81.

64 Máirtín Ó Cadhain, *Páipéir Bhána agus Páipéir Bhreaca* (Dublin: An Clóchomhar, 1969), p. 40.

65 'Translator's Introduction', in Fyodor Dostoyevsky, *The House of the Dead* (London: Penguin, 2003), p. 7.

66 'Faoi dhó a tháinig mé amach go hÉirinn nó gur saoradh faoi dheire thiar mé beagnach cheithre bliana go leith in a dhiaidh sin.' (Twice I came out to Ireland until I was eventually freed almost four and a half years after that.) Máirtín Ó Cadhain Papers, Trinity College, Dublin, M/2/31, p. 7. See also Claire Wills, *That Neutral Island: a cultural history of Ireland during the Second World War* (London: Faber, 2007), pp. 333–43.

67 In a talk given to mark the fiftieth anniversary of the 1916 Rising, also entitled 'An Aisling', Ó Cadhain asks what has happened to this 'vision', claiming that if they could return to the present the leaders of the Rising would see an Ireland that was more like England than it was in their own time; Máirtín Ó Cadhain, *An Aisling* (Dublin: Coiste Cuimhneacháin Náisiúnta, 1966), p. 23.

68 'Bhí mé i mo oidhre ar an bhuaireamh a fuair sé.' (I was heir to the vexation he endured.) Bhí sí in m'intinn agus crá agus teas an údair in mo chuid fola. (It

was in my mind and the torment and heat of the author in my blood.) Seosamh Mac Grianna, *Dá mBíodh Ruball ar an Éan* (Dublin: An Gúm, 1992), pp. 5, 55.

69 The first three of five characteristics of film noir cited by Christine Gledhill are '1) the investigative structure of the narrative; 2) plot devices such as voice-over or flashback, or frequently both; 3) proliferation of points of view'; Christine Gledhill, 'Klute 1: a contemporary *film noir* and feminist criticism', in Ann E. Kaplan (ed.), *Women in Film Noir* (London: British Film Institute, 1978), p. 14.

70 Mac Grianna, *Dá mBíodh Ruball ar an Éan*, p. 29.

71 'In Ainm Dé agus Shlóite na Marbh'; ibid. p. 25.

72 This trend has been characterised by Seamus Deane: 'Since the death of Parnell, modern Irish writing has been fond of providing us with the image of the hero as artist surrounded by the philistine or clerically-dominated mob'; Deane, *Celtic Revivals*, p. 31.

73 'Ba í an mhéin rúin sin a thug orm gan teacht in éifeacht riamh' (It was that secret mien/mind which prevented me from ever succeeding in life); Mac Grianna, *Dá mBíodh Ruball ar an Éan*, p. 3.

74 'Murab é gur rugadh faoin chinniúint mé nárbh fhéidir mo thabhairt in éifeacht.' Mac Grianna, 'Filí gan Iomrá', p. 139. Aodh Ó Dónaill should not be confused with Aodh Mac Domhnaill (1802–67) of County Meath.

75 'Thráigh an tobar sa tsamhradh, 1935. Ní scríobhfaidh mé níos mó. Rinne mé mo dhícheall agus is cuma liom.' (The well dried in the summer of 1935. I will write no more. I did my best and I don't care.) Mac Grianna, *Dá mBíodh Ruball ar an Éan*, p. 89. This comes after several clues that the novel, like national liberation, will not achieve its full course but will instead be put into abeyance, one instance being Mánas' assertion that when this book is complete, the first period of his life will come to a close; ibid. p. 5.

76 Máirtín Ó Cadhain Papers, Trinity College, Dublin, M/2/31, p. 3.

77 The other occasion where Ó Cadhain was temporarily released from prison was when he was taken to hospital for an X-ray; Máirtín Ó Cadhain Papers, Trinity College, Dublin, M/2/31, pp. 7–8.

78 'Máirtín Ó Cadhain Papers, Trinity College, Dublin, M/2/31, p. 8.

79 Ó Laighin (ed.), *Ó Cadhain i bhFeasta*, pp. 129–69.

80 Ibid. pp. 151, 155.

81 Ibid. p. 139.

82 The full English definition of *cré* is 'clay; earth, dust'; Ó Dónaill (ed.), *Foclóir Gaeilge–Béarla*, p. 312. The text of the lecture on folklore, 'Béaloideas', is divided under three main headings: An chré (the clay; earth), An chré mharbh (the dead clay; earth) and An chré bheo (living clay; earth). The text is also replete with references to clay/earth qualified by various adjectives. An important example of this is where Ó Cadhain speaks of the provenance of various cultural achievements as having risen from 'an chré the' (the hot clay; earth), 'an chré uaibhreach' (the proud clay/earth), and, referring to the Celtic Twilight's 'Kiltartanese' and 'living speech', 'as an gcré chéasta … an chré dhiamhair arb aisti a thig sa deireadh gach feart urlabhra maraon le gach fás' (from the tortured clay/earth … the mysterious clay/earth from which comes eventually every

miracle of speech as well as all growth); Ó Laighin (ed.), *Ó Cadhain i bhFeasta*, p. 157.

83 Ó Cadhain, *The Dirty Dust/Cré na Cille*, p. 112.

84 Ó Laighin (ed.), *Ó Cadhain i bhFeasta*, pp. 132, 135.

85 See for example his review of Patrick Kavanagh's *Tarry Flynn* (1948), which he praises for its authentic, insider's portrayal of rural life, and contrasts with the 'beautiful life' described by newspaper columnists who had never spent a week working on a farm; Ó Cadhain, 'Tarry Flynn', p. 28.

86 In regard to Ó Cadhain's championing of the *Gaeltacht*, Alan Titley writes that 'It is almost, but not entirely, true to say that whatever he [Ó Cadhain] did in the public arena he did for the people of the Gaeltacht'; Alan Titley, *Nailing Theses* (Belfast: Lagan Press, 2011), p. 293.

87 At the beginning of a talk given to the Irish Soviet Friendship Society in 1962, Ó Cadhain declared, 'I am not now nor never was in the Communist Party. I am a Christian, a Catholic'; Máirtín Ó Cadhain Papers, Trinity College, Dublin, M/2/29, p. 1.

88 '… an t-oileáinín spioradáltachta ar leith san aigne dhaonna arb é an Gael é'; Ó Laighin (ed.), *Ó Cadhain i bhFeasta*, p. 132.

89 'Is obair thíolaicthe í, beart spriodáilte ar bhealach an-áirid'; Máirtín Ó Cadhain Papers, Trinity College, Dublin, M/2/47, p. 45.

90 Anthony D. Smith, *National Identity* (London: Penguin, 1991), p. 96. See also Hutchinson, *The Dynamics of Cultural Nationalism*, p. 207.

91 'Dúinne is rud comhiomlán doroinnte an stair agus an 'folk tradition'. Is é a sintéis ár ndóchas as Náisiún Gael.' (For us history and folk tradition are an aggregate and indivisible thing. Their synthesis is the basis of our hope in the Nation of the Gael); Ó Laighin (ed.), *Ó Cadhain i bhFeasta*, p. 142.

92 Ó Cadhain, *Páipéir Bhána agus Páipéir Bhreaca*, pp. 9, 14. See also Alan Titley, *An tÚrscéal Gaeilge* (Dublin: An Clóchomhar, 1993), pp. 232–3; Aindrias Ó Cathasaigh, *Ag Samhlú Troda* (Dublin: Coiscéim, 2002), pp. 6–7, 11 for a discussion of both the origin of the term 'local organic community' and Ó Cadhain's reference to its development after Eliot by English writers such as Raymond Williams and Richard Hoggart.

93 Ó Laighin (ed.), *Ó Cadhain i bhFeasta*, p. 142; T.S. Eliot, *What Is a Classic?* (London: Faber & Faber, 1945), p. 25.

94 Ó Laighin (ed.), *Ó Cadhain i bhFeasta*, p. 146. Eliot, *What Is a Classic?*, p. 30. Ó Cadhain did not include the second part of this quotation – perhaps since his intention was to emphasise the importance of believing in the future while being aware of the past.

95 'Ní shéanaim ach oiread gur leas, uaireanta, iad 'traidisiúin' bhréige fearacht an rud a thionscail Iolo Morgannwg agus ar léir a shliocht in Eisteddfod na Breataine Bige fós.' (I don't deny either the advantage that accrues, at times, from false 'traditions' such as that initiated by Iolo Morgannwg, the legacy of which is still evident in the Welsh *Eisteddfod*.) Ó Laighin (ed.), *Ó Cadhain i bhFeasta*, p. 146. For a detailed discussion of the influence of competitions such as the Oireachtas in the development of the oral tradition in twentieth-century Ireland, see Éadaoin Ní Mhuircheartaigh, 'Drámaíocht ó Dhúchas? Stáitsiú na

nealaíon béil san fhichiú haois', PhD thesis, Ollscoil na hÉireann Gaillimh, 2012.

96   Mícheál Briody, "'Is Fearr an tAighneas ná an tUaigneas": Máirtín Ó Cadhain agus Bailiú an Bhéaloidis', *Bliainiris 9* (Ráth Chairn: Carbad, 2009), pp. 7–49. See also Ríonach Uí Ógáin, 'Máirtín Ó Cadhain agus Saol an Bhéaloidis', in Máire Ní Annracháin (ed.), *Saothar Mháirtín Uí Chadhain, Léachtaí Cholm Cille XXXVII* (Maigh Nuad: An Sagart, 2007), pp. 131–56.

97   Ó Cadhain, *Páipéir Bhána agus Páipéir Bhreaca*, p. 37.

98   This visit appears to have been organised by the Irish Soviet Friendship Society. Ó Cadhain gave a lecture to this society, based on the experience of his visit, in November 1962, and mentions 'Mairéad Nic Maicín' who was also part of the visiting group. According to the Ainm.ie biographical entry for Maighréad Nic Mhaicín, she was a member of the council of the Irish Soviet Friendship Society. Nic Mhaicín's husband, Patrick Breslin, was a victim of Stalinist repression, and died in prison in Kazan in 1942. There is an account of Nic Mhaicín's (known in English as Daisy McMackin) and Breslin's life in 1930s Russia in Barry McLoughlin, *Left to the Wolves: Irish victims of Stalinist terror* (Dublin: Irish Academic Press, 2007), pp. 53–70.

99   Máirtín Ó Cadhain Papers, Trinity College, Dublin, M/2/29, pp. 7–8.

100   H.M. Chadwick and N.K. Chadwick (eds), *The Growth of Literature*, vol. 3 (Cambridge: Cambridge University Press, 1940); George Thomson, *Marxism and Poetry* (London: Lawrence & Wishart, 1945); W. Radlov [V.V. Radlov], *Proben der Volksliteratur der Türkischen Stamme* (St Petersburg, 1866).

101   Máirtín Ó Cadhain Papers, Trinity College, Dublin, M/2/29, p. 7.

102   Ibid. p. 22.

103   'No one would be gladder to be proven wrong in the matter than myself. But from a number of impressions I came to the conclusion that there is definite Russianisation'; Máirtín Ó Cadhain Papers, Trinity College, Dublin, M/2/29, p. 33.

104   Ibid. p. 34.

105   Ibid. pp. 30–1. The most likely source for this assertion is in Colm Ó Gaora's autobiography; Colm Ó Gaora, *Mise* (Dublin: Oifig an tSoláthair, 1969), p. 169. I am grateful to Máirín Nic Eoin for this reference.

106   Thomson, *Marxism and Poetry*, pp. 55–6.

107   Ibid. p. 56.

108   Ibid. p. 58.

109   Ibid. In a recent study of Central Asian culture, the author points to claims that the secretaries appointed to transcribe the work of the native *akyns* (oral poets) 'edited' their compositions in order to accentuate the Stalinist cult of personality; Razia Sultanova, *From Shamanism to Sufism: women, Islam and culture in Central Asia* (London: I.B. Tauris, 2011), pp. 14–16. There is an anecdotal unsubstantiated theory that Jamboul had actually died at the age of seventy, and that the compositions attributed to him from the 1930s onwards were originally Russian compositions.

110   Colm de Bhailís, *Amhráin Chuilm de Bhailís* (Dublin: Connradh na Gaedhilge, 1904), p. xxi. See also Denvir, 'Decolonizing the Mind', pp. 57–9.

111 One important example is Fintan Mac Bóchna, whose memory stretches back to the time of the Flood and is called upon by the men of Ireland to identify the original site of Tara; see Nagy, *Conversing with Angels and Ancients*, p. 5.

112 'IRISHMEN AND IRISHWOMEN: In the name of God and of the dead generations from which she receives her old tradition of nationhood, Ireland, through us, summons her children to her flag and strikes for her freedom.' There are many examples one might cite here, but the essay 'Ghosts' is of particular relevance: 'The ghosts of a nation sometimes ask very big things; and they must be appeased whatever the cost'; Pearse, 'Ghosts', p. 221.

113 Pearse, 'Fragment of Autobiography by Patrick Pearse', p. 26. See also Róisín Ní Ghairbhí, 'A People That Did Not Exist? Reflections on some sources and contexts for Patrick Pearse's militant nationalism', in Ruán O'Donnell (ed.), *The Impact of the 1916 Rising: among the nations* (Dublin: Irish Academic Press, 2008), pp. 161–86.

114 For Croker, see Deirdre Nic Mhathúna, 'A Journey from Manuscript to Print: the transmission of an elegy by Piaras Feiritéar', in James Kelly and Ciarán Mac Murchaidh (eds), *Irish and English: essays on the Irish linguistic cultural frontier, 1600–1900* (Dublin: Four Courts Press, 2012), pp. 252–3; for Gregory, see Colm Tóibín, *Lady Gregory's Toothbrush* (London: Picador, 2002), p. 42; for Blythe, see Earnán de Blaghd, *Trasna na Bóinne* (Dublin: Sáirséal & Dill, 1957), pp. 16–17.

115 Alexander Pushkin, *Eugene Onegin*, trans. Stanley Mitchell [1833] (London: Penguin, 2008), p. xvi.

116 See Ó Conchubhair, *Fin de Siècle na Gaeilge*, pp. 119, 290; Sisson, *Pearse's Patriots*, pp. 38, 205.

117 Conradh na Gaeilge, *The Language and National Identity: where stands Conradh na Gaeilge? Where do you stand?* (Dublin: Conradh na Gaeilge, 1966), p. 4 (my italics). The copy consulted, in which the same phrase has been underlined, is contained in the Máirtín Ó Cadhain Papers, Trinity College, Dublin, M/2/26.

118 Conradh na Gaeilge, *The Language and National Identity*, p. 1. The quasi-religious nature of the text is also evident in the format of questions and answers in the style of a school catechism.

119 'Céard ba mhíréasúnaí ná Seachtain na Cásca? Marach cho míréasúnach is bhí cine Gael ariamh anall is fadó gur imithe as an stair a bheadh muid'; Ó Cadhain, *An Aisling*, p. 31.

120 'Sé an dóchas an mhaidhmiú chuartach, an chain detonation, a fheicim ariamh anall i stair na tíre. (Hope is the chain detonation that I see going right back in the history of the country.) Ibid. p. 1.

121 Walter Benjamin, *Illuminations* (New York: Schocken Books, 2007), pp. 254, 263.

122 Conradh na Gaeilge, *The Language and National Identity*, p. 5.

123 C. Ó Giollagáin and S. Mac Donncha (eds), *Staidéar Cuimsitheach Teangeolaíoch ar Úsáid na Gaeilge sa Ghaeltacht: tuarascáil chríochnaitheach* (Galway: Ollscoil na hÉireann Gaillimh, 2007).

124 Fredric Jameson, 'The End of Temporality', *Critical Inquiry*, vol. 29, no. 4 (summer 2003), p. 709.

125   Brian Ó Conchubhair (ed.), *Twisted Truths: stories from the Irish* (Indreabhán: Cló Iar-Chonnacht, 2011), p. 19; Diarmuid Ó Giolláin, *An Dúchas agus an Domhan* (Cork: Cork University Press, 2005), p. 136.

126   Máirtín Ó Cadhain Papers, M/2/47, p. 41. The same phrase is used to comic effect by the pretentious Nóra Sheáinín in *Cré na Cille*; see Kiberd, *Irish Classics*, p. 589.

127   Máirtín Ó Cadhain Papers, M/2/47, p. 47. See also Máirtín Ó Cadhain, *An Ghaeilge Bheo: destined to pass* (Dublin: Coiscéim, 2002), p. 7.

128   O'Driscoll, *Stepping Stones*, pp. 315–16.

Chapter 6: Utopia, Place and Displacement from Myles na gCopaleen's Corca Dorcha to Nuala Ní Dhomhnaill's *Murúcha*

1   'Aontaím leis an Easbog Berkeley, a chreid nach féidir fuaim gan cluais ag éisteacht, agus an rud nach bhfeictear – níl sé ann. Ní féidir litríocht gan lucht léite. Níl aon lucht léite gur fiú trácht air againn i nÉirinn'; Máirtín Ó Cadhain Papers, Trinity College, Dublin, M/2/17. The debate took place on 9 March 1952. Berkeley (1685–1753) was famous for defending the philosophy of idealism, which held that all reality consists entirely of minds and their ideas. For his importance to the Irish philosophical tradition, see Harry Bracken, 'George Berkeley, the Irish Cartesian', in Richard Kearney (ed.), *The Irish Mind: exploring intellectual traditions* (Dublin: Wolfhound Press, 1985), pp. 107–18. For Ó Nualláin's affinity with Berkeley's ideas, see Alf Mac Lochlainn, 'The Outside Skin of Light Yellow: Flann O'Brien's tribute to Berkeley', in Anne Clune and Tess Hurson (eds), *Conjuring Complexities: essays on Flann O'Brien* (Belfast: Institute for Irish Studies, QUB, 1997), pp. 83–7; Terry Eagleton, *Crazy John and the Bishop and Other Essays in Irish Culture* (Cork: Cork University Press/Field Day, 1998), pp. 29–30.

2   Myles na gCopaleen, *An Béal Bocht* (Dublin: An Press Náisiúnta, 1941). Quotations here are taken from the Mercier Press edition of 1986 (the most widely available edition), in spite of some occasional textual inconsistencies, most importantly the name *Corca Dorcha*, which is incorrectly rendered *Corca Dhorcha*. See also the English translation, Myles na gCopaleen, *The Poor Mouth: a bad story about the hard life*, trans. Patrick C. Power (London: Paladin, 1973).

3   '"An bhfuilir cinnte," arsa mise, "gur daoine na Gaeil?"'; na gCopaleen, *An Béal Bocht*, p. 90. It is worth noting that the Aran Islands poet Máirtín Ó Direáin (1910–88) invoked the philosophy of Berkeley to account for the loss of the utopian island of his youth, which, viewed retrospectively in 1960s Dublin, existed only in his mind; see Máirtín Ó Direáin, 'Berkeley', in idem, *Tacar Dánta/Selected Poems*, eds Tomás Mac Síomóin and Douglas Sealy (Dublin: Goldsmith Press, 1984), pp. 106–7.

4   See Caitríona Ó Torna, *Cruthú na Gaeltachta, 1893–1922* (Dublin: Cois Life, 2005).

5   Nuala Ní Dhomhnaill, *The Fifty Minute Mermaid* (Oldcastle: Gallery Press, 2007).

6   See for example R. Schaer, G. Claeys and L.T. Sargent (eds), *Utopia: the search*

for the ideal society in the Western world (New York/Oxford: Oxford University Press, 2000).

7   Tom Moylan, 'Irish Voyages and Visions: pre-figuring, re? configuring utopia', in *Utopian Studies*, vol. 18, no. 3 (2007), p. 312.

8   Ibid. p. 304.

9   See Lyman Tower Sargent, 'Utopian Traditions: themes and variations', in R. Schaer, G. Claeys and L.T. Sargent (eds), *Utopia: the search for the ideal society in the Western world* (New York/Oxford: Oxford University Press, 2000), p. 8.

10   Adam Philips (ed.), *The Penguin Freud Reader* (London: Penguin, 2006), p. xiv.

11   Quoted in Régine Detambel, *Les Livres Prennent Soin de Nous: pour une bibliothérapie créative* (Arles: Actes Sud, 2015), p. 18.

12   See Jacques Lacan, 'Seminar on "The Purloined Letter"', in idem, *Écrits*, trans. Bruce Fink (New York: W.W. Norton, 2006), pp. 6–57. See also remarks in the author's 'Ouverture', ibid. p. 4.

13   Jacques Lacan quoted by Marcus Pound in idem, *Žižek: a (very) critical introduction* (Michigan: William B. Eerdmans, 2008), p. 10.

14   David Macey, 'Introduction', in Jacques Lacan, *The Four Fundamental Concepts of Psychoanalysis* (London: Penguin, 1994), p. xxi.

15   Ibid. p. 45.

16   See Dylan Evans, *An Introductory Dictionary of Lacanian Psychoanalysis* (London: Routledge, 1996), p. 38.

17   Antonis Balasopoulos, 'Varieties of Lacanian Anti-utopianism', in A. Blaim and L. Gruszewska-Blaim (eds), *Spectres of Utopia: theory, practice, conventions* (Frankfurt: Peter Lang, 2012), pp. 69–80.

18   Macey, 'Introduction', p. xxvi.

19   Charles Rycroft, *A Critical Dictionary of Psychoanalysis* (London: Penguin, 1995), p. 39.

20   Ó Torna, *Cruthú na Gaeltachta*, p. 44.

21   The first of these was held in 1926; see Rialtas na hÉireann, *Gaeltacht Commission: report* (Dublin, Oifig an tSoláthair, 1926). See also John Walsh, *Díchoimisiúnú Teanga: Coimisiún na Gaeltachta, 1926* (Dublin: Cois Life, 2002).

22   For a general introduction to structuralism, see Terence Hawkes, *Structuralism and Semiotics* (London: Methuen, 1977).

23   Darach Ó Scolaí, *Coinneáil Orainn* (Indreabhán: Leabhar Breac, 2005); *An Braon Aníos* (The Leak) (Indreabhán: Leabhar Breac, 2007); *Craos* (Gluttony) (Indreabhán: Leabhar Breac, 2008).

24   'Dá mhéid Gaeilgeoirí a fostaíodh chun an teanga a shábháilt, is lú a bhí fanta chun í a labhairt'; Ó Scolaí, *Coinneáil Orainní*, p. 41.

25   'Nuair a aimseoidh an cigire deireanach na Gaeilgeoirí deireanacha agus nuair a thabharfaidh sé an deontas dhóibh, beidh deireadh leis an rud ar fad'; ibid. p. 42.

26   Ibid. p. 67.

27   J.P. Mahaffy, 'The Recent Fuss About the Irish Language', *Nineteenth Century: a monthly review*, vol. 46, no. 270 (1899), p. 222.

28   'Ní bhaineann sibh leis an oileán in ar chuir Dia sibh, tá sibh mar dhaoine

crochta suas leath-bhealaigh idir an spéir agus an talamh. Ní bhaineann sibh-se le tír ná le talamh'; Hyde, *Selected Plays Douglas Hyde*, p. 148.

29 Ó Scolaí, pp. 50–1.

30 Jean Baudrillard, *Simulacra and Simulation*, trans. Sheila Faria Glaser (Michigan: University of Michigan Press, 1994), p. 7. See also Robin Hemley, *Invented Eden: the elusive, disputed history of the Tasaday* (Lincoln: University of Nebraska Press, 2003).

31 Samuel Beckett, *The Beckett Trilogy: Molloy, Malone Dies, The Unnameable* (London: Picador, 1976), pp. 267, 382.

32 Samuel Beckett, *Waiting for Godot* (London: Faber & Faber, 2010), pp. 41–2.

33 'Tá sé chomh deacair agam smaoineamh ar an gcinniúint atá á bagairt orainn, ní áirím labhairt ná scríobh faoi, is atá sé agam mo bhás féin a shamhlú'; Darach Ó Scolaí, unpublished lecture given to students of the MA in language planning at NUI Galway, 2010.

34 *Eachtra Pheadair Dhuibh* was first published in the journal *Inis Fáil* (Márta 1933), pp. 63–4. For an English translation by Jack Fennell of this story, 'The Tale of Black Peter', see Neil Murphy and Keith Hopper (eds), *The Short Fiction of Flann O'Brien* (Champaign, IL: Dalkey Archive Press, 2013), pp. 42–5.

35 See Breandán Ó Conaire, *Myles na Gaeilge* (Dublin: An Clóchomhar, 1986), p. 10, and Ian Ó Caoimh, 'Timpeall chun an teampaill: idirthéacsúlacht iar-nua-aoiseach *An Béal Bocht*', *Comhar*, vol. 73, no. 1 (Eanáir 2013), pp. 15–18, and idem, 'Timpeall chun an teampaill: idirthéacsúlacht iar-nua-aoiseach *An Béal Bocht*, cuid a dó', *Comhar*, vol. 73, no. 2 (Feabhra 2013), pp. 17–21.

36 The 'foreign government's' introduction of a scheme, in which each family is given a grant of £2 for each member that speaks English rather than Irish, is of course a parody of the grant scheme introduced by the Free State government in 1934 with the opposite intention; see John Walsh, *Contests and Contexts: the Irish language and Ireland's socio-economic development* (Bern: Peter Lang, 2011), p. 180. The speech given by the vice-president of the *feis* (festival), where he doubts that the government is serious about the Irish language or 'Gaelic in their hearts', implies a native government that was supposed to be both of these things.

37 Séamus Ó Grianna, *Caisleán Óir* (Cork: Mercier Press, 1976), pp. 7–8.

38 Tomás Ó Criomhthain, *An tOileánach* (Dublin: Talbot Press, 2002); Thomas O'Crohan, *The Islandman*, trans. Robin Flower (Dublin: Talbot Press, 1934). The definitive work on the various influences to be discerned in *An Béal Bocht* is Ó Conaire, *Myles na Gaeilge*. See also Brian Ó Conchubhair, '*An Béal Bocht* and *An tOileánach*: writing on the margin: Gaelic glosses or postmodern marginalia', *Review of Contemporary Literature*, vol. 31, no. 3 (fall 2011), pp. 191–204, 237; Sarah McKibben, '*An Béal Bocht*: mouthing off at national identity', *Éire-Ireland*, vol. 38, nos 1–2 (spring/summer 2003), pp. 37–53; Louis de Paor, 'Myles na gCopaleen agus Drochshampla na nDea-leabhar', *Irish Review*, no. 23 (1998), pp. 24–32.

39 Ó Conaire, *Myles na Gaeilge*, p. 122.

40 Both Irish and English forms are given for the family's domestic servant, Bridget Peoples, then fourteen years of age; see http://www.census.nationalarchives.ie/reels/nai003401874 (accessed 28 November 2016).

41   Ciarán Ó Nualláin, *Óige an Dearthár* (Dublin: Foilseacháin Náisiúnta Teoranta, 1973), pp. 24–5. This memoir is available in English as *The Early Years of Brian O'Nolan/Flann O'Brien/Myles na gCopaleen*, trans. Róisín Ní Nualláin (Dublin: Lilliput Press, 1998).

42   Ernest Gellner, *Nations and Nationalism* (Oxford: Blackwell, 1983), p. 57.

43   Ó Nualláin, *Óige an Dearthár*, pp. 62–5.

44   Ibid. pp. 85–90.

45   Ibid. pp. 86, 88–90.

46   Ibid. pp. 79–84. See Ian Ó Caoimh's highly nuanced reading of the *Gaeltacht* episodes in *Óige an Dearthár* and their relation to *An Béal Bocht*; Ian Ó Caoimh, 'The ideal and the ironic: incongruous Irelands in *An Béal Bocht*, *No Laughing Matter* and Ciarán Ó Nualláin's *Óige an Dearthár*', in Ruben Borg, Paul Fagan and John McCourt (eds), *Flann O'Brien: problems with authority* (Cork: Cork University Press, 2017), pp. 226–53.

47   An important thread in O'Nolan's critique of 'the pathology of revivalism' was what he regarded as the failure of revivalists to engage with reality: 'To them the non-Gaelic world is unreal, they detest it and shrink from it, huddling together in the "reality" of their Gaelic dream'; Myles na gCopaleen, 'The Revival of Irish', unpublished manuscript, Flann O'Brien Papers, MS 97–27, John J. Burns Library, Boston College.

48   Ó Caoimh, 'The Ideal and the Ironic', p. 230.

49   Anthony Cronin, *No Laughing Matter: the life and times of Flann O'Brien* (New York: Fromm, 1998), p. 11.

50   Feargus Ó Nualláin to Seán MacLellan, 'Memorandum on the Typescript of "Beatha Dhuine a Thoil", an Autobiography Written by the Late Very Revd Dr Gearóid Ó Nualláin', National Archives, An Gúm Files, N0812 (hereafter 'Memorandum', N0812)

51   Letter from Caoimhin Ó Nualláin to An Gúm, National Archives, An Gúm Files, N0812.

52   Ibid. and 'Draft Memorandum on the Typescript of "Beatha Dhuine a Thoil", an Autobiography Written by the Late Very Revd Dr Gearóid Ó Nualláin', National Archives, An Gúm Files (hereafter 'Draft Memorandum', N0812). In the 'Memorandum' the authors explain that, having initially only read portions of the typescript, their original criticisms in the draft memorandum were based on the strictures of a relative who had read 'the complete script'. Remarking that 'it has since transpired that his reading was only cursory', they go on to give their own definitive response (based on five readings of the typescript) in which they conclude that the clichés and repetitions were only really a problem in certain passages, and that the priority is to excise three chapters and various passages that they feel would impair the work if published; 'Memorandum', N0812.

53   Ó Conaire, *Myles na Gaeilge*, p. 93. Fr Gearóid considered Fr Peadar to have taught Irish writers how to write Irish, and that to ignore this example would be a matter of regret not only to the writers but to the language itself; see Gearóid Ó Nualláin, *Beatha Dhuine a Thoil* (Dublin: Oifig an tSoláthair, 1950), p. 256.

54   See for example the end of Chapter 14, where the author apologises for the

digressions in this chapter, adding that he is simply recording his thoughts as they appear to him; ibid. p. 74. Fr Gearóid's brothers refer to his 'rambling narrative' in their 'Memorandum', but explain this as being a pure expression of personality in the way that Fr Peadar's work is also a revelation of personality; 'Memorandum', N0812.

55   'Cé gurbh é mí an Iúil a bhí ann, bhí sé ana-fhuar, agus bhí sé chómh dorcha le hIfreann sul ar bhaineamair an áit amach'; Ó Nualláin, *Beatha Dhuine a Thoil*, p. 48.

56   Myles na gCopaleen, *An Béal Bocht* (Cork: Mercier Press, 1986), p. 39.

57   Ó Nualláin, *Beatha Dhuine a Thoil*, p. 49.

58   Ibid. p. 48.

59   Na gCopaleen, *An Béal Bocht*, p. 42.

60   Ó Nualláin, *Beatha Dhuine a Thoil*, p. 49.

61   Ibid.

62   See endnote 38 in the previous chapter.

63   The essay on Fr Peadar reprinted in his autobiography is particularly apposite. Here Fr Gearóid eulogises Fr Peadar's gift for showing that the Irish language was the best medium for expressing the thoughts of the Irish, his own great love for the Irish language and his particular understanding of 'the vigourness, beauty, usefulness and excellence of the Irish language' (… bríoghmhaire agus breaghthacht, feidhm agus feabhas na Gaoluinne), Ó Nualláin, *Beatha Dhuine a Thoil*, p. 256.

64   Rev. Gearóid Ó Nualláin to Seán MacLellan, An Gúm, 3 March 1938, National Archives, An Gúm Files, N0812.

65   'Draft Memorandum', N0812.

66   Ibid.

67   'We adhere to our opinion expressed in the draft memo that "autobiography is one of the most difficult forms of literary art and that only five or six great outstanding autobiographies exist in the whole course of literature." We should not be surprised if "Beatha Dhuine a Thoil" came eventually to be recognised as a sixth or a seventh in that most exclusive category.' 'Memorandum', N0812.

68   'Draft Memorandum', N0812; 'Memorandum', N0812. An Gúm's own reader, 'Torna' (Tadhg Ó Donnchadha), also likened Fr Gearóid to a child whose innocence might not be appreciated by those who might take offence at some of the passages in the book; Torna, 15 April 1938, National Archives, An Gúm Files, N0812.

69   This first quotation is taken from Myles' Cruiskeen Lawn column of 20 January 1944: 'To be a Gael one had to change oneself, clothes, brogue and all, into the simulacrum of a western farm labourer … Try to imagine the monstrous perversion of townies pretending they are peasants! That then is the root of the trouble. Our young people perceive about Gaelicism a loutish and mealy-mouthed quality – something quite unknown in the Gaeltacht itself'; Ó Conaire, *Myles na Gaeilge*, pp. 84–5; on Brian Ó Nualláin's reaction to first reading *An tOileánach*, see Ó Conaire, *Myles na Gaeilge*, pp. 121–2.

70   Ó Nualláin, *Óige an Dearthár*, p. 78. See also Ian Ó Caoimh's critique of Anthony Cronin's mistranslation of this passage, which, Ó Caoimh argues,

has given an exaggerated sense of idealisation by occluding key qualifiers in the phrasing; Ó Caoimh, 'The Ironic and the Ideal', pp. 235–8.

71 See Ó Conaire, *Myles na Gaeilge*, pp. 224–5, and Kiberd, *Inventing Ireland*, pp. 497–8.

72 Cronin, *No Laughing Matter*, p. 196. The story was published in the *Bell* in 1954 while Cronin was its editor, and has been reproduced in Murphy and Hopper (eds), *The Short Fiction of Flann O'Brien*, pp. 84–9.

73 Myles na gCopaleen, 'Cruiskeen Lawn', *Irish Times*, 10 February 1943.

74 James Joyce, *A Portrait of the Artist as a Young Man* [1916] (London: Everyman's Library, 1991), p. 317.

75 Maebh Long, *Assembling Flann O'Brien* (London: Bloomsbury, 2014), pp. 99–101.

76 Ó Conaire, *Myles na Gaeilge*, p. 95.

77 Fr Gearóid Ó Nualláin to Seán McLellan, An Gúm, 03/03/38, National Archives, An Gúm Files, N0812.

78 Na gCopaleen, *An Béal Bocht*, pp. 50–1.

79 Ó Conaire, *Myles na Gaeilge*, p. 94.

80 This was certainly Ó Grianna's default policy, with very few exceptions, as recalled by Séamus Ó Saothraí, who worked with him in the publications branch of the Department of Education in the 1950s; see Séamus Ó Saothraí, 'An Seanchaí, an Scéalaí agus an Scríbhneoir: cuimhní fánacha ar Chlann Mhic Grianna', *An tUltach*, vol. 59, no. 6 (1982), pp. 46–8.

81 Ibid. p. 94.

82 'Ceapadóireacht liteardha i nÉirinn nó i dtír ar bith eile – gné sibhialta no "cathrdha" [*sic*] seadh í. Bhí 'béim ghutha' na n-údar nGaelach riamh ar an nGaeltacht'; Máirtín Ó Cadhain Papers, Trinity College, Dublin, M/2/17.

83 'Tá an cainnteoir ó dhúchas maith-go-leor, ach is CAINNTEOIR é. Tá pé litríocht Gaeilge atá againn truaillithe le cúigeachas, paróisteachas, aineloas [*sic*], etc. lucht na Gaeltachta.' (The native speaker is all very well, but he is a SPEAKER. Any literature we have has been ruined by the provincialism, parochialism, ignorance etc. of those from the *Gaeltacht*); ibid.

84 Na gCopaleen, *An Béal Bocht*, pp. 36–7.

85 Letter from Ciarán Ó Nualláin to Seosamh Ó Duibhginn, dated Good Friday, 1957, Seosamh Ó Duibhginn Papers, University College, Dublin, P172/378. I am grateful to Mícheál Briody for bringing this letter to my attention.

86 Seosamh Mac Grianna, *Mo Bhealach Féin* (Dublin: An Gúm, 1940). He had written a favourable review of Mac Grianna's *Eoghan Ruadh Ó Néill* (1931), and in the late 1940s was part of a campaign to raise funds for the Donegal author, whose situation had become increasingly fraught with the onset of mental illness. In a letter advertising this campaign, Ó Nualláin described him as one of the most talented and stylistically accomplished Irish-language authors; Brian Ó Conchubhair, 'Seosamh Mac Grianna: a bhealach féin', in John Walsh and Peadar Ó Muircheartaigh (eds), *Ag Siúl an Bhealaigh Mhóir: aistí in ómós don Ollamh Nollaig Mac Congáil* (Dublin: LeabhairCOMHAR, 2015), pp. 139–40.

87 See Gearóid Denvir, *Aistí Phádraic Uí Chonaire* (Indreabhán: Cló Chois Fharraige, 1978), pp. 80–1, 306–7. Ó Conaire's essay *Páistí Scoile: an bhfuil*

siad ag milleadh nualitríocht na Gaeilge (Schoolchildren: are they destroying modern Irish literature) was first published in 1917.

88 *An Phoblacht,* letter from 'Máire' [Séamus Ó Grianna], 6 August 1932.

89 Ibid. 25 June 1932.

90 Éamon Ó Ciosáin, *An t-Éireannach, 1934–1937: páipéar sóisialach Gaeltachta* (Dublin: An Clóchomhar, 1993).

91 *Dá mBíodh Ruball ar an Éan* was published initially as an appendix to *Mo Bhealach Féin* in 1940, when it became clear to Mac Grianna in the summer of 1935 that he could write no more.

92 'bealach nach bpillfeadh'; Mac Grianna, *Mo Bhealach Féin*, p. 5.

93 Ibid. p. 7.

94 Ibid. p. 69. For the poems attributed to Colm Cille in which he gives himself the name *Cúl re hÉirinn*, see Ó Rathile, *Measgra Dánta II*, pp. 120–1, 126–8, 267.

95 Mac Grianna, *Mo Bhealach Féin*, p. 112.

96 Chuto (ed.), *The Collected Works of James Clarence Mangan, Vol. II* (Dublin: Irish Academic Press, 1996), p. 292.

97 In his discussion of Mangan, Terry Eagleton remarks that 'His view of himself as "a plural [man] – a Protean", his assumption of translations as so many masks, and his deep distrust of anything which emanated directly from himself, are signs of a colonial crisis of identity'; Terry Eagleton, *Heathcliff and the Great Hunger: studies in Irish culture* (London: Verso, 1995), p. 234.

98 See Homi Bhabha's 'Remembering Fanon', published as the foreword to Frantz Fanon, *Black Skins, White Masks* (London: Pluto Press, 1986).

99 Edward Said, *Culture and Imperialism* (London: Vintage, 1993), p. 259.

100 Nic Eoin, *Trén bhFearann Breac.*

101 Yeats, *Michael Robartes and the Dancer*, p. 19; Chinua Achebe, *Things Fall Apart* (London: Heinemann, 1958).

102 Nic Eoin, *Trén bhFearann Breac*, pp. 267–9.

103 Ibid, see especially pp. 278–81.

104 Ibid, see Chapter 6.

105 Ibid. pp. 265–6. See Nuala Ní Dhomhnaill, *Feis* (Maigh Nuad: An Sagart, 1991), p. 119: 'Fós cluinim scéalta nua uaidh [an Chonair] gach uile uair/ léasanna tuisceana a chuireann/ na carraigeacha ina seasamh i lár an bhóthair orm/ faoi mar a bheadh focail ann.'

106 Nuala Ní Dhomhnaill, *An Dealg Droighin* (Cork: Mercier Press, 1981), pp. 81–2. See Nic Eoin, *Trén bhFearann Breac*, pp. 288–9.

107 Nuala Ní Dhomhnaill, *Cead Aighnis* (Maigh Nuad: An Sagart, 1998); Nuala Ní Dhomhnaill, *The Fifty Minute Mermaid*. These poems have been submitted to perspicacious readings by Pádraig de Paor, Máirín Nic Eoin and Ríona Ní Fhrighil in particular; Pádraig de Paor, *Tionscnamh Filíochta Nuala Ní Dhomhnaill* (Dublin: An Clóchomhar, 1997); Nic Eoin, *Trén bhFearann Breac*, Chapter 7; Ríona Ní Fhrighil, *Briathra, Béithe agus Banfhilí: filíocht Eavan Boland agus Nuala Ní Dhomhnaill* (Dublin: An Clóchomhar, 2008).

108 Ní Dhomhnaill, *The Fifty Minute Mermaid*, pp. 26–9.

109 Ibid. pp. 30–3.

110 Ibid. p. 161.

111 Ibid. p. 155.

112 Ibid. p. 159.

113 Ibid. p. 161.

114 Ibid. p. 39.

115 Ní Fhrighil, *Briathra, Béithe agus Banfhilí*, pp. 209–11.

116 Ernst Bloch, *The Principle of Hope*, vol. 2, trans. Neville Plaice, Stephen Plaice and Paul Knight (Cambridge, MA: MIT Press, 1995), pp. 762–5.

117 Herbert Marcuse, *One-dimensional Man: studies in the ideology of advanced industrial society* (Boston: Beacon Press, 1964), p. 257.

118 See Slavoj Žižek, *The Fragile Absolute: or, why is the Christian legacy worth fighting for?* (London: Verso, 2000). For a discussion of the relation of Žižek's work to theology, see also Pound, *Žižek*. See also Terry Eagleton, *Reason, Faith, and Revolution: reflections on the God debate* (New Haven, CT: Yale University Press, 2010).

119 As mentioned in the previous chapter, Ó Cadhain had no hesitation in explaining this duality to an audience of the Ireland Soviet Friendship Society in 1962, declaring, 'I am not now nor never was in the Communist Party. I am a Christian, a Catholic. Putting these two statements in juxtaposition does not mean that I believe that one cannot be a communist and a Christian. One may choose neither, or one, or the other, or both.'

120 Ernst Bloch, *The Utopian Function of Art and Literature: selected essays* (Cambridge, MA: MIT Press, 1988), p. 216; Benjamin, *Illuminations*, p. 263.

121 Ó Cadhain, *An Ghaeilge Bheo*, p. xvi.

122 See Ruth Levitas, *The Concept of Utopia* (Hertfordshire: Philip Allan, 1990), pp. 86–7.

123 Ernst Bloch, *The Principle of Hope*, vol. 3 (Cambridge, MA: MIT Press, 1995), p. 1376.

124 Frederic Jameson, *Archaeologies of the Future: the desire called utopia and other science fictions* (London: Verso, 2005), p. 416.

125 Francis Fukuyama, *The End of History and the Last Man* (Harmondsworth: Penguin, 1992); Peter Thomson and Slavoj Žižek (eds), *The Privatization of Hope: Ernst Bloch and the future of utopia* (Durham: Duke University Press, 2013), p. 3.

Conclusion

1 Pádraig Ó Conaire, *An Sgoláire Bocht agus Sgéalta Eile* (Dublin: Clódhanna/ Connradh na Gaedhilge, 1913), pp. 1–35; Pádraic Ó Conaire, *Seacht mBua an Éirí Amach/Seven Virtues of the Rising*, trans. Diarmuid de Faoite (Galway: Arlen House, 2016), pp. 233–67.

2 See Pádraigín Riggs, *Pádraic Ó Conaire: deoraí* (Dublin: An Clóchomhar, 1994), pp. 65, 67–8.

3 Besides the instrumentalisation of the Irish language by the Protestant Bible societies, the story also reflects the fatal response of some of the Catholic clergy, who deemed any reading material in Irish as suspect thereafter. The Donegal

Gaelic Leaguer P.T. Mac Fhionnlaoich spoke of the dislike the older clergy had for the Irish language during the early days of the Gaelic League revival, and recalled how his mother had at an earlier period been 'fined in confession for the offence of reading Irish to earn fees – from a Protestant Society – at the bidding of a travelling teacher'; see P.T. Mac Fhionnlaoich, 'The Language Movement and the Gaelic Soul', in William G. Fitzgerald (ed.), *The Voice of Ireland: a survey of the race and nation from all angles by the foremost leaders at home and abroad* (Dublin and London: Virtue & Company Ltd, 1924), pp. 445, 449.

4 It is likely that the figure of Peadar Ó Dónaill was inspired by Seán Mac Diarmada, and that the tobacconist's shop in which Peadar spends time is based on Tom Clarke's tobacconist's. Being a hub for insurgents, Clarke's shop represents the flipside of the antique shop. For a discussion of these similarities, see Aindrias Ó Cathasaigh, *Réabhlóid Phádraic Uí Chonaire* (Dublin: Coiscéim, 2007), p. 82.

5 Ó Conaire, *Seacht mBua an Éirí Amach*, p. 252.

6 Ibid. p. 257.

7 Ó Conaire, *An Sgoláire Bocht agus Sgéalta Eile*, pp. 1–2.

8 Homi K. Bhabha, *The Location of Culture* (London: Routledge, 1994), p. 172.

Bibliography

ARCHIVAL SOURCES
British Library
Add MS 70992, Morgan-Grenville Papers (ser. II), vol. I (f. 86)

Bureau of Military History Witness Statements
WS 889, James Kavanagh
WS 724, Desmond Ryan
WS 923, Ignatius Callender

John J. Burns Library, Boston College
Flann O'Brien Papers, MS 97–27
Myles na gCopaleen, 'The Revival of Irish', unpublished manuscript, Flann O'Brien
  Papers, MS 97–27

National Archives
An Gúm Files, *Beatha Dhuine a Thoil*, N0812

National Library of Ireland
MS G 416
MS 3254
EPH A275

New York Public Library
Lady Gregory Collection of Papers
Foster-Murphy Collection

Pearse Museum, Rathfarnham
'Fragment of Autobiography by Patrick Pearse', unpublished typescript

Royal Irish Academy
RIA 23 I 30
RIA 24 K 4

Trinity College, Dublin
Máirtín Ó Cadhain Papers, MS 10878

University College, Dublin
Muiris Ó Droighneáin Papers, P154
Seosamh Ó Duibhginn Papers, P172

CENSUS REPORTS

The Census of Ireland for the Year 1851, Part VI: general report
The Census of Ireland for the Year 1861, Part II, Vol. II: reports and tables
Census of Ireland, 1891, Part II: general report
Census 2011: this is Ireland (part 1), http://www.cso.ie/en/census/census2011reports/
    census2011thisisirelandpart1
http://www.nisra.gov.uk/census/2011/results/population.html
http://www.census.nationalarchives.ie/reels/nai003401874

GOVERNMENT REPORTS

Rialtas na hÉireann, *Gaeltacht Commission: report* (Dublin: Oifig an tSoláthair, 1926)
___, *Athbheochan na Gaeilge: the restoration of the Irish language* (Dublin: Oifig an tSo-
    láthair, 1965)

NEWSPAPERS AND PERIODICALS

An Claidheamh Soluis
An Phoblacht
An tUltach
Ancient Ireland: a Weekly Magazine
Belfast News-letter
Bell
Comhar
Inis Fáil
Irish Times
Keltic Journal and Educator
Morning Post
Nation
United Irishman

ELECTRONIC RESOURCES

Dictionary of Irish Biography: from the earliest times to the year 2002, http://dib.cam-
    bridge.org
Tobar na Gaedhilge, http://www.smo.uhi.ac.uk/~oduibhin/tobar
Ainm.ie, www.ainm.ie

AUDIO-VISUAL RESOURCE

RTÉ, *Survivors*, television project recorded in 1964–65, http://www.rte.ie/archives/exhi-
    bitions/1993–easter-1916/2017–survivors/608845–the-survivors-desmond-ryan

SECONDARY SOURCES

Achebe, Chinua, *Things Fall Apart* (London: Heinemann, 1958)
Alcock, Deborah, *Walking with God: a memoir of the venerable John Alcock* (London,
    1887)
Anderson, Benedict, *Imagined Communities* (London: Verso, 2006)
Anderson, Christopher, *Historical Sketches of the Native Irish and Their Descendants*
    (Edinburgh, 1828)

Anon., *The Concise Oxford English Dictionary* (Oxford: Oxford University Press, 2008), online edition

Arnold, Matthew, *On the Study of Celtic Literature and Other Essays* (London, 1910)

Ashcroft, B., G. Griffiths and H. Tiffin (eds), *Post-colonial Studies* (London: Routledge, 2000)

Assmann, Aleida, 'Canon and Archive', in Astrid Erll and Ansgar Nünning (eds), *Cultural Memory Studies: an international and interdisciplinary handbook* (Berlin: Walter de Gruyter, 2008)

Augusteijn, Joost, *Patrick Pearse: the making of a revolutionary* (London: Palgrave Macmillan, 2010)

Balasopoulos, Antonis, 'Varieties of Lacanian Anti-utopianism', in A. Blaim and L. Gruszewska-Blaim (eds), *Spectres of Utopia: theory, practice, conventions* (Frankfurt: Peter Lang, 2012)

Baudrillard, Jean, *Simulacra and Simulation*, trans. Sheila Faria Glaser (Michigan: University of Michigan Press, 1994)

Beckett, Colm (ed.), *Fealsúnacht Aodha Mhic Dhomhnaill* (Dublin: An Clóchomhar, 1967)

___, *Aodh Mac Domhnaill: dánta* (Dublin: An Clóchomhar, 1987)

Beckett, Samuel, *The Beckett Trilogy: Molloy, Malone Dies, The Unnameable* (London: Picador, 1976)

___, *Waiting for Godot* (London: Faber & Faber, 2010)

Bellamy, Edward, *Looking Backward, 2000–1887* (Boston, 1888)

Bencivenga, Ermanno, *Hegel's Dialectical Logic* (New York: Oxford University Press, 2000)

Benjamin, Walter, *Illuminations* (New York: Schocken Books, 2007)

Bergin, Osborn (ed.), *Irish Bardic Poetry* (Dublin: Dublin Institute of Advanced Studies, 1970)

Bergson, Henri, *Matter and Memory*, trans. N.M. Paul and W.S. Palmer (New York: Zone Books, 1991)

Bhabha, Homi K., *The Location of Culture* (London: Routledge, 1994)

Black, Ronald, 'The Gaelic Academy: the cultural commitment of the Highland Society of Scotland', *Scottish Gaelic Studies*, vol. 14, no. 2 (1986)

Blaney, Roger, *Presbyterians and the Irish Language* (Belfast: Ulster Historical Foundation and Ultach Trust, 1996)

Bloch, Ernst, *The Principle of Hope*, 3 vols, trans. Neville Plaice, Stephen Plaice and Paul Knight (Cambridge, MA: MIT Press, 1995)

___, *The Utopian Function of Art and Literature: selected essays*, trans. Jack Zipes and Frank Mecklenburg (Cambridge, MA: MIT Press, 1988)

Bourdieu, Pierre, *The Logic of Practice*, trans. Richard Nice (Cambridge: Polity Press, 1990)

Bourke, Angela, 'The Imagined Community of Pearse's Short Stories', in Róisín Higgins and Regina Uí Chollatáin (eds), *The Life and After-life of P.H. Pearse/Pádraic Mac Piarais: saol agus oidhreacht* (Dublin: Irish Academic Press, 2009)

Bracken, Harry, 'George Berkeley, the Irish Cartesian', in Richard Kearney (ed.), *The Irish Mind: exploring intellectual traditions* (Dublin: Wolfhound Press, 1985)

Bradshaw, Brendan, 'Native Reaction to the Westward Enterprise: a case-study in

Gaelic ideology', in K.R. Andrews, Nicholas P. Canny and P.E.H. Hair (eds), *The Westward Enterprise: English activities in Ireland, the Atlantic and America, 1480–1650* (Liverpool: Liverpool University Press, 1978)

___, 'Manus the Magnificent': O'Donnell as Renaissance prince', in A. Cosgrave and D. McCartney (eds), *Studies in Irish History Presented to R. Dudley Edwards* (Dublin: UCD Press, 1979)

___, 'Reading Seathrún Céitinn's *Foras Feasa ar Éirinn*', in Pádraig Ó Riain (ed.), *Geoffrey Keating's Foras Feasa ar Éirinn: reassessments* (Dublin: Irish Texts Society, 2008)

Braudel, Fernand, 'Histoire et Sciences Sociales: la longue durée', *Réseaux*, vol. 5, no. 27 (1987)

Breton, André, *Manifestoes of Surrealism*, trans. Richard Seaver and Helen R. Lane (Michigan: University of Michigan Press, 1972)

Briody, Mícheál, '"Is Fearr an tAighneas ná an tUaigneas": Máirtín Ó Cadhain agus Bailiú an Bhéaloidis', *Bliainiris 9* (Ráth Chairn: Carbad, 2009)

Brown, Michael, *The Irish Enlightenment* (Cambridge, MA: Harvard University Press, 2016)

Buckley, Jerome Hamilton, *The Triumph of Time: a study of the Victorian concepts of time, history, progress, and decadence* (Cambridge, MA: Harvard University Press, 1967)

Bunting, Edward, *The Ancient Music of Ireland* (Dublin: Hodges & Smith, 1840)

Buttimer, Cornelius G., '*Cogadh Sagsana Nuadh Sonn*: reporting the American Revolution', *Studia Hibernica*, no. 28 (1994)

Caball, Marc, *Poets and Politics: continuity and reaction in Irish poetry, 1558–1625* (Cork: Cork University Press, 1999)

___, 'Innovation and Tradition: Irish Gaelic responses to early modern conquest and colonization', in Hiram Morgan (ed.), *Political Ideology in Ireland, 1541–1641* (Dublin: Four Courts Press, 1999)

Calder, George (ed.), *Auraicept na n-Éces: the scholars' primer* (Edinburgh: John Grant, 1917)

Carlyle, Thomas, *Critical and Miscellaneous Essays*, 4 vols (London: Chapman & Hall, 1888)

Carney, James (ed.), *A Genealogical History of the O'Reillys* (Cavan: Cumann Sheanchais Bhreifne, 1959)

Carney, James, 'Literature in Irish, 1169–1534', in Art Cosgrove (ed.), *A New History of Ireland, II: medieval Ireland, 1169–1534* (Oxford: Clarendon Press, 1987)

Carroll, Claire Lois, *Exiles in a Global City: the Irish and early modern Rome, 1609–1783* (Leiden: Brill, 2018)

Carson, Ciarán, *The Midnight Court* (Oldcastle: Gallery Press, 2005)

Castle, Gregory, 'Irish Revivalism: critical trends and new directions', *Literature Compass*, vol. 8, no. 5 (2011)

Chadwick, H.M. and N.K. Chadwick (eds), *The Growth of Literature*, 3 vols (Cambridge: Cambridge University Press, 1940)

Champion J.A.I., 'John Toland, the Druids, and the Politics of Celtic Scholarship', *Irish Historical Studies*, vol. 32, no. 127, May, 2001

Chuto, Jacques (ed.), *The Collected Works of James Clarence Mangan, Vol. II: poems 1838–1844* (Dublin: Irish Academic Press, 1996)

Chuto, Jacques, Rudolf Patrick Holzapfel, Peter MacMahon, Patrick Ó Snodaigh, Ellen Shannon-Mangan, Tadhg Ó Dúshláine and Peter van de Kamp (eds), *Collected Works of James Clarence Mangan, Vol. IV: poems 1848–1912* (Dublin: Irish Academic Press, 2002)

Comerford, R.V., *The Fenians in Context* (Dublin: Wolfhound Press, 1998)

___, *Ireland (Inventing the Nation)* (London: Bloomsbury, 2003)

Comyn, David (ed.), *Foras Feasa ar Éirinn le Seathrún Céitinn/The History of Ireland by Geoffrey Keating, Part 1* (London: Irish Texts Society, 1902)

Connellan, Owen, *The Annals of Ireland, Translated from the Original Irish of the Four Masters* (Dublin, 1846)

Conradh na Gaeilge, *The Language and National Identity: where stands Conradh na Gaeilge? Where do you stand?* (Dublin: Conradh na Gaeilge, 1966)

Coolahan, Marie-Louise, *Women, Writing and Language in Early Modern Ireland* (Oxford: Oxford University Press, 2010)

Corkery, Daniel, *The Hidden Ireland* (Dublin: M.H. Gill & Son, 1924)

Crombie, I.M., *An Examination of Plato's Doctrines, Volume Two: Plato on knowledge and reality* (London: Routledge & Kegan Paul, 1963)

Cronin, Anthony, *No Laughing Matter: the life and times of Flann O'Brien* (New York: Fromm, 1998)

Crowley, Brian, '"His Father's Son": James and Patrick Pearse', *Folk Life*, vol. 43 (2004–05)

___, '"I am the son of a good father": James Pearse and Patrick Pearse', in Róisín Higgins and Regina Uí Chollatáin (eds), *The Life and After-life of P.H. Pearse* (Dublin: Irish Academic Press, 2009)

Crowley, Tony, *The Politics of Language in Ireland, 1366–1922* (London: Routledge, 2000)

Cunningham, Bernadette and Raymond Gillespie, 'Cultural Frontiers and the Circulation of Manuscripts in Ireland, 1625–1725', in James Kelly and Ciarán Mac Murchaidh (eds), *Irish and English: essays on the Irish linguistic and cultural frontier, 1600–1900* (Dublin: Four Courts Press, 2012)

Cunningham, Bernadette, *The World of Geoffrey Keating: history, myth and religion in seventeenth-century Ireland* (Dublin: Four Courts Press, 2000)

Curtis, L. Perry, *Apes and Angels: the Irishman in Victorian caricature* (Washington: Smithsonian Institution Press, 1997)

Daly, Mary, 'A Second Golden Age: the Irish Franciscans, 1918–63', in E. Bhreatnach, J. MacMahon and J. McCafferty (eds), *The Irish Franciscans, 1534–1990* (Dublin: Four Courts Press, 2009)

Darmody, Merike and Tania Daly (eds), *Attitudes Towards the Irish Language on the Island of Ireland* (Dublin: ESRI/Foras na Gaeilge, 2015)

Darragh, Paul Mervyn, 'Epidemiological Observations on Episodes of Communicable Psychogenic Illness', PhD thesis, Queen's University Belfast, 1988

Darwin, Charles, *On the Origin of Species by Means of Natural Selection* (London: Murray, 1859)

Davis, Thomas, *Thomas Davis: essays literary and historical*, ed. D.J. O'Donoghue (Dundalk, 1914)

de Bhailís, Colm, *Amhráin Chuilm de Bhailís* (Dublin: Connradh na Gaedhilge, 1904) de Bháll, Tomás, 'A West Limerick Anthology', *Irish Book Lover* (September/October 1936)

de Blaghd, Earnán, *Trasna na Bóinne* (Dublin: Sáirséal & Dill, 1957)

de Brún, Fionntán (ed.), *Belfast and the Irish Language* (Dublin: Four Courts Press, 2006)

___, 'Expressing the Nineteenth Century in Irish: the poetry of Aodh Mac Domhnaill (1802–67)', *New Hibernia Review*, vol. 15, no. 1 (earrach/spring 2011)

___, '"Society in Ulster Seems Breaking Up": an tionsclú, an imirce agus pobal na Gaeilge sa naoú haois déag', in F. de Brún and S. Mac Mathúna (eds), *Éigse Loch Lao: teanga agus litríocht na Gaeilge sa naoú haois déag* (University of Ulster, 2012)

___, 'Aodh Mac Domhnaill: tuiscint, cuimhne is toil shaor', in M. Ní Úrdail and C. Mac Giolla Léith (eds), *Mo Ghnósa Leas an Dáin: aistí in ómós do Mháirtín Ó Direáin* (Maigh Nuad: An Sagart 2014)

de Brún, Pádraig, 'Forogra do Ghaelaibh, 1824', *Studia Hibernica*, no. 12 (1972)

___, '"Gan Teannta Buird ná Binse": scríobhnaithe na Gaeilge, *c.* 1650–1850', *Comhar*, vol. 31, no. 11 (samhain 1972)

___, 'The Irish Society's Bible Teachers, 1818–27', *Éigse*, vol. 19, no. 2 (1983)

___, *Scriptural Instruction in the Vernacular: the Irish Society and its teachers, 1818–1827* (Dublin: Dublin Institute for Advanced Studies, 2009)

de Fréine, Seán, 'The Dominance of the English Language in the Nineteenth Century', in Diarmaid Ó Muirithe (ed.), *The English Language in Ireland* (Cork: Mercier Press, 1977)

de Nie, Michael, *The Eternal Paddy: Irish identity and the British press, 1798–1882* (Madison, WI: University of Wisconsin Press, 2004)

de Paor, Louis, *Faoin mBlaoisc Bheag Sin: an aigneolaíocht i scéalta Mháirtín Uí Chadhain* (Dublin: Coiscéim, 1991)

___, 'Myles na gCopaleen agus Drochshampla na nDea-leabhar', *Irish Review*, no. 23 (1998)

de Paor, Pádraig, *Tionscnamh Filíochta Nuala Ní Dhomhnaill* (Dublin: An Clóchomhar, 1997)

___, *Na Buachaillí Dána: Cathal Ó Searcaigh, Gabriel Rosenstock agus Ról Comhaimseartha an fhile sa Ghaeilge* (Dublin: An Clóchomhar, 2005)

___, *Áille na hÁille: gnéithe de choincheap na híobartha* (An Daingean: An Sagart, 2013)

Deane, Seamus, *Celtic Revivals: essays in modern Irish literature, 1880–1980* (London: Faber & Faber, 1985)

___, *Strange Country: modernity and nationhood in Irish writing since 1790* (Oxford: Oxford University Press, 1997)

___, 'Review of *Captain Rock: the Irish agrarian rebellion of 1821–1824*', *History Ireland*, vol. 18, no. 6 (November/December 2010)

Deleuze, Gilles, *Nietzsche and Philosophy*, trans. Hugh Tomlinson (London: Athlone Press, 1983)

___, *Bergsonism*, trans. Hugh Tomlinson and Barbara Habberjam (New York: Zone Books, 1988)

___, *Negotiations* (New York: Columbia University Press, 1995)

Denvir, Gearóid (ed.), *Aistí Phádraic Uí Chonaire* (Indreabhán: Cló Chois Fharraige, 1978)

___, *An Cadhan Aonair: saothar liteartha Mháirtín Uí Chadhain* (Dublin: An Clóchomhar, 1987)

___, *An Dúil is Dual* (Indreabhán: Cló Iar-Chonnacht, 1991)

___, *Litríocht agus Pobal* (Indreabhán: Cló Iar-Chonnacht, 1997)

___, 'Decolonizing the Mind: language and literature in Ireland', *New Hibernia Review*, vol. 1, no. 1 (spring 1997)

___, 'Literature in Irish 1800–1890, from the Act of Union to the Gaelic League', in Margaret Kelleher and Philip O'Leary (eds), *The Cambridge History of Irish Literature, Vol. 1, to 1890* (Cambridge: Cambridge University Press, 2006)

Denvir, John, *The Life Story of an Old Rebel* (Dublin: Sealy, Bryers & Walker, 1910)

Detambel, Régine, *Les Livres Prennent Soin de Nous: pour une bibliothérapie créative* (Arles: Actes Sud, 2015)

Dewar, Daniel, *Observations on the Character, Customs, and Superstitions of the Irish* (London, 1812)

Dillon, Charles, '*An Ghaeilg Nua:* English, Irish and the south Ulster poets and scribes in the late seventeenth and eighteenth centuries', in James Kelly and Ciarán Mac Murchaidh (eds), *Irish and English: essays on the Irish linguistic and cultural frontier, 1600–1900* (Dublin: Four Courts Press, 2012)

Dinneen, Patrick, *Filidhe na Máighe* (Dublin: Gill & Sons, 1906)

Donlevy, Andrew, *An Teagasg Críosduidhe do réir Ceasda agus Freagartha, air na Tharruing go Bunudhasach as Bréithir Shoilléir Dé, agus as Toibreacaibh Fíorghlana Oile. The Catechism, or Christian Doctrine by Way of Question and Answer, Drawn Chiefly from the Express Word of God, and Other Pure Sources* (Paris, 1742)

Donnelly, James S. Jr, 'Pastorini and Captain Rock: millenarianism and sectarianism in the Rockite movement of 1821–4', in Samuel Clark and J.S. Donnelly Jr (eds), *Irish Peasants: violence and political unrest, 1780–1914* (Wisconsin: University of Wisconsin Press, 1983)

___, *Captain Rock: the Irish agrarian rebellion of 1821–1824* (Cork: Collins Press, 2009)

Dostoyevsky, Fyodor, *The House of the Dead* [1860] (London: Penguin, 2003)

Doyle, Aidan, *A History of the Irish Language* (Oxford: Oxford Linguistics, 2015)

Dudley Edwards, Owen, *Complete Works of Oscar Wilde* (Glasgow: Harper Collins, 1994)

Dudley Edwards, Ruth, *Patrick Pearse: the triumph of failure* (London: Victor Gollancz, 1977)

Duffy, Thomas, 'Artisan Sculpture and the Stone Carving Firms of Dublin, 1859–1910', PhD thesis, National College of Art and Design, Dublin, 1999

Dyson, F.W., 'Standard Time in Ireland', *Observatory*, vol. 39 (1916)

Eagleton, Terry, *Heathcliff and the Great Hunger: studies in Irish culture* (London: Verso, 1995)

___, *Crazy John and the Bishop and Other Essays in Irish Culture* (Cork: Cork University Press/Field Day, 1998)

___, *Reason, Faith, and Revolution: reflections on the God debate* (New Haven, CT: Yale University Press, 2010)

Eliade, Mircea, *The Myth of the Eternal Return: cosmos and history*, trans. Willard R. Trask (New Jersey: Princeton University Press, 1954)

Eliot, T.S., *What Is a Classic?* (London: Faber & Faber, 1945)

Evans, Dylan, *An Introductory Dictionary of Lacanian Psychoanalysis* (London: Routledge, 1996)

Fanon, Frantz, *Black Skins, White Masks*, trans. Charles Lam Markmann (London: Pluto Press, 1986)

Farrell, Joseph and Damien P. Nelis (eds), *Augustan Poetry and the Roman Republic* (Oxford: Oxford University Press, 2013)

Feeney, Brian, *16 Lives: Seán Mac Diarmada* (Dublin: O'Brien Press, 2014)

FitzGerald, Garret, 'Estimates for Baronies of Minimum Level of Irish-speaking Amongst Successive Decennial Cohorts: 1771–1781 to 1861–1871', *Proceedings of the Royal Irish Academy*, vol. 84C (1984)

___, 'Irish-speaking in the Pre-Famine Period: a study based on the 1911 census data for people born before 1851 and still alive in 1911', *Proceedings of the Royal Irish Academy*, vol. 103C [5] (2003)

Flanagan, Thomas, 'Literature in English, 1801–91', in W.E. Vaughan (ed.), *A New History of Ireland, V: Ireland under the Union, I, 1801–70* (Oxford: Clarendon Press, 1989)

Foster, R.F., *Paddy and Mr. Punch: connections in Irish and English history* (London: Penguin, 1995)

___, *W.B. Yeats, a Life, Vol. I: the apprentice mage: 1865–1914* (Oxford: Oxford University Press, 1997)

___, *W.B. Yeats, a Life, Vol. II: the arch-poet 1915–1939* (Oxford: Oxford University Press, 2003)

___, *Vivid Faces: the revolutionary generation in Ireland, 1890–1923* (London: Penguin, 2014)

Freeman, Philip, *War, Women and Druids: eyewitness reports and early accounts of the ancient Celts* (Austin: University of Texas Press, 2002)

Freud, Sigmund, *The Standard Edition of the Complete Psychological Works of Sigmund Freud*, vol. v (London: Vintage, 2001)

Fukuyama, Francis, *The End of History and the Last Man* (Harmondsworth: Penguin, 1992)

Gaelic League, *Imtheachta an Oireachtais/Full Report of the Proceedings at the Oireachtas* (Dublin: Gaelic League, 1897)

Garrigan-Mattar, Sinéad, *Primitivism, Science, and the Irish Revival* (Oxford: Oxford University Press, 2004)

Garvin, Tom, *Nationalist Revolutionaries in Ireland, 1858–1928* (Oxford: Clarendon Press, 1987)

Gellner, Ernest, *Nations and Nationalism* (Oxford: Blackwell, 1983)

Gibbons, Luke, *Gaelic Gothic: race, colonization and Irish culture* (Galway: Arlen House, 2004)

Gillies, William, 'A Poem on the Downfall of the Gaoidhil', *Éigse*, vol. 13, pt 3 (1970)

Gledhill, Christine, 'Klute 1: a contemporary *film noir* and feminist criticism', in Ann E. Kaplan (ed.), *Women in Film Noir* (London: British Film Institute, 1978)

Godden, Richard H., 'The Medieval Sense of History', in Stephen J. Harris and Bryon L. Grigsby (eds), *Misconceptions about the Middle Ages* (London: Routledge, 2008)

Graves, Alfred Perceval, *The Book of Irish Poetry* (Dublin: Talbot Press, 1914)

Gray, John, *The Immortalization Commission: the strange quest to cheat death* (London: Penguin, 2012)

Gregory, Lady Augusta, *Poets and Dreamers: studies and translations from the Irish* (Dublin: Hodges, Figgis & Co.), 1903)

___, *Gods and Fighting Men: the story of the Tuatha De Danaan and of the Fianna of Ireland* (London: John Murray, 1904)

Gwynn, Stephen, *A Lay of Patrick and Ossian with Other Verses* (Dublin: Hodges, Figgis & Co., 1903)

Habermas, Jürgen, 'An Awareness of What Is Missing', in Jürgen Habermas et al., *An Awareness of What Is Missing: faith and reason in a post-secular age*, trans. Ciaran Cronin (Cambridge: Polity Press, 2010)

Hardiman, James, *Irish Minstrelsy or Bardic Remains of Ireland*, 2 vols (London: John Robins, 1831)

Harrison, Alan, *Béal Eiriciúil as Inis Eoghain: John Toland, 1670–1722* (Dublin: Coiscéim, 1994)

Hatab, Lawrence J., *Nietzsche's Life Sentence: coming to terms with eternal recurrence* (London: Routledge, 2005)

Hawes, J., 'Religious Revivals in America', *Orthodox Presbyterian* [Belfast], vol. 4 (1833)

Hawkes, Terence, *Structuralism and Semiotics* (London: Methuen, 1977)

Heaney, Seamus, *Stations* (Belfast: Ulsterman Publications, 1975)

___, *Sweeney Astray: a version from the Irish* (Derry: Field Day, 1983)

___, *The Midnight Verdict* (Oldcastle: Gallery, 2000)

___, *Electric Light* (New York: Farrar, Strauss & Giroux, 2002)

___, *Human Chain* (London: Faber & Faber, 2010)

Heidegger, Martin, *Being and Time*, trans. John Macquarrie and Edward Robinson (Oxford: Blackwell, 1962)

Hemley, Robin, *Invented Eden: the elusive, disputed history of the Tasaday* (Lincoln: University of Nebraska Press, 2003)

Herity, Michael (ed.), *Ordnance Survey Letters Donegal* (Dublin: Four Masters Press, 2000)

Hill, Rosemary, *God's Architect: Pugin and the building of Romantic Britain* (London: Allen Lane, 2007)

Hobsbawm, Eric and Terence Ranger (eds), *The Invention of Tradition* (Cambridge: Cambridge University Press, 1983)

Hollingdale, R.J. (ed.), *A Nietzsche Reader* (London: Penguin, 1977)

Holmes, Janice, *Religious Revivals in Britain and Ireland, 1859–1905* (Dublin: Irish Academic Press, 2000)

Hughes, A.J., '*An Dream Gaoidhealta Gallda*: east Ulster poets and patrons as Gaelic and Irish Crown *personae*', *Études Celtiques*, vol. 34 (1998–2000)

___, 'Gaelic Poets and Scribes of the South Armagh Hinterland in the Eighteenth and Nineteenth Century', in A.J. Hughes and William Nolan (eds), *Armagh: history and society: interdisciplinary essays on the history of an Irish county* (Dublin: Geography Publications, 2001)

Hunt, Tristam, *Building Jerusalem: the rise and fall of the Victorian city* (London: Phoenix, 2004)

Hutchinson, John, *The Dynamics of Cultural Nationalism: the Gaelic Revival and the creation of the Irish nation state* (London: Allen & Unwin, 1987)

Hyde, Douglas, *A Literary History of Ireland from Earliest Times to the Present Day* [1899] (New York: Charles Scribner's Sons, 1901)

___, *Abhráin atá Leagtha ar an Reachtúire: songs ascribed to Raftery. Being the fifth chapter of the songs of Connacht* (Dublin: Gill, 1903)

___, *Language, Lore and Lyrics*, ed. Breandán Ó Conaire (Dublin: Irish Academic Press, 1986)

___, *Selected Plays Douglas Hyde: 'An Craoibhín Aoibhinn'* (Gerrard's Cross: Colin Smythe, 1991)

Inwood, Michael, *A Hegel Dictionary* (Oxford: Blackwell, 1992)

Jameson, Frederic, 'The End of Temporality', *Critical Inquiry*, vol. 29, no. 4 (summer 2003)

___, *Archaeologies of the Future: the desire called utopia and other science fictions* (London: Verso, 2005)

Joyce, James, *A Portrait of the Artist as a Young Man* [1916] (London: Everyman's Library, 1991)

Kavanagh, Patrick, *A Soul for Sale: poems* (London: Macmillan, 1947)

___, 'From Monaghan to the Grand Canal', *Studies: an Irish Quarterly Review*, vol. 48, no. 189 (1959)

Keating, Geoffrey, *The History of Ireland from the Earliest Period to the English Invasion. By the Reverend Geoffrey Keating, D.D.*, ed. John O'Mahony (New York: P.M. Haverty, 1857)

Kelleher, Margaret (ed.), *Irish University Review* (special issue on the Irish Literary Revival) (Cork: Cork University Press, 2003)

Kelleher, Margaret and Philip O'Leary (eds), *The Cambridge History of Irish Literature, Vol. 1, to 1890* (Cambridge: Cambridge University Press, 2006)

___, *The Cambridge History of Irish Literature, Vol. 2, 1890–2000* (Cambridge: Cambridge University Press, 2006)

Kenny, Anthony, *A Brief History of Western Philosophy* (Oxford: Blackwell, 1998)

Kiberd, Declan, *Inventing Ireland* (London: Vintage, 1996)

___, *Irish Classics* (London: Granta, 2000)

Killeen, Jarlath, *Gothic Ireland: horror and the Irish Anglican imagination in the long eighteenth century* (Dublin: Four Courts Press, 2005)

___, *Gothic Literature, 1825–1914* (Cardiff: University of Wales Press, 2009)

Kirkland, Richard, *Cathal O'Byrne and the Revival in the North of Ireland, 1890–1960* (Liverpool: Liverpool University Press, 2006)

Knox, Robert, *The Races of Man* (Philadelphia: Lea & Blanchard, 1850)

Lacan, Jacques, *The Four Fundamental Concepts of Psychoanalysis*, trans. Alan Sheridan (London: Penguin, 1994)

___, *Écrits*, trans. Bruce Fink (New York: W.W. Norton, 2006)

Le Goff, Jacques, *Time, Work and Culture in the Middle Ages*, trans. Arthur Goldhammer (Chicago: University of Chicago Press, 1981)

Leerssen, Joep, *Remembrance and Imagination: patterns in the historical and literary representation of Ireland in the nineteenth century* (Cork: Cork University Press/Field Day, 1996)

___, 'Celticism', in Terence Brown (ed.), *Celticism*, Studia Imagologica: Amsterdam Studies on Cultural Identity (Amsterdam: Rodopi, 1996)

___, *Mere Irish and Fíor-Ghael: studies in the idea of Irish nationality, its development and literary expression prior to the nineteenth century* (Cork: Cork University Press/Field Day, 1996) *gles by the foremost leaders at home and abroad* (Dublin and London: Virtue & ompany Ltd, 1924)

olla Chomhaill, Anraí, *Bráithrín Bocht ó Dhún: Aodh Mac Aingil* (Dublin: An óchomhar, 1985)

ianna, Seosamh [Iolann Fionn], 'Filí Gan Iomrá' [1926], in Gearóid Mac Giolla omhnaigh and Gearóid Stockman (eds), *Athchló Uladh* (Muineachán: Comhaltas adh, 1991)

ghan Ruadh Ó Néill (Dublin: An Gúm, 1931)

o Bhealach Féin [1940] (Dublin: An Gúm, 1965)

Druma Mór (Dublin: An Gúm, 1969)

í mBíodh Ruball ar an Éan [1940] (Dublin: An Gúm, 1992)

chlainn, Alf, 'The Outside Skin of Light Yellow: Flann O'Brien's tribute to rkeley', in Anne Clune and Tess Hurson (eds), *Conjuring Complexities: essays on ann O'Brien* (Belfast: Institute for Irish Studies, QUB, 1997)

athúna, Liam, *Béarla sa Ghaeilge: cabhair choigríche: an códmheascadh Gaeilge/ arla i litríocht na Gaeilge, 1600–1900* (Dublin: An Clóchomhar, 2007)

erisimilitude or Subversion? Probing the interaction of English and Irish in ected warrants and macaronic verse in the eighteenth century', in James Kelly d Ciarán Mac Murchaidh (eds), *Irish and English: essays on the Irish linguistic and tural frontier, 1600–1900* (Dublin: Four Courts Press, 2012)

arais, Pádraic [Patrick Pearse], *Íosagán agus Scéalta Eile* (Dublin: Conradh na eilge, 1907)

Mháthair (Dundalk: Wm Tempest, Dundalgan Press, 1916)

am, Robert, 'The Archaeology of Ulster', *Ulster Journal of Archaeology*, 1st ser., l. 1 (1853)

nagh, Oliver, *The Life of Daniel O'Connell, 1775–1847* (London: Weidenfeld Nicolson, 1991)

ean, John (ed.), *Duanaire Dháibhidh Uí Bhruadair: the poems of David Bruadair. Part 1* (London: Irish Texts Society, 1910)

uanaire Dháibhidh Uí Bhruadair: the poems of David Ó Bruadair. Part 2 (London: sh Texts Society, 1913)

d, Norman, 'To the Rev. George Bellis, Secretary to the Presbyterian Missionary ciety for Ireland', *Orthodox Presbyterian* [Belfast], vol. 5 (1834)

Letter to the Rev. G. Bellis, by Norman McLeod D.D.', *Orthodox Presbyterian* lfast], vol. 6 (1835)

raid nan Gaidheal/The Friend of the Gael: a selection of his writings (Edinburgh: n Grant, 1910)

hon, Joseph, 'The Silent Century, 1698–1829', in E. Bhreatnach, J. MacMahon d J. McCafferty (eds), *The Irish Franciscans, 1534–1990* (Dublin: Four Courts ss, 2009)

rson, James, *Fingal: an ancient epic poem in six books by Ossian the son of Fingal* dinburgh, 1761)

nora: an ancient epic poem, in eight books: together with several other poems, nposed by Ossian, the son of Fingal (London, 1763)

eney, P.M., *A Group of Nation-builders: O'Donovan, O'Curry, Petrie* (Dublin: tholic Truth Society, 1913)

___, *Remembrance and Imagination: patterns in the histo*
    of Ireland in the nineteenth century (Cork: Cork Uni

___, *Hidden Ireland, Public Sphere* (Galway: Arlen Hous

Levitas, Ruth, *The Concept of Utopia* (Hertfordshire: Phil

Liddell, Henry and Robert Scott (eds), *Greek–English L*
    Brothers, 1883)

Lloyd, David, *Irish Times: temporalities of modernity* (
    Naughton Institute, 2008)

Lloyd, John, *A Short Tour or an Impartial and Accurate De*
    (Ennis, 1780)

Long, Maebh, *Assembling Flann O'Brien* (London: Bloon

Lyons, F.S.L., *Ireland Since the Famine* (London: Fontana

Mac Aodha, Breandán S., 'Was This a Social Revolution?
    Gaelic League Idea (Cork: Mercier Press, 1993)

Mac Aonghusa, Proinsias, *Ar Son na Gaeilge: Conradh na*
    Conradh na Gaeilge, 1993)

Mac Cana, Proinsias, *Collège des Irlandais Paris and Ir*
    Institute for Advanced Studies, 2001)

Mac Cathmhaoil, Nioclás, *Muiris Ó Gormáin: beatha agu*
    2012)

Mac Cionnaith, Láimhbheartach, *Dioghluim Dána* (Dubl

Mac Cóil, Liam, *An Dochtúir Áthas* (Indreabhán: Leabha

___, *Fontenoy* (Indreabhán: Leabhar Breac, 2005)

___, *An Litir* (Indreabhán: Leabhar Breac, 2011)

___, *I dTír Strainséartha* (Indreabhán: Leabhar Breac, 20

Mac Craith, Mícheál, 'Cioth na Baoise', *Béaloideas*, vol. 5

___, 'Gaelic Ireland and the Renaissance', in G. Willian
    Celts and the Renaissance: tradition and innovation (
    Press, 1990)

___, 'The Political and Religious Thought of Florence Con
    in A. Ford and J. McCafferty (eds), *The Origins of S*
    Ireland (Cambridge: Cambridge University Press, 20

___, 'Literature in Irish, *c.* 1550–1690', in M. Kellehe
    Cambridge History of Irish Literature, Vol. 1, to 18
    University Press, 2006)

___, '… The false and crafty bludsukkers, the Observaun
    beartacha: na hObsarvaintigh', in D. Finnegan, É. Ó
    The Flight of the Earls: Imeacht na nIarlaí (Derry: Gu

___, 'Clár Fichille agus Coinín Baineann Bán: gaibhni
    seachtú haois déag', in Ríona Nic Congáil, Máirí
    Úrdail, Pádraig Ó Liatháin and Regina Uí Chollatái
    ar fud an Domhain: cruthú, caomhnú agus athbheo
    LeabhairCOMHAR, 2015)

Mac Eoin, Gearóid S., 'Mise Raifterí 1', *Éigse*, vol. 12, pt

Mac Fhionnlaoich, P.T., 'The Language Movement and t
    G. Fitzgerald (ed.), *The Voice of Ireland: a survey of*

Magee, Glen Alexander, *The Hegel Dictionary* (London: Continuum Books, 2010)

Mahaffy, J.P., 'The Recent Fuss About the Irish Language', *Nineteenth Century: a monthly review*, vol. 46, no. 270 (1899)

Marcuse, Herbert, *One-dimensional Man: studies in the ideology of advanced industrial society* (Boston: Beacon Press, 1964)

Martin, Augustine, 'Inherited Dissent the Dilemma of the Irish Writer', *Studies: an Irish Quarterly Review*, vol. 54, no. 213 (spring 1965)

Mason, Andrew S., *Plato* (Durham: Acumen, 2010)

Mathews, P.J., *Revival: the Abbey Theatre, Sinn Féin, the Gaelic League and the co-operative movement* (Cork: Cork University Press, 2003)

___ and Declan Kiberd (eds), *Handbook of the Irish Revival: an anthology of Irish cultural and political writings, 1891–1922* (Dublin: Abbey Press, 2015)

Maturin, Charles, *Melmoth the Wanderer* [1820] (London: Penguin, 2006)

McCormack, W.J., 'Irish Gothic and After: 1820–1945', in Seamus Deane (ed.), *The Field Day Anthology of Irish Writing*, vol. 2 (Derry: Field Day Publications, 1991)

McCrea, Barry, *Languages of the Night: minor languages and the literary imagination in twentieth-century Ireland and Europe* (New Haven, CT: Yale University Press, 2015)

McGarry, Fearghal, *The Rising: Ireland, Easter 1916* (Oxford: Oxford University Press, 2010)

McGuinness, Philip, Alan Harrison and Richard Kearney (eds), *John Toland's Christianity Not Mysterious: text, associated works and critical essays* (Dublin: Lilliput Press, 1997)

McKay, J.P., B.D. Hill and J. Buckler (eds), *A History of Western Society: from the Renaissance to 1815* (Boston: Houghton Mifflin, 1987)

McKenna, Lambert, 'Poem to Aodh Mag Uidhir by Eochaidh Ó hEoghusa', *Irish Monthly*, vol. 48, no. 569 (November 1920)

McKibben, Sarah, '*An Béal Bocht*: mouthing off at national identity', *Éire-Ireland*, vol. 38, nos 1–2 (spring/summer 2003)

___, *Endangered Masculinities in Irish Poetry, 1540–1780* (Dublin: UCD Press, 2010)

McLoughlin, Barry, *Left to the Wolves: Irish victims of Stalinist terror* (Dublin: Irish Academic Press, 2007)

McMahon, Timothy G., *Grand Opportunity: the Gaelic Revival and Irish society, 1893–1910* (Syracuse: Syracuse University Press, 2008)

McManus, Henry, *Sketches of the Irish Highlands: descriptive, social and religious* (London, 1863)

McNeill, J. [Eoin Mac Néill], 'How and Why the Irish Language Is to Be Preserved', *Irish Ecclesiastical Record*, vol. 12 (December 1891)

McQuillan, Peter, 'Loneliness Versus Delight in the Eighteenth-century Aisling', *Eighteenth-century Ireland/Iris an Dá Chultúr*, vol. 25 (2010)

Memmi, Albert, *The Colonizer and the Colonized*, trans. Howard Greenfield (London: Earthscan, 2003)

Mhág Craith, Cuthbert, *Dán na mBráthar Mionúr* (Dublin: Dublin Institute for Advanced Studies, 1967)

Mhic Sheáin, Brighid agus Séamus Mac Diarmada (eds), *Robert Shipboy MacAdam in Albain, 1848* (Dublin: Coiscéim, 2009)

Mill, John Stuart, *On Bentham and Coleridge* (London: Chatto & Windus, 1950)

Minihane, John, 'Hiding Ireland', *Dublin Review of Books*, http://www.drb.ie/essays/hiding-ireland (accessed 6 September 2016)

Mitchel, John, *Jail Journal* [1854] (London: Sphere Books, 1983)

Moore, Thomas, *Memoirs of Captain Rock*, ed. Emer Nolan (Dublin: Field Day/Keough-Naughton Institute of Irish Studies, 2008)

Morales, Oscar Recio, *Ireland and the Spanish Empire, 1600–1825* (Dublin: Four Courts Press, 2010)

Morel, Jean-Pierre, 'Breton and Freud', *Diacritics*, vol. 2, no. 2 (summer 1972)

Morley, Vincent, *An Crann os Coill: Aodh Buí Mac Cruitín, c. 1680–1755* (Dublin: Coiscéim, 1995)

___, *Washington i gCeannas a Ríochta: cogadh Mheiriceá i litríocht na Gaeilge* (Dublin: Coiscéim, 2005)

___, *Ó Chéitinn go Raiftearaí: mar a cumadh stair na hÉireann* (Dublin: Coiscéim, 2011)

___, 'The Popular Influence of *Foras Feasa ar Éirinn*', in James Kelly and Ciarán Mac Murchaidh (eds), *Irish and English: essays on the Irish linguistic and cultural frontier, 1600–1900* (Dublin: Four Courts Press, 2012)

___, *Aodh Buí Mac Cruitín: dánta* (Dublin: Field Day/Keough Naughton Institute of Irish Studies, 2012)

___, *The Popular Mind in Eighteenth-century Ireland* (Cork: Cork University Press, 2017)

Moylan, Tom, 'Irish Voyages and Visions: pre-figuring, re? configuring utopia', in *Utopian Studies*, vol. 18, no. 3 (2007)

Mueller, Gustav E., 'The Hegel Legend of "Thesis, Antithesis, Synthesis"', *Journal of the History of Ideas*, vol. 19, no. 3 (June 1958)

Murphy, Neil and Keith Hopper (eds), *The Short Fiction of Flann O'Brien* (Champaign, IL: Dalkey Archive Press, 2013)

Murray, Damien, *Romanticism, Nationalism and Irish Antiquarian Societies, 1840–80* (Maynooth: Dept. of Old and Middle Irish, 2000)

Na gCopaleen, Myles [Brian Ó Nualláin], *An Béal Bocht* [1941] (Cork: Mercier Press, 1986)

___, *The Poor Mouth: a bad story about the hard life*, trans. Patrick C. Power (London: Paladin, 1973)

Nagy, Joseph, *Conversing with Angels and Ancients: literary myths of medieval Ireland* (Dublin: Four Courts Press, 1997)

Nahir, Moshe, 'Micro Language Planning and the Revival of Hebrew: a schematic framework', *Language in Society*, vol. 27, no. 3 (September 1998)

Ní Bhroiméil, Úna, *Building Irish Identity in America, 1870–1915* (Dublin: Four Courts Press, 2003)

Ní Dhomhnaill, Cáit, *Duanaireacht: rialacha meadarachta fhilíocht na mbard* (Dublin: Oifig an tSoláthair, 1975)

Ní Dhomhnaill, Nuala, *An Dealg Droighin* (Cork: Mercier Press, 1981)

___, *Feis* (Maigh Nuad: An Sagart, 1991)

___, *Cead Aighnis* (An Daingean: An Sagart, 1998)

___, *The Fifty Minute Mermaid* (Oldcastle: Gallery Press, 2007)

Ní Dhonnchadha, Eibhlín, *Tomás Ó Conchubhair agus a Chuid Filidheachta* (Dublin: Oifig an tSoláthair, 1953)

Ní Fhrighil, Ríóna, 'Scéal na Murúch i bhFilíocht Nuala Ní Dhomhnaill', in Breandán Ó Conaire (ed.), *Aistí ag Iompar Scéil* (Dublin: An Clóchomhar, 2004)

___, *Briathra, Béithe agus Banfhilí: filíocht Eavan Boland agus Nuala Ní Dhomhnaill* (Dublin: An Clóchomhar, 2008)

Ní Ghairbhí, Róisín and Eugene McNulty (eds), *Patrick Pearse: collected plays/drámaí an Phiarsaigh* (Dublin: Irish Academic Press, 2013)

Ní Ghairbhí, Róisín, 'A People That Did Not Exist? Reflections on some sources and contexts for Patrick Pearse's militant nationalism', in Ruán O'Donnell (ed.), *The Impact of the 1916 Rising: among the nations* (Dublin: Irish Academic Press, 2008)

Ní Mhuircheartaigh, Éadaoin, 'Drámaíocht ó Dhúchas? Stáitsiú na nealaíon béil san fhichiú haois', PhD thesis, Ollscoil na hÉireann Gaillimh, 2012

Ní Mhunghaile, Lesa, 'An Dearcadh a Léirítear ar Fheidhmiú an Dlí in Éirinn i bhFoinsí Gaeilge ón 18ú agus 19ú hAois', *Studia Hibernica*, no. 36 (2009–2010)

___, 'Bilingualism, Print Culture in Irish and the Public Sphere, 1700–*c.*1830', in James Kelly and Ciarán Mac Murchaidh (eds), *Irish and English: essays on the Irish linguistic and cultural frontier, 1600–1900* (Dublin: Four Courts Press, 2012)

Ní Mhurchú, Dóirín, 'Philip Barron: man of mystery', *Decies* [Waterford], no. 2 (May 1976)

Ní Úrdail, Meidhbhín, *The Scribe in Eighteenth- and Nineteenth-century Ireland: motivations and milieu* (Münster: Nodus Publikationen, 2000)

___, 'Máire Bhuí Ní Laoghaire: file an "Rilleadh Cainte"', *Eighteenth-century Ireland/ Iris an Dá Chultúr*, vol. 17 (2002)

___, 'Ón gCnocán Aoibhinn go dtí Londain Shasana: Tomás "An tSneachta" Ó Conchubhair (1798–*c.*1870)', *Celtica*, no. 28 (2016)

Nic Eoin, Máirín, *Trén bhFearann Breac: an díláithriú cultúir agus nualitríocht na Gaeilge* (Dublin: Cois Life, 2005)

Nic Mhathúna, Deirdre, 'A Journey from Manuscript to Print: the transmission of an elegy by Piaras Feiritéar', in James Kelly and Ciarán Mac Murchaidh (eds), *Irish and English: essays on the Irish linguistic cultural frontier, 1600–1900* (Dublin: Four Courts Press, 2012)

Nietzsche, Friedrich, *Thus Spoke Zarathustra*, trans. R.J. Hollingdale (London: Penguin, 1969)

___, *The Gay Science*, trans. Walter Kaufmann (New York: Random House, 1974)

___, *Beyond Good and Evil*, trans. R.J. Hollingdale (London: Penguin, 2003)

___, *The Birth of Tragedy*, trans. Shaun Whiteside (London: Penguin, 2003)

Nilsen, Kenneth E., 'The Irish Language in New York, 1850–1900', in Ronald H. Bayor and Timothy J. Meagher (eds), *The New York Irish* (Baltimore: Johns Hopkins University Press, 1996)

Ó Baoill, Colm, 'Norman MacLeod, *Cara na nGael*', *Scottish Gaelic Studies*, vol. 13, no. 2 (summer 1981)

Ó Baoill, Mánus (ed.), *Ceolta Gael 2* (Cork: Mercier Press, 1986)

Ó Beaglaoich, Conchobhar, *The English Irish Dictionary: an focloir Bearla Gaoidheilge* (Paris, 1732)

Ó Briain, Liam, *Cuimhní Cinn* (Dublin: Sáirséal & Dill, 1951)

Ó Briain, Pádraic, 'Beagán Focal Timchioll Aondacht na Gaedhilge', *Irisleabhar na Gaedhilge*, no. 25 (1887)

Ó Buachalla, Breandán, *I mBéal Feirste Cois Cuain* (Dublin: An Clóchomhar, 1968)

___ (ed.), *Peadar Ó Doirnín: amhráin* (Dublin: An Clóchomhar, 1969)

___, *Aisling Ghéar: na Stíobhartaigh agus an tAos Léinn, 1603–1788* (Dublin: An Clóchomhar, 1996)

___, 'Canóin na Creille: an file ar leaba a bháis', in Máirín Ní Dhonnchadha (ed.), *Nua-léamha: gnéithe de chultúr, stair agus pholaitíocht na hÉireann* c. *1600–*c. *1900* (Dublin: An Clóchomhar, 1996)

Ó Buachalla, Séamus (ed.), *The Letters of P.H. Pearse* (Gerrards Cross: Colin Smythe, 1980)

Ó Cadhain, Máirtín, 'Tarry Flynn', *Comhar*, vol. 8, no. 3 (Márta 1949)

___, *Cré na Cille* (Dublin: Sáirséal & Dill, 1949)

___, *An Aisling* (Dublin: Coiste Cuimhneacháin Náisiúnta, 1966)

___, *Páipéir Bhána agus Páipéir Bhreaca* (Dublin: An Clóchomhar, 1969)

___, '[Review of] *Studia Hibernica*, Uimh. 2 1962', in Seán Ó Laighin, *Ó Cadhain i bhFeasta* (Dublin: Clódhanna Teoranta, 1990)

___, *An Ghaeilge Bheo: destined to pass* (Dublin: Coiscéim, 2002)

___, *The Dirty Dust/Cré na Cille*, trans. Alan Titley (New Haven, CT: Yale University Press, 2015)

___, *Graveyard Clay*, trans. Liam Mac Con Iomaire and Tim Robinson (New Haven, CT: Yale University Press, 2016)

Ó Caoimh, Ian, 'Timpeall chun an Teampaill: idirthéacsúlacht iar-nua-aoiseach *An Béal Bocht*', *Comhar*, vol. 73, no. 1 (Eanáir 2013)

___, 'Timpeall chun an Teampaill: idirthéacsúlacht iar-nua-aoiseach *An Béal Bocht*, cuid a dó', *Comhar*, vol. 73, no. 2 (Feabhra 2013)

___, 'The Ideal and the Ironic: incongruous Irelands in *An Béal Bocht*, *No Laughing Matter* and Ciarán Ó Nualláin's *Óige an Dearthár*', in Ruben Borg, Paul Fagan and John McCourt (eds), *Flann O'Brien: problems with authority* (Cork: Cork University Press, 2017)

Ó Cathasaigh, Aindrias, *Ag Samhlú Troda* (Dublin: Coiscéim, 2002)

___, *Réabhlóid Phádraic Uí Chonaire* (Dublin: Coiscéim, 2007)

Ó Ceallaigh, Seán, *Filíocht na gCallanán* (Dublin: An Clóchomhar, 1967)

Ó Ciardha, Éamonn, *Ireland and the Jacobite Cause, 1685–1766: a fatal attachment* (Dublin: Four Courts Press, 2002)

Ó Cíobháin, Pádraig, *Desiderius a Dó* (Dublin: Coiscéim, 1995)

___, 'Dúchas agus Toil mo Chinn', *Comhar*, vol. 57, no. 6 (1998)

Ó Ciosáin, É., P. Ó Macháin and C. O'Scea, 'Two Letters in Irish from Domhnall Mac Suibhne OSA in Nantes (1640) [with index]', *Archivium Hibernicum*, vol. lxvii (2015)

Ó Ciosáin, Éamon, *An t-Éireannach, 1934–1937: páipéar sóisialach Gaeltachta* (Dublin: An Clóchomhar, 1993)

Ó Coigligh, Ciarán (ed.), *Filíocht Ghaeilge Phádraig Mhic Phiarais* (Dublin: An Clóchomhar, 1981)

___, *Raiftearaí: amhráin agus dánta* (Dublin: An Clóchomhar, 1987)

Ó Conaire, Breandán, *Myles na Gaeilge* (Dublin: An Clóchomhar, 1986)

Ó Conaire, Pádraic, *Deoraíocht* [1910] (Dublin: Talbot Press, 1973)

___, *An Sgoláire Bocht agus Sgéalta Eile* (Dublin: Clódhanna/Connradh na Gaedhilge, 1913)

___, *Seacht mBua an Éirí Amach/Seven Virtues of the Rising*, trans. Diarmuid de Faoite (Galway: Arlen House, 2016)

Ó Conchubhair, Brian, *Fin de Siècle na Gaeilge: Darwin, an Athbheochan, agus smaointeoireacht na hEorpa* (Indreabhán: An Clóchomhar, 2009)

___, 'An Béal Bocht and An tOileánach: writing on the margin: Gaelic glosses or post-modern marginalia', *Review of Contemporary Literature*, vol. 31, no. 3 (fall 2011)

___, *Twisted Truths: stories from the Irish* (Indreabhán: Cló Iar-Chonnacht, 2011)

___, 'Seosamh Mac Grianna: a bhealach féin', in John Walsh and Peadar Ó Muircheartaigh (eds), *Ag Siúl an Bhealaigh Mhóir: aistí in ómós don Ollamh Nollaig Mac Congáil* (Dublin: LeabhairComhar, 2015)

Ó Corráin, Ailbhe, *The Pearl of the Kingdom: a study of a 'Fhir Léghtha an Leabhráin Bhig' by Giolla Brighde Ó hEódhasa* (Oslo: Institute for Comparative Research in Human Culture, 2011)

Ó Corráin, Donnchadh, 'Foreword', in Séamus Ó Ceallaigh, *Gleanings from Ulster History* (Ballinascreen: Ballinascreen Historical Society, 1994)

Ó Criomhthain, Tomás, *An tOileánach* (Dublin: Talbot Press, 2002)

Ó Cuív, Brian, 'Rialacha do Chúirt Éigse ó Chontae an Chláir', *Éigse* 11, pt 3 (1965–66)

___, 'Irish Language and Literature, 1691–1845', in T.W. Moody and W. Vaughan (eds), *A New History of Ireland, IV: eighteenth-century Ireland, 1691–1800* (Oxford: Clarendon Press, 1986)

Ó Dálaigh, Brian, 'Tomás Ó Míocháin and the Munster Courts of Gaelic Poetry, c. 1730–1804', *Eighteenth-century Ireland/Iris an Dá Chultúr*, vol. 27 (2012)

Ó Dálaigh, Pádraig (ed.), *Roibárd Bheldon: file an chomaraigh* (Dublin: Comhlucht Oideachais na hÉireann, 1903)

Ó Danachair, Liam, 'Memories of My Youth', *Béaloideas*, vol. 17 (1947)

Ó Direáin, Máirtín, *Tacar Dánta/Selected Poems*, eds Tomás Mac Síomóin and Douglas Sealy (Dublin: Goldsmith Press, 1984)

Ó Doibhlin, Breandán, *An Branar Gan Cur* (Dublin: Sáirséal-Ó Marcaigh, 1979)

___, *Sliocht ar Thír na Scáth* (Dublin: Coiscéim, 2018)

Ó Domhnaill, Maoghnas (ed.), *An Bheatha Chrábhaidh* (Dublin: An Gúm, 1939)

Ó Dónaill, Niall (ed.), *Foclóir Gaeilge–Béarla* (Dublin: Rialtas na hÉireann, 1977)

Ó Donnchú, Donncha (ed.), *Filíocht Mháire Bhuidhe Ní Laoghaire* (Dublin: Oifig an tSoláthair, 1931)

Ó Drisceoil, Proinsias, *Seán Ó Dálaigh: éigse agus iomarbhá* (Cork: Cork University Press, 2007)

Ó Dúshláine, Tadhg, *An Eoraip agus Litríocht na Gaeilge, 1600–1650: gnéithe den bharócachas Eorpach i litríocht na Gaeilge* (Dublin: An Clóchomhar, 1987)

Ó Fiaich, Tomás (ed.), *Art Mac Cumhaigh: dánta* (Dublin: An Clóchomhar, 1973)

___ and Liam Ó Caithnia (eds), *Art Mac Bionaid: dánta* (Dublin: An Clóchomhar, 1979)

Ó Fiannachta, Pádraig, *An Barántas* (Maigh Nuad: An Sagart, 1978)

Ó Flaithearta, Liam, *Dúil* (Dublin: Sáirséal & Dill, 1953)

Ó Flannghaile, Tomás, *For the Tongue of the Gael* (London: City of London Book Depot, Gill, 1896)

___, *De Prosodia Hibernica* (Dublin: Gill & Son, 1908)

Ó Gallchóir, Seán (ed.), *Séamus Dall Mac Cuarta: dánta* (Dublin: An Clóchomhar, 1971)

Ó Gaora, Colm, *Mise* (Dublin: Oifig an tSoláthair, 1969)

Ó Giollagáin, C., and S. Mac Donncha (eds), *Staidéar cuimsitheach teangeolaíoch ar úsáid na Gaeilge sa Ghaeltacht: tuarascáil chríochnaitheach* (Galway: Ollscoil na hÉireann Gaillimh, 2007)

Ó Giolláin, Diarmuid, *An Dúchas agus an Domhan* (Cork: Cork University Press, 2005)

Ó Grianna, Séamus, *Caisleáin Óir* (Cork: Mercier Press, 1976)

___, *Saoghal Corrach* (Dublin: An Press Náisiúnta, 1945)

Ó Háinle, Cathal,'Ó Chaint na nDaoine go dtí an Caighdeán Oifigiúil', in K. McCone, D. McManus, C. Ó Hainle, N. Williams and L. Breatnach (eds), *Stair na Gaeilge* (Maynooth: Roinn na Sean-Ghaeilge, 1994)

___ (ed.), *Gearrscéalta an Phiarsaigh* (Dublin: Cló Thalbóid, 1999)

___, *Scáthanna* (Dublin: Coiscéim, 2008)

Ó hEodhasa, Bonaventúra, *An Teagasg Críosdaidhe* [1611], ed. Fearghal Mac Raghnaill (Dublin: Dublin Institute for Advanced Studies, 1976).

Ó hÓgáin, Dáithí, *Duanaire Osraíoch: cnuasach d'fhilíocht na ndaoine ó Cho. Chill Chainnigh* (Dublin: An Clóchomhar, 1980)

___, *The Hero in Irish Folk History* (Dublin: Gill & Macmillan, 1985)

Ó hUiginn, Ruairí, 'Captain Somhairle and His Books Revisited', in Pádraig Ó Macháin (ed.), *The Book of the O'Conor Don: essays on an Irish manuscript* (Dublin: Dublin Institute for Advanced Studies, 2010)

___, 'Transmitting the Text: some linguistic issues in the work of the Franciscans', in R. Gillespie and R. Ó hUiginn (eds), *Irish Europe, 1600–1650: writing and learning* (Dublin: Four Courts Press, 2013)

___, 'Éireannaigh, Fir Éireann, Gaeil agus Gaill', in C. Breatnach and M. Ní Úrdail (eds), *Aon don Éigse: essays marking Osborn Bergin's centenary lecture on bardic poetry (1912)* (Dublin: Dublin Institute for Advanced Studies, 2015)

Ó Liatháin, Donnchadh, *Tomás Ó Flannghaile: scoláire agus file* (Dublin, 1940)

Ó Macháin, Pádraig (ed.), *The Book of the O'Conor Don: essays on an Irish manuscript* (Dublin: DIAS, 2010)

___, '"One Glimpse of Ireland": the manuscript of Fr Nioclás (Fearghal Dubh) Ó Gadhra, OSA', in Raymond Gillespie and Ruairí Ó hUiginn (eds), *Irish Europe, 1600–1650: writing and learning* (Dublin: Four Courts Press, 2013)

Ó Maolmhuaidh, Froinsias, *Grammatica Latino–Hibernica* (Rome: Propaganda Fide, 1677)

___, *Lucerna Fidelium*, ed. Pádraig Ó Súilleabháin (Dublin: Dublin Institute for Advanced Studies, 1962)

Ó Maolmhuaidh, Proinsias, *Athair na hAthbheochana: Uilleog de Búrca* (Dublin: Foilseacháin Náisiúnta Teoranta, 1981)

Ó Maonaigh, Cainneach (ed.), *Scáthán Shacramuinte na hAithridhe: Aodh Mac Aingil O.F.M.* (Dublin: Dublin Institute for Advanced Studies, 1952)

___, 'Scríbhneoirí Gaeilge an Seachtú hAois Déag', *Studia Hibernica*, no. 2 (1962)

Ó Mórdha, Séamus P., 'Arthur Bennett's Correspondence with Robert S. Mac Adam', *Seanchas Ardmhacha*: *Journal of the Armagh Diocesan Historical Society*, vol. 2, no. 2 (1957)

Ó Muirgheasa, Énrí, *Amhráin Airt Mhic Chubhthaigh agus Amhráin Eile* (Dundalk: Dundalgan Press, 1916)

___, *Amhráin na Midhe* (Dublin: Cómhlucht Oideachais na hÉireann, 1933)

___, *Dhá Chéad de Cheoltaibh Uladh* (Dublin: Oifig Díolta Foillseacháin Rialtais, 1934)

Ó Muirithe, Diarmaid, *Tomás Ó Míocháin: filíocht* (Dublin: An Clóchomhar, 1988)

Ó Muirthile, Liam, *An Colm Bán/La Blanche Colombe* (Dublin: Cois Life, 2014)

Ó Muraíle, Nollaig (ed.), *Turas na dTaoiseach nUltach as Éirinn: from Ráth Maoláin to Rome* (Rome: Pontifical Irish College of Rome, 2007)

___, 'Tadhg Ó Cianáin and the Significance of His Memoir: "The only work of its kind in Irish literature"', in Fearghus Ó Fearghail (ed.), *Tadhg Ó Cianáin: an Irish scholar in Rome* (Dublin: Mater Dei Institute of Education, 2011)

Ó Murchú, Liam P. (ed.), *Cúirt an Mheon-oíche* (Dublin: An Clóchomhar, 1982)

Ó Murchú, Máirtín, 'Language and Society in Nineteenth Century Ireland', in G.H. Jenkins (ed.), *Language and Community in the Nineteenth Century* (Cardiff: University of Wales Press, 1998)

___, *Cumann Buan-choimeádta na Gaeilge: tús an athréimnithe* (Dublin: Cois Life, 2001)

Ó Nualláin, Ciarán, *Óige an Dearthár* (Dublin: Foilseacháin Náisiúnta Teoranta, 1973)

___, *The Early Years of Brian O'Nolan/Flann O'Brien/Myles na gCopaleen*, trans. Róisín Ní Nualláin (Dublin: Lilliput Press, 1998)

Ó Nualláin, Gearóid, *Beatha Dhuine a Thoil* (Dublin: Oifig an tSoláthair, 1950)

Ó Rathile, Tomás (ed.), *Measgra Dánta II* (Cork: Cork University Press, 1927)

Ó Ríordáin, Seán, *Brosna* (Dublin: Sáirséal & Dill, 1964)

Ó Saothraí, Séamus, 'An Seanchaí, an Scéalaí agus an Scríbhneoir: cuimhní fánacha ar Chlann Mhic Grianna', *An tUltach*, vol. 59, no. 6 (1982)

Ó Scolaí, Darach, *Coinneáil Orainn* (Indreabhán: Leabhar Breac, 2005)

___, *An Braon Aníos* (Indreabhán: Leabhar Breac, 2007)

___, *An Cléireach* (Indreabhán: Leabhar Breac, 2007)

___, *Craos* (Indreabhán: Leabhar Breac, 2008)

___, unpublished lecture for MA in language planning at NUI Galway, 2010

Ó Súilleabháin, Muiris, *Fiche Blian ag Fás* (Dublin: Clólucht an Talbóidigh, 1933)

Ó Súilleabháin, Seán, 'Scáthán an Chrábhaidh: foinsí an aistriúcháin', *Éigse*, no. xxiv (1990)

Ó Táilliúir, Pádraig, 'Ceartliosta de Leabhair, Paimfléid, etc. Foilsithe in Éirinn ag Connradh na Gaedhilge, 1893–1918', *Comhar* (Feabhra, 1964)

___, 'Ceartliosta de Leabhair, Paimfléid, etc. Foilsithe in Éirinn ag Connradh na Gaedhilge, 1893–1918, Cuid a Dó', *Comhar* (Márta 1964)

___, 'Ceartliosta de Leabhair, Paimfléid, etc. Foilsithe in Éirinn ag Connradh na Gaedhilge, 1893–1918, Cuid a Trí', *Comhar* (Aibreán 1964)

___, 'Ceartliosta de Leabhair, Paimfléid, etc. Foilsithe in Éirinn ag Connradh na Gaedhilge, 1893–1918, Cuid a Ceathair', *Comhar* (Bealtaine 1964)

___, 'Ceartliosta de Leabhair, Paimfléid, etc. Foilsithe in Éirinn ag Connradh na Gaedhilge, 1893–1918, Cuid a Cúig', *Comhar* (Meitheamh 1964)

___, 'Ceartliosta de Leabhair, Paimfléid, etc. Foilsithe in Éirinn ag Connradh na Gaedhilge, 1893–1918, Cuid a Sé', *Comhar* (Iúil 1964)

___, 'Ceartliosta de Leabhair, Paimfléid, etc. Foilsithe in Éirinn ag Connradh na Gaedhilge, 1893–1918, Cuid a Seacht/Deireadh', *Comhar* (Lúnasa 1964)

Ó Torna, Caitríona, *Cruthú na Gaeltachta, 1893–1922* (Dublin: Cois Life, 2005)

Ó Tuairisc, Eoghan, *Dé Luain* [1966] (Dublin: Sáirséal & Ó Marcaigh, 1998)

Ó Tuama, Seán and Thomas Kinsella (eds), *An Duanaire: poems of the dispossessed, 1600–1900* (Dublin: Dolmen Press, 1994)

Ó Tuama, Seán, 'Brian Merriman and his Court', *Irish University Review*, vol. 11, no. 2 (autumn 1981)

Ó Tuathaigh, Gearóid, *I mBéal an Bháis: the Great Famine and the language shift in nineteenth-century Ireland* (Connecticut: Quinnipiac University Press, 2015)

O'Brien, Sylvester (ed.), *Measgra i gCuimhne Mhichíl Uí Chléirigh* (Dublin: Assisi Press, 1944)

O'Connell, F.W., 'The Philosophy of Aodh Mac Domhnaill', *Journal of the County Louth Archaeological Society*, vol. 3, no. 4 (November, 1915)

O'Connor, Frank, *The Backward Look: a survey of Irish literature* (London: Macmillan, 1967)

O'Crohan, Thomas, *The Islandman*, trans. Robin Flower (Dublin: Talbot Press, 1934)

O'Daly, John, *Reliques of Irish Jacobite Poetry* (Dublin: Samuel J. Machen, 1844)

O'Driscoll, Dennis, *Stepping Stones: interviews with Seamus Heaney* (London: Faber & Faber, 2008)

O'Halloran, Claire, *Golden Ages and Barbarous Nations: antiquarian debate and cultural politics in Ireland, c. 1750–1800* (Cork: Cork University Press/Field Day, 2005)

O'Leary, Philip, *The Prose Literature of the Gaelic Revival, 1881–1921: ideology and innovation* (Pennsylvania: Pennsylvania State University Press, 1994)

___, *Gaelic Prose in the Irish Free State, 1922–1939* (Dublin: UCD Press, 2004)

___, *Irish Interior: keeping faith with the past in Gaelic prose, 1940–1951* (Dublin: UCD Press, 2010)

___, 'Reasoning Why After Fifty Years: the Easter Rising in Eoghan Ó Tuairisc's *Dé Luain* (1966)', *Proceedings of the Harvard Celtic Colloquium*, vol. 31 (2011)

___, *Writing Beyond the Revival: facing the future in Gaelic prose, 1940–1951* (Dublin: UCD Press, 2011)

O'Rahilly, Cecile, *Five Seventeenth-century Political Poems* (Dublin: Dublin Institute for Advanced Studies, 1977)

O'Rahilly, Thomas F. (ed.), *Desiderius, Otherwise Called Sgáthán an Chrábhaidh by Flaithrí Ó Maolchonaire* (Dublin: Dublin Institute for Advanced Studies, 1975)

O'Riordan, Michelle, *Irish Bardic Poetry and Rhetorical Reality* (Cork: Cork University Press, 2007)

O'Sullivan, Maurice, *Twenty Years A' Growing*, trans. Moya Llewelyn Davis and George Thomson (London: Chatto & Windus, 1933)

___, *Vingt Ans de Jeunesse*, trans. Raymond Queneau (Paris: Gallimard, 1936)

Palm, Ralph, 'Hegel's Concept of Sublation: a critical interpretation', PhD thesis, Catholic University of Leuven, 2009

Pastorini, Signor [Charles Walmesley], *General History of the Christian Church from Her Birth to Her Final Triumphant States in Heaven Chiefly Deduced from the Apocalypse of St. John the Apostle* (1771)

Pearse, Mary Brigid (ed.), *The Home Life of Pádraig Pearse* (Dublin: Mercier Press, 1979)

Pearse, P.H., 'Review: *Séadna* and the future of Irish prose', *An Claidheamh Soluis*, 24 September 1904

___, 'About Literature', *An Claidheamh Soluis*, 26 May 1906

___, *Complete Works of Pádraic H. Pearse: songs of the Irish rebels and specimens from an Irish anthology* (Dublin: Maunsel & Co., 1918)

___, *The Story of a Success*, ed. Desmond Ryan (Dublin: Maunsel, 1918)

___, *Collected Works of Pádraic H. Pearse: plays, stories, poems* (Dublin: Phoenix, 1924)

___, *Collected Works of Pádraic H. Pearse: political writings and speeches* (Dublin: Phoenix, 1924)

Philips, Adam (ed.), *The Penguin Freud Reader* (London: Penguin, 2006)

Pim, Herbert Moore, *Unknown Immortals in the Northern City of Success* (Dublin: Talbot Press, 1917)

Plato, *Phaedrus*, trans. Reginald Hackforth (Oxford: Oxford University Press, 1952)

___, *Protagoras and Meno*, trans. W.K.C. Guthrie (London: Penguin, 1970)

___, *Phaedo*, trans. David Gallup (Oxford: Clarendon Press, 1975)

Plummer, Charles (ed.), *Vitae Sanctorum Hiberniae*, vol. 2 (Oxford: Clarendon Press, 1910)

Pound, Marcus, *Žižek: a (very) critical introduction* (Michigan: William B. Eerdmans, 2008)

Pugin, A.N.W., *Contrasts; or a Parallel Between the Noble Edifices of the Fourteenth and Fifteenth Centuries, and Similar Buildings of the Present Day; Shewing the Present Decay of Taste* (London, 1836)

Pushkin, Alexander, *Eugene Onegin*, trans. Stanley Mitchell [1833] (London: Penguin, 2008)

Queneau, Raymond, *On est Toujours Trop Bon Avec Les Femmes* [1947] (Paris: Gallimard, 1971)

___, *We Always Treat Women Too Well*, trans. Barbara Wright [1981] (New York: New York Review Books, 2003)

Radlov, W. [V.V. Radlov], *Proben der Volksliteratur der Türkischen Stamme* (St Petersburg, 1866)

Ramelli, Ilaria, *The Christian Doctrine of Apokatastasis: a critical assessment from the New Testament to Eriugena* (Leiden: Brill, 2014)

Reddin, Kenneth, 'A Man Called Pearse', *Studies: an Irish Quarterly Review*, vol. 34, no. 134 (June 1945)

Riggs, Pádraigín, *Pádraic Ó Conaire: deoraí* (Dublin: An Clóchomhar, 1994)

___, 'The Origins of the Irish Texts Society', *History Ireland*, vol. 6, no. 1 (1998)

Robinson, Paul, *Freudian Left: Wilhelm Reich, Geza Roheim, Herbert Marcuse* (Ithaca: Cornell University Press, 1990)

Rosemann, Philipp, *The Charred Root of Meaning: continuity, transgression and the Other in Christian Tradition* (Michigan: Wm B. Eerdmans, 2018)

Ryan, Desmond, *Remembering Sion: a chronicle of storm and quiet* (London: Arthur Barker, 1934)

Rycroft, Charles, *A Critical Dictionary of Psychoanalysis* (London: Penguin, 1995)

Said, Edward, *Culture and Imperialism* (London: Vintage, 1993)

Sargent, Lyman Tower, 'Utopian Traditions: themes and variations', in R. Schaer, G. Claeys and L.T. Sargent (eds), *Utopia: the search for the ideal society in the Western world* (New York/Oxford: Oxford University Press, 2000)

Sedgwick, Peter R., *Nietzsche: the key concepts* (London: Routledge, 2009)

Sewell, Frank (ed.), *Selected Poems: Seán Ó Ríordáin* (New Haven, CT: Yale University Press, 2014)

Sisson, Elaine, *Pearse's Patriots: St Enda's and the cult of boyhood* (Cork: Cork University Press, 2004)

Small, Robin, 'Being, Becoming and Time in Nietzsche', in Ken Gemes and John Richardson (eds), *The Oxford Handbook of Nietzsche* (Oxford: Oxford University Press, 2013)

Smith, Anthony D., *Theories of Nationalism* (New York: Harper & Row, 1972)

___, *National Identity* (London: Penguin, 1991)

___, *Nationalism and Modernism* (London: Routledge, 1998)

Stavrakakis, Yannis, *The Lacanian Left: psychoanalysis, theory, and politics* (Edinburgh: Edinburgh University Press, 2007)

Stevens Curl, James (ed.), *The Oxford Dictionary of Architecture* (Oxford: Oxford University Press, 1999)

Stokes, Gale, 'The Underdeveloped Theory of Nationalism', *World Politics*, vol. 31, no. 1 (October 1978)

Stokes, Whitley, 'Acallamh na Senórach', in Whitley Stokes and Ernst Windisch (eds), *Irische Texte*, ser. iv, vol. 1 (Leipzig, 1900).

Sullivan, A.M., *The Story of Ireland* (Dublin, 1867)

Sultanova, Razia, *From Shamanism to Sufism: women, Islam and culture in Central Asia* (London: I.B. Tauris, 2011)

Synge, J.M., *Four Plays and the Aran Islands* [1907] (London: Oxford University Press, 1962)

Taylor-FitzSimon, B. and J.H. Murphy (eds), *The Irish Revival Reappraised* (Dublin: Four Courts Press, 2004)

Thomson, George, *Marxism and Poetry* (London: Lawrence & Wishart, 1945)

Thomson, Peter and Slavoj Žižek (eds), *The Privatization of Hope: Ernst Bloch and the future of utopia* (Durham: Duke University Press, 2013)

Thomson, R.L. (ed.), *Foirm na nUrrnuidheadh: John Carswell's Gaelic translation of the Book of Common Order* (Edinburgh: Scottish Gaelic Texts Society, 1970)

Thornley, David, 'Patrick Pearse and the Pearse Family', *Studies: an Irish Quarterly Review*, vol. 60, nos 239–40 (autumn/winter 1971)

Tierney, Michael, D.A. Binchy, Gerard Murphy, John Ryan and Sean O'Faolain, 'Politics and Culture: Daniel O'Connell and the Gaelic past', *Studies: an Irish Quarterly Review*, vol. 27, no. 107 (September 1938)

Titley, Alan, *An tÚrscéal Gaeilge* (Dublin: An Clóchomhar, 1993)

___, *Nailing Theses* (Belfast: Lagan Press, 2011)

Tóibín, Colm, *Lady Gregory's Toothbrush* (London: Picador, 2002)

Townshend, Charles, *Easter 1916: the Irish rebellion* (London: Penguin, 2006)

Trumpener, Katie, *Bardic Nationalism: the Romantic novel and the British Empire* (Princeton: Princeton University Press, 1997)

Ua Duinnín, Pádraig, *Spioraid na Saoirse: aisling draoidheachta ar an mbliadhain 1916* (Dublin: M.H. Gill & Son, 1919)

Ua Laoghaire, Peadar, *Séadna*, ed. Liam Mac Mathúna (Dublin: Cois Life, 2011)

Ua Muireadhaigh, Lorcán, *Amhráin Shéamais Mhic Chuarta* (Dundalk: William Tempest, 1925)

Uí Chollatáin, Regina, *An Claidheamh Soluis agus Fáinne an Lae, 1899–1932: anailís ar phríomhnuachtán Gaeilge ré na hAthbheochana* (Dublin: Cois Life, 2004)

Uí Ógáin, Ríonach, 'Máirtín Ó Cadhain agus Saol an Bhéaloidis', in Máire Ní Annracháin (ed.), *Saothar Mháirtín Uí Chadhain, Léachtaí Cholm Cille XXXVII* (Maigh Nuad: An Sagart, 2007)

Walsh, J., B. O'Rourke and H. Rowland (eds), *Tuarascáil Taighde ar Nuachainteoirí na Gaeilge* (Dublin: Foras na Gaeilge, 2015)

Walsh, John, *Díchoimisiúnú Teanga: Coimisiún na Gaeltachta, 1926* (Dublin: Cois Life, 2002)

___, *Contests and Contexts: the Irish language and Ireland's socio-economic development* (Bern: Peter Lang, 2011)

Walsh, Paul, *Gleanings from Irish Manuscripts* (Dublin: Sign of the Three Candles, 1933)

Welch, Robert (ed.), *The Oxford Companion to Irish Literature* (Oxford: Clarendon Press, 1996)

Whelan, Irene, *The Bible War in Ireland: the 'Second Reformation' and the polarization of Protestant–Catholic relations, 1800–1840* (Wisconsin: University of Wisconsin Press, 2005)

Whelan, Kevin, 'Between Filiation and Affiliation: the politics of postcolonial memory', in Clare Carroll and Patricia King (eds), *Ireland and Postcolonial Theory* (Cork: Cork University Press, 2003)

Williams, N.J.A., *Pairlement Chloinne Tomáis* (Dublin: Dublin Institute for Advanced Studies, 1981)

Williams, Raymond, *The Politics of Modernism: against the new conformists* (London: Verso, 1989)

Wills, Claire, *That Neutral Island: a cultural history of Ireland during the Second World War* (London: Faber, 2007)

Wolf, Nicholas, *An Irish-speaking Island: state, religion, community, and the linguistic landscape in Ireland, 1770–1870* (Wisconsin: University of Wisconsin Press, 2014)

Yeats, W.B., *The Celtic Twilight* (London: A.H. Bullen, 1902)

___, *Michael Robartes and the Dancer* (Dundrum: Cuala Press, 1920)

Žižek, Slavoj, *The Sublime Object of Ideology* (London: Verso, 1989)

___, *The Fragile Absolute: or, why is the Christian legacy worth fighting for?* (London: Verso, 2000)

___, 'The Counterbook of Christianity', in Marcus Pound, *Žižek: a (very) critical introduction* (Michigan: Wm B. Eerdmans, 2008)

Index

252